The Evolution of Inequality

MANUS I. MIDLARSKY

The Evolution of Inequality

*War, State Survival, and Democracy
in Comparative Perspective*

STANFORD UNIVERSITY PRESS
STANFORD, CALIFORNIA

STANFORD UNIVERSITY PRESS
Stanford, California

© 1999 by the Board of Trustees of the Leland Stanford Junior University

Printed in the United States of America

CIP data appear at the end of the book

To my family, most of whom were fortunate enough to avoid the political depredations of the twentieth century, and to the memory of those who perished in the Holocaust, in this, the sixth decade after the liberation of the camps.

PREFACE

"The Thunderbird is a legendary, eagle-like bird, so big it could pick up whales in its claws. It told the ancestors of the people, 'You will know I am around when you hear the thunder; it is the sound of my wings flapping. You will know I am around when you see the lightning coming from my blinking eyes. If you hear me during rough weather, the weather will change for the better. If you hear me during fair weather, it will change for the worse'" (Wallas and Whitaker 1989, 49).

This legend of the Kwakiutl tribe of the Pacific Northwest nicely illustrates the tendency of human beings to seek parsimonious, if mythical, explanations for the world around them. All of the vagaries of the weather are accounted for by the huge creature whose eyes give rise to lightning and whose wings lead to the sound of thunder as well as to the changes from one set of weather conditions to the next. Nothing could be simpler or more certain as a source of explanation for climatic conditions, for it all resides in one being.

Modern physical and social sciences also seek parsimony and simple structure, although with much less of an emphasis on certainty. The physical sciences are further along this road, for even the explanation of the fundamental forces—gravity, electromagnetism, and the strong and weak nuclear forces—are in the process of unification within a single theoretical framework, albeit one subject to indeterminacy conditions.

We in the social sciences are less fortunate in this regard, yet like the physicist and electromagnetism or the chemist and molecular bonding there are clear and palpable foci of analysis. One of these is inequality. As with the importance of the weather for agricultural and riverine peoples, or electromagnetism and the bonding of molecules for physical scientists, inequality in the sociopolitical sphere is ubiquitous for the social analyst. As Kenneth Waltz put it for one branch of the social sciences, "international politics is mostly about inequalities" (1979, 94). To understand the sources and consequences of inequality is to make sense of an ever-present phenomenon that strongly conditions the economic, political, and social universe in which we live.

And so this book will proceed in the analysis of inequality, not within the mythical or legendary domain, but under the rubric of modern social science, using its concepts, tools, models, and metaphors. Yet in a functional sense, there is little to choose between the myths of traditional peoples and the empirically based theories of modern physical and social sciences. Logic and empirical verification, of course, are decisive in matters of material truth but do not help much to understand the human quest for certainly that establishes either priesthoods of Kwakiutl shamans or hierarchies of scientific administrators and practitioners in national capitals and university research centers. The quest proceeds in varying forms appropriate for different societies and different ages. As for the science and accuracy of weather prediction, the original domain of the Kwakiutl Thunderbird, clearly we have not progressed as far along the road to certainty as we would like. Yet our repeated failures in predicting have, in part, given rise to a new science of indeterminacy, that of chaos theory (Gleick 1987), and we can now set out the limits to certainty of prediction with far greater precision than was possible before the scientific quest for certainty. One of the basic components of chaos theory—fractals—is one of the principal tools of analysis used in this book. As a component of probability theory, along with others, it establishes an inherent indeterminacy of explanation.

It is in this spirit that this book is written, seeking the boundaries of certainty for the sources of inequality and its consequences and attempting to understand the nature of the indeterminacy that delimits those boundaries. Although it would be enormously satisfying psychologically to proclaim some enduring certainties concerning sources of the human condition, that, as we now know, is the stuff of legend.

Several agencies deserve thanks for their contributions to this effort. First, the University of Colorado at Boulder generously funded the Center for International Relations, which in turn supported the initial stages of this inquiry. Rutgers University, New Brunswick and the Back family generously supported the Moses and Annuta Back Professorship of International Peace and Conflict Resolution that enabled me to finish this book. The National Science Foundation, Grant Number 1-5-34855, and the United States Institute of Peace, Grant Number SF-96-12, also aided the process of inquiry. Highly competent research assistance was provided by Hochul Lee, Han Jung Kim, Richard Nolan, and Susan Craig. I am indebted to Greg Manco for his highly competent emendations of the mathematical derivations. In addition, this effort would not have been completed without the diligent secretarial support of Donna Pelican, Mirah Riben, and Beth Vallario. All errors of course are my own.

The following journals generously gave permission for material to be reprinted here. Materials in Chapters 2 and 7 are reprinted in part from the *Journal of Conflict Resolution* (Midlarsky 1982, 1992a, 1995) and the *Interna-

tional Studies Quarterly (Midlarsky 1998), while portions of Chapter 8 were originally published in the *American Political Science Review* (Midlarsky 1988). Much of the substance of Chapter 9 was published in the *Humboldt Journal of Social Relations* (Midlarsky 1986).

M.M.

CONTENTS

Figures and Tables — xiii

PART I. INTRODUCTION

1 Theoretical Overview — 3
2 Scarcity and Inequality — 18

PART II. STATE FORMATION AND DISSOLUTION

3 Warfare and the Origins of the State — 47
4 Decline and Fall of Empires and States — 89

PART III. DEMOCRACY

5 The Timing of the "Social Problem" and Democratization — 151
6 Failures of State Formation and Democratization — 165
7 Sources of Democracy — 185

PART IV. VIOLENCE AND COOPERATION

8 Inequality and Political Violence — 231
9 Equality and Cooperation or Helping — 248

PART V. CONCLUSION

10 Paradoxes of Democracy and State Survivability — 263

APPENDIX A. Mathematical Derivations of the Equations for the Exponential and Fractal (EI) Distributions — 285
APPENDIX B. Countries Included in the Analysis of Chapter 7 — 295

Notes — 301
Bibliography — 309
Index — 339

FIGURES AND TABLES

FIGURES

Figure 2.1. Comparison of Distribution of Value Under Conditions of Scarcity and Infinite Abundance — 20

Figure 2.2. Comparison of Distribution of Value Under Conditions of Scarcity and Relative Abundance — 21

Figure 2.3. Observed and Theoretical Distributions of Landholdings for Malta and Gozo — 22

Figure 2.4. Fractal Formation as the Result of Expansion — 26

Figure 2.5. Fractal Formation in the Sierpinski Gasket — 27

Figure 2.6. Fractal Formation in Resettlement — 29

Figure 2.7. Fractal Formation in an Administrative Hierarchy — 30

Figure 2.8. The Dependence of the Measure of Inequality on the Number of Available Utiles — 42

Figure 6.1. A Thought Experiment on Church-State Relations and Landownership Patterns — 179

Figure 8.1. Goodness of Fit of the Exponential Distribution to Income Levels of African-Americans, 1950–70 — 244

Figure 8.2. Poverty Rates of African-American and White Families Headed by Men and Odds of Being in Poverty by Household Type, 1959–86 — 246

Figure 10.1. Relationship Between Inequality and Democracy — 266

Figure A.1. Fractal Formation on a Straight-Line Segment — 290

TABLES

Table 2.1. Dutch Shipping Hegemony in 1786: Observed and Predicted EI and Exponential Distributions — 32

Table 2.2. Colonial Populations of the European Powers in 1914: Observed and Predicted EI and Exponential Distributions — 33

Table 2.3. Russian Farms in 1911, as a Percentage of Those of 1882 (EI distribution) — 34

Table 2.4. Observed and Predicted Patterns of Tenancy in Negros Oriental, Philippines, in 1958 (EI distribution) — 35

Table 2.5. Observed and Predicted Upper Portions of Land Distributions for Peru (1961) and Ecuador (1954) (EI distribution) — 36

Table 2.6. Observed and Predicted Nearest-Neighbor Distances in the Uruk Hierarchy (EI distribution) — 37

Table 2.7. Observed and Predicted Distribution of Population in Core Chinese Cities in 1893 (EI distribution) — 37

Table 2.8. The Number of Countries with r Utiles, Total Utiles κ and $m = 5$ (random distribution) — 41

Table 4.1. Change in the Proportion of Families of the Various Economic Groupings in the District of Pan-yu, Kwangtung, China, 1928 and 1933 — 97

Table 7.1. Regression of the Political Rights, Liberal Democracy, and Polity III Indexes on the Initial Explanatory Variables — 215

Table 7.2. Regression of the Political Rights, Liberal Democracy, and Polity III Indexes on the Initial Explanatory plus Environmental Variables — 217

Table 7.3. Regression of the Political Rights, Liberal Democracy, and Polity III Indexes on the Explanatory Variables, Adding Land Inequality and Substituting Size of Military Personnel — 219

Table 8.1. Tests of the Exponential and EI Models of Landholdings in El Salvador, 1960 — 237

Table 8.2. Results of the Exponential and EI Analyses of Land Distribution in Twenty Latin American Countries — 239

Table 8.3. Association Between Patterned Inequality and Political Violence for the Twenty Latin American Countries — 241

Table 9.1. Occupational Distribution of Jews and Opponents of Antisemitism in Germany, the Rhine Province, and the Governmental District of Düsseldorf — 259

The Evolution of Inequality

PART I

Introduction

CHAPTER 1

Theoretical Overview

This book is about inequalities as they evolve and influence the political process. Various forms of political violence, including war and revolution, are to be analyzed, along with the origins and dissolution of the state, and sources of cooperation; all of these are to be viewed analytically through the prism of inequality. The genesis of democracy also will be understood as a consequence of processes to be detailed in the following chapters.

Why study inequality? Although the answer might appear to be self-evident, it is worthwhile to consider reasons for its importance, or even centrality, in the etiology of processes to be considered here. First, definitions of politics have at least implicitly included inequality as a principal component or outcome of the political process. Whether it be David Easton's "authoritative allocation of value" (1965, 51) or Harold Lasswell's "who gets what, when, and how" (1936), there are some who get and others who do not. Typically, political scientists have centered on the decision processes by which such allocations are made, treating inequalities as the effective consequence of choices made in centers of political decision making.

I propose to attack the problem in a different way, one that derives in part from the field of international politics. When Kenneth Waltz states that "international politics is mostly about inequalities" (1979, 94), he does not mean that some central decision-making entity has ordained that these inequalities exist, as implied by Easton's and Lasswell's definitions. Instead, he sees that certain structural configurations have evolved over time, which, in themselves, constitute a set of inequality relations (e.g., major powers vis-à-vis small powers). It is this process of evolution that I seek to emphasize in this book.

The emergence of inequality will be used as a theoretical "cut" into the substantive material. In place of a multivariate and multifaceted inquiry into the admittedly big questions that occupy center stage here (which would probably prove intractable), the role of inequality alone will be examined across a range of these important issues. Of course, where possible and with available data, controls will be introduced into the analyses. Ultimately, in the concluding chapter, these investigations will yield outcomes that are relevant to policy making in democracies and to their survivability. The basic assumption is that the processes associated with inequality formation are of such key importance that they have profound influence on policy and political systems.

One indication of the importance of these processes is the emphasis placed on them by eminent scholars. No less a personage than Fernand Braudel expresses wonderment at the inequality relations he observes. I shall quote him at length because of the vast amount of research that he has done in connection with his monumental series of volumes on civilization and capitalism and the manner in which he expresses his surprise. Thus, according to Braudel:

> Conspicuous at the top of the pyramid is a handful of privileged people. Everything invariably falls into the lap of this tiny group: power, wealth, a large share of surplus production. This is the group that governs, administers, directs, takes decisions, sees to the continuity of investment and thus of production. To this group flow all goods, services, currencies. Below it ranges the multitude of economic agents, workers of every rank, the mass of the governed. And below everyone else, stretches that huge social scrapheap, the world of the unemployed.... What is so surprising is that the privileged should *always* be so few. Since social advancement does exist, and since this tiny elite has always depended on the surplus provided by the labour of the non-privileged, whenever that surplus increased, the tiny elite at the top ought to have expanded too. But it never has—even in the twentieth century.... Is there not in short, whatever the society and whatever the period, an insidious law giving power to the few, an irritating law it must be said, since the reasons for it are not obvious. And yet this is a stubborn fact, taunting us at every turn. We cannot argue with it: all the evidence agrees. (1982, 466–67; emphasis in original)

The evidence referred to by Braudel is drawn by him from a variety of sources. In Venice, a major Mediterranean power for several centuries prior to 1575, the *Nobili* never numbered more than 10,000 persons, and this was no more than 5 percent of the total population. From the late sixteenth century there was a steady decline in the absolute size of the nobility until the early eighteenth century. In Nuremberg, by the fourteenth century, power was in the hands of a small aristocracy, approximately 150 to 200 persons out of a total of 20,000 people in the town and another 20,000 in the surrounding district. In the Netherlands, in the seventeenth century, the ruling aristocracy counted for no more than 10,000 out of a total population of two million.

These are some of the many instances adduced by Braudel (1982, 466–72). Other scholars also have recognized both the importance and the poorly understood status of the processes that drive inequality relations. William McNeill, for example, observes in connection with the Hellenistic world that *"obscure* economic factors apparently favored the growth of large estates tilled by hired hands or slaves, while the old-fashioned citizen farmer with his family property disappeared by degrees. An impoverished proletariat gathered in the cities.... Under these circumstances, the few tended to become richer, the rest poorer" (1963, 286–87; emphasis added). Or as Chester Starr puts it, in examining the early rise of the Greek aristocracy and consequent inequality relations, "The manner in which loans became so mighty a machine of oppression is mysterious" (1986, 63–64).

Throughout all of the ancient and modern periods that will be considered in this volume, the same or similar inequality relations appear. Braudel's affirmation of the universality of such inequality will be confirmed, as will McNeill's observations on ancient Greece and its *sequelae*. But whereas others, such as Marx or Hobbes, have attributed the outcome of inequality to specific economic structures or more generally to human greed and perhaps even to human venality, I shall take a far more simple-minded view. Occam's razor will be asserted to hold, in the simple—but, I shall claim, important—random processes of allocation, subdivision, or expansion, as the case may be.

Part I lays the overall theoretical groundwork for the remainder of the book. After the overview provided in this chapter, Chapter 2 provides the theoretical-probabilistic argument that links scarcity and inequality. Evidence for this relationship will be presented in the form of an exponentially declining probability of attaining valued commodities under conditions of scarcity. Moreover, the greater the scarcity, the more rapid the exponential decline. This clearly is a recipe for the emergence of inequality under scarce conditions and requires *no additional assumptions* beyond that of scarcity and randomness. In other words, we need make no assumptions concerning human nature or structural economic relations in order to derive the existence of inequality.

One example should suffice to illustrate the basic contours of the argument. Concerning the emergent scarcity of land as the result of border closings among the Kirghiz of Northeastern Afghanistan, Allen Johnson and Timothy Earle write:

The border closings have greatly increased the stratification and political centralization of the Kirghiz. Formerly they moved freely through the Pamir largely as independent family camps, although leaders existed for specific functions in ceremonial exchange and dispute resolution. But after 1950 camps and kin clusters laid claim to strips of land transecting the valley to ensure their access to all the microenvironments they need for year-round subsistence. And with the construction of permanent houses, corrals, and irrigation works, the ownership of carefully defined plots of land has become common. *One result has been the differential accumulation of wealth.* (1987, 190; emphasis added)

But, as we shall see, this is only one half of the argument. The exponential distribution exists under the condition of a scarce commodity to be distributed. Under conditions of expansion—outward movement of populations, conquest, and/or the resettlement of conquered populations—a distribution of even greater inequality emerges, namely the Pareto or, as it will be referred to here, the fractal or the distribution of extreme inequality (EI distribution). I will argue that this distribution of vastly greater inequality is associated with state formation and interestingly, under different conditions, with the dissolution of states.

It is in this extreme inequality that we see the beginnings of an absence of mutual identification between rulers and ruled, although in the early stages of state formation this does not appear to be especially injurious. Only in the later histories of empires and states do severe inequalities and a consequent absence of mutual identifications presage state collapse. This theme of inequality and the resultant absence of identification will reappear throughout this book, beginning in Chapter 4, and will be especially developed in Part IV, with its treatment of political violence and cooperation or helping. Recent events and data analyses of individual behavior can be drawn on to develop a theory of identification beyond that of the historical inferences that will be made, mostly by implication, in the earlier chapters. Thus, the theory of exponential subdivision under scarcity and fractal formation upon expansion will be supplemented where possible (because of data availability) by a theory of the presence or absence of identification between populations under certain societal conditions.

A common precursor of state decline, as we shall see, is the decline of middle groups in society, whether it be lesser nobility in Venice and Rome (mainly *curiales*), middle peasantry in the case of China, or lesser nobility and a consequent decline of the *Landtage* in Germany. Such middle groups can constitute "ladders of identification" whereby, for example, although it is extraordinarily difficult for an inner city African-American youth to identify with a white corporate executive in a far suburb, it is possible to identify with a black middle-level manager living in the city or a near suburb. The middle group of society establishes a conduit of identification, as it were, between the upper and lower levels. Those who would not dream of identifying with and aspiring to a societal level far above them could do so in relation to one closer in status. Without such a middle group, the gap between elite and mass is so wide that any number of consequences may follow, including political violence or societal ennui and ultimately decay.

In my analysis warfare will not be understood as a necessary condition for state formation, only as a sufficient one. If warfare occurs, then the state can indeed evolve. But if warfare does not occur, then the state can evolve by other means. Expansion in and of itself, whether it includes warfare or not, will be seen as both necessary and sufficient for the origins of the state.[1] In turn, state dissolution and, more specifically, the breakup of empires will be examined from the perspective of inequality. Several different types of inequality will be associated with the decline and fall of empires, some including the onset of domestic violence, others not.

Inequality and its role both in state formation and dissolution and in political democracy will occupy much of the remainder of this volume, with special attention to the role of warfare in connection with each of these. Additionally, the onset of mass (domestic) political violence will be considered from the perspective of the two inequality distributions, as will the relationship between equality and cooperation.

Given this theoretical development, Part II investigates the origins of states and their dissolution. After attacking the supposed inextricable link between warfare and state formation,[2] Chapter 3 examines the origins of states from the perspective of inequality relations. Specifically, there exists an initial status differentiation that emerges from the exponential distribution of scarce quantities. This initial, somewhat tempered inequality, under conditions of expansion and/or warfare, yields a fractal distribution of extreme inequality that, especially in the form of land ownership, provides a material basis for the incipient state.

Although Chapter 3 will examine mainly pristine states for evidence of state formation, it is instructive, by way of illustration, to examine briefly the medieval origins of the modern state, simply because we know so much more about it. Evidence of the bases of the modern state are found precisely in those areas subject to fractal expansion and a consequent feudalization. As Joseph Strayer remarks, "Curiously enough, the drive towards improved judicial and financial institutions was especially strong in some of the larger feudal lordships. . . . In some areas, notably northern France, the more competent feudal lords took some of the first steps in state-building" (1970, 18–19). Indeed, "the first permanent [state] functionaries were estate-managers—the reeves and shire-reeves (sheriffs) of England, the *prévôts* of France, the ministerials of Germany" (Strayer 1970, 28).

The Black Death of the fourteenth century appears to have accelerated the process of fractal expansion and hastened the coming of the modern state. Vast areas of Europe lay depopulated and ripe for the plucking by ambitious and contentious feudal leaders.³ And "in an age when the economy was stagnant, if not regressive, the easiest way for a ruler to increase his income and power was to try to gain control of new territories" (Strayer 1970, 59). In this fashion, feudal principalities expanded, as did the bureaucracies staffed initially by estate managers.

The evolution of inequality resulting from scarcity and its political consequences drive the following causal sequences examined here. Given a *pristine system*,⁴ that is, one that is not preceded by or affected by earlier states,

Resource scarcity → Status and/or economic inequality → Chiefdom (religious and/or political) → Expansion via fractal (EI) formation → State

Note that the early chiefdom can be religious or secular or some combination of the two, but as we shall see, over time the early religious forms tended to give way to more secular ones (Kramer 1963; Oppenheim 1977).

Several state trajectories are examined in Chapter 3, specifically ancient Mesopotamia, Egypt, Crete, China, Mesoamerica, and the Andes. These instances are chosen because most of these societies are acknowledged to be pristine, generally by virtue of a geographical isolation. An exception, Crete (and possibly Egypt), is extraordinarily interesting in its own right, not least because of the possible emergence of proto-democracies in early societies, with Crete and especially Sumer and China as cases in point.

State dissolution is analyzed in Chapter 4. Here the fractal or EI distribution is already formed and has long since been used as the initial basis for state formation. Two circumstances differ between the analyses of state formation in Chapter 3 and state dissolution in Chapter 4. First, in contrast to prehistory, with its absence of documentation and confirmed observation, state dissolution can be analyzed using historical documents and the observations of ancient historians. Simply the advent of writing makes the latter process far more accessible. The second distinction is not historiographic but analytical. Although the formation of states occurred under conditions of extreme inequality, that inequality is, in the period of terminal decline, even more vastly exacerbated. A quality of fractals as they grow (absent redistribution) is a growing inequality between the earliest arrivals in an expansionary process and those who come later (Ball, Blunt, and Spivack 1989; Willson 1986).⁵ Thus, whereas there is some opportunity for personal gain shortly after state formation (as in the instance of Roman soldiers given plots of land for farming, either in recently conquered portions of Italy or later in North Africa), little such opportunity exists in later periods. Expansion generally has ceased, some processes of contraction have even begun, and opportunity has now become extremely limited. Landlordism, or the growth of large estates with many tenants or serfs, is a product of the continued fractal formation. As Robert Wesson remarks, "A landlord power seems to have grown up in all vast empires that lasted long enough" (1967, 261). There are variants of this basic pattern with equally varied consequences.

There are two fundamental processes of dissolution, each giving rise to at least two consequences. The first has a single state or empire experiencing either scarcities due to overpopulation or contraction as the result of enemy conquest at the borders. Fractal formations continue to grow, generally as a consequence of the sale of small, barely tenable holdings to larger landowners. The resulting large estates and an oppressed serf-like population become easy prey for marauding tribes. Examples of this process include the later Roman Empire, the later Byzantine Empire, and in a variation on these themes, ancient Israel and Egypt. The second process also is one entailing resource scarcity and fractal formation, but there exists as well a continuing exponential subdivision of lands by the growing peasant population without the growth of enormous landlord-owned fractals. Recurrent political violence results that actually constitutes a periodic renewal of the polity, albeit transformed each time in fundamental ways. Chinese history contains strong elements of this process. Thus, given a *single state or empire*

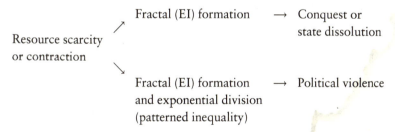

There is yet another pattern of state dissolution unique to a multipolar environment, generally consisting, historically, of city-states in a situation of competition, which under conditions of resource scarcity leads to open warfare. Because of the scarcities often associated with warfare, inequalities *within* city-states also can increase, thus superimposing a domestic inequality on that occurring between the system units. If continued, as is often the case, this warfare can yield either mutual destruction and abandonment or conquest by an external power. The ancient Maya constitute an illustration of the first sequence while the ancient Greek and the Italian Renaissance city-states offer instances of the second. Thus, given a *multipolar environment*

```
                                                       ↗ Destruction or
                                                          abandonment
  Resource scarcity        Warfare between
                      →    political aggregates
  or contraction            of fairly equal power
                                                       ↘ External conquest
```

Specific historical instances are treated at some length—Rome, Byzantium, the Maya, ancient China, ancient Israel and Judah, and ancient Egypt. In some cases, these instances overlap with those treated in Chapter 3, in others not. They were chosen, not for consistency with the histories of state formation, but for their own intrinsic analytic properties of state dissolution, to be compared with other equally interesting cases. Theoretically, as a final comparison, the analysis extends to the Aztec and Inca, which seemed to disappear politically solely as the result of rapid conquest through superior technology, but in fact reveal analytic commonalities with the other instances examined.

A special feature of the analysis concerns the timing of state collapse. Scholars have expressed considerable puzzlement at the sudden collapse of civilizations, the ancient Maya being a case in point. Although there is an emerging agreement on the general causes of the Maya collapse, the rapidity of that disintegration still generates surprise if not dismay. It turns out that both of the models of inequality considered here indeed predict that in the face of resource depletion (which is the emerging consensus explanation for the fall; see, e.g., Sabloff 1990) there should be a sudden worsening of conditions, so quick in fact that there would be little time to prepare for it. The implications of this argument for our present condition are apparent. There already exists substantial evidence for the effects of inequality on modern societies, particularly in the form of various forms of ill health and declines in longevity, that can signal the onset of an eroding social fabric (Wilkinson 1996).

The remaining chapters present alternatives to decline and political violence. First, democracy is understood to be a form of political activity substitutable for political violence. And the origins of democracy in agrarian society present yet another avenue for the exploration of the consequences of inequality, explicitly land inequality and its consequences for political rights.

Part III examines the role of factors pertaining to democracy. Initially, in Chapter 5, elements of the societal sources of state dissolution presented in

Chapter 4 are isolated and related to failures to democratize as general sources of state weakness. In particular, the timing of what I call the "social problem" relative to the occurrence of war is of extreme importance. If that problem—namely, the pressures for reform resulting from existing massive societal inequalities—is resolved in some fashion *prior* to major international warfare that requires serious funding efforts, then parliamentary supremacy may take hold, as in the English Civil War and its aftermath, the Glorious Revolution of 1688. If, however, the problem is not resolved successfully prior to major warfare, as in the War of the Spanish Succession for France and the Napoleonic Wars for Spain, then monarchical or other forms of authoritarian rule can develop.

Failure to democratize at an early moment in history can be the result of societal factors, as discussed in Chapter 5. Even more extreme are instances of early state failure that include elimination of the bases for later democratization. Chapter 6 treats the Germano-Roman and the Abbasid empires as cases in point. In each, the failure to distinguish clearly between the domains of church and state and even, as in the Germano-Roman case, to distinguish between the state core and more peripheral areas, doomed these states to early dissolution. Processes of democratization were arrested by incessant warfare and a decline of the lesser nobility, along with the virtual dissolution of representative institutions such as the *Landtage*. Similar problems of an essential union of church and state and the absence of a strong landed base plagued the Abbasid monarchy. On the other hand, the contrast between Germany west of the Elbe and Prussia to the east is an instructive one. The fractal formation of steady eastward expansion facilitated the formation of a strong Prussian state.

The theoretical and historical materials treated thus far lay the foundation for a more systematic treatment of democracy in Chapter 7. Three major categories of variables emerge from the preceding treatments: (1) land incquality, (2) environmental impacts, namely aridity and the threat of warfare, and (3) ideological impacts, such as that of Islam. The first is reflected in this book's central concern with inequality and, equally, its emphasis on fractal formation as the basis of a strong state. The threat of warfare, also one of the principal foci of the book, will be seen as an environmental variable, along with rainfall, the absence of which we will examine in the case of irrigation and state formation. Finally, following certain of the implications of Chapter 6, Islam is examined in relation to democracy. The findings are intriguing, for they suggest that different measures of democracy—here an index of basic political rights, an index of liberal democracy, and one reflecting institutional forms—may yield different conclusions. Culturally related variables such as islam or British colonial heritage demonstrate far more of an impact on the liberal democracy measure than on the more rudimentary political rights index. Perhaps most important is the finding that land inequality is positively related to the three measures of democracy while the threat of war is negatively related to all three. The outcome related to war is intuitively appealing, but that pertaining to land inequality is much less so. Why should land inequality be positively related to democracy? The answer, developed more fully in Chapter 7, resides in the argument pointing to a strong state as a precursor for the early granting of small political rights by long-term, hence relatively secure conquest elites.

Finally, Part IV juxtaposes the inequality relations specified in patterned inequality and political violence with the equality inherent in mutual identification and cooperation or helping.[6] Chapter 8 develops the theory of patterned inequality, wherein the combination of fractal distributions at the higher end of land distributions and exponential distributions at the lower combine to increase the probability of political violence as a result of the absence of a mutual identification between peasant and landlord. Hence,

Patterned inequality (conjunction of fractal [EI] and exponential distributions) $\rightarrow$ Absence of mutual identification between social strata $\rightarrow$ Political violence

These arguments are applied in the instances of Latin American land distributions and income distributions of African-Americans, both subject to serious scarcity conditions. But this violence is not necessarily associated with the termination of the state or empire. Indeed it can sometimes actually enhance the likelihood of state survival, at least in altered form. On the other hand, the presence of only one of these distributions, the fractal (EI) distribution, in the relative absence of others, will decrease the probability of state survival, even in the absence of political violence.

Similarly, equality and the presence of a mutual identification can enhance cooperation and helping, as shown in Chapter 9. Equality of circumstance and a consequent mutual identification of a religious, political, and socioeconomic nature is associated with increased helping of Jews by non-Jews during the Holocaust. Equality of circumstance between German opponents of Nazism and their Jewish counterparts and a consequent helping of Jews is particularly impressive, especially as it defies prediction by other, equally compelling frameworks. The argument here takes the form of:

Equality of circumstance $\rightarrow$ Mutual identification $\rightarrow$ Cooperation and helping

This is a fitting way to conclude our analysis, for it suggests reasons why even under the most favorable conditions for cooperation among equals the political scenario can give way to hierarchy and inequality, although perhaps of a benevolent sort. A tension between the conditions necessary for democracy and those needed for cooperation are here evident. Yet cooperation itself may be a requisite of stable democracy. This tension, perhaps even paradox, of democracy will be developed more fully in the Conclusion, which attempts to resolve many of these apparently conflicting streams of theory and findings.

A comment or two is necessary concerning the mode of inquiry adopted here. Aside from the obvious use of mathematical models (mercifully relegated to appendixes, except where absolutely necessary), this book is an exercise in historical scholarship. But this is not history as a typical historian would write it; rather it follows from Stephen Jay Gould's injunctions concerning evolutionary biology as a historical science:

> History subverts the stereotype of science as a precise, heartless enterprise that strips the uniqueness from any complexity and reduces everything to timeless, repeatable, controlled experiments in a laboratory. Historical sciences are different, not lesser. Their methods are comparative, not always experimental; they explain, but do not usually try to predict; they recognize the irreducible quirkiness that history entails, and acknowledge the limited power of present circumstances to impose or elicit optimal solutions. (1985, 18)

Because this book is about the evolution of inequality, it is entirely appropriate that Gould's definition be adopted here. But there is another perspective on evolution that also deserves mention for its similarities and differences with that undertaken here. This is the understanding of history enunciated by Friedrich Engels (1940) in establishing the bases of historical materialism. This understanding proceeds from a virtual equality of circumstance in primitive society, termed primitive communism by him, through inequalities that evolved as a result of private property sequestration in the feudal and later capitalist periods, followed by a mature communism in the industrial era. Chapters 2–3 of this book emphasize a commonality with Engels's framework, in that only relatively minor inequalities and even proto-democracies existed in prehistory and early historical times. And indeed it is private property in the form of land ownership that establishes bases for the state in my argument as well as in Engels's treatment (developed more fully in Chapter 3). But whereas Engels, and of course Marx, saw private property and state formation as a virtual evil, or at least a historical anomaly in the modern "revolutionary" era, the understanding here is radically different.

Although certainly the basis for eventual state formation, land inequality later begins to serve various purposes. While providing the basis of capital accumulation and, particularly in the English case, early industrialization, it also has certain unintended consequences of providing a secure basis of control for the landed elite, which then slowly, and in many cases peacefully, can devolve political rights on other societal groupings. In other words, as inequality evolves, whether it be based on land or income, it can serve purposes beyond those of the manifest sort emphasized by Engels. The understanding of democracy as an eventual outcome stemming from an earlier land inequality is totally alien to the views of Marx and Engels and later of Lenin and Stalin because of the derogation of parliamentary democracy as a sham foisted on a virtually helpless public by the landed elite. For parliaments changed, and gradually the earlier control by the elite gave way to more inclusive forms.

Perhaps the basic error of the Marxian view is the treatment of the modern period as virtually equivalent to the ancient in regard to elasticity of production modes. G. E. M. de Ste. Croix could write a book entitled *The Class Struggle in the Ancient Greek World* in which class has the explicitly Marxian interpretation of "the social embodiment of the fact of exploitation" (de Ste. Croix 1981, 3) based on ownership of the means of production. Interestingly, this nineteenth-century understanding was indeed applicable to the ancient world, with land as the basic source of production and increasingly limited in availability as population levels rose. In the industrial world, on the other hand, modes of production and technology could expand, enlarging incomes and increasingly rendering the Marxian view inapplicable to the understanding of the modern economy and society. Whereas Marx likely was entirely correct in his view of land ownership in ancient societies as a basis for state-sponsored oppression, thus justifying revolution as the only means of breaking the elite stranglehold on society, that understanding is far less applicable to modern society with elastic incomes and, in particular, evolving parliamentary forms that only in their genesis required a substantial land inequality.

The theory of land inequality as a progenitor of democracy is developed in Chapter 7, particularly in relation to Athenian democracy. But for now, we can observe that such processes are continuing even at the present time. Recent interviews with South Carolina political figures are revealing. According to State Senator Michael Rose, "There's a real deference to authority here. It's like we began with a system of feudal lords who created a hierarchical structure, and it's always more or less been that way." And as then Governor Carroll Campbell put it, "I think you see a transition in the state. We have gone from a state that, like some others, was dominated by rural barons who operated under their own code and who operated in a non-threatening society, to a state that now has a competitive two-party system. We had something of an oligarchy down here for a lot of years, and now we're making a transition from it" (Applebome 1991, 16).

I will close this chapter with what appears to be an extravagant claim, namely that one reason I chose this particular approach is the seed of predictability contained within it. Prediction here, I hasten to add, is not the microprediction of the time and place of a particular event. Instead, it is the macroprediction of long-term trends and probable outcomes, such as state decline and ultimate dissolution. It is for this reason I avoided such contemporary approaches as collective action (e.g., Olson 1965), which despite its many virtues is avowedly nonpredictive.[7] There is no necessity to avoid macro-prediction; we now know, for example, that despite the apparent failure to predict the demise of the Soviet Union, the actual record on this score of Sovietologists is better than is generally supposed (J. S. Berliner, cited in Keep 1995).

Further, one can make reasonably secure predictions in constrained systems. For example, it was possible to predict the onset of the recent Croatian War against Serb-held Krajina, as it was to predict the second Reagan victory in 1984. The Croatian offensive was part of a mobilization war consequent upon the earlier structural war of 1991 between Serbia and Croatia.[8] The second Reagan victory prediction was based exclusively on time-series election data extending only through 1980 (Midlarsky 1984, 938). These were not necessarily difficult predictions to make. I simply invoke them to demonstrate that prediction in the social sciences certainly is not impossible.[9] Given a long-term tendency with fairly clearly specified parameters, then high probabilities can be attached to certain general outcomes. The more constrained the system, as in a two-party alternation in power, the more specific the prediction. The less constrained the system, the less specific a successful prediction is likely to be. Both structural and mobilization wars and party systems are highly constrained. War focuses attention on an enemy and trumps virtually all other concerns. Two-party systems virtually by definition are highly constrained, as one party focuses almost exclusively on the other. In the context of this book, inequality in extremis may have similar focusing power of one group on another, as we shall see in Chapter 4. Given the uncertainties of contemporary rapid social change, it is virtually incumbent on the social scientist to at least attempt to detect long-term trends that could yield deleterious results. State dissolution under conditions of widespread violence or the demise of democracy are cases in point.

At the same time, as we shall see in the concluding chapter, the theory presented here has predictive power, not for predicting an event at some point $t + n$ number of years in the future, but for aspects of societies either ancient or modern that are not evident at the present time. For example, discoveries have recently been made concerning gender equality in certain nomadic societies that could have been predicted by the present theoretical framework.

This effort is consistent with the overall philosophy of inquiry that suggests a strong empirical base conjugate with our theoretical base. This surely is a hallmark of science, but interestingly it is also a basis for certain artistic efforts. Piet Mondrian, for example, attempted to establish an art abstracted from reality in common with many other mid-twentieth century artists. He wanted to "reveal an essential order hidden beneath the veil of natural appearances" (Kernan 1995, 6). In doing so, he carried his abstractions to the point of extreme formalism, as in his Compositions. Effectively, he sought to establish an ideal order in which each change from the previous abstraction would be only a marginal alteration in that particular order. In other words, the referent became the abstraction itself, to which all future changes referred.

In certain ways, this is not terribly different from what scientists have done in attempting to create models that are isomorphic to reality, and then the models themselves are tinkered with or altered. The danger here, of course, as Mondrian himself saw in his last years, is that the abstraction can become an end in itself instead of a means to an end. It is ultimately reality that we are concerned with, contrary to the view of one social scientist who, questioned at a conference about his simulation effort, responded "reality is a crutch." In his last years in New York, Mondrian inserted wild colors into his previously maximally trichromal abstractions and in a sense edged closer to the reality underpinning his art. It is said that he died happy. Our current efforts in the social sciences, it is to be hoped, will avoid the Scylla of excessive formalisms that become self-referential and thereby scientifically sterile and the Charybdis of "thick description" that eschews any effort at modeling or abstraction.

In one important sense, this book tells a story, namely what happens when the two distributions identified here, the exponential and the EI, take hold. Stratification begins, states form and decline, political violence or cooperation can exist depending on societal circumstances and especially on mutual identification or its absence between societal groupings, and, most importantly, democracy can be strongly influenced by inequality conditions. Along this theoretical-historical pathway other variables are found to be salient, and so they must be examined as well. These distributions, to be defined mathematically in Chapter 2, and their sequencing constitute the theoretical core of the book. All else, including historical narratives and later systematic empirical analyses, follows from these initial conditions.

The "storytelling" aspect of the book emerges from a coincidence of theoretical conditions and historical time. In the evolution of human societies, stratification and its exponential description necessarily precede the formation of states, at least in earlier times before the state as an organizational principle became well known worldwide. State formation and its associated fractals follow in time, with democracy sometimes in tandem, most often not. State decline and disappearance in relation to later fractal formation, is one potential outcome of these evolving stories. Democracy can be an antidote to such tendencies toward state dissolution, although it certainly does not have to be. But because democracy is of such potential importance not only to the health of the state but also to a neo-Kantian perpetual peace, the concluding chapter will emphasize paradoxes of democracy and the conditions of state survivability. A symbiosis of the earlier theoretics and empirics will, in the end, yield analytic elements that verge on the policy-making process. There are many stories to be told in the succeeding chapters, all in the service of examining the basic theories. A thorough empirical investigation using prehistorical or early historical materials requires a fair degree of narration.

A final comment is in order on the organization of this volume. Beyond the theoretical material in the first two chapters, Chapters 3 and 4 use the materials of prehistory and history, respectively, in comparative analyses, while Chapters 5 and 6 use similar methods of focused historical comparison to answer questions raised by the earlier inquiry. In Chapters 7–9, we deal with more systematic analyses applied to the contemporary period, using many of the basic ideas developed in the earlier chapters. For readers less concerned with the mathematical and systematic empirical basis of the book and more interested in the historical, both Chapter 2 and Chapter 8 can be skimmed for their basic concepts.

CHAPTER 2

Scarcity and Inequality

How does inequality evolve? Two forms of a basic theorem govern this inquiry. They reveal a link between the ecological circumstances of a community and its state of unequal distribution of desired commodities. The strong form of the theorem asserts that given *equal opportunity for random access to the acquisition of these desiderata, their scarcity limits equality of distribution*; it is called "strong" because it posits the existence of inequality *independent* of the characteristics of the actors in question. In other words, the distribution is dependent only on the amount of available resources or, in practice, as we shall see, the mean value of these commodities. The second or weak form of the theorem is one that claims *certain differences between actors, which then lead to an even more extreme inequality of distribution*. It is the existence of these differences among actors that results in this greater inequality. A third variant of the scarcity-inequality nexus is applied specifically to units in a multipolar system and is akin to the exponential decline in resource acquisition. For purposes of clarity of exposition, it is presented last in the following sequence.

Because this book has evolutionary concerns, it is appropriate to consider them in some detail. The following quote neatly summarizes a basic argument of evolutionary theory:

Both Darwin and Wallace saw that there must be competition for limited resource supplies. And they also realized that with the exception of some pairs of twins, no two organisms within a population are ever exactly alike. Such natural variation ensures that the competition will be unequal: it will be in the nature of things for some organisms to be more vigorous, more viable, more "fit"—generally more able by dint of overall better health, or equipped with a superior version of some feature vital to survival. . . . And that's all there is to natural selection: in the competition for resources, the variability in the population means that some organisms will be better equipped to survive. (Eldredge 1985, 35)

Here, in a nutshell, we have the basic argument that relates the characteristics of actors, in this case organisms, to the inequality of distribution—the "weak" form of our theorem. There exists variability in the distribution of genetic characteristics that enable some to prevail more readily than others under conditions of scarcity. It is the endowment from nature that allows some to acquire more than others when there are limited sources. As might be expected, such inequality will be greater than that which would arise under conditions of no postulated differences among the participant actors, that is, random equal access for indistinguishable actors (the strong form of the theorem).

How do these two scenarios—equal opportunity for indistinguishable actors and for distinguishable actors, yielding unequal access to scarce resources—play out in practice? And what do these distributions look like? As a note to the history of this book, the two distributions were arrived at independent of considerations of evolutionary theory but have strong theoretical links with it; it is worthwhile for descriptive purposes to present them sui generis.

The Exponential Distribution

Let us now consider the strong form of the basic theorem, which postulates no differences among actors yet yields inequality under conditions of scarcity. This is called the exponential distribution. In the approach to this investigation, we first consider the obverse circumstance of infinite abundance, in which indistinguishable actors have equal opportunity to achieve any one of several commodities. If all commodities have the same value, then obviously there is no inequality. Infinite abundance insures that all receive the same amount of value. But supposing that the commodities are of unequal value. Even under conditions of infinite abundance, there will be some inequality of distribution, for random access will ensure that some persons will be assigned to "better" categories (those with more valuable resources) than others. The mathematics underlying this distribution are given in Appendix A, although the intuitive argument presented here is reasonably straightforward. Equation 2.1 expresses the scarcity-inequality argument mathematically, while Figure 2.1 represents it graphically. The predicted values for the exponential distribution are given by

$$p_i = A(k)e^{-kx_i} \qquad k > 0, \ 0 \leq x_i < \infty, \ i = 1, 2, 3, \ldots. \qquad (2.1)$$

where p_i is the proportion of holdings held by the ith category x_i; k is a constant, generally estimated from the empirical distribution (least squares or maximum likelihood); and $A(k)$ is a normalization constant designed to make the sum of the p_i equal to one.

In Figure 2.1, there exists an equal number of persons in each of the unequally valued categories (scale of increasing value) under the infinite abun-

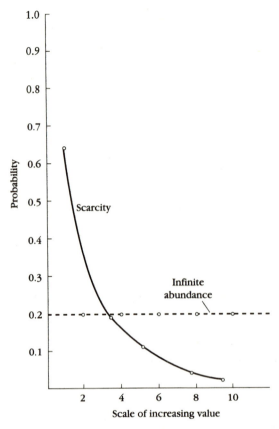

Figure 2.1. Comparison of distribution of value under conditions of scarcity and infinite abundance.

dance condition, but when we impose the scarcity constraint, the situation changes radically. No longer are there equal numbers of persons in each of the categories, but a far greater proportion are found in the lower, least-valued categories (i.e., the probability is highest for the lesser values).

It is easily shown that the greater the scarcity, the greater the proportion in the lower-value categories, hence the greater the inequality. In Figure 2.2 a moderate constraint is imposed in the form of the relative abundance curve, to be contrasted with the scarcity curve. As the figure shows, the proportion of persons in the lower-value categories is much greater under the scarcity condition than under relative abundance, thus establishing a greater inequality between poor and rich.

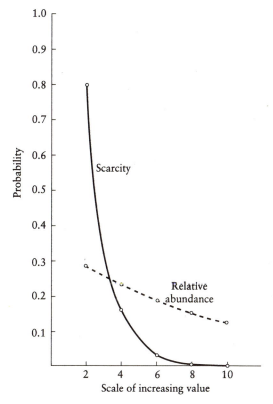

Figure 2.2. Comparison of distribution of value under conditions of scarcity and relative abundance.

We require now a fixed commodity that can serve to illustrate the scarcity condition. Agricultural land clearly qualifies, because such land is a finite resource and beyond a certain point no more can be generated (as from the clearing of forest for agricultural purposes).

Societies with high population densities which already have developed virtually all of their arable land could qualify for our example, because new amounts of this resource cannot be found. Island societies in particular would satisfy this requirement. Let us take the case of Malta (including Gozo, a much smaller neighboring island), which has one of the highest population densities of any society in the contemporary period (1,024 persons per sq km); its distribution of agricultural land ownership is published by the United Nations (Food and Agriculture Organization 1966, 124). The theoretical and observed exponential distributions for Malta and Gozo are shown in Figure 2.3, the value of k,

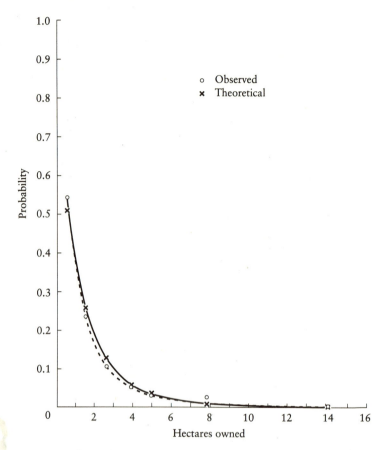

Figure 2.3. Observed and theoretical distributions of landholdings for Malta and Gozo, 1960.

estimated by the reciprocal of the mean, is equal to .6032 and A, the normalizing constant, is equal to .7106. The fit is reasonably good, especially given the restrictive assumptions required for a good fit.

The exponential distribution, in fact, has been used by others to describe agricultural landholdings. Folke Dovring (1973) first put forward the use of this distribution (he had previously described it in mimeo form), and R. F. Boxley (1971) applied it successfully to eastern portions of the United States—but, interestingly, not as successfully to western states, which have lower population densities. An additional application to India can be found in Clark 1972. All of these applications, including Dovring's, are largely empirical, and none of these contain the justification in probability theory found here.

The Geometric Distribution

It is noteworthy that a scheme devised at the level of probability theory should be applicable to actual landholdings. This can be understood through the use of the geometric distribution in the following way. Consider an approximately equal distribution of persons per unit of land in some initial situation. Over a period of time, there is some probability p that each of the landholdings would be divided because of the birth of several males per family (in the absence of primogeniture) and the absence of additional land for expansion, as in island or other constrained societies. Here, the scarcity condition is fully operative.

Given family size as a geometric distribution (Feller 1968, 141) and in particular, the survival of s male carriers of the family name in the nth generation as a geometric distribution (Feller 1968, 294; Lotka 1939, 123-36), then the distribution p_s of the number of persons per unit land over time must follow a geometric distribution given by

$$p_s = qp^{s-1} \qquad s = 1, 2, \ldots \text{ for } 0 < p < 1. \tag{2.2}$$

Now the exponential distribution is the limiting continuous form of the geometric (Feller 1968, 458; Kleinrock 1975, 39), and so the preceding explanation applies here directly, especially as a consequence of the large numbers that would accumulate over time. Note that the scarcity condition is incorporated directly; the derivation does not allow for migration to new lands or some other relief of the circumstance of scarcity. The families reproduce over the generations only within the confines of the given territory of the island or other restricted domain.

This is, in effect, a parallel derivation to the more formal argument leading to Equation 2.1 but one that reveals the specific mechanisms by which land distributions are derived. It also has an additional advantage. Equation 2.1 (and its discrete analogue, Equation 2.2) provides a "snapshot" of the distribution of holdings at any given point in time, but does not indicate the dynamics of evolution of a contemporaneous set of landholdings. This, however, can be constructed from the preceding argument.

In the early stages of this process, the holdings are approximately equal in size, or there at least exists an equality of opportunity to be born into or to inherit a large set of holdings along lines suggested by the softly curvilinear relative-abundance plot in Figure 2.2. However, with each new generation and subsequent divisions of the holdings according to Equation 2.2, the pattern of holdings steadily becomes more unequal, as suggested by the transformation of the gently sloping relative-abundance plot into the more sharply decelerating scarcity curve in that figure. Succeeding generations, therefore, are confronted not only with the greater likelihood of smaller holdings relative to earlier generations, but also with a growing inequality between the mass of the population and the more fortunate few on the far right tail of the distributions.

When directly applied to landholdings, the geometric distribution can, on occasion, provide a better fit than the exponential, especially in the right-hand portion of the distribution. However, for sufficiently large N confined to a small enough land area, the continuity assumptions of the exponential are more nearly met, and there is no significant difference between the two forms. Further, the exponential is more flexible in its application, a fact that will have considerable importance later in analyzing the effects on inequality of the transition from scarcity to abundance. For this reason, there will be no further reference to the geometric distribution in this chapter.

The Fractal (EI) Distribution

What of the second of our two basic models, that dependent on differences among the actors competing for scarce resources? Here there are various possible paths along which such differences may be played out. There exist formal proofs of this distributional form, one of which is included in Appendix A. The fractal or extreme inequality (EI; also known as log-exponential or Pareto-Lévy) model is given by

$$P_i^1 = A_1(k_1)\, e^{-k_1 \log_e x_i} \qquad k_1 > 0,\ 1 \leq x_i < \infty,\ i = 1, 2, 3, \ldots, \qquad (2.3)$$

where as before k_1 and A_1 (normalization) are constants. Here, I will present only expository justifications for the use of this distribution in this context. The possible pathways for the acting out of differences among persons are listed here, not merely for purposes of taxonomy, although that in itself could prove to be useful, but as a means for later establishing the absence of war as a necessary condition for state formation.

The possible avenues for the emergence of inequalities based on differential capabilities (among persons, tribes, nation-states . . .) are (1) expansion over a relatively empty space, (2) conquest and/or settlement, (3) resettlement, and (4) administrative hierarchy. Any one of these processes, separately or in combination with others from this set, can yield the distribution of extreme inequality.

There is now ample evidence for the emergence of fractal distributions upon the expansion of units across a defined space. Fractal distributions are inherently those of extreme inequality because of the self-similarity characteristics at whatever stage of magnification. The distribution appears the same, hence the aggregate of smallest holdings and largest together forms one distribution of extreme inequality. This can be seen in the following illustration.

We begin with ones in the following positions:

1
11

Each subsequent line contains one additional number, and each number in a line will be the sum of the number directly above it (zero if none is explicitly there) and the number at its upper left. Thus, after several moves, one obtains

1
11
121
1331
14641

The pattern moves to the right and is not immediately obvious until all even numbers are treated as zeros and all odd numbers are ones (Chaitin 1987, 8–11). The zeros now occupy a set of triangles with a ratio of areas that is fractal (EI). In Figure 2.4 the zeros are removed, leaving blank spaces, to highlight the fractal pattern.

The areas encompassed by the ones tend to be equal to one another, in contrast to the inequality inherent in the fractal formation. This contrast between the two forms the basis for what I have called *patterned inequality*, for as a consequence of the growth or expansion on the conquest space giving rise to the inequality of a fractal formation, there are the equal areas remaining to be subdivided by the remaining peasantry. The fractal areas—the blanks in Figure 2.4—correspond to the upper tail of a land distribution, and the subdivided areas of the "ones" correspond to an exponential distribution, at the lower end.

The contrast between the expanding space made available by conquest and that remaining to the peasantry can be seen even more clearly in Figure 2.5, which depicts what is known as the Sierpinski gasket. One-fourth of the interior triangular space is removed initially, followed by successive fourths of the remaining areas, thereby giving rise to the fractal (EI) distribution shown in the white areas. The dark sections of equal area correspond to those formed by ones in Figure 2.4, to be subdivided through succeeding generations and giving rise to the geometric-exponential distribution. Illustrations of patterned inequality in landholdings will be offered in the more extended analysis in Chapter 8.

In addition to a straightforward expansion on a defined space, there exists

```
1
11
1 1
1111
1       1
11      11
1 1   1 1
11111111
1               1
11              11
1 1             1 1
1111            1111
1   1         1   1
11  11        11  11
1 1 1 1       1 1 1 1
1111111111111111
1               1
11              11
1 1             1 1
1111            1111
1   1         1   1
11  11        11  11
1 1 1 1       1 1 1 1
11111111        11111111
1       1       1       1
11      11      11      11
1 1   1 1     1 1   1 1
1111  1111    1111  1111
1 1 1 1 1 1 1 1
11 11 11 11 11 11 11 11
1 1 1 1 1 1 1 1 1 1 1 1 1 1 1 1
1111111111111111111111111111111111
```

Figure 2.4. Fractal formation as the result of expansion (after Chaitin, 1987, 12).

a random variant, in which a lottery, coin toss, or any other random selection procedure can define movement across this space (Willson 1986). The end result is the same, namely a fractal pattern that appears identical to that obtained with the steady expansion process of Figure 2.4, but accomplished in a fitful manner.

How do individual differences figure into this process? Those who are fortunate enough to be first in the process and obtain the largest or at least one of the larger portions clearly are at the salutary end of the inequality pattern. How do they get there? Generally, positioning at the head of a queue of potential ac-

Figure 2.5. Fractal formation in the Sierpinski Gasket (after Feder 1988, 25).

quisitors, by whatever means will do the trick. Clearly they would have to be prescient enough to observe the unfolding pattern and also have the financial or military resources to stake their claim and keep it.

Individual differences appear even more directly in the second mode of attaining the EI distribution. Here, a sequential acquisition takes place in which the first arrival in a particular area either settles the best or largest piece of land or conquers it from the indigenous inhabitants. A second arrival appears and takes the next best or largest sector, followed by a third, fourth, etc. Each of the holdings is proportionately smaller than that of the preceding arrival (with the exception of course of the first), thus yielding the distribution of extreme inequality once again.

Each of the earlier arrivals has some operating advantages (technical or otherwise) over the later ones. These could take the form of earlier development of ocean-going vessels or navigational instruments (e.g., Portugal, Spain) or the building of a larger navy (Britain) or any other development that would enhance access over other potential contenders. Here, too, the process can be diagrammed, as in Figures 2.4 and 2.5. The pictorial depiction does not distinguish between expansion with opposition, as in conquest, and without opposition, as in simple expansion over an empty space. Once again, the mathematics can be found in Appendix A.

Let us now look at the third pattern, that of resettlement. How would the fractal pattern appear in this instance? Consider one possible variant. An indigenous population occupies certain territories. If their original territory is successively reduced at regular stages and the population is simultaneously relocated to other (probably outer) portions of the land area, a fractal pattern emerges. This can be seen in the Figure 2.6; the word FRACTAL has been reduced by a copying machine at successive stages and relocated to corners of its original triangular area. The amount of territory now occupied by the indigenous population, shown by the dark letters in the word FRACTAL, is less, and the remainder of the territory, shown in white and now presumably occupied by the conquerors, is fractal. This, incidentally, is probably an approximate model for the fate of indigenous populations such as American Indians after the Iberian conquests.

The final model, that of an administrative hierarchy, emerges after some elementary considerations. If one begins with a fixed area and divides it into successive fractions — ½, ¼, ⅛, 1/16 . . . of the original area — one arrives at a fractal distribution. If one assumes that each level requires a multiple of its area (or population) below it (½ is twice ¼, etc.), then this fractal model approximates a tree-like administrative hierarchy as shown in Figure 2.7. One can conceive of the boxes at the top of the tree as the administrative centers, with the lower "trunk" as the small and numerous villages administered by the centers. Each of the administrative units governs an area or population size that is some multiple of the one immediately below it.

All of these are also EI models. They not only represent extreme inequality but also reflect an abundantly clear hierarchy. Each of the layer areas "above" is some multiple of the one below. The largest is several multiples in size above that of the smallest.

What unites all four models is what is typically called a Markovian process, in which each state of the system is dependent only on the preceding state. Put another way, the future is dependent only on that which exists in the present, not on any past overall pattern. In a stochastic Markovian process (some random variation), no pattern is readily discernible other than dependence on the preceding state of the system. Illustrations of such processes will be introduced shortly. This stands in contrast to the exponential model that was applied to the subdivision of land, in which a purely random process operates. In most agrarian societies, the number of children per peasant family is a random variable independent of the state of the agricultural land distribution at any given time. This basic difference between the two models, shown by the contrast between the fractal pattern on the one hand and the equal areas to be subdivided

FRACTAL

FRACTAL

FRACTAL FRACTAL

FRACTAL

FRACTAL FRACTAL

FRACTAL   FRACTAL

FRACTAL FRACTAL FRACTAL FRACTAL

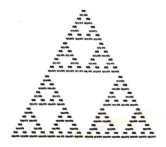

Figure 2.6. Fractal formation in resettlement. (From "The Language of Fractals," Hartmut Jürgens, Heinz-Otto Peitgen, and Dietmar Saupe. © 1990 by Scientific American, Inc. All rights reserved.)

Figure 2.7. Fractal formation in an administrative hierarchy. (Reproduced by permission of the authors from H.-O. Peitgen, P. H. Richter, H. Jürgens, and D. Saupe, *The Beauty of Fractals: Images of Complex Dynamical Systems* [Berlin: Springer, 1986]).

on the other in Figures 2.4 and 2.5, gives rise to implications for the onset of political violence that will be treated later.

Now, although the four fractal models are conceptually distinct insofar as they embody different social mechanisms, mathematically they are indistinguishable; they all result from the same mathematical operations. Nevertheless, it is useful to provide illustrations of the EI distribution resulting from the four separate processes. This will provide some "feel" for the kind of real-world expansions (and in one instance, a contraction) that lead to these distributions. The systematic empirical applicability is especially important, for the historical (and prehistorical) materials of Chapters 3 and 4 are dependent on the validity of these arguments concerning fractal formation.

First, we will consider sequential acquisitions in the form of shipping and colonies. These reflect the serial nature of hegemonic or at least extreme hierarchical control. Data here are drawn from Dutch shipping in the late eighteenth century, which was the beneficiary of the early centuries of Dutch hegemony in shipping. If the distribution of extreme inequality (EI) is an appropriate model, then it should demonstrate a close fit between observation and prediction under conditions of hegemony. After all, this is probably the quintessential example of extreme inequality. Of the 1,504 ships docking in the Amsterdam harbor in 1786, as observed by the French consul, only 44 were not Dutch-registered (2.9 percent). Because Amsterdam was the gateway to all of Northern Europe (England excepted), this amounted to a near monopoly of trade. Table 2.1 presents both observed and theoretical distributions for this shipping, first for all ships and then for the Dutch-registered ships. The fit is extremely good for the EI distribution, with little, if any difference between the degree of fit of the theoretical to the observed distributions in both cases.

For purposes of comparison, Table 2.1 also shows the exponential distribution applied to both cases with correspondingly worse results. The criterion here is the fit between observed and predicted distributions as measured by the chi-square distribution. A higher probability value, p, for the chi-square statistic implies a better fit between observation and prediction while a lower value implies a poorer fit. In order to adopt a conservative policy on acceptance of either the EI or the exponential model, a model will be rejected at $p < .20$ (instead of the usual $p < .05$), which indicates of course that any probability levels higher than .20 imply acceptance of the model. As the p values in the table show, the exponential distribution applied to both data sets should clearly be rejected, but the EI distribution is accepted.

We must consider not only the likely sequential acquisition process that gave rise to this distribution, but an additional underpinning as well. As Braudel indicates,

TABLE 2.1
Dutch Shipping Hegemony in 1786:
Observed and Predicted EI and Exponential Distributions

Average number of ships by category[a]	Number of locations[b]	Observed percentage of countries	Predicted percentage of countries	
			EI distribution	Exponential distribution
A. *Total number*				
24.86	7	53.85	53.03	39.22
87.67	3	23.08	25.07	32.57
238.00	2	15.38	13.84	20.87
591.00	1	7.69	8.06	7.34
			$k_1 = .594$, $A_1(k_1) = 3.581$ $\chi^2 = .359$, df = 2, $p < .90$	$k = .003$, $A(k) = .422$ $\chi^2 = 9.677$, df = 2, $p < .01$
B. *Dutch-registered*				
20.29	7	53.85	54.22	39.66
87.00	3	23.08	23.94	32.44
238.00	2	15.38	13.60	20.58
581.00	1	7.69	8.24	7.32
			$k_1 = .562$, $A_1(k_1) = 2.941$ $\chi^2 = .304$, df = 2, $p < .90$	$k = .003$, $A(k) = .422$ $\chi^2 = 9.107$, df = 2, $p < .02$

SOURCE: Braudel 1984, 238.

[a] Average number of ships coming from thirteen European, Mediterranean, and American locations docking in Amsterdam harbor, in each of four statistical categories, aggregated from the source, with the corresponding number of countries in the second column. For the total number of ships, the statistical categories are 12–55, 74–109, 200–300, and 500–600 respectively. For the Dutch-registered ships, they are 12–35, 72–109, 200–300, and 500–600, respectively. The total in either A or B can be obtained by summing the products of the first two columns equally, respectively equaling 1504 and 1460 ships.

[b] Locations include countries such as Prussia and Russia or places such as the Levant or individual American colonies (not the United States).

Storage and warehousing lay at the heart of Dutch commercial strategy.... The Amsterdam entrepôt trade verged on a monopoly. And if the Dutch really were "the Carryers of the World, the middle Persons in Trade, the Factors and Brokers of Europe," as Defoe wrote in 1728, this was not, as Le Pottier de la Hestroy thought because "all the other nations were willing to suffer it to be so," but because they were unable to prevent it. The Dutch system was built on a network of commercial relations of interdependence which combined to produce a series of virtually obligatory channels for the circulation and redistribution of goods. (1984, 238–39)

Here in a nutshell, Braudel describes the establishment of commercial hegemony by the Dutch, a principal basis of which is the creation of a circumstance of extreme scarcity. They held the reins of the warehousing system that was necessary for the commercial redistribution process. And it was only through

TABLE 2.2
Colonial Populations of the European Powers in 1914:
Observed and Predicted EI and Exponential Distributions

Colonial population size (mean)	Number of countries[a]	Observed percentage of countries	Predicted percentage of countries	
			EI distribution	Exponential distribution
691,560	5	41.67	49.40	32.28
9,754,540	4	33.33	24.55	31.25
39,493,121	2	16.67	16.97	28.08
375,710,827	1	8.33	9.09	8.38
			$k_1 = .264$,	$k = 3.596 \times 10^{-9}$,
			$A_1(k_1) = 17.241$	$A(k) = 0.324$
			$\chi^2 = 4.418$,	$\chi^2 = 7.507$,
			df = 2, $p < .20$	df = 2, $p < .05$

SOURCE: *Statesman's Year-Book* 1914.

[a] The countries represented by the four rows are, from top to bottom: (1) Austria-Hungary, Denmark, Italy, Spain, and Sweden; (2) Belgium, Germany, Portugal, and Russia; (3) France and the Netherlands; (4) Great Britain.

the Dutch that the merchants of Europe could function effectively. In a clear sense, this was an artificially induced and managed scarcity of warehousing space, which in turn led to Dutch commercial hegemony.

Another distribution arose from sequential acquisition that also encountered a scarcity of desiderata, this time not incurred and managed by human beings but imposed by nature in the form of a limited resource. This is the distribution of colonial population held by the European powers at the outbreak of World War I in 1914. All of the available territory in what is now mostly the Third World had already been "parceled out" by the Europeans, so that a scarcity condition was fully operative. The first arrival gets the lion's share, the second a proportionally smaller colonial population, the third still smaller and so forth through the last of these. As shown in Table 2.2, the "eyeball" fit between observation and prediction is reasonably good, although certainly not as strong as in the case of Dutch shipping, and based on our conservative criterion of $p < .20$ must be rejected. The condition of hegemony in colonial holdings before World War I was not as extreme as in the instance of Dutch shipping, perhaps allowing a sufficient degree of competition among the colonial powers to fuel the fires of that war. In any case, the fit of the exponential distribution, shown on the far right of the table, is not nearly as good.

Turning to the second of our patterns, that of random expansion, we can also find two illustrations of the process. The first emerges from a rather interesting set of statistics on Russian land distributions, comparing farms in 1911 with farms in 1882 (Chayanov 1966). They are published for 1911 as a percentage of those of 1882, for farms that increased their sown area and farms that died out,

TABLE 2.3
Russian Farms in 1911, as a Percentage of Those of 1882 (EI distribution)

Sown area (in desyatinas)	Number of farms[a]	Observed percentage of farms	Predicted percentage of farms (EI)
Farms that increased sown area, as a percentage of those that divided since 1882			
1.5	72.8	67.60	68.17
4.5	18.0	16.71	17.04
7.5	11.2	10.40	8.94
10.5	5.7	5.29	5.85
			$k_1 = 1.262$, $A_1(k_1) = 1.137$ $\chi^2 = .301$, df = 2, $p < .90$
Farms that died out, as a percentage of those existing in 1882			
1.5	32.5	64.23	65.96
4.5	10.4	20.55	17.83
7.5	4.2	8.30	9.71
10.5	3.5	6.92	6.50
			$k_1 = 1.191$, $A_1(k_1) = 1.069$ $\chi^2 = .690$, df = 2, $p < .70$

SOURCE: Chayanov 1966, 246–47.

[a] These numbers, given in the data source, essentially are normed (divided by) a base number that in the source happens to be that for 1882. The numbers allow us to examine expansion or contraction relative to a fixed quantity existing at an earlier time.

respectively as a percentage of those divided since 1882 and the total number in 1882 (see Table 2.3). The data for farms that increased conform almost exactly to the EI distribution while again, for purposes of comparison, applying the exponential distribution (not shown here in order to avoid redundancy) gives $\chi^2 = 4.881$, df = 2, $p < .10$ and can be rejected. Another condition of extreme scarcity is found in the instance of farms that die out, largely as the result of subdivision and/or poor soil, and are sold to landlords who then increase their holdings as part of their expansion process. Table 2.3 shows a strong conformity of the dying farms to the EI distribution. The exponential, for comparative purposes, is much less applicable at $\chi^2 = 3.962$, df = 2, $p < .20$.

Unfortunately, we have no Russian data on landlord holdings or its obverse, farm tenancy, but in the Philippine archives we find such data on the island of Negros Oriental. As in the Russian data, random births and deaths bring about the disappearance of farms that then are incorporated into the growing possession of the landlords. Data on farming tenancy in Negros Oriental are examined in Table 2.4, and the EI distribution, once again, conforms to the data, while the exponential at $\chi^2 = 85.201$, df = 4, $p < .001$ does not.

TABLE 2.4
Observed and Predicted Patterns of Tenancy
in Negros Oriental, Philippines, 1958 (EI distribution)

Size of parcels (in gantas of corn seeds)	Number of parcels cultivated by tenants ($N = 597$)	Observed percentage of tenant-cultivated parcels	Predicted percentage of tenant-cultivated parcels (EI)
3.5	535	89.61	82.62
9.0	48	8.04	11.37
15.0	6	1.01	3.89
24.0	4	0.67	1.45[a]
40.0	3	0.50	0.50
65.0	1	0.17	0.18

$$k_1 = 2.100, A_1(k_1) = 11.471$$
$$\chi^2 = 4.126, df = 4, p < .50$$

SOURCE: Pal 1963, 338.
[a] In order to maximize possibilities for rejecting the goodness-of-fit hypothesis thus yielding a conservative estimate, categories were not combined in the tail of the distribution.

We now move from the case of expansion—here the random dying out and incorporation of farms into new, larger holdings—to those of conquest, resettlement, and administration. Latin America gives us probably the most comprehensive data on the consequences of conquest and resettlement. The Iberian conquests and invasions of the sixteenth century led to massive depopulations as the result of disease, forced labor in mines that resulted in the virtual disappearance of villages, and the outright seizure of the best land by the Iberian colonists (McAlister 1984). Table 2.5 shows the analysis for upper portions of land distributions for Peru and Ecuador, as principal Andean-Inca centers of conquest and resettlement in South America. (Upper and lower portions are discussed more fully in Chapter 8.) Significantly, few, if any, land redistributions had occurred in these two countries prior to these recorded data, unlike what occurred in Mexico—the other major center for conquest and resettlement—after the revolution of 1910-17. Of all of the Latin America countries with land distributions conforming to the EI distribution at the upper end, Ecuador and Peru stand near the top in goodness of fit. Only Cuba (with its depopulation due to disease of the Carib Indians), Panama, and Honduras have slightly better fits between observation and prediction (see Table 8.2).

Two examples of administrative hierarchies constitute the last of our instances of EI distributions. The first of these is a distribution of distances among sites in ancient Sumer, more specifically in the Late Uruk period. Distances are used because of the uncertainty of the actual settlement size excavated (Johnson 1975). Center to center distances, however can be calculated with a fair degree of accuracy and can serve as a surrogate variable for actual size because

36 / INTRODUCTION

TABLE 2.5
Observed and Predicted Upper Portions of Land Distributions
for Peru (1961) and Ecuador (1954) (EI distribution)

Size of holding (in hectares)	Number of holdings	Observed percentage of holdings	Predicted percentage of holdings (EI)
A. Peru			
75.0	6,643	39.22	40.19
150.0	4,284	25.29	26.77
350.0	3,400	20.07	16.29
750.0	1,519	8.97	10.42
1,750.0	1,093	6.45	6.34

$k_1 = .586, A_1(k_1) = 5.054$
$\chi^2 = 1.186, \text{df} = 3, p < .80$

B. Ecuador			
35.0	19,415	56.02	52.65
75.0	8,327	24.03	25.09
150.0	3,452	9.96	12.79
350.0	2,335	6.74	5.61
750.0	664	1.92	2.68[a]
1,750.0	464	1.34	1.17

$k_1 = .972, A_1(k_1) = 16.693$
$\chi^2 = 1.205, \text{df} = 3, p < .80$

SOURCE: Peru: Food and Agriculture Organization 1966–70; Ecuador: Wilkie and Perkal 1985.
[a] Bottom two categories combined for the chi-square test. Without combining categories, the chi-square value actually was significant at $p < .90$ with the additional degree of freedom, but is recorded as above to maintain consistency with the findings reported in Table 8.2.

of the expectation of larger distances between larger centers and smaller distances between smaller villages. There are four levels of sites: large centers, small centers, large villages, and villages. Given an EI distribution of settlements, the distances between them should also reflect an EI distribution—and this is precisely what we find shown in Table 2.6. Although each of the size classes is averaged in the source, thus likely eliminating much of the random variation, the fit between observation and prediction is indeed impressive. This suggests that distance hierarchies, at least in ancient societies, reflected the dominance of a small number of large centers and proportionately larger numbers of smaller centers for purposes of administration and/or redistribution.

This hierarchical property also is found in core populations of central places in China in 1893; the more recent planned exercises of the Chinese Communists are, of course, not evident. Once again, the EI distribution demonstrates an excellent fit to the data, as shown in Table 2.7. The interpretation here, as in the case of the Sumerian data, is that administrative hierarchies evolve from economic ones that satisfy the basic requirements of redistribution, namely, efficiency of transport and movement of goods from one node of

TABLE 2.6
Observed and Predicted Nearest-Neighbor Distances
in the Uruk Hierarchy (EI distribution)

Types of sites	Number of sites	Average distances between sites within each type (km)	Observed percentage	Predicted percentage (EI)
Large centers	5	18.16	57.14	56.40
Small centers	8	11.52	29.59	29.89
Large villages	29	4.58	8.16	8.85
Villages	56	2.83	5.10	4.86

$k_1 = 1.319$, $A_1(k_1) = 2.224$
$\chi^2 = .079$, df $= 2, p < .98$

SOURCE: Johnson 1975, 317.

TABLE 2.7
Observed and Predicted Distribution of Population
in Core Chinese Cities in 1893 (EI distribution)

Mean populations of core cities	Number of cities	Observed percentage	Predicted percentage (EI)
210	13,242	70.29	68.06
690	3,905	20.73	21.86
2,330	1,163	6.17	6.84
7,800	360	1.91	2.16
25,500	108	0.57	0.70
73,500	38	0.20	0.25
217,000	18	0.10	0.09
667,000	6	0.03	0.03

$k_1 = .955$, $A_1(k_1) = 112.083$
$\chi^2 = .259$, df $= 6, p < .99$

SOURCE: Skinner 1978, 15.

the system to another, generally, at a different level of the hierarchy. Agricultural products collected at the lowest points of the hierarchy, in the rural areas, would then be filtered up to the top. Similarly, goods imported into one region from another or outside the country would be filtered successively down the hierarchy, depending on need and demand. This model is appropriate for an agrarian society without the accouterments of modern transportation and communication. Now, bureaucratic administrations should follow the contours of this hierarchy, and that is precisely what G. William Skinner found, at least in the case of China. His argument is: "Elites were disproportionately concentrated in more favorably situated, richly endowed, 'urbanized' marketing systems, so that the nonofficial elite and, a fortiori, the bureaucratic elite would be far more numerous in a central marketing system whose node was a greater city in the regional core than in a central marketing system whose node was a central market town situated in the far periphery" (1978, 65).

The Multipolar Environment

A variant of the exponential model, although similar in all major respects, will be used in a special context. This is an interunit, interstate, or international context. As in the exponential and fractal (EI) models, this model is subject to the scarcity condition, but makes explicit the dependence of the measure of inequality on the number of available *utiles*, or systemic desiderata.

I begin the analysis with three basic assumptions. First, what we generally regard as multipolarity (or bipolarity for that matter) was situated historically within European and other regional and world systems of some fairly widely accepted scope and definition. That is, the units or countries within the setting constituted a system in which the actors were aware of each other as system members and openly acknowledged that membership. Second, inequalities among system members are more destabilizing than equalities. Envies and political intrigues that can result in war are far more likely under the former circumstance. Third, in the absence of a centralized administration, the system is subject to random processes that have an impact on the system members.

The first assumption derives from treatments, such as Edward Gulick's (1955), that posit the historical balance of power as one existing within a common cultural frame of reference. Post-Reformation Christian Europe provides an interesting example. A secular political culture, but one based on fairly widely accepted norms of behavior, emerged following the Treaty of Westphalia. The Abbé de Pradt found that Europe formed "a single social body which one might rightly call the European Republic" (1800, 86–87). Emmerich de Vattel declared that the practices of balance-of-power politics "make of modern Europe a sort of Republic" (1870, 251), and Friedrich von Gentz called it a "European commonwealth" (1806, 69). The shared experience of the European states led to the emergence of shared norms that were established within what was commonly held to be a balance-of-power framework. As Georg von Martens summarized it, "the resemblance in manners and religion, the intercourse of commerce, the frequency of treaties of all sorts, and the ties of blood between sovereigns, have so multiplied the relations between each particular state and the rest, that one may consider Europe (particularly the Christian states of it) as a society of nations and states" (1795; quoted in Gulick 1955,

10–11). Morton Kaplan's rules of the balance-of-power system are a precise articulation of these norms of system behavior, which are generally acknowledged by all of the system participants (for example, "Treat all essential actors as acceptable role partners"; see Kaplan 1957, 23).

The second assumption follows from the current and still widely accepted observation that equality is more conducive to political stability than inequality. We find the virtual equation of justice with equality in Artistotle's *Politics* as we do in John Rawls's (1971) second principle of justice, which demands equal access to all social and economic opportunities. Even more directly, entire theories of instability and their empirical confirmation have been based on the premise of severe inequalities. Included among these are theories based on relative deprivation, rapidly declining economic circumstances, and scarcity of valued commodities.[1] It is the last of these that will directly concern us in evaluating the relevant properties of multipolar systems. Given a particular society of states, equalities among the members are more likely to yield stability in the long run than are inequalities. The particular dynamics by which inequality-induced conflicts among states occur will be treated later. For now, we will simply observe that in the modern period the most stable societies by far are those with industrialized economies and their associated equalities, in comparison with the severe inequalities found in the instability-prone, largely agrarian countries.

The last assumption is almost axiomatic in international politics.[2] Without a central administration, the only other significant system forces that can exist, *ceteris paribus*, are random ones.

Formal Distinctions

A bipolar system composed of two major powers will now be formally compared with a multipolar one consisting of three or more major powers. All major powers initially will have no small powers associated with them. The number of powers in the multipolar system will be taken to be five initially in order to conform to the existence of five major powers throughout much of eighteenth and nineteenth century Europe. The case of three major powers also will be treated but will be shown to demonstrate essentially the same dynamics.

Consider now the existence of κ utiles to be distributed among m major powers. The utiles are international desiderata or resources and can be allies, which generally are smaller powers to be associated politically with the great powers or colonies to be absorbed politically by the great powers. There could also be other international utiles (for example, access to natural resources).

If κ items (utiles) are distributed randomly among m recipients (countries) with equal probability for each recipient, then $E(n_r)$, the expected number of recipients with r items in the long run after a steady state has been reached is given by the following distribution:[3]

$$E(n_r) = m \binom{\kappa}{r} \left(\frac{1}{m}\right)^r \left(1 - \frac{1}{m}\right)^{\kappa - r} \qquad r = 0, 1, 2, \ldots, \kappa. \qquad (2.4)$$

$$\binom{\kappa}{r} = \frac{\kappa!}{r!(\kappa - r)!}$$

With $m = 5$ and allowing r to assume successively larger values, we obtain the number of powers, n_r, with r utiles. Table 2.8 presents these values. Thus, we see in Table 2.8 that, with only 15 utiles to be distributed, a random result is that one of the five countries will receive one utile while another receives 2 utiles, and so forth through the fifth country that receives 5 utiles. Compare this with the distribution to be expected when 180 utiles are randomly distributed. Again, there is a disparity among adjacent recipient countries of one utile difference, but the relative contrast of each receiving between 32 and 36 utiles is far less, as will be discussed below. Additional calculations were made with $m = 3$ and $\kappa = 15, 30, 60, 120,$ and 180 as well as with $m = 7$ and associated values of κ and are used later in the construction of Figure 2.8.

What is required now is a measure of inequality to reflect the disparities in random allocation of the κ utiles. This is suggested by the prior use in studies of inequality of the difference between allocations to the upper and lower proportions of society.[4] This measure also has shown strong correlation with the Gini index of inequality, which is a fairly standard measure (see, e.g., Park 1986). Using the top and bottom 20 percent for $m = 5$, the country lowest in distributed resources or utiles would be compared with that which is highest. The difference between the two is treated as a percentage of the amount held by the least-favored country recipient. Thus, for $\kappa = 15$, the measure of inequality is $I = [(5 - 1) / 1] \times 100$, or there is a 400 percent difference between the top and bottom countries in possession of resources. For $\kappa = 30$, the difference is $[(8 - 4) / 4] \times 100 = 1 \times 100$ or 100 percent, while for $\kappa = 180$, the difference declines dramatically to approximately 12 percent.

Thus the relationship between κ available utiles and I, the inequality between least- and most-favored recipient, clearly is curvilinear and of an exponential form. The inequality is greatest when the number of available resources is small and diminishes rapidly in extent as the number of available resources increases. This relationship is plotted in Figure 2.8 for values of $m = 3, 5,$ and 7, leading to the three curves shown. The value $m = 5$, as noted, is chosen to cor-

TABLE 2.8
The Number of Countries with r Utiles (n_r),
Total Utiles κ and m = 5 (random distribution)

r	κ				
	15	30	60	120	180
1	1				
2	1				
3	1				
4	1	1			
5	1	1			
6		1			
7		1			
8		1			
9					
10			1		
11			1		
12			1		
13			1		
14			1		
.					
.					
.					
20				1	
21				1	
22				1	
23				1	
24				1	
.					
.					
.					
32					1
33					1
34					1
35					1
36					1

SOURCE: Midlarsky 1993.
NOTE: All values below 0.5 are treated as zero; all values equal to or greater than 0.5 are shown as 1.

respond to the existence of five great powers during much of eighteenth- and nineteenth-century Europe, while $m = 7$ corresponds to the emergence of a wider global system at the beginning of the twentieth century with the addition of three great powers, the United States, Italy, and Japan, and the decline of an older one, Austria-Hungary. The value $m = 3$ corresponds to a much older instance of emerging tripolarity to be explored shortly.

It turns out that the relationship indicated here is a special case of the more general relationship between scarcity and inequality identified earlier. The exponential approach to greater equality under increased abundance emerged from a general mathematical-theoretical treatment. Here, the approach is more specific but yields an additional dividend. Whereas in that approach, the ex-

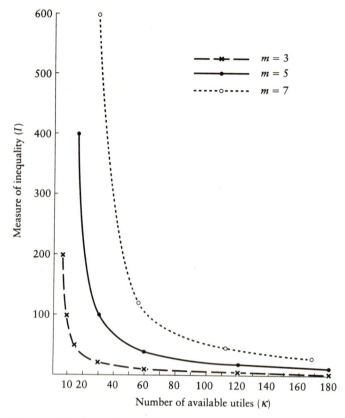

Figure 2.8. The dependence of the measure of inequality, I, on the number of available utiles, κ, for three values of m.

ponential formula could generally and in an abstract way be identified as a measure of inequality, here this is no longer true. The exponential inequality measure, I, has a very specific meaning of difference between best- and worst-off in the context of several international seats of power and, moreover, is consistent with earlier usages, such as that of Chenery and Syrquin (1975) in the analysis of inequality.

What is most striking about these results is not so much the rapid decline of inequality with increased available resources but the contrast with bipolarity. For in that event, there is the equal division of resources in the long run between the two power centers ($m = 2$). This can be easily seen by substituting the value $m = 2$ in Equation 2.4 for any value of κ. The equality is independent of the number of resources in the system; it applies equally to $\kappa = 30$ and to $\kappa = 180$.

In the former instance each side receives 15 utiles, in the latter each receives 90. This is in contrast to the case of $m = 5$ poles where there is a large difference of 100 percent between the most and least favored actor for $\kappa = 30$ but only approximately 12 percent for $\kappa = 180$. The case of equality for bipolarity may be represented as a horizontal line across the bottom of Figure 2.8 at $I = 0$.

Another interpretation of these results, then, is that there is not a great deal of difference between bipolarity and multipolarity for a large number of available utiles (κ large), where values of I for multipolar systems begin to approach the horizontal on the right side of Figure 2.8. For a small number of available resources or conditions of scarcity (small κ), on the other hand, the strong contrast between the two structural conditions is evident.

With this treatment, we have now completed the analysis of the three forms of inequality formation—exponential-geometric, fractal (EI), and a multiunit system comprised of autonomous entities. All three will find direct counterparts in the investigation of state dissolution in Chapter 4. With this theoretical and empirical grounding, we can now turn to the essentially historical materials in Part II that treat the knotty problems of state formation and dissolution.

PART II

State Formation and Dissolution

CHAPTER 3

Warfare and the Origins of the State

We turn now to the origins of the state in human prehistory. Following a discussion of other theories and a comparison of those with the one presented here, several illustrations will be examined in depth: Mesopotamia, Egypt, China, Mesoamerica, and the Andes. Now, granted that anthropologists and archaeologists have had an abiding interest in this subject for decades, why should political scientists (such as myself), historians, economists, sociologists, geographers, and other social scientists concern themselves with this question? After all, it is a question whose answer lies in the distant, mostly unrecorded past. Why should it concern us now?

There are at least two answers to this question, one general and the other specific. Generally, as human beings we have a compelling need to know the origins of our political arrangements. And historical analysis, the principal vehicle of investigation for succeeding chapters, provides that understanding suggested by R. G. Collingwood:

> The four characteristics of history . . . [are] (a) that it is scientific, or begins by asking questions, whereas the writer of legends [such as the Kwakiutl Thunderbird mentioned in the Preface] begins by knowing something and tells what he knows; (b) that it is humanistic, or asks questions about things done by men at determinate times in the past; (c) that it is rational, or bases the answers which it gives to its questions on grounds, namely appeal to evidence; (d) that it is self-revelatory, or exists in order to tell man what man is by telling him what man has done. (1994, 18)

When such an examination of origins is applied to the realm of politics and specifically to the origins of the state, the fundamental qualities of human political arrangements become evident.

The more specific reason for delving into early political causation concerns a particular hypothesis suggested to explain the origins of the state. This is the oft-cited nexus between warfare and the state, or as it has been put succinctly as a paraphrase of writers such as Otto Hintze (1975): "War made the state and the state made war." In this conception, political leadership arose to respond to the needs of a hostile human environment. In order to defend itself, the unit (tribe, kinship/ethnic group, incipient nation) had to appoint a leadership in times of external threat. Somehow or other (the exact process is almost never spelled out in detail), this leadership becomes the nucleus of a permanent political edifice now called the "state." In order to continue to wage war, either in defense or offense, the state increases its resources via taxation, thus expanding its foundation. Another war requires additional taxation, and the state continues to expand.

I will not challenge the theory of the spiraling *expansion* of the state as the result of war. There is, in my view, ample evidence for this process. It is the contention that the *origin* of the state is to be found in war that I seek to examine. Specifically, I will argue that although warfare (more specifically, violent territorial acquisition or defense) may combine with other antecedent processes to constitute a sufficient condition for the establishment of a state, it is not a necessary one. There are other mechanisms, essentially peaceful ones, that can lead to state formation. In approaching this problem of warfare and the state, I will have to examine the problem of state origins generally, for alternative mechanisms will have to be specified if the hypothesis of necessity is to be falsified. Of course, one or more illustrations will have to be adduced as well.

This problem of the supposed inextricable nexus between warfare and state origins, of course, has additional implications beyond that of a historical curiosity, albeit an important one. Warfare and the state are both omnipresent institutions created by human beings. Eulogies have been written for the state as an outmoded institution, however, particularly after the rise of the multinationals during the post–World War II era. Yet we see a massive resurgence of nationalism in Eastern Europe and a desire for separate states for the various nationalities that devolved from the Soviet Union and the former Yugoslavia. Warfare too has been periodically declared obsolete, but the recent Iran-Iraq and Gulf wars, not to mention the civil strife in Yugoslavia, belie this notion. (A particularly interesting example of the effort to consign warfare to the dustbin of history is found in a work by Norman Angell published in 1911 — shortly before the onset of World War I.)

But for all its persistence in history, warfare still is episodic. There are long stretches of historical time when warfare is absent or at least maintained at a fairly low level. Much of the nineteenth century in Europe and the contemporary Cold War era were without system-destroying wars. Any conflicts were contained at a relatively low level of violence in comparison with such instances as the Napoleonic Wars, World War I, and World War II. There are countries, such as Sweden, which have not experienced war for nearly two centuries and others, such as Switzerland, for even longer than that.

The state, however, is truly ubiquitous. Virtually all of humanity is organized into states and has been for a very long time. For us to acknowledge that there is an inextricable linkage between warfare and the state as an institution (separate from the question of state expansion) is to bow to a kind of inevitability of war that in fact is at least partially belied by the historical record, as we have seen. Our view of ourselves as human beings inevitably prone to interstate violence would be falsely enhanced by the acceptance of this linkage. If the state does not disappear, neither will war, goes the argument, and so this linkage must now be examined with great care. To do so we must turn to general theories of the origins of stratification and of the state to understand the specific role that warfare may take within the general theory. First I will put forward my theory of state origins in rudimentary form and then reflect on its relationship to other theories. As will be seen, there are relationships to be developed with other approaches, not necessarily to contradict any but to emphasize the complexity in already discovered key relationships and to simplify others, as well as to offer the salient characteristics of the present theory.

A Comparison of Theories

Briefly, the origins of the state are to be found in a two-stage mechanism reflecting the exponential and fractal (EI) distributions identified in Chapter 2. First, given the scarcity of valued commodities such as agricultural land, there is bound to be inequality. The greater the scarcity, the greater the inequality. Alternatively, the greater the population density, as another method of generating scarcity, the greater the inequality. As we saw in Chapter 2, the two approaches are effectively interchangeable. This degree of inequality, however, is not likely to yield anything as complex as a state or even a complex chiefdom. It simply suggests that in some settlement areas, there is likely to exist a degree of stratification between those who have more and those who have less. Interestingly, this process can be reversed; the amelioration of scarcity can lead to the diminution or disappearance of hierarchy, as apparently occurred in northern Melanesia. According to Jonathan Friedman, the Trobriand "hierarchy collapsed into the present-day more egalitarian big-man system as a result of European distribution of formerly scarce valuables" (1982, 184).

At some point in the social evolutionary process, as population grows and the pressure on resources increases, thus exacerbating inequality and widening the distance between strata, the community (settlement, tribe, kinship group) will expand into neighboring territory, thus easing the pressure on resources and consequent inequality. If this expansion is sizable enough, it can begin to approximate one of the four models for the EI distribution described in Chapter 2: sequential acquisition, random expansion, conquest and resettlement, or administrative hierarchy. Clearly any of these alternatives can involve warfare, but sequential acquisition, random expansion, or even administrative hierarchy, do not necessarily involve warfare. Merely the expansion process can yield the EI distribution.

It is suggested that the EI distribution provides a basis for state formation. Instead of the more moderate gradient of the exponential distribution, there is a much steeper gradient of inequality that has at least two consequences. First, the existence of a small category consisting of those with resources much greater than others implies the existence of a clear hierarchy, one much more evident than in the exponential distribution. A leadership then can clearly arise, governing both the older settlement areas and the newly acquired territory. The first steps toward regional hierarchy have been taken. The second consequence is that this leadership can provide the foundations of a redistributive system that lies at the basis of virtually every polity (Service 1975), certainly those that survive the longest. Given a large differential between the most favored and least favored, potlatch ceremonies or other forms of redistribution are much easier to carry out. A political system based on hierarchy and redistribution is now possible. The former pressures of population on resources are alleviated in the redistribution process, a remedy that could not have been so easily effected prior to the expansion process and the establishment of an EI distribution.

Of course, there are many varieties of the expansion process. One of the most important is that which arises when the initial community does not itself expand but sends out "colonies" that establish new communal associations at some distance from the first. The result, however, is the same, as can be seen in the following manner. Assuming this pattern persists, several such communities may evolve, placing simultaneous pressure on the available resources. Confrontation and eventually warfare may result from a scarcity induced as the result of population increase. Indeed, this multipolar variant of the scarcity-inequality scenario developed in Chapter 2 has at least one of the competing communities emerging as more favored than others (Midlarsky 1993). Either through its command of its own resources or through a coalition with other threatened communities, one victor is likely to emerge from the conflict. The net result still is an expansion over space of a particular leadership, which then constitutes an EI distribution or an incipient state.

If the victory is only temporary or there emerges a pattern of continual strife, then a weakening of the emergent city-state system may invite aggression from outside. As William McNeill observes in connection with the rise of great powers on the periphery of warring smaller or at least weaker powers, "The rise of such march states to dominance over older and smaller polities located near a center where important innovation first concentrated is one of the oldest and best-attested patterns of civilized history" (1982, 148). Examples given by McNeill include Aggad (ca. 2350 B.C.) in Mesopotamia, Ch'in (221 B.C.) in what is contemporary China, the Amerindian states (Aztec and Inca), and Macedon. We will examine the first three in detail in this and subsequent chapters, but for now, let us observe that all of these societies experienced intense internecine conflicts among their component city-states or other constituent units which weakened them sufficiently to allow for eventual external domination. But again, although warfare is a significant component of this particular scenario, it does not *have* to be the case. At least two, if not three, important instances of state formation seem to have occurred without the significant presence of warfare, as we shall see.

Probably the most typical of these instances was the formation of chiefdoms and then complex chiefdoms, followed in some instances by state formation. Timothy Earle (1997) demonstrates how the political economy of the emerging society was used by chiefs to gain power and then augment it in three cases: Hawai'i, Denmark, and Peru. The economic basis of chiefdoms probably was most evident in Hawai'i, with its well-developed irrigation systems controlled by chiefs, and in Denmark, with its trade in prestige goods as the basis of scarcity and a consequent inequality. Yet even in the Peruvian Wanka society, where warfare appears to have had a role in the initial formation of a chiefdom, as Earle remarks, "warfare as a primary source of social power proved to be limited" (1997, 195), and irrigated lands later became the basis of social power.

Now let us compare this understanding with others that have been put forward. Probably the earliest exponent of the modern view of state formation is Morton Fried (1967, 1978). His formulation bears similarities to my own but exhibits key differences as well. First, a major similarity is the basis of his theory of the origin of the state in social stratification. As he tells it,

Central to the concept of state ... is an order of stratification, specifically a system whereby different members of a society enjoy invidiously differentiated rights of access to the productive necessities of life. It is not enough that the society should provide different or even grossly unequal levels of prestige for its members; it is essential that such differences of rank be intertwined with regulations of economic access. Indeed the state needs something more than this—a formal organization of power but going beyond the social control functions of kinship. This formal organization of power has as its central task the protection (and often extension) of the order of stratification. (1978, 36)

Thus Fried sees stratification resulting from differential access to necessary resources as the principal event, followed by the building of a structure of power (really, force) to protect it. In this, the theory proposed here is in essential agreement with his view, as it concurs with the temporal priority of stratification over war. My theory in fact suggests that warfare came *after* the occurrence of stratification, not before, because the leadership needed for warfare and/or expansion would not necessarily have been in place before stratification occurred. In any event, the historical record shows many instances when leadership in time of war was temporary, with the successful leader retiring with suitable honors once the threat had diminished.[1] Fried's theory also requires some societal emphasis on private ownership of property, as does mine. Later, I will provide evidence for the existence of such ownership principles or at least customs of continued access in early societies.

In one key respect, however, there is a fundamental difference between Fried's approach and my own. This is revealed by his use of the term "invidious" to characterize the differential access to the necessities of life. Whereas the term "invidious" connotes lack of fairness or absence of justice in distribution, perhaps perpetrated by some agency of the state, the theory proffered here makes no such attribution. Instead, it is only the random distribution of access that governs the possession of resources. The greater the scarcity of the resources to be distributed, the greater the inequality of distribution. The notion of "invidious" differential access to the necessities of life certainly is not unique to Fried. Indeed, Charles Tilly (1998) has recently coined the term "categorical inequality" to suggest a very similar sort of exclusionary process wherein certain societal categories of people (e.g., managers, technically trained personnel) horde opportunities or exploit others to foster a durable inequality. Perhaps for these reasons, A. B. Atkinson (1996) suggests the establishment of an official poverty line in the United Kingdom to parallel those already existing in the United States and the European Union. An official recognition of a persistent inequality between the poor and the remainder of society, or between the haves and have-nots, would probably make it easier to institute redistributive reforms.

Even scholars not typically associated with liberal governmental intervention have used pejorative language. Vilfredo Pareto (1964), for example, uses the term "spoliation" to describe the activities of the ruling elite, while Gaetano Mosca (1939) refers to a minority clientelistic "political class" that governs virtually all polities, including democracies. The theories of Marx and Engels examined briefly in Chapter 1, of course, carry with them the pejorative connotation of "exploitation" of the masses by political-economic elites. A comparison of these linguistic usages is found in Hirschman (1996).

The absence of pejorative attribution here makes the present theory consistent with another prominent approach championed by Elman Service (1975). Instead of the emphasis on differential access to resources and the conflict generated thereby, according to Service there exists a "governance by benefit. This general factor is, so far as I can see now, a universal in the formation of all persevering power relationships" (1975, 223).

"Benefit," as Service suggests, means redistribution, in addition of course to the physical protection against external enemies provided by the state's armies. He further suggests that the integrative benefits of redistribution outweigh the impact of stratification in the genesis of the "pristine" state (one without any antecedents, neighboring or otherwise; see Fried 1967). Whatever stratification existed was, according to Service, "thus mainly of two classes, the governors and the governed—political strata, not strata of ownership groups" (1975, 285).

My theory does not distinguish between the importance of stratification and that of redistributive benefits in state formation. What it does do, in addition to strongly implying stratification given the existence of ownership groups, is to suggest that redistribution is desirable in the interests of societal harmony. If in a kinship system or other relatively cohesive grouping some are more advantaged than others as the result of any of the several processes detailed in Chapter 2, then it may become desirable to redistribute the benefits that have been accrued by the more fortunate group members. If by chance, certain kinship members have by some process attained agricultural land on the river alluvium while others did not (because of the need to keep the clan geographically intact or some other reason), then the interests of the group as a whole may demand the redistribution to others of at least a portion of the more fortunate members' abundant produce. Either permanent stratification in the form of maintaining the advantage ordained by chance processes or a redistribution scheme to ameliorate its effects are possible outcomes. What is mandatory in any case is the existence of stratification in the form of inequality as the result of the scarcity of desirable commodities such as alluvial farmland.

The consequences of scarcity are also to be found in Robert Carneiro's (1970) theory of the origins of the state, but with circumscription as the principal variable; a recent multivariable model incorporating a similar idea is found in Chase-Dunn and Hall 1997 (107). In Carneiro's work, we find a full-blown theory of the origins of the state that has three main foci, circumscription, population growth, and warfare. The circumscribed territory keeps the burgeoning population from fleeing the growing state power necessary to the waging of war against other social groups that are feeling the same pressure as the amount of available arable land shrinks. This is a parsimonious and in many respects appealing theory of the state; certainly it has been influential in suggesting new research topics during the past several decades. However, it only fully agrees with the present theory with regard to one variable, circumscription. It is mixed in regard to the impact of population growth, as we shall see, and negative in its positing the necessity for war as a prerequisite for state formation.

Even the major consequences of circumscription in my theory differ from those suggested by Carneiro. In his approach, circumscription decreases the likelihood of residents fleeing the area when oppressive state institutions are imposed (e.g., taxation). Further, the likelihood of conflict is intensified within the circumscribed area when pressures on resources increase. In the present theory, circumscription implies scarcity, if only in that there is a fixed amount of arable land available. This scarcity *in itself* yields the inequality and stratification that form the basis of state power and/or redistribution efforts to offset the effects of the inequality. Riverine areas should be especially susceptible to the scarcity-inequality nexus because of the limited amount of riverfront and/or alluvium-rich locations available for settlement. Scarcity and its consequence, inequality, would be emphasized by such locations. Circumscription alone, on the other hand, would not specify an outcome of inequality, one that in fact appears to be critical to the formation of the pristine state. Although important, as we shall see shortly in our discussion of peer polity interaction, the concept of "pristineness" probably is not critical to the argument here. With the exception of Mesoamerica, *all* of the pristine states identified thus far — in Mesopotamia, ancient Egypt (perhaps), northern China, the Indus Valley, and the Central Andes — were formed in riverine or maritime environments. Later we shall see another consequence of the riverine system in facilitating the expansion of the early states (or even just stratified societies) in seeking to ameliorate the consequences of resource scarcity and inequality.

Despite these important differences of nuance, the significance Carneiro assigns to circumscription agrees with the overall approach adopted here. It is in the consequences of population growth and its link with warfare that we disagree. Specifically his contention that population growth leads to warfare and consequently to state formation will be challenged in at least one important instance that in fact points to significant pacific aspects even of war-prone states. I will begin by examining the origins of several important early states in Mesopotamia, Egypt, China, Mesoamerica, and the Andes. Although with one possible exception all of these are pristine states, this concept will prove to have only limited utility. Egypt, though one of the earliest states, may have had contact with Mesopotamia before its first dynasty and perhaps even earlier than that (Hoffman 1991; J. Wilson 1951). But beyond that there is an argument that is seldom, if ever, expressed but is, I believe, crucial to the whole matter of origins. That is, even if the state exists in some neighboring territory, why should the observing population allow itself to be similarly governed? After all, the early states tended to be despotic in the extreme, even to the point of employing human sacrifice in China (Chang 1986), Egypt (Hoffman 1991), and Mesoamerica (Harris 1977), and slavery was not uncommon. To observe such subservience of course is to be repelled (unless there is peer polity legitimation within a common settlement area, to be discussed below),[2] especially if the observers are nomadic tribes accustomed to being free of the fetters of state citizenship, even in the most benign of obligations, that of taxation. Thus, whether a state is pristine or not probably is not critical. What is crucial is that it be early enough to have developed pretty much on its own without the experience of conquest and the imposition of alien rule.

As we shall see, Crete, although probably not a pristine state, does meet this criterion of early native development during the Minoan period and shows a pattern of state formation that is extremely informative. Further, such indigenous development often does not take place in isolation, but proceeds as the result of repeated contacts among several adjacent settlements in a process that Colin Renfrew calls peer polity interaction. Each of the settlements influences the others in competition, emulation of ceremonies, and structural homologies such as architectural forms or numerical and symbolic systems (Renfrew 1986, 5). The competition often occurs over scarce resources, leading to considerable conflict, as we shall see shortly in the instances of ancient Mesopotamia and the Maya, among others. Thus, Renfrew's theory and my own, specifically concerning warfare in multipolar (or multisettlement) systems, are mutually supportive.

For purposes of clarification now, and to distinguish between a *state* and a *civilization*, a civilization can be seen as

a group or cluster of states sharing a number of common features. These usually include closely similar political institutions, a common system of weights and measures, the same system of writing (if any), essentially the same structure of religious beliefs (albeit with local variations, such as a special patron deity), the same spoken language, and indeed generally what the archaeologist would call the same "culture," in whatever sense he might choose to use that term. The individual political units—the states—are often fiercely independent and competitive. (Renfrew 1986, 2)

Ostensibly, the civilization may exist with or without the persistence of a particular type of state or states system. Yet in virtually all of the cases to be presented here, in both the rise and the decline of states, the connection between civilization and type of state has been strong. The existence of states has been required to allow the civilization to flourish, and when a particular state or states system collapsed, often the contours of the civilization changed radically or disappeared altogether. Examples include the transition from Sumer to Aggad (city-state to empire) or Imperial Rome to feudal principalities (empire to baronies). Even an apparent exception, China, proves the rule, for although it appears as if Chinese civilization persisted over time despite the disappearance of many states, all of these states adopted very similar contours, even after conquest from without, differing from each other more in nuance than in essential detail (see Chapter 4). The same may be said for Western civilization currently. The disappearance of the democratic states system in the West would indicate a major transformation of the civilization itself.

Although the theories discussed so far have been mostly monocausal, with my own emphasizing inequality relations, it is clear that state formation, like most other social outcomes, has multiple causes (see, e.g., certain chapters in Ehrenreich, Crumley, and Levy 1995; and in Patterson and Gailey 1987). My theoretical emphasis on inequality and state formation not only examines the consequences of inequality across a broad spectrum of social processes but, more importantly, specifies a model both verbally and mathematically and then empirically examines that model, adding additional variables where they seem necessary and where the historical documentation allows. It is extraordinarily difficult to specify multicausality in prehistory or in early history, but later, in the empirical analysis of democracy in the contemporary period, multivariate models will be introduced.

An additional clarification concerns the role of multiple causes or even more specifically multiple hierarchies, in which several hierarchies exist simultaneously, each of which is unranked relative to the others, or in which a re-ranking occurs based on societal need. Carole Crumley (1987a, 1995) calls this heterarchy, and it has broad application to social systems. One of the best extended definitions of this concept is given by Elizabeth Brumfiel (1995).[3] Although such simultaneity undoubtedly exists in more mature civilizations, it is unlikely to be found at the point of origin of stratification, or if it does exist, it is likely to be subordinated at that time. Here, it is scarcity that provides the first societal need (resulting in inequality) able to subvert the existence of simultaneous hierarchies. Concomitantly, Friedman (1981) notes that increased abundance as the result of external exchange corrupts the path to hierarchy, which in an obverse sense, is in agreement with the present theory.[4]

Mesopotamia

It is fitting that we begin with Mesopotamia as the region with the first known state formation. As early as the fifth millennium B.C., there is evidence of social stratification in the lower Euphrates, a portion of the Tigris-Euphrates region in Southwestern Iran, where settlements are found with raised platforms for storage and segregated elite residences, signified by status goods. These early settlements occurred during the Susa period (Southwestern Iran) or terminal Ubaid (Southern Iraq), approximately 4000 B.C. or somewhat earlier (Wright and Johnson 1975, 273). Two hierarchical or control levels existed at that time, but these societies did not evolve into an actual state, which is generally considered to require three or more levels of hierarchical control (Wright 1986). After the partial destruction and abandonment of the earliest settlements around Susa, a new settlement system began to emerge at the beginning of the fourth millennium. This is termed the Early Uruk period, which gave rise to the Late Uruk and then the dynastic period of Sumerian civilization, the justly famed earliest "high" civilization of humankind.

That this was a circumscribed area with the associated scarcities is not subject to debate. The valley of the Euphrates and its tributaries, which supported most of the earliest settlements, is not susceptible to dry farming. Some water must be made available to counter the relative absence of rainfall at critical times. Most surrounding areas were either desert or mountain regions that were far less hospitable to a settled existence. Interestingly, the first settlements somewhat to the east were situated in areas where dry farming was possible (Nissen 1988, 58; Wright 1986, 332) on the Susiana plain, but for whatever reason, most likely raiding by nomads, these settlements were abandoned. The society that arose in the Uruk area to the west in the broad southern plain gave rise to what we can call the first stratified society approximating a state.

The Uruk settlement system arose on a broad plain that nevertheless required relatively densely sited villages and towns because of the common need for water channels. By contrast the earlier Ubaid civilization to the east, which had relied on dry farming, could have village centers a fair distance apart from each other.

Possibilities for all sorts of economic and, later, political cooperation obviously were enhanced by this proximity. This is not to say, in passing, that irrigation and its associated administrative complexities were required for this early state to emerge, as is argued by Karl Wittfogel (1957). There is ample evidence that whatever bureaucratic structures existed in ancient Mesopotamia came into being far later in the history of the city-states (Adams 1966, 1981). General arguments against Wittfogel's theory of state formation have been presented by Michael Mann (1986, 94–98). In the stage of early development that occupies our attention, there were existing water channels that had been left after the general water levels receded as a consequence of climatic changes. These channels were sufficient to draw water for irrigation purposes without the need for any complex administration. At the same time, these channels constituted a scarce resource that would automatically establish status differentials between those who resided in close proximity to them and those who were unlucky enough to be removed from them. It is also quite likely that some forms of redistribution emerged to provide at least a partial equalization of this essentially unfair circumstance and that this led to the first administrative structures. This, of course, would not have been expected in the dry farming regions nearby, wherein the settlement system did not, in fact, progress to the higher administrative stages of the Uruk region.

Receding water levels not only resulted in the emergence of these channels in the vicinity of the Euphrates River but also gave rise, at least temporarily, to fertile land that could be farmed. This availability of land apparently attracted the Sumerians from the north, who then mixed with the indigenous proto-Euphrateans, as they have been called (Kramer 1963). Here, for the first time, the number of settlements increased markedly, in contrast to the earlier Susa phase in which no such rapid increase occurred. What is more important, the Susa settlement sites, even after some period of time, continued to be so far apart that little structured contact was likely among them. In Uruk, on the other hand, the number of settlements was seen to increase "tenfold from one period to the next and the aggregate settlement area jump from 60 to 440 hectares" (Nissen 1988, 67). There were thus a larger number of settlements in closer proximity to each other. At the point of state formation during the early Uruk period, in which the society moved to at least three or four administrative levels, there occurs a nucleation of settlements. The number of settlements declines markedly, but the overall area of settlement grows (Nissen 1988, 68). The area of Uruk itself increased steadily into the Early Dynastic I period (ca. 3000 B.C.), when a wall was built defining the city limits. The size of settlements such as Uruk also was quite extraordinary, especially given its antiquity. The wall enclosed an area of 5.5 sq km, which is sizable indeed when compared with Athens after its expansion under Themistocles to an area of only about 2.5 sq km. Jerusalem after its growth under Agrippa reached a size of 1 sq km. The growth of the overall settlement area and of Uruk itself conforms at least qualitatively to the EI distribution.

This extension of area and population was also associated with the growth of administrative and coercive structures, especially the rise of the Sumerian kings. In fact, this may be a particular instance of the relationship between the number of levels of administrative structures and population size. As social units extend to include additional settlements or to found new ones within an administrative catchment area, population should increase within the overall administrative unit or polity, and this is what was found for a group of Micronesian polities at the time of the European conquest (Cordy 1986). Population was found to vary positively with the number of administrative levels. This is in contrast to the population *density* of these polities, which varied negatively with the number of administrative (or coercive) levels. More will be said on this later when we treat the origins of democracy in agrarian society.

Perhaps the most important aspect of our treatment here is the matter of warfare. Simply put, to what extent is the origin of one of the earliest states (more accurately city-state) such as Uruk the consequence of warfare? The answer is, at first appearance, a fairly simple one. Despite Uruk's origins in the early fourth millennium B.C., the first signs of fortification do not appear until the early Dynastic period of about 2800 B.C., almost a full millennium later (Nissen 1988). And this despite the existence and hence example of walled cities in the Middle East as early as the eighth millennium B.C.; the well-known instance of Jericho is a case in point (Negev 1986, 143). Fortifications are a sure sign of persistent warfare within a civilization, or at least of the necessity to defend against frequent attacks by nomads (Cohen 1978). Their absence does not assure the absence of fighting, but does suggest that this was not an endemic feature of that society, especially when there exist nearby models of protection, such as fortifications, within a region in which communications were fairly extensive as a result of trade (Wright and Johnson 1975).

This conclusion is complicated somewhat by the presence of the nearby earlier Ubaid culture, which was partially destroyed and then abandoned, possibly as the result of fighting around the time of the beginnings of Uruk. Exactly how this occurred, of course, we do not know. Nomadic incursions or a form of civil strife might have led to the end of this culture. But the similarities with Early Uruk suggest that whatever the nature of the destruction, it was not sufficient to propel Early Uruk into the building of fortifications, in the manner of, for example, Jericho and Ai (Negev 1986), at much earlier dates. This fact, in itself, suggests the presence of marauding nomads was infrequent. The relatively low probability of political violence for the Ubaid culture is reinforced by the absence of the density of settlement found for example in nearby Uruk, which could ultimately lead to civil strife among communities contesting for the same piece of scarce land.

In Uruk itself, we have evidence of a fair degree of social control by the elite *before* the building of the city wall. The Epic of Gilgamesh tells us that Gilgamesh had to suppress the population in order to construct the city wall. It is highly likely that Gilgamesh was a ruler during the Early Dynastic period, in any event, far later than the foundation of the city-state itself (Nissen 1988, 95). We have pictorials that depict scenes of siege and battle on cylinder seals dating from the Late Uruk period, just before the Early Dynastic when the city wall was erected (Nissen 1988, 109).

The Early Dynastic period is one not only in which fortifications and the potential for war became permanent, but in which the interrelationship among resources, state power, and interstate conflict developed. A hallmark of this period is the lowering of the water level of the Persian Gulf and the nearby land on which Uruk was built. This natural event had several consequences. First, it reduced the number of water channels, which made it necessary for the first time to build irrigation works to manage the now scarce water. This administrative requirement of course augmented state power, for water was the single most essential scarce resource required to sustain the expanding Sumerian civilization. At the same time, the channels that remained cut more deeply into the earth, thus drawing even more water away from the now rapidly diminishing channels that would soon disappear. Settlements that were deprived of water likely merged with those fortunate enough to retain theirs. As a consequence, the remaining settlements grow much larger while smaller ones disappeared. Hans Nissen (1988, 130–31) records that there were 62 settlements in the Early Dynastic I period; the number diminished to 29 in the Early Dynastic II period. Most of the population was now to be found in the large urban centers; nine-tenths of the population lived in settlements larger than 30 hectares.

But these receding waters and their geopolitical consequences were not the only important historical phenomena of the period. A change in the course of the Euphrates River had led to the rise of new city-states, not the least of which was Umma, which now proceeded to challenge Uruk in importance. The population density of Uruk declined after the Early Dynastic I period.

The rise of Umma and its relationship to other city-states now can be understood as prototypical of a larger process identified at the end of Chapter 2 (Equation 2.4). With the rise of several city-states along the new river course, such as Adab, Zabalam, and Umma, spheres of influence developed between neighboring cities. Evidence for this comes from fairly regular stretches of land—generally between 12 and 15 km—with no settlements between city-states. A few smaller settlements are found in close proximity to city walls but beyond these there generally were no settlements in areas that could be claimed by more than one city-state. One would expect there to be conflict between these city-states, especially if they were competing for the same scarce resource, namely water. And this is precisely what we find, in a protracted conflict between Umma and Girsu, whose fields were irrigated by the same stretch of the Euphrates River. It is tempting to think that virtually all of the other conflicts among the now numerous city-states would have similar causes.

In any event, the rise of new city-states ushered in a period of conflict among them, beginning in the Early Dynastic II period. These conflicts existed not only between city-states but between an individual city-state and a higher centralized authority. It is around this period that the world *lugal* appears for the first time, connoting not merely the religious-political governor of a city-state (*ensi*) but a monarch, generally of several city-states if not of an entire region. It is noteworthy that, although this word for "king" or "monarch" does not appear before the Early Dynastic period, words for "elder" and "assembly" do appear in earlier times (Frankfort 1971, 92) suggesting a popular, if not democratic, development in the formative period of the Sumerian city-state; this will be treated more fully in Chapter 7. For now, we may observe that although the monarchy, or other forms of individual autocratic leadership, may have been fostered by the arrival of widespread warfare, the state itself in its earlier non-autocratic incarnation likely arose as the result of other causes such as those detailed in Chapter 2. This early democracy or protodemocracy bears certain similarities to the concept of heterarchy mentioned above, as the relatively egalitarian absence of ranking among societal elements or the potential for ranking in different ways (Crumley 1987a, 1995).

It is in the Early Dynastic III period that we find a preoccupation with war (Gadd 1971a, 121). Inscriptions from this period, for example, refer to the fairly incessant conflict between Umma and Lagash, neighboring city-states that warred over territory between them and especially over an irrigation channel in that territory. This famous rivalry was typical of a variety of such conflicts in southern Babylonia at the time. We know that increased salinity of the irrigated land became a problem toward the end of the early period (Oppenheim 1977) and probably increased competition and ultimately violent conflict for the remaining arable land.

At a higher level were struggles for supremacy over Sumer itself. The three-cornered conflict among Kish, Ur, and Uruk was perhaps the best known of these (Kramer 1963, 50). As is so often the case in multipolar systems, a ruler, by the name of Lugalzaggesi, subsequently arose from one of these cities, Umma, and destroyed the power of Lagash, among others, before conquering Uruk, Ur, and other Sumerian cities. This "unification" from within then set the stage for conquest from without, when the united but weakened state could not withstand the Aggadean conquest by Sargon, the first great imperial ruler of Babylonia (Gadd 1971b, 420). Although from the earliest times, there had been a significant admixture of Semitic peoples and language within the Sumerian society, now for the first time a different language, the Semitic Aggadean and its accompanying rulership dominated Sumer. It is interesting in light of the scarcity-inequality relationship that the period of Aggadean rule was one of diminished luxury compared with earlier periods (Gadd 1971b, 452). Materials for jewelry and even tin, necessary for making bronze, are not found as frequently as in earlier times, suggesting that scarcities may have existed in the time of Lugalzaggesi's conquests and may have exacerbated conflicts among the city-states, thus facilitating conquest by the leadership of Umma and ultimately the emergence of the Aggadean imperial rule. Expansion by Aggad continued the spatial and administrative fractal formations begun by the Sumerian city-states, especially by Umma in the final stages of Sumerian independent existence.

Egypt

Turning now to the Egyptian case, we have what can be properly called a controlled naturalistic experiment. Four different environments existed in close proximity to each other in the Nile River region. Given the theory of scarcity-induced inequality and the consequent stratification expected to emerge, these regions should yield differing patterns. Three regions lie directly on the Nile: to the north is the Delta with its web of arterial waterways; then the Nile River valley and the alluvial deposits along the banks extend southward until the first cataract; south beyond the first cataract the Nile valley narrows considerably and the desert frequently comes up to the shores of the river. In the following treatment, the northern region will be called the Delta or Lower Egypt; the Nile River region to the south will be called Upper Egypt; and the region south of the first cataract, Nubia. The fourth zone, the Fayum, lies to the west of the river and is a region defined by Lake Fayum and its environs.

As noted, expectations differ for stratification patterns in the four regions. Perhaps the Fayum and Nubia are easiest to characterize because they have fairly evident ecologies. The Fayum region is dominated by Lake Fayum, which provides an ideal environment for fishing and hunting. At the same time,

> The Fayum has not provided any evidence for the kind of agricultural or urban development seen elsewhere in the [Nile] Valley during later Predynastic times. . . . The high productivity and stability of the fauna and flora of the marshes would have lured the population toward fishing, hunting, and gathering. . . . Fish and aquatic sources were more prolific and easier to obtain than in the Nile Valley. It is significant to recall the observation . . . concerning the absence of large permanent settlements in the Fayum until the Middle Kingdom and the lack of large settlements until the lake was partially drained in New Kingdom and Ptolemaic times. (Hassan 1988, 150)

Thus, abundance of natural resources in effect prevented the development in the Fayum of the agricultural settlements so characteristic of the Nile Valley itself.

Similarly, the absence of arable soil in Nubia characterized its development. In contrast to Upper Egypt and even certain places in Lower Egypt, which early developed social stratification, there is no early evidence for it in Nubia (Hoffman 1991, 260). This agricultural-pastoral society was more or less egalitarian until the Egyptian model made itself felt, roughly around 3300–3100 B.C. Indeed, the succeeding history of Nubia must be seen through the filter of Egypt as the defining political and cultural force during that formative period. Much of the Egyptian cultural hegemony, at least initially, resulted from proximity to Asia and the control of African trade with southwest Asia. This cultural hegemony was reinforced by "the diffusion of Egyptian political symbolism up the Nile" (Hoffman 1991, 262).

Why was this society egalitarian when neighboring societies to the north were yielding clear patterns of status and stratification? The answer given by Bruce Trigger is wholly consistent with the scarcity-inequality arguments put forward here: "There were no opportunities for land to acquire special value, which in turn would reinforce the development of a public authority and of the state" (1965, 75). In the absence of desirable river frontage or alluvial soils, an egalitarian society could continue until such time as it would be influenced directly by Egyptian culture.

Our discussion now will center on the contrast between the two major regions of Egypt, Upper and Lower Egypt, and in particular on why a highly stratified and politically organized society first arose in Upper Egypt to the south and not in Lower Egypt to the north. After all, was not the Delta region in Lower Egypt exposed more fully to Mesopotamian influences that would have provided a model of stratification and early state formation? In fact, the rise of more fully stratified societies earlier in the south may argue strongly against the demonstration effect and consequent geopolitical diffusion of statehood, and more for indigenous stratification as a harbinger of the state.

With the limited alluvial deposits along the Nile in Upper Egypt we have an ideal prescription for the scarcity-inequality induced emergence of stratified society. And at Nagada in the heart of Upper Egypt, just to the north of Thebes, were found the earliest remains of highly stratified societies. At a time when villages to the north in the Delta were burying their dead in communal graves, at Nagada the wealthy were segregated from the remainder in rather elaborate tombs that actually prefigured the splendor of the tombs and pyramids of Early Dynastic Egypt (Hoffman 1991, 124). Even before 4000 B.C. the Predynastic people of Upper Egypt buried their surplus wealth with them, in contrast to the people of the Delta, who did not bury social wealth (Hoffman 1991, 110).

By 3600 B.C., the inhabitants of the Nile Valley had achieved a fully agricultural mode of existence, with little dependence on hunting. Although the initial dispersion of settlements along the Nile was fairly regular, about 2 km apart, Fekri Hassan (1988, 158) has calculated that it would take only about 220 years for the entire narrow floodplain (1-2 km in width) between Mehdi in the north and Nagada in the south to be filled with people. Thus, once agriculture became the dominant mode of subsistence, it would take only several hundred years for the most desirable land along the river to be filled with people, thus invoking one version of the scarcity-inequality nexus (Equation 2.3) and rendering those who come later less equal in the quality of their holdings. This differential access could operate either within communal villages or between them; in either event the same result would follow, namely the emergence of an elite based on the superior quality of its holdings and/or the instituting of efforts at redistribution that in themselves would require some central administration and hence an elite.

Not only at Nagada, where so many grave sites were found, but also at Hierankopolis somewhat farther to the south evidence has been found for differentials in power and wealth. And here too, as Hoffman observes, "the trend toward the development of a power elite who buried themselves in splendor reflects directly the growth of a social order that was a direct predecessor to that of Dynastic Egypt" (1991, 259). Hierankopolis is significant because it was from here that Narmer, the legendary unifier of Upper and Lower Egypt, launched his "war of unification."

Two additional facts stand out in this connection. First is the exacerbation of the scarcity problem that had developed prior to the Dynastic period as a result of the decline in rainfall between about 3300 and 3000 B.C. and a consequent decline in the average depths of the Nile inundation. Such a decline in water available for agricultural production clearly would have an impact on the scarcity-inequality nexus. The second consideration is the site from which the actual unification began, Hierankopolis. Clearly, the nucleus of the Egyptian state must have been in the most advanced stage of state development in this general vicinity. It is also likely to have been a location with one of the narrowest floodplains and thus a particularly dense population, or as Hassan put it, "It is perhaps no accident that Hierankopolis, which would have been hard hit because of the narrow floodplain in this region, produced the legendary Narmer, the warrior King who supposedly led the unification wars" (1988, 173). Karl Butzer (1976) has estimated that Hierankopolis had one of the highest population densities in all of Egypt.

Let us now contrast this Upper Egyptian pattern with that for Lower Egypt. The small towns or villages were located on branches of the Nile in the Delta. Food sources were rich, both within the river branches and as a result of the rich black soil deposited by the waters. There was much empty land between villages, both for farming and for pasturage. Hoffman puts the contrast between the two forms of settlement in stark terms:

> Unlike their Upper Egyptian neighbors whose towns, villages, and hamlets were strung out like evenly spaced beads on a necklace, parallel to the Nile or along the main desert water courses, the people of Lower Egypt grew up in a world where boundaries were, of necessity drawn more by social and political convention than by nature. Their villages, surrounded on all sides by expanses of open space, dotted the landscape like knots in a net rather than beads on a necklace—and this pattern has persisted from the pharaohs to the present. (1991, 170)

A consequence of this abundance was the absence of patterns of stratification and in particular the absence of funerary practices such as the burial of valuables. In Upper Egypt, clusters of rich graves were set apart from the poorer ones as at Nagada. It is likely that the existence of some differentials in wealth fueled the desire for more of the same and generated class consciousness by providing a graded series of items, the possession of which was a reflection of the owner's rank.

It is possible to notice fine differences in the tendency toward stratification, even in cities of rather close geographical proximity but different ecology. Merimda is a Lower Egyptian site on the Delta that has been heavily excavated, with few or no grave goods found in the local cemeteries dating from the fifth millennium B.C. Indeed, in common with many communal societies, the dead were buried within the confines of the village. Only 60 km to the south a group of sites called Omari, on the Nile itself, reveal different practices indicative of much greater stratification. Although the village huts are of a similar structure to those at Merimda, important social practices differed. The dead were buried in cemeteries outside the settlement instead of within it. Also grave offerings indicative of status differentials were found at Omari. Some graves, removed from others, had piles of stones on top of them, probably indicative of higher status. Equally significant is the skeleton of a man who probably was a chief or ruler, found holding a wooden staff or scepter, carved at both ends, foreshadowing the *ames*-staff carried by Egyptian kings and gods. Thus, within only a small area, two different ecologies, one blessed with the abundance of the Delta and the other subject to the scarcities and vagaries of the Nile Valley, demonstrated two different societal outcomes regarding stratification and the emergence of a ruling elite.

We can follow Egyptian history forward in time and witness the consequences of a de-emphasis on scarcity during the New Kingdom period. As the center of gravity of the Egyptian polity moved northward in the confrontation between Egypt and Asia Minor and as the riches of empire increased, we see the greater equality that would be predicted by the scarcity-inequality framework put forward here. The various functioning capitals of Egypt were no longer to the south but were found now in the north near the great abundance of the Delta region and its abutting empire. That this was "a period of great prosperity cannot be doubted" (Gardiner 1961, 268). At the same time, as John Wilson put it, "The Eighteenth Dynasty ... surpassed previous ages in the acknowledged influence of women" (1951, 202). In addition to political influence, we know that Egyptian women "held property in their own names and had money invested in businesses" (Budge 1977, 21). They were also seen as fully competent in the law-courts (Gardiner 1961, 270). Thus, as Egypt fully utilizes its "almost unlimited agricultural potential" (Kemp 1989, 32), augmented by the riches of empire, we also witness the emergence of a near-modern gender equality, as would be predicted by the scarcity-inequality nexus.

We should now consider briefly the role of population density, a matter that will be given more detailed consideration later. It is apparent that population generally increased prior to unification, and it is likely that the density of population—or concentration, as Hoffman (1991, 309) puts it—played a critical role in the emergence of civilization in Upper Egypt. Whether it played a critical role in the rise of individual city-states in the Delta or of *nomes* (roughly, principalities) in the south is another question entirely and will be dealt with later. For now, we will treat the unification process and the obvious warfare that attended it. As Butzer (1984) observes, there were serious political consequences that likely attended changes in the level of the Nile. Competition and conflict between neighboring principalities was probably aggravated by the falling water levels. And, as we have observed, the region around Hierankopolis, home of Narmer, the unifier of Egypt, must have been hard hit because of the narrow floodplain there.

It is likely then, that this scenario conforms to the model for the genesis of warfare that was found to be applicable to the wars among the Sumerians prior to unification under the empire of Aggad. It is quite likely that, as Hassan (1988, 174) points out, Narmer's first conquest would have been Nagada, slightly to the north, and then on to the Delta region further to the north. The scarcity-inequality nexus applied to several political regions is operative here. Although we have no records of such warfare, it probably occurred under these conditions of a scarcity-induced inequality among the various nomes and later the walled towns to the north. Indeed the Narmer palette, one of the best records we have of this period, shows the king wearing the crowns of both Lower and Upper Egypt (in different locations of the palette), while a rampant bull—a traditional symbol of the pharaohs—smashes in the walls of a town. Such a walled city could only have been found in the north. The role of Hierankopolis on the southern fringes of the Egyptian civilization might have been similar to that of Aggad. It is possible that the northern towns of the Delta and even certain of the nomes somewhat further to the south could have been more advanced culturally. Certainly there is evidence of fairly extensive trade with southwest Asia in the northern towns (Hassan 1986, 160), which could have, via diffusion processes and other forms of intermingling, led to a more advanced culture, much as the Semites and Sumerians appear to have developed in the ancient Sumerian city-states. The conquest from the south then could take the form of a more stratified and politically organized culture but one less advanced in other ways (degree of urbanization, for example) overwhelming a somewhat more developed way of life. In this sense, the "unification" of Egypt could conform to McNeill's dictum, mentioned earlier, that the conquest of more advanced societies by external, more primitive forces is one of the best attested elements of civilized history. From this point on, the fractal formations associated either with administration or with control of large land areas would be characteristic of the Egyptian state.

But if warfare was only the ultimate unifier of Egypt, what was the basis of the earlier political organization of the nomes to the south and of the walled cities to the north? The likely candidate is redistribution. Although Egypt could produce legendary food surpluses, the country also suffered from periodic losses of grain harvests as the result of insufficient inundation or high and destructive flooding. Since we know that there was almost a total absence of hunting by the Middle Predynastic period (Hassan 1988, 167), there must have been other ways of mitigating the shortages. Three possibilities are (1) the integration of resources among neighboring communities, (2) increases in cultivable land, and (3) an increase in the yield per unit area. In early agricultural societies, there are distinct limits to the latter two possibilities. In the narrow floodplain, land quickly runs out, and the yield per unit area would have decisive limitations in such a prescientific era. At some point, then, central storage systems would likely have come into existence as a simple expedient to guard against the next agricultural shortfall. As time went on, not only would there be the need to administer these storage systems, even in a primitive way, but in times of plenty, the periodic concentration of large numbers of persons needed to undertake public works would be facilitated by the stored agricultural surplus. Tomb construction, so characteristic even of Predynastic Egyptian society, the building of town walls, and care of the growing local irrigation systems (really only canals at this stage) would have been facilitated by this redistribution process. Local leaders could use whatever surplus wealth accrued to establish their own differential wealth and status vis-à-vis the remainder of the population. Conspicuous consumption of grave goods would have been amplified, reinforcing the tendency toward funerary cults among the elite. Thus the basis for the religious ideation of the Egyptian state would have been laid fairly early.

Hoffman (1991, 329) finds certain striking parallels between the function of funerary rites among contemporary tribes such as the Berawan of Borneo and the Predynastic Egyptians. Specifically, the funeral rites for a political leader allow for a sumptuous display that focuses not only on the dead leader but also on the succession process that often is included as well. In this manner, political continuity is maintained and even augmented over time.

Minoan Crete

A major part of my argument relies on the assumption of the existence of peaceful, largely socioeconomic processes leading to statehood. But certainly substantial evidence of warfare has been found in our two illustrations, ancient Mesopotamia and Egypt. Fortunately there is one polity that demonstrates little if any, evidence of warfare during its period of ascendancy, namely Minoan Crete. Although Crete generally is not listed among the "pristine" states because of evidence of contact with the Levant and Egypt, this is not a critical consideration here. As argued earlier, knowledge of the existence of a state should not necessarily effect its initiation elsewhere. If anything, some knowledge of coercive practices in other locations could lead to their explicit rejection. And indeed we find that certain characteristic practices of Mesopotamia, such as the building of major fortifications around cities and towns, simply are not found in Minoan Crete. Only later (as at Mallia) is there any evidence of walled fortifications, but this is well after the building of the Old Palaces that were harbingers of the Minoan state. Here then is clear evidence for the rise of the state without any evidence of war. To what then do we owe the origins of the Minoan state?

To begin, it is useful to compare ancient Crete with ancient Messenia as a region of Greece which, like Crete, had cultivable land and a fairly dense population. Indeed the population growth patterns of both are almost identical (Renfrew 1972, 254-58), yet Crete emerged with statelike structures without any evidence of warfare while Messenia did experience war, at least as indicated by the presence of fortifications and hilltop locations for villages as bases of security. As Renfrew observes, regarding the Old Palaces of ancient Crete, "The Palace principalities can thus be regarded as minor states, effectively organized economically, but in other respects not differing strikingly from chiefdoms" (1972, 369). It is the presence of effective redistribution, the presence of the throne in the palace at Knossos, the existence of the Minoan navy, and the palace as an institution of Cretan society that suggests this conclusion.

The number of large palaces in Crete (Knossos, Phaistos, Mallia, Katxakro) and the extent of the storage areas for redistribution, especially at Knossos, suggest a contrast with Messenia. For at Pylos, the one large palace found thus far in Messenia, the storage area was not so extensive, and no other large palaces have thus far been found. And the much larger redistribution area in the Cretan palaces occurs with a lesser population density (Renfrew 1972, 253). By the Middle Bronze Age, the density for Messenia was almost twice as large as for Crete (41.2 vs. 26.1 persons per sq km) and by the Late Bronze Age it exceeded twice that for Crete.

As we shall see, trade is the likely source of many of the goods that found their way into the redistribution area. At the outset, however, it was not trade but the differing ecological environments that set Crete and Messenia on different trajectories, both achieving state structures, but the former without war and the latter with at least defense needs requiring political organization.

The major ecological difference between the two is the percentage of cultivable land, as would be suggested by the differing population densities. Whereas most of Messenian land is cultivable (witness the later use of Messenia as the "breadbasket" of Sparta), only approximately 30 percent of Cretan land is (Allbaugh 1953, 54). And these arable lands are found at some distance from each other, thus suggesting a circumscribed condition not terribly different from that of the river valleys of the Nile, the Tigris-Euphrates, the Indus, or the Yellow River in China. Evidence of overpopulation is at once apparent. Colonies, as at Kythera, were established by the Early Minoan period, which precedes the building of the Old Palaces (Branigan 1970, 189). We also know that large families appeared to be the norm, as suggested by a late Neolithic village excavated at Knossos. The house plans reflecting a large number of small rooms discovered there appeared to be typical of those in use throughout the island (Branigan 1970, 37–38). It appears as if population rapidly increased prior to the foundation of the palaces at the beginning of the second millennium. Afterward, the rate of increase of population diminished (Renfrew 1972, 252).

Population growth and the consequent exacerbation of scarcities leading to inequalities answers one question put by John Cherry in conjunction with his treatment of peer polity interaction: "Generalised patterns of interaction between such units [small residential groups] existed throughout the one-and-a-half millennia of the Cretan Early Bronze Age and even earlier during the Neolithic period. Why then was it only in the two or three centuries immediately preceding palace emergence that there begin to be seen the first signs of incipient stratification and regional differentiation?" (1986, 43).

The old palaces grew up principally as redistribution centers spurred by local cultivation. What would have been the impetus for such redistribution? The answer probably is given by the relatively small percentage of farm area devoted to cereals (19 percent), whereas grapes, mostly for wine, and olives for oil together made up 27 percent of the cultivated area. Most of the remaining cultivable land either lay fallow (18 percent) or was used for pasture (24 percent) (Renfrew 1972, 302). The discovery that Cretan hillsides could be used for growing olives and grapes likely had an effect on increasing population density, for these products could be used in exchange for staples such as cereal and for export, as in fact later occurred. Palace redistribution centers could have made such increased horticulture possible by providing facilities for storage and later redistribution.

Trade however, was not the impetus for the building the Old Palaces, although it might have affected the construction of the newer ones. As Keith Branigan observes,

> There is no evidence of the Minoans ever producing specifically for the "export market" and certainly this was not the case in the Early Bronze Age. With the rise of the palaces overseas trade may have become well organized and the commodities involved may well have come under the control of a central authority, but in the Early Bronze Age the various crafts were practiced as village industries and were all interconnected as part of the village economy. Production was principally for consumption within the village and its environs, and this may well explain the remarkable variety and individuality which pervades so much of the Early Minoan material which remains to us." (1970, 90)

Renfrew concurs with this view, pointing to the infrequent trading contracts between Crete and Egypt as well as with the Levant. When compared with trade, "the local redistribution of foodstuffs and other goods must have taken place on a very much larger scale" (1972, 478).

Thus, it is fairly clear that we can take the origin of the Old Palaces to lie in the redistribution of commodities. Certainly defense, given the absence of any signs of fortifications, is not a plausible explanation. Religion also is an unlikely candidate, for as F. Matz points out, "As Minoan representational art was developing during this period, the absence of cult images is striking" (1973, 161). But we also know that the New Palaces that came into existence after the destruction of the old by earthquake had greatly expanded functions. Not only were there large storage facilities, but there were also rooms obviously devoted to religious observances, as well as the throne rooms at Knossos and Pylos in Messenia. Communal ritual was an important property of the late Minoan "city-state;" it became the responsibility of the palace leader and even apparently was influenced by the Mesopotamian representation of gods. Even then, there were no cult images or idols; these did not appear until after the Late Palace period. Domestic commerce and trade were apparently still an increasingly major redistribution function of the palaces. The importance of trade is underscored by the more recent discovery of a Minoan palace at Kato Zakro in an area with little or no arable land (Graham 1987, 250). The other large palaces all were located in or near highly cultivable land. This fact, coupled with Kato Zakro's location at the eastern end of the island, suggests its importance as a redistribution center almost solely concerned with trade, especially with Syria. Artifacts discovered at the site support this interpretation.

Of paramount importance, of course, is the nature of the Minoan polity and administration. In the absence of contemporary historical records we must rely on inferences from the archaeological record as well as later accounts. Nevertheless, we can piece together a fairly detailed picture. It is inferred first, that the king ruled with the support of a nobility. The luxurious dwellings of the nobility are placed round the palaces at Knossos and at Mallia. Their burial places also are distinct, as in the Messara region. They resided in villages scattered all through the countryside. We are not aware of the exact relationship between king and nobles in this Late Palace period, but it is likely that the lords of smaller palaces (intermediate between villas and the great palaces) ruled at the discretion of the king. We are not even certain that there was a single Minoan state, for it is possible that several principalities existed around the several great palaces. However, the references to King Minos and the existence of a single Minoan navy suggest a unified polity, at least during the Late Palace Period.

There is clear evidence of stratification in Crete, indicated not only by the presence of the noble residences and the public works projects, such as the palaces and harbors, that would have required extensive labor, but also by written historical accounts. Aristotle for example, tells us that a "caste-system" prevalent in Crete in his own time had been established by Minos (Willetts 1965, 47). The existence of such a system is foreshadowed by the scarcity-inequality arguments leading first to the exponential distribution in scarce environments and then to the EI distribution as an expression of elite hegemony. The emergence of specialized crafts such as metallurgy, pottery, and stoneworking in response to increased trade and an expanding economy also would have reinforced the stratified gap between artisan and peasant or serf.

Other, related societies not considered directly here also provide evidence for early stratification. For example, regarding ancient Greece and the Aegean, Antonio Gilman remarks that "evidence for stratification precedes the development of centers for higher-order regulation by several centuries" (1981, 8).

The route to such a highly stratified society, however, could traverse a fairly democratic period. At first, despite all of the indications of stratification, the power of the king appears to have been limited. As M. I. Finley comments, "there is nothing majestic or central about the throne-room at Cnossos whether in size or in its wall-decoration. . . . Even the throne is not particularly regal. Not a single picture exists which portrays a historical event or which reveals administrative or judicial activity or any other manifestation of political power in action" (1981, 41). This physical evidence is coupled with additional evidence drawn from the Early Minoan period.

During this time, the Minoan communities most likely had an elected leader, as in the early Sumerian towns, most probably an individual selected by reason of birth, tradition, or wealth, or some contribution of all three. Early Minoan tombs suggest that large numbers of people within a community were considered to be of approximately equal status, at least for burial purposes. There were no exclusive burial sites for an elite during this period, indicating the absence of an imposed leadership from above. The bodies interred in these tombs varied very little in their material possessions.

There is even reason to speculate that the period of tenure for an elected leader was eight years. As Branigan notes, "The legends which relate the octennial offering of Athenian youths to the Minotaur and the octennial departure of Minos to commune with Zeus are thought to indicate that this was the period of tenure during the political era and such an important tradition would very probably have its roots in the origins of the system, which seem to be in the Early Bronze Age" (1970, 119). We can conclude from these arguments that some degree of democracy, or at least the absence of serious imposition of rule from above, accompanied the development of Cretan society. Whether that was true at the end, at the time of the presumed Mycenaean invasion and takeover in the fifteenth century B.C., is another matter.

Before proceeding further, it is useful to consider one of the potential explanations of the origin of Minoan society, namely diffusion from abroad, most likely the Near East. This is of some concern here because of the question of the potential "importation" of the state to Crete from Egypt or Mesopotamia, which would render our arguments here less critical in their implications for the origins of the state without war. Virtually every modern writer concerned with Crete dismisses the idea of importation, while still acknowledging that there were outside influences. Renfrew, as we have seen, notes the small number of trading contracts, or, as he puts it, "trading contacts in the third millennium [just prior to the building of the Early Palaces] with Egypt were few, and with the Near East even fewer" (1972, 478). Clearly there were repeated contacts and emulations of Near Eastern models *after* the building of the palaces. As Cherry remarks, "My own reading of the Minoan case suggests that the Near Eastern exemplars emulated by different Minoan polities provided a *medium* for competitive display and self-aggrandizement, yet they were not the *cause* either of such competition or of the rise of the competing political entities themselves" (1986, 42; emphasis in original). Contacts within the Aegean were far greater both in terms of innovation and economics.

But aside from the absence of early contacts numerous enough to generate significant diffusion, there is indigenous evidence for the internal development of Minoan society. As R. F. Willetts observes, "The palace economy of the Middle Bronze Age of Crete developed over a period of about five hundred years with an enterprise which suggests little interference with the basic structure of social life. Thus the very planlessness of Minoan palace architecture, its apparently haphazard, 'cellular' growth, with the addition of structures in varying sizes have been traced to a similar pattern in the building of neolithic dwellings" (1965, 41). Or as Rodney Castleden puts it in a summary judgment, "Minoan Crete may be seen as a cradle of civilization on a level with the Nile, Indus, Tigris, and Euphrates valleys" (1990, 3).

China

Turning now to ancient China we see similar patterns at work. First there is evidence for ranking and stratification and, later, remains of fortifications and organized violence. And, as in the instances of Sumer and Crete, we shall see evidence of a vestigial democracy at work, even after the occurrence of warfare.

Kinship or clan society, perhaps even more than in the other instances, will be seen to affect the trajectory of Chinese civilization. As in the rise of Sumer, the centers of Chinese civilization occurred in an area of intersecting rivers and wetlands. As the paleontologist Chou Pen-hsiung put it, "It can be estimated that, from the Neolithic to the historic period, the Yellow River and the Huai-ho River plains were crisscrossed with rivers and densely dotted with large and small lakes and were covered with a full vegetation" (quoted in Chang 1986, 162). This combination of marshy landscape with riverfronts and their alluvia affording more desirable landholdings set the stage for the particular pattern of early Chinese civilization. Major regions of the Late Shang, the earliest recorded dynastic Chinese civilization, are found either along tributaries of the Yellow River (more inhabitable than the often severely flooded main river beds) or in areas lying between such tributaries (Keightley 1983, 544).

The first evidence of stratification is found in various Chinese cemeteries dating anywhere from 5000 to 2000 B.C. In the earliest graves, the variation in furnishings is not terribly large, although frequently one individual with many more objects will stand out—in one instance a boy, three or four years old (Chang 1986, 119). Later in this period, the evidence of ranking or stratification is more compelling. "The variation in the amount of grave furnishings suggests a society at a sophisticated level; this is also indicated by the huge number of painted signs on pottery" (Chang 1986, 150). It was in the third millennium that the stratification patterns were intensified. In one cemetery from the middle of the third millennium not only are there distinctions in the grave furnishings, but the graves of the rich are in one section of the cemetery while those of the poor are in another (Chang 1986, 169). Even within lineages, there are clear distinctions in burial patterns. There are, for example, individual clusters in well-defined areas of a prehistoric cemetery, but four distinct classes of graves are found in each of the three clusters (Chang 1986, 249).

Here now is a clue to the reason for rank and status differentials even under conditions of fairly sparse settlement. As Charles Hucker observes for a later society, "Shang civilization was not characterized by population density and urban civilization on a scale comparable to those of Mesopotamia and the Indus River Valley, but the Shang cities were large and multi-functional and the Shang population was differentiated by rank, status, and occupation" (1975, 27). Without a high population density, how was the scarcity-inequality nexus operational? The answer is provided by the ancient and pervasive Chinese clan and lineage system that essentially required members of the kinship group to remain in close proximity to each other unless an absolutely compelling reason should arise for the departure of some members. There would be no opportunity to range over a wide area for purposes of equalizing holdings. Rich alluvial land bordering rivers would be farmed only by certain clan members and not others. As time proceeded, the inequality condition would worsen, thus leading to rank and status differences both within and between clans. And when irrigation was introduced along the Yellow River and its tributaries, then this effect was more pronounced. The presence of irrigated water tends to foster nuclear families with implied inequalities among them, while the absence of such irrigation has been shown in Chinese society to augment joint families or clan-like settlement (Pasternak 1978) with common holdings and hence equality of circumstance. Families possessing irrigated water simply can "go it alone" without the necessity for other family members to provide labor or other forms of sustenance in difficult times. Without such water, joint families are required virtually as insurance against the difficulties induced by drought. Equality automatically would be enhanced by the equality of holdings experienced by those dwelling in common.

This sui generis emergence of stratification is of course a strong argument for the absence of any conquering civilization that imposed its will on the indigenous population. Referring to Shang civilization as the first dynastic period for which we have recorded king lists, Kwang-chih Chang tells us that "as the Shang class system was characterized more by intralineage and interlineage differentiation than by conqueror/conquered stratification in any ethnic sense, there is no evidence that the Shang civilization was linguistically diverse in terms of familial classification" (1980, 329).

Nor should we be persuaded that there was a significant diffusion effect that formed Chinese civilization. In matters of "intensified differentiation of society and qualitatively higher degrees of achievement in the arts" the various stages of early Chinese civilization exhibit "remarkable continuity" (Chang 1986, 364).

The matter of warfare of course is central, and here there is considerable evidence for the emergence of fortifications and violence *after* an intensified stratification. As early as 4500–4000 B.C., the Ta-wen-k'ou culture exhibited strong differences in burial furnishings (Chang 1986, 162), but not until the later Lung-shan culture (around 2500–2000 B.C.) do we find not only demonstrated intensified stratification but the first evidence of fortifications and violence. The earliest such remains thus far discovered are found at Ch'eng tzu-yai in Shantung (Chang 1986, 248), in which an enclosure of hard brick was found. Perhaps even more compelling is the analysis of the written characters of the Shang. (Shang script is an ancestor of later Chinese writing; Pulleyblank 1984.) Such analysis demonstrates that the character for settlement and that for defense bear strong similarities, that both show the essence of a settlement was a walled enclosure (Chang 1980, 134). The Lung-shan culture of this period also yields the first evidence of violence against people (Chang 1986, 270), including signs of blows, decapitation, and scalping. (It is tempting to speculate on the possibility of a climate change that affected China and Mesopotamia equally around the beginning of the third millennium, when the earliest signs of fortifications were found in both. Perhaps a global warming made certain lands cultivable and therefore more desirable, thus precipitating conflict; alternatively, a cooling period might have led to scarcities and their consequent inequalities that also could have induced conflict. However, recent evidence, at least concerning one well-known period, tends to discount possibilities for a common global climate effect, although regional common effects certainly are possible [Hughes and Diaz 1994]. The possible influence of global climate changes, although not common worldwide effects, is treated in Chapter 4.)

Thus, warfare follows stratification, and this precedence also occurs in the larger context of emergent inequality among contending states, as seen in Mesopotamia and as suggested in the model of multipolar inequality. Indeed, the last period prior to the unification of China under the Ch'in was the Warring States period, which saw the emergence of one state, Ch'i, then another, Ch'u, and finally the ultimate victory of Ch'in in the third century B.C. (Hucker 1975, 41).

Perhaps of even greater interest is the evidence of a vestigial democracy in the documents of the Shang society. And the relative stability of Shang society as measured by the low frequency of war in comparison with other periods (Cioffi-Revilla and Lai 1995) will find echoes in the later systematic analysis of democracy and war in Chapter 7. The term "vestigial democracy" as used here certainly does not refer to a process of election such as would normally be associated with a mature functioning democracy. Instead, it is intended to suggest certain limitations on the rights of monarchs that would not normally be associated with a hereditary monarchy. First, the kingship could not stay within the same *kan* unit; this is explored more fully below. Second, the king had to fulfill his obligations toward his subordinate lords or he would be considered fit to be overthrown (Chang 1980, 201). As the first of these is the more startling, let us consider it in more detail.

Shang society was ruled by a ruling class of consanguineal origin (the Tzu clan). Within this ruling class, ten ritual segments were organized into *kan* units, which were political entities. In turn, these *kan* units were organized into two divisions, traditionally labeled A and B. Now when the kingship succession stayed within the same generation, it could remain in the same division but went to a member of a different *kan* unit. But when there was a generational change, the kingship had to go to a member of the other division (see

Chang 1980, 181). Further, the king was assisted by a prime official who had to be from the opposite division from the king. In the history of the Shang dynasty, roughly six centuries, the kingship shifted between divisions six times (Chang 1980, 187). Although this certainly is not democracy in any currently accepted sense, nevertheless, this "two-party" division of the ruling elite and the requirement for alteration either between *kans* or divisions suggests a vestige of shared power that very likely had a more popular form prior to the emergence of the Shang dynasty.

The Chinese history of warfare conforms to the classic supposition of the influence of nomadic tribesman on settled agricultural populations (Cohen 1978). Settled populations in China were always watching to the north and the west for the next barbarian or semibarbarian incursion from barely civilized groups, which led ultimately to the building of the Great Wall during the Ch'in dynasty in the third century B.C. (Hucker 1975, 44). Without such incursions, it is possible that here too more democratic or at least less authoritarian forms would have developed, as apparently was the case in Crete, early Sumer, and as we shall see shortly, in parts of early Mesoamerica.

The overall pattern of the genesis of Chinese civilization has additional implications for the foundations of the theory of scarcity and inequality as the basis of the state. Chinese civilization apparently did not appear in one place in North China and then spread from there. Instead, the recent archeological evidence argues for the simultaneous emergence of that civilization in many areas of China geographically remote from each other (Chang 1986). The concept of "tribe" that has been so widely used for the past century and a half is not particularly useful for understanding the rise of Chinese civilization. According to Fried (1983), different unilineal kinship groups or clans can settle in separate locations and through simultaneous social influences evolve to a ranked and stratified society constituting virtually an incipient state. The tribe as an intermediary form is not necessary for that process to take hold. Likewise, the theory of scarcity-induced inequality does not rely on the concept of tribe. Indeed, kinship groupings can be exposed to such inequalities simply by virtue of unequal access to scarce resources such as alluvial soil; even within the same kinship grouping such inequalities can occur. The tribe as a collection of kinship groupings presumably descended from a common ancestor is unnecessary to this formulation. Thus, my theoretical framework makes Fried's position on the inessentiality of the tribe more understandable, for inequality and the consequent path to state formation can emerge directly upon the exposure to scarcity.

I hasten to add that in no way does this argument reflect on the actual existence of tribes, for as we know, tribes have existed historically and do so today (see, for example, Birdsell 1973). It is the status of the tribe as a *necessary* condition for the transition to statehood that is called into question both by Fried and by my theory of scarcity-induced inequality. As we will see in succeeding chapters, population growth alone, leading to agricultural density in settled populations and increased land scarcity, has many consequences, one of which is the establishment of political rights as a basis for state formation.

Mesoamerica

Ancient Mesoamerica is probably the most extensively researched area in the Western Hemisphere. This is in large part because of the fascination and semi-mythical status of the Maya remains discovered in the Yucatan peninsula and the attraction of the pyramids of Teotihuacan in the Valley of Mexico. Mesoamerica also is widely acknowledged to be the location of pristine states. In the following treatment I will concentrate on the Valley of Oaxaca, the Valley of Mexico, and the Eastern (Maya) Lowlands, where so much archaeological investigation has taken place.

In the Early Formative period of the Valley of Oaxaca (1500–850 B.C.) sedentary farming villages were located throughout the valley. During the early, or Tierras Largas, phase, there is no evidence of stratification, despite the fairly large number of villages, but by the second, or San Jose phase (1150–850 B.C.), such evidence does appear, and it is this phase that interests us. Specifically, the question is, what are the circumstances surrounding the appearance of stratification and more especially why is it found in one location—San Jose Mogote in the Etla area—and not in others? In fact, most of the population growth during the later period, as well as the stratification, occurs in only this one area, out of the entire river system in the Valley of Oaxaca. We can understand the consequences of stratification as the result of population growth, but why should that growth be restricted to one location of the valley, when there are rivers in other portions that easily could have absorbed the excess population? Richard Blanton and his colleagues (1981, 53) suggest that the centering of ritual activity in the Etla area likely caused the population to congregate in that location.

This is certainly a plausible argument, and not inconsistent with the preceding arguments of this book, but it is not necessary to invoke this sort of explanation. Flannery, Marcus, and Kowalewski (1981) conclude that the iconography found on pottery were motifs of descent groups such as clans (also see Adams 1991, 80). If so, then the growth of an extended kinship structure could have led to the population density at that point in the valley. Loath to abandon their kin, the "surplus" individuals may then have lived under less than egalitarian conditions with their extended family. The growth of extended kinship structures leading to inequality within them at riverine locations is, of course, a theme developed in this and earlier chapters.

The question of warfare is also of great importance, and here the evidence is ambiguous. Marcus Winter claims that the period from 600 to 1 B.C. appears to have been a time of peace. Population grew at a more rapid rate than during the preceding San Rosario phase. Monte Albán, an extensively excavated site, became the focus for the rapidly increasing population within the Valley of Oaxaca (Winter 1984, 209). It is during this period that a developed state begins to emerge, appearing in full consolidated form around 200 B.C. (Adams 1991, 235; Flannery, Marcus, and Kowalewski 1981). According to Winter, evidence of conflict begins to appear only *after* 1 B.C., extending for several centuries thereafter. The causes of the conflict are not known, but may have been related to the efforts of the new large and monumental Monte Albán civilization to extend its influence and particularly to integrate the surrounding communities into its market system, trading in obsidian, ceramics, jade, and greenstone, which had grown extensively during the preceding period.

Flannery, Marcus, and Kowalewski, however, note that there was warfare as early as 700–500 B.C. and that it escalated during the later period preceding and subsequent to the formation of the Monte Albán state. They date the fortification of the city by about 100 B.C., suggesting the presence of warfare at least at that time. Blanton and his colleagues (1981, 76) argue that work began on a large defensive wall as early as 200 B.C. Thus warfare may well have been associated with state formation in this case.

Another view emerging from the present theory, however, suggests that warfare began *after* the consolidation of the very early state, which may or may not have been autocratic. After all, evidence of stratification is found for several centuries, if not almost a millennium before 200 B.C., the acknowledged time of full state formation. Might not smaller polities have evolved in a quasi-democratic form earlier, the emergence of Monte Albán then followed, along the lines of the scarcity-induced inequality among several states, as we saw earlier in the instance of Sumer and possibly China? The favored actor, Monte Albán, could have risen to prominence in conflict with other city-states, but *after* state formation in each instance. (The decline in population in the valley itself after state formation suggests some nucleation, but also possibly the results of malnutrition and disease attendant upon widespread conflict.) Indeed, this is the conclusion reached by Blanton and his colleagues. Interpreting various monuments (*Danzantes*) indicating captured leaders, they suggest "that the

Danzantes monuments indicate that other people of the southern highlands, during period I [500-200 B.C.], were organized into small, autonomous polities. The monuments may indicate that Monte Albán carried out punitive raids in response to military threats, or that Monte Albán conquered these polities in an attempt to gain access to their resources" (1981, 85). If Blanton and his colleagues are correct, then the model of competition and ultimately warfare among already formed polities may have led to the rise of Monte Albán as the premier city and its later fortification. They go on to assert that Monte Albán entered a new imperial phase shortly after this period of subjugating the valley (1981, 85-87). Empire formation was now feasible during the period 200 B.C.-A.D. 300, much as Athens, Rome, and other ascendant city-states embarked on the path of empire after rising to preeminence in their own regions and subjugating the competing regional polities.

As in the case of the Valley of Oaxaca, the dynamics of the growth of Maya civilization, at least during the Formative period, are attributed principally to population growth (Willey 1987, 83). According to William Sanders (1977), who developed a model for the rise of Lowland Maya civilization, population growth followed by a shortage of agricultural land led to competition and inequalities in the control of the land and so to social ranking and finally stratification. We even see differences in political centralization based on quality of agricultural land. For example, in the Rosario polity, there are two major environmental zones, the upper valley, with less favored agricultural land, and the lower zone, with more favored valley bottomlands. The elite proportion of the total population in the lower section is nearly twice that of the upper, and the total elite population is almost five times as large in the lower as in the upper, suggesting a substantial difference in political centralization between the upper (more centralized under conditions of scarce good agricultural land) and lower (less centralized) sections (de Montmollin 1989, 225).

This finding of course agrees strongly with the exponential model. When one adds competitions between centers on some observable social process—say, competition for scarce lands—the inequalities both within and between communities emerge purely as the result of scarcities, even assuming equal initial access for all of the participants.

Although there is early evidence of ranking and stratification (Adams 1991; Blanton et al. 1981) and later evidence of warfare (Hammond 1988), there is also evidence of early egalitarian and representative practices. Even at the time warfare began, during the Late Formative period (circa 250 B.C.-A.D. 250), "there is evidence that assemblies and councils of lineage heads were the principal governing bodies. By the Classic period, many of the heads of lineages had evidently parlayed their advantages into hereditary superior status" (Adams 1991, 189). In another analysis, Evon Vogt (1971) developed an egalitarian model for ancient Maya civilizations. Rotating civil and religious offices allowed for relatively open access to higher status positions. Fulfilling less important offices allowed one to advance to higher positions. But, as Richard Adams indicates, an increasing aristocratic principle of favoring the elite worked to establish a hereditary control. This occurred, of course, after the advent of warfare during the Late Formative period. This also is the period that witnessed the first of the fortifications that eventually became widespread throughout the Maya area during the Classic period. Indeed, during these periods, the Maya built more fortifications than any other Mesoamerican civilization (Adams 1991, 161).

Warfare among the Maya during the Classic period and later, approximates what we know about the Sumerians. There was constant competition and later warfare among the various city-states in an environment of increasing scarcity, which required intensified agricultural methods (Blanton et al. 1981; Sabloff 1990). The Maya, in fact, offer an interesting sidelight on the impact of warfare in exacerbating an already resource-poor situation. In a relatively peaceful setting, all of the land lying between city-states in the Formative period is available for farming. However, as we saw in the instance of Sumer, "spheres of influence" develop within which there will be one or more areas of "no-man's-land" not available for cultivation. Cultivable land is removed from agriculture; as a result the scarcity-induced inequality that led to the rise of certain centers is reinforced, and the inequalities among city-states intensify, leading to warfare and the rise of one preeminent city-state. As a consequence, "The evidence is heavily in favor of the development of regional states by the beginning of the Classic period" (Adams 1991, 174). This, of course, is reminiscent of the role of Ur, Umma, and Lagash, which served at various times as heads of the regional Sumerian polities.

In contrast to the Valley of Oaxaca and the Valley of Mexico, the area in which Lowland Maya civilization grew up is not heavily circumscribed. It is a broad land area with water and vegetation, although with increased population growth various horticultural methods such as raised fields and irrigation had to be introduced. Nevertheless, these ecological differences among the three instances will have certain consequences to be explored later.

Finally, let me briefly consider the Valley of Mexico and, in particular, Teotihuacan, first as an urban center and then as the likely capital of an extended regional state or empire. Teotihuacan was a large city, probably the largest of ancient Mesoamerica, with a population of 150,000 at its peak (Spence 1984). The rise of Teotihuacan bears certain similarities with that of Monte Albán, although it was much larger and had more of its administration contained in the city itself (Blanton et al. 1981, 233); by contrast, Monte Albán relied on secondary and tertiary administrative centers. The Teotihuacan political and economic sphere extended even into the Maya highlands, as at Kaminaljuyu, and included influences on the Maya Classic period at Tikal (Adams 1991, 225–29). The issue of concentrated versus dispersed administration raises the question of earlier democratic or at least egalitarian and representative forms. If even at Teotihuacan, with its *image* of centralized despotism, we find some vestiges of decentralization, then there may have been earlier democratic forms. Here we have the problem, posed by George Cowgill (1983), of why such a large structure as the Ciudadela, apparently home of the ruling elite, has apartments covering so small an area. His answer, developed more fully in Chapter 7, is that there likely was decentralized control for most of the history of that city-state, with changes in the architecture of the Ciudadela occurring only close to the fall of the city. This observation is consistent with the hypothesis, also explored more fully in Chapter 7, that there exists a positive relationship between the emergence of external threat and the rise of autocratic rule.

The contrast of Teotihuacan as a large capital of a regional polity (if not empire), Monte Albán as a smaller regional center, and the dispersed competing polities of the Maya civilization suggests certain relationships between polity development and ecology. A broad, open terrain such as that of the Maya apparently gave rise to the competing and ultimately warring Classic centers, whereas primary centers arose at Teotihuacan in the Valley of Mexico and Monte Albán in the Valley of Oaxaca (Blanton et al. 1981, 218–19). These circumscribed areas, which led ultimately to greater scarcity, may have helped generate the inequality of one center rising above all of the others and a fractal distribution leading to a larger state formation. Yet there are limits to this explanation. Teotihuacan was a large center of trade in obsidian, jade, and various craft productions. As such, it could easily have risen to dominance by virtue of its opportunities for a large labor pool. We know that Teotihuacan grew during its Classic period while the remainder of the Valley of Mexico actively declined in population (Blanton et al. 1981), supporting the rapid urbanization process at Teotihuacan. Yet we know that trade in itself, for the most part, is not a progenitor of state formation (see Drennan and Nowack 1984; Hirth 1984; Willey 1987, 135). Thus, although the rise of trade is a possible explanation for the *expansion* of Teotihuacan and Monte Albán, once formed, it is not a strong candidate for explaining the origins of these polities. Far more likely is the earlier scarcity-inequality nexus within a circumscribed area, followed by state expansion driven largely by trade. In this sense, trade and warfare may be functionally interchangeable as mechanisms of expansion. Certainly a fractal EI distribution can result from trade, as seen in Table 2.1, demonstrating the Dutch shipping hegemony.

Andean Civilization

The last of our examples, the Andes, provides an exceptionally interesting case study, for here, in a sense, the exception will prove the rule. The difference between this case and the preceding ones, and in fact all instances of the rise of pristine civilizations, is the apparent origin of Andean civilization in a maritime setting. Other civilizations arose in circumscribed riverine settings; here the earliest settlements are found on the Pacific coast of what is today Peru. This unique circumstance has given rise to an intense debate among anthropologists over the accuracy of the claim that Andean civilization did indeed have its origins in this maritime, coastal setting.

On the one hand, writers such as Michael Moseley (1975, 1992) assert that sea life such as anchovies and shellfish is superabundant on the Peruvian coast as the result of its unique temperatures and tides, offering ample food for early populations. On the other hand, critics of Moseley (and of others, cf. Lanning 1967), question the caloric value of the likely foodstuffs eaten (mollusks, for example) and whether the absence of significant plant remains at archaeological sites really indicates their non-use, given that significant deterioration in such remains would have taken place over time (Raymond 1981; D. J. Wilson 1981). Still others (such as Quilter and Stocker 1983) aver that foodstuffs from the sea supplemented by others on land nearby would have been sufficient to support a mostly maritime existence. Whatever the outcome of this debate, there is general agreement that after 1800 B.C. settlements moved upland into river valleys and assumed a sedentary agricultural existence, comparable to the early phases of other pristine civilizations. Population density on the coast and a consequent increased pressure on available resources very likely was the principal cause of such a generalized movement (Pineda 1988, 70).

What is fascinating about the early coastal settlements is the appearance of stratification; virtually all scholars of Peruvian prehistory agree that this stratification existed. Whatever its interest to anthropologists and archaeologists, it is doubly interesting here because of our theory that inequality should appear only after significant societal scarcities have been experienced. Maritime abundance should mitigate against any such scarcities, yet inequality in the form of a probable two-level stratification is found (Carneiro 1987).

First, the notion of abundance must be clarified in this context, for, as noted above, there is significant disagreement among anthropologists whether maritime food resources would have been sufficient to support populations of the size found in the coastal villages. Providing strong support for the negative position, David Wilson (1981), for example, argues that it would have required a hundred times the probable caloric availability from the sea in order to support the typical population sizes in coastal villages, and J. Scott Raymond (1981) comes to similar conclusions. Further, this region does share one characteristic in common with riverine locations giving rise to civilizations, in that aside from the river valleys and the coast itself, the area is mostly desert. Hence, the food must come either from the sea or from agriculture practiced at the mouths of river deltas and in the valleys themselves. Thus, a kind of circumscription is found that prevents people from simply wandering off and living where they pleased. Thus *any* increased population pressure on the available resources, maritime or otherwise, would lead to the dynamics of Equation 2.1 and a resultant increase in inequality. It is likely then that once the inequality and consequent stratification appeared, the newly emergent leadership could make the decision to increase the agricultural base of the community by moving upland into the river valleys. It is significant here that virtually all observers agree on the increased population density during the later phases of coastal village life and its very likely impingement on the necessary resource base per person or per family. According to Moseley, "Some authorities estimate that maritime societies on the central coast experienced a 30-fold increase in their numbers during the Preceramic period" (1992, 107).

Given the presence of maritime resources, it is clear that the scarcities of foodstuffs would probably not have been severe, and the extent of hierarchy probably would not have been extreme. In such a circumstance and given the absence of any indications of fortifications (Fiedel 1992; Pineda 1988), suggesting the absence of warfare, a primitive sort of democracy probably would have existed—again not terribly different from other instances we have examined and will examine in more detail in Part III. And this is precisely the sort of decision-making process that Moseley suggests operated in the villages "in which capable individuals rotate through a formal hierarchy of leadership positions, ... because there is little mortuary evidence of an élite class or of chiefs who inherited their offices" (1992, 107). This absence of a hereditary elite consequent upon more extreme stratification is consistent with the absence of both extreme resource scarcities and warfare. Thus despite the exceptional ecological circumstances found in comparison with other societies, the dynamics of Equation 2.1 and the theory of scarcity-induced inequality are operative here. It is only with later state formation associated with societies such as the Moche and, most spectacularly, the Incas and their extraordinary expansion into the highlands and down the Pacific coast (Métraux 1970) that we find the fractal formations associated with conquest and the emergence of a strongly articulated state and empire.

It is significant that resource scarcities of various types apparently drove the Inca expansion. In one version of this dynamic, the practice of split inheritance, which came to the Inca from the Chimu, also an expansionary polity, played a significant role. This split inheritance effectively kept any material possessions from the new ruler upon the death of the old, or, as Geoffrey Conrad and Arthur Demarest put it,

> Upon the death of an Inca emperor (the *Sapa Inca*, or "Unique Inca"), the rights to govern, to wage war, and to impose taxes on the realm passed to one of his sons, who was his successor and principal heir. However, *the chroniclers emphatically state that the new ruler received no material legacy from his predecessor*. The deceased emperor's palaces in Cuzco and the countryside, servants, chattel, and other possessions continued to be treated as his property and were entrusted to his *panaqa*, a corporate social group containing all of his descendants in the male line except his successor. These secondary heirs did not actually own the items named above. Instead, ownership remained vested in the dead king. *Panaqa* members received some of their support through their ancestor's "generosity" — ceremonial redistribution of part of his continuing income. They derived the rest of their sustenance from the *panaqa*'s own separate holdings. (1984, 113; emphasis added)

Thus, in order to develop his own material holdings, effectively beginning at ground zero, the new ruler had to expand significantly beyond the confines of the then-existing polity. This would account for the extremely rapid expansion of the Inca state between 1463 and 1525 (Fiedel 1992, 343).

This, effectively, is an ideologically driven scarcity, for it demands that new resources be acquired by the new ruler as the result of virtually a funerary mortgaging of the deceased ruler's possessions for sacral purposes. Whatever its source, the scarcities are extreme. Some scholars (see Fiedel 1992; Paulsen 1981) attribute the expansion not to an ideological sequestering of older resources but to actual or potential environmental stresses engendering new scarcities that require the acquisition of new resources. In any event, it is a resource scarcity — whether actual or perceived — that drives the imperial expansion.

An important point to emphasize is that there is little evidence of warfare during the period of state formation. Instead, the Cuzco region, the heart of the Inca state "was marked by the gradual consolidation and centralization of economic authority in Cuzco during the Killke period [an early period of state formation] rather than through the heroic actions of a single leader. . . . It is suggested that the centralization of regional authority and the development of a stratified social hierarchy in the Cuzco region were already occurring during the Killke Period" (Bauer 1992, 141). The stratification mentioned by Brian Bauer originates in a regional class of producers that formed the heart of the Inca state prior to its major period of expansion in the fifteenth century. Indeed, the major groups occupying the area south of Cuzco, or the Inca de Privilegio of that region, apparently were integrated into the Inca-dominated Cuzco region without warfare. There is no evidence of fortified communities during the Killke period. Instead, various groups south of Cuzco existed in small, widely scattered hamlets and unfortified villages (Bauer 1992, 105). Here we see the operation of peaceful dynamics suggested by Equation 2.3 (fractal expansion over a relatively uninhabited or unopposed space) and only later, after the consolidation of the early state, do we find a concerted effort to expand beyond the initial confines of that state. At this later point, somewhat different dynamics of Equation 2.3 come into play, which of course may involve warfare in the conquest and expansion over the desired territory. Hence the famous victory of the Inca over the Chanca some time during the late fifteenth century is not essential to Inca state formation as is sometimes thought (e.g., Dwyer 1971; Niles 1987; Rowe 1985) but a part of, albeit an important part of, the process of expansion of the already existing state.

Similar dynamics of early stratification are found in another Andean setting, this time originating in a river valley in central Peru. Local political centralization arose before the arrival of the Inca, and the manner in which it did so is of interest. Initially, in what is called the Wanka I phase, small farming and herding villages were scattered throughout the valley areas and lower hillsides. These hamlets were self-sufficient locally, and there is little evidence of inequality and its associated stratification. In the latter portion of the earlier period, evidence of agricultural intensification is found, with little pressure on resources and no physical evidence of intersite tensions, suggested by the absence of defensive walls (Hastorf 1990). In the second stage, Wanka II, we see evidence of what Christine Hastorf calls "incipient inequality" (1990, 141). Further, the proportion of upland sites away from the valleys is much greater, and the villages are larger, with many having protective walls. "An increase in internal boundedness and tensions over local territories and resources" (144) is suggested to account for this increased inequality and the emergence of an economic elite. There also is evidence of an irrigation canal that further suggests the frequently found association between irrigated lands and the emergence of an economic elite. In a sense, the two stages of Wanka civilization reflect a similar pattern to that found in the movement from maritime to upland riverine settings, although apparently the threat of war and the search for protective hillside settings is more prevalent in the case of the Wanka civilization.

Unifying Themes and Differences

What have we learned from this exercise in comparative history—or anthropology? First, the presence of significant scarcities is associated with the origins of all the civilizations, as suggested by the basic theorem indicated by Equation 2.1. There are variations on this theme as in the apparent maritime origins of Andean civilization, but all conform to the presence of scarcities induced by population pressure, circumscription, or some combination of the two, leading to the initial presence of stratification.

It is in the eventual process of state formation along the lines of EI fractal formations suggested by Equation 2.3 that variations on this theme become significant. Whereas the Monte Albán society and especially Teotihuacan expanded within the Mexican valleys, thus yielding a likely fractal formation based on conquest and/or simple expansion over an empty land space, the Sumerians, Mayans, and very likely the Chinese went through a significant period of conflict among city states prior to significant imperial expansion by ultimate conquerors such as Aggad or Ch'in. This may also be the case for conflict among nomes in Upper Egypt before the advance down the Nile leading to the unification of Egypt, but here the evidence is less secure. The unification of a civilization by means of the emergence of one preeminent power or by such an attempt and failure, followed by conquest from without, results from the emergence of inequality in a multipolar setting leading to warfare and a consequent state formation, suggested by Equation 2.4. In this sense, the dynamics of conflict within a multipolar setting precede the conquest and later expansion of fractal formation.

One rather famous case not considered in detail here, that of the Peloponnesian War, follows this model (Midlarsky 1988a, ch. 3). Athens rose to preeminence among the contending Greek city-states (including Corinth, Sparta, and Thebes) and a major war followed, the consequence of which was the ultimate emergence of an external power, Macedon, that unified the older, now exhausted civilization and began the rapid imperial expansion. This better-known example parallels the model considered here of warfare among the Sumerian city-states followed by the Aggadean conquest. Again, these are the dynamics suggested by the emergence of inequality in a multipolar setting, consequent upon earlier scarcities probably fueled by population pressure.

To be sure, there are significant variations in historical detail among all of the cases considered here. Nevertheless, when one considers them within a comparative setting, the similarities emerge. Salient among them are the origins of stratification after the emergence of scarcities and later state formation, as the result of either direct fractal formations consequent upon expansion or warfare among city-states that weakens the civilization and allows for later external conquest, followed by an imperial expansion.

CHAPTER 4

Decline and Fall of Empires and States

We are now prepared to tackle one of the more difficult problems of human civilization, that of the decline and ultimate fall of empires and states. The approach adopted here, namely, the inequality emergent in mature empires, should carry us far in understanding the various patterns of decline—but also, in other instances, of revival. As in my treatment of the origins of states and empires, their decline and fall and/or revival will be examined by means of several cases: Rome, Byzantium, ancient China, the Maya, ancient Israel and Judah (including a brief comparison with Ammon), and ancient Egypt; a final comparison includes two civilizations that died suddenly as the result of conquest, the Aztec and the Inca. Analyses of state decline do not typically include these last two cases precisely because the sudden death was due to conquest, but somewhat surprisingly certain of the processes to be identified in this chapter will apply to the Aztec and Inca as well. Note that these cases overlap only in part with those treated in Chapter 3. This is simply because I am interested in *processes* of state and empire formation and dissolution, not necessarily in particular historical instances. The illustrations chosen in Chapter 3 were pristine or near-pristine states, hence their intrinsic interest for state formation, whereas those analyzed here either are large, well-known empires or possess uniquely interesting characteristics of state decline.

Note that there are two sets of comparisons within the overall number of cases. These are Rome and Byzantium and Israel and Judah. In both of these sets, each of the pair emerged from the same civilization but had strikingly different historical trajectories. Rome and Byzantium were, respectively, the western and eastern halves of the original Roman Empire, while Israel and Judah developed from the united Davidic and Solomonic kingdom. Byzantium survived for a thousand years after the fall of Rome, and while Judah survived only some 136 years after the fall of Israel, it provided a basis for the survival of a variant of Judaic civilization into the present day.

Although the discussion does not group them in this manner, these cases represent three basic patterns of decline. The first is the basic fractal formation resulting from conquest and expansion, represented by Rome, Byzantium in its later years, and variants on this theme found in Israel, Egypt, the Aztecs, and the Incas. The second pattern, reflected in China, is what I call patterned inequality, an exponential land division in the lower levels of society and incipient or fully realized fractal formations in the upper levels, leading to frequent rebellions. Finally, the Maya present the consequences of inequality and warfare in a multipolar setting; a brief comparison with the early Greek city-states also is included. All of these distributional consequences were presented in Chapter 2.

Before treating these cases individually, it might be useful to consider one small instance that can illustrate temporally certain of the processes to be considered here. This example may in fact be uniquely illustrative because of its small size, which yields a clarity of focus. The examination of Venice during its rise to greatness, especially given its small size (its population was never more than 190,000 [Lane 1973, 324]), and then analysis of its decline might lend considerable clarity to the arguments that will be applied in the other, primary cases.

Two major intertwined themes govern this historical trajectory. First is the initial financial success of Venice resulting from Mediterranean trade, to be followed thereafter by an emphasis on possessions on the Italian mainland. Second is the emergence of the Venetian nobility as a virtual caste preceding the period of decline.

Venetian greatness began with trade with the East fostered by those who settled on the land masses within the lagoons of the northern Adriatic and the nearby river waterways. Early attachment to Byzantium, which then began to decline, and a simultaneous refusal to recognize the suzerainty of the Frankish kingdom allowed for a gradual Venetian emergence to independence, certainly by 1000. Before the fifteenth century, Venice's wealth came almost entirely from trade. It became a world market, based not only on actual trade with both the East and the West, but on shipbuilding and an increasingly hegemonic control first of the Adriatic and then of the Mediterranean itself (Lane 1973, 14). But in the fifteenth and early sixteenth centuries, increasing competition from the East, especially from the Ottoman Empire, and in the West from the Habsburgs led to some diminution of emphasis on the sea and more on land possession. "Governmental revenue increased by more than 50 percent early in the fifteenth century with the conquest of the mainland state.... It was about

1,000,000 ducats a year in the late fifteenth century and then grew again to reach about 2,000,000 ducats before 1570" (Lane 1973, 323). The nobility — in particular certain portions of it — benefited more than did the remainder of the population, while others, even some of noble status, remained impoverished or became increasingly so as wealth accrued to the landed minority (Lane 1973, 324).

As Lauro Martines comments,

The promise and opportunities of Venice's mainland empire, acquired after 1405, worked a profound change in the Venetian patriciate. Providing it with new concerns, with land, governorships, and other lucrative offices, the mainland lulled the entrepreneurial initiative of the nobility, gradually rendering it more sedentary. In Pareto's classic formulation, entrepreneurs turned into *rentiers*. Almost as soon as Venice grabbed the surrounding mainland, complaints at home alleged that Venetian noblemen were turning away from overseas trade and getting no experience of the sea. Before 1500 the complaint had become plangent. The government toiled to find enough noblemen with the experience needed to command Venetian ships, one of their inveterate occupations. (1988, 171–72)

This emphasis on landed wealth was expressed in the building of country villas, at least 85 in the fifteenth century and more than 250 in the sixteenth (Martines 1988, 173). But nobles of modest incomes could not benefit to the same extent from this new emphasis on the land. Nor were the opportunities available in trade as they were earlier (Davis 1962, 43). "Division between rich and poor ran through the Great Council [the governing assembly of which all male nobles were members]. Priuli [an important diarist] estimates that three-fourths of the patriciate could be classed as 'poor,' that is, dependent on offices for a livelihood" (Finlay 1980, 75). And during the War of the League of Cambrai in the early sixteenth century, "loss of the *terraferma*, decline of trade, suspension of Monte payments, increase in taxation, and growth of the Great Council all worked to create a patriciate hungry for office" (Finlay 1980, 175). The poverty of so many of the nobles placed increasing pressures on the state to provide jobs for them. We shall see echoes of this essential subdivision of state finances in the history of the late Roman Empire.

Thus, one important theme that emerges from the Venetian expansion is the differential benefits accrued to a class, and especially to the more fortunate few within a class such as the nobility, after a significant expansion on land. Although initially considerable (relative to the small city size of Venice), in the long run, the returns on land provided only a fixed amount, proportionate to the size of the land mass. "Land could not do for a nobleman of modest means in 1600 what commerce had done for Andrea Barbarigo almost two centuries earlier" (Davis 1962, 43).

The stage is then set for the next important act in Venetian history, the emergence of the Venetian nobility as a caste, with of course only a small proportion benefiting directly from that status. It is clear that from the beginning of the fifteenth century it was virtually impossible to gain entry to the nobility. The government began to keep records of the births of male nobles in 1506 and two decades later recorded the marriages of all noblemen (Davis 1962, 19). Along with the emphasis on land there now began the emergence of the nobility as a clearly demarcated caste that one could enter only by means of birth. The consequences of this combination of limited economic opportunity and a closed caste were enormous. To begin with, according to James Davis, "Unable to increase their wealth, the families elected to decrease their size" (1962, 66). The numbers of noble families with only one child began to increase dramatically. The purpose of their limited procreation, of course, was to maintain each noble holding intact and not have to divide it among many children. Along with the losses due to war and plagues in the sixteenth and seventeenth centuries, their limited procreation would ultimately lead to a decrease in the number of nobles. Between 1513 and 1797, when a limited number of noble families later could be added, the number of noblemen declined from 2,570 to 1,090 and their percentage of the population decreased from approximately 2 percent to 0.8 percent (Davis 1962, 58). As a result there were governmental positions left unfilled—or filled by incompetent nobles, for only nobles were eligible. Military commissions also were left empty or filled badly.

The fideicommissum was an additional voluntary avenue for limitations on the number of the nobility. This was a form of legalized primogeniture found in wills, stipulating that property could be inherited by only one heir and that it was indivisible. The fideicommissum ultimately reduced the number of landowners, and it was said of its consequences by Gaetano Filangieri, a Neapolitan legal writer:

A father who can afford to have only one of his sons rich wants to have only one son. In the others he sees just so many dead weights for his family. The degree of unhappiness in a family is computed by the number of sons. . . . So many younger sons deprived of property, and consequently of the right to marry, oblige as many girls to remain single. Deprived of husbands, under pressure from their fathers, these unfortunate creatures are often obliged to shut themselves up in cloisters, where with their bodies they bury forever their posterity. (quoted in Davis 1962, 69)

In addition to the cloistering of daughters, many noble sons entered the priesthood.

Economic decline supplemented the decline in quality of government and the numbers of the nobility. Non-nobles with talent and ambition for economic success clearly set out to do well elsewhere, for there were laws limiting their activity so as not to threaten the increasingly impoverished nobility (Lane 1973, 301). The critical lack of talent, especially nobles capable of filling governmental posts, is credited as an extremely important factor in the Venetian decline. It was the dependence on land for wealth after an initial expansion, thus empowering only a few, combined with the consequent emergence of a noble caste that was to make more precipitous the Venetian decline. Of course, the identification between rulers and ruled would be absolutely minimal under these conditions. These themes of a fractal formation after expansion that benefits only a few along with dependence on fixed resources such as land will find echoes in the succeeding cases to be examined. In particular, Rome, with its vast expansion and consequent fractal formation in landholdings combined with the rigidification of Roman society after the Diocletian reforms, is a case in point.

Rome

First I turn to the case of Rome, the cadaver that has perhaps been most dissected by historians for clues about the demise of empires. This deep and pervading interest has of course resulted in a wealth of publications on this subject, which even to this day shows no signs of abating. Such a store of information can prove to be extremely useful for our purposes here. For these reasons, the portion of this chapter devoted to Rome will be larger than those devoted to other cases.

The emphasis here is on land inequality and its evolution over time. As in most preindustrialized societies, land was the basis of Roman wealth. Here there seems to be little doubt that there was a considerable increase in inequality, especially as Rome began to pass into the Imperial period. Initially, during the Etruscan period, the tribal structure of Roman society emphasized a fairly egalitarian distribution of land (Ward 1988). Plots tended to be small and of relatively equal size. But by the second century B.C., there were signs of discontent among the Roman population. Peasants had their smaller holdings bought by wealthier proprietors, leading to increasingly large holdings; although these were initially fragmented, later, during the Imperial period, they were consolidated into huge estates (Hopkins 1978, 49). As M. I. Finley puts it: "The trend in antiquity was for a steady increase in the size of landholdings; not a simple straight line upward, as much [as] an accumulation of scattered, sometimes very widely scattered, estates as a process of consolidation; but a continuing trend nevertheless" (1973, 102). This process was advanced principally by the absence of primogeniture so that the Roman farm generally was divided equally among the children (Finley 1973, 106) along the lines of Equation 2.1. As population increased, so did the number of smaller holdings, many of which became untenable as bases for sustenance. Hence, they were sold to larger landowners who consequently were able to increase their holdings in this fashion. As Lorne Ward notes, "The peasantry arose primarily from a combination of impoverished, limited-acreage farmers who went into debt to bigger landholders; and surplus people with no land at all who became the big holders' totally dependent peasant-clients" (1988, 418).

Part of the process was ameliorated by grants of land to demobilized soldiers. In the last century of the Roman Republic there is evidence that a quarter of a million veteran families were given land in Italy alone by Sulla, Caesar, members of the triumvirate, and Augustus (Finley 1973, 80). But often these were too small to sustain a family, especially if they were to be eventually subdivided one or more times. For example, Caesar's bill of 59 B.C. gave only slightly more than six acres to a veteran or poor man with three or more children.

As a consequence of such processes, large numbers of peasants were displaced, while the rich concentrated their land holdings and built up their estates. Roman cities grew, and there was as well a vast immigration to provincial lands that were cheaper. To a large extent, land formerly held by free peasants now was cultivated by slaves, who frequently were the booty of war as the Republic, the Principate, and later the Empire expanded. Here in fact was a dynamic for imperial expansion — not only the material war booty that enriched Rome but the land for settlement of veterans and the slaves to work the newly created large estates were consequences of that expansion.[1]

The problem of land accumulation had presented itself fully by the second century B.C. Plutarch summarizes well the processes leading up to the reforms of Tiberius Gracchus:

Whenever the Romans annexed land from their neighbours as a result of their wars, it was their custom to put a part up for sale by auction: the rest was made common land and was distributed among the poorest and most needy citizens, who were allowed to cultivate it on payment of a small rent to the public treasury. When the rich began to outbid and drive out the poor by offering higher rentals, a law was passed which forbade any one individual to hold more than 500 *iugera* [125 ha] of [state] land. For a while this law restrained the greed of the rich and helped the poor, who were enabled to remain on the land which they had rented, so that each of them could occupy the allotment which he had originally been granted. But after a time the rich men in each neighbourhood, by using names of fictitious tenants, contrived to transfer many of these holdings to themselves, and finally they openly took possession of the greater part of the land under their own names. The poor, when they found themselves forced off the land, became more and more unwilling to volunteer for military service or even to raise a family. The result was a rapid decline of the class of free small-holders all over Italy, their place being taken by gangs of foreign slaves, whom the rich employed to cultivate the estates from which they had driven off the free citizens." (Plutarch, quoted in Hopkins 1978, 58-59)

In 133 B.C. there began the series of laws associated with the Gracchi, which redistributed land away from those who had gained it at the expense of the poor. Two points are noteworthy. First, as Plutarch tells us, this was "public" or "common" land that had been established as the result of war and the consequent annexation of territory. Second, all that Tiberius Gracchus, and later his brother Gaius, attempted to do was to restore the Roman distribution of landholdings to some facsimile of the condition that existed before the expansions in Italy. The law, limiting the size of holdings to 500 *iugera*, had never been repealed (Hopkins 1978, 63), despite the violations Plutarch describes. Although Tiberius Gracchus was assassinated by supporters of the Senate after less than a year in office, several of his reforms remained in force, and land was distributed to several thousand citizens.

The attempts of both Tiberius and later Gaius Gracchus (also assassinated) to do battle with an institution as powerful as the Roman Senate, seat of the large landowning class, indicates the extent of the maldistribution problem. Both leaders had strong popular support among the landless or near-landless, and both also understood the scope of the problems, which required enormous risk-taking, to their eventual ruin. The episode of the Gracchi suggests how difficult the problem had become even before the Imperial period. As the large landowners increased their holdings, problems continued to worsen, ultimately prompting Pliny's famous remark that "the large estates ruined Italy" (quoted in Hopkins 1978, 54). By the fourth century A.D., the major landowners had amassed "estates and wealth on an enormous scale" (Cameron 1993, 117).

Among historians of the ancient world there is considerable agreement on the emergence of large estates as a central cause of the decline of the Empire. In the words of A. H. M. Jones, "If I may venture a generalization on the economic effects of the Roman empire, I would say that its chief effect was to promote an ever increasing concentration of land in the hands of its governing aristocracy at the expense of the population at large" (quoted in de Ste. Croix 1981, 328). Elsewhere Jones notes, "The basic cause of the economic decline of the empire was in fact the increasing number of (economically speaking) idle mouths—senators with their vast households, decurions, civil servants, lawyers, soldiers, clergy, citizens of the capitals—as compared with the number of producers. The resultant burden of taxation and rents proved too much for the peasantry, who slowly dwindled in numbers" (1966, 367).

Ferdinand Lot concurs, emphasizing the importance of the city to the Roman world and the decay of the city as a consequence of the formation of large estates: "At the end of the Empire, the large estate, which formed an economic, fiscal, juridical, and even religious unit lived an independent life apart from the City. Reduced to a chief town which was now merely a fortress and inhabited by the poorer country landowners, bankers, and lawyers who henceforth constituted the *curia* ... the City in the fourth century entered upon a process of incurable decay" (1961, 126).

What was the dynamic through which the large estates led to the decline of Rome? First, as we have seen in the enormous popular support of the Gracchi, there was already widespread dissatisfaction with the emergence of these large estates. With the displacement of the smallholder in Italy and the increased use of slaves largely captured in war in his stead, the possibility of slave rebellions grew. Indeed, it has been said that "the imperial state was born amid the great slave revolts of the late republic" (Dockès 1982, 89). Gradually, in part as a result of the slave revolts, slaves were in turn replaced by displaced tenant farmers, who by this time, during the early Empire, were in short supply. It was Diocletian who then introduced reforms that were to save the Empire temporarily but at the same time sowed the seeds for its eventual destruction. Among these reforms was the legal tying of the tenant to the large estate; only with permission of the authorities was he allowed to leave. Effectively, this central reform of Diocletian began a process of enserfment for the previously free tenant farmer—a condition he was eager to flee from whenever the opportunity safely permitted.

Second, although the large landholders were barred from the military, they increasingly dominated the civil service, either within the Senate or without. As the only power base outside the Imperial court itself, the landowning aristocracy came virtually to control the civil bureaucracy. Because taxation was the principal preoccupation of the bureaucracy, effectively this most crucial aspect of the imperial administration was dominated by the large landholders, mostly for their own benefit. Taxes were increased many times over, not only for the support of the Imperial administration, but especially for the support of the military that was hard-pressed by the invasions of barbarian tribes. At the same time, however, an increasingly large number of landowners were less concerned with the welfare of the Empire than with their own well-being. With barbarian —chiefly Germanic—tribes being settled on Imperial lands, the owners of the large and by now mostly self-contained estates, or villae, began to make their own individual arrangements with the barbarian chieftains. As Pierre Dockès puts it, "The latifundists, the patrons fought against the state—and the state

TABLE 4.1.
Change in the Proportion of Families of the Various Economic Groupings in Ten Representative Villages in the District of Pan-yu, Kwangtung, China, 1928 and 1933

Category	Percent of the total number of families		Index for 1933 (1928 = 100)
	1928	1933	
Landlords[a]	2.6	2.9	111.5
Rich peasants	9.3	8.8	94.6
Middle peasants	17.3	16.0	92.5
Poor peasants	42.2	44.7	105.9
Agricultural laborers	7.0	6.9	98.6
Others	21.6	20.7	95.8

SOURCE: After Chen Han-Seng 1936, 139.
[a] Includes only individual and residential landlords; excludes clan-owned lands.

struck back at patronage; as a result, latifundists frequently entered into alliances with the Germanic tribes. In the fifth century we find clear indications of a quarrelsome collusion among barbarian chieftains, latifundists, and 'Roman' military leaders" (1982, 84–85).

Here we now see one of the reasons for the absence of large-scale uprisings in Rome after the slave revolts at the beginning of the Imperial period. Instead of fomenting revolt, both landowners and peasants could simply enter into collusion with the barbarian tribes, thus simultaneously gaining protection from the newer arrivals and escaping from the onerous requirements (taxation, military service) of the late Roman period. In fact, C. R. Whittaker (1994, 265) considers many of these landlords more akin to warlords in their degree of autonomy and large numbers of retainers.

Another consequence of the growth of the large estates was the concomitant decline of the middle groups in Roman society—smaller landowners and curial officeholders in the cities. As we saw in Chapter 2, especially in the case of China, the small landowner is one of the first to suffer subdivision processes. Whereas the large landowner will often have enough land to survive such subdivision or alternatively be able to expand his holdings at the expense of those with very small holdings, and the peasant with tiny holdings will hold on tenaciously to a sliver of land, the middle-size landowner tends to face relentless subdivision. With less capital available to augment his holdings, the subdivision process continues until one sees the sort of change in only a five-year period shown in Table 4.1.

Growth of the large estates and the perceived necessity by Diocletian to bind the peasantry to them had a parallel consequence for the curial class, who also tended to be property owners but with smaller holdings. These were the men who made up the councils of cities, both of the *poleis* of the Greek east and the corresponding *civitates* of the west. These town councilors were already a hereditary caste by the time of Diocletian, for if they had the requisite property qualifications, they were obliged to serve unless they could claim a legal exemption. Decurions or *curiales*, as they were called, were forbidden to join the army, but they could assume administrative posts, which wealthier decurions took in order to escape from the onerous burden of having to be town councilor. If they were wealthy enough, they entered the equestrian class, the knights, or even the Senate, thus diminishing the size of this middle class. Their decline paralleled, and perhaps was in part a cause of, the decline of the cities.

At the same time, this "leakage" augmented the upper classes, thus magnifying the already substantial inequality in the empire. As G. E. M. de Ste. Croix comments:

But the *curiales*, although I often refer to them as a class, when contrasting them with the imperial aristocracy (the senators and equestrians) on the one hand, and the poor free men, *coloni*, and slaves on the other, were a class with a considerable "spread," those at the very lowest end of the scale hardly falling within my "propertied class," while those at the top end might be very rich and might hope to become members of the imperial aristocracy themselves. And the key to the understanding of the position of the curial class in the fourth and fifth centuries is the realisation of two facts. First, the richer the decurion, the more likely he was to be able to escape upwards into the ranks of the imperial *honorati*, or to obtain by influence or bribery some position (in the imperial civil service in particular) which exempted him from curial duties, thereby increasing the burden on the poorer members of the order who were left, sometimes to the point of actual ruin and loss of property. And secondly, curial burdens, far from being distributed in proportion to wealth, tended to fall heavily on the poorer decurions in a given Council. (1981, 471)

In the western provinces there are signs that the cities, and especially the smaller towns, were experiencing economic decline by the end of the fourth century. If members of the city guilds abandoned their positions, they were to be brought back forcibly, according to a series of laws promulgated from 395 onward (Jones 1966, 250).

In the face of the decline of the cities, "a very large proportion of the burden of taxation fell on agriculture" (Jones 1966, 178). And this burden was exacerbated by the increase in the proportion of nonproducers. The army had grown to gargantuan proportions by the standards of the ancient world—as many as 533,000 men by one estimate (Lot 1961, 229) or some 600,000 by another (Jones 1966, 228); Ramsay MacMullen (1988, 174) gives a lower estimate of

400,000. Although some of the soldiers farmed while not participating in a campaign, many did not, increasing the number of idle mouths to feed.

The rise of the Christian church also placed increasing burdens on the tax base, which was, as we have noted, principally land. From the time of Constantine, the Church had accumulated ever-growing endowments of land that were used to support an ever-increasing number of clergy (Jones 1964, 1046). Although some lands had been set aside for pagan gods, especially in Egypt, their allotted size nowhere near approached that which was evolving in the later, Christianized empire.

Added to this was the custom of feeding 120,000 citizens of Rome and 80,000 citizens of Constantinople. But not only at the lower end of urban society did such consumptive activity appear. Many of the large landowners were absentees, financially supporting large houses or palaces in the cities through the burden placed on the peasantry forced to remain on the rural latifundia.

Depopulation, or at least diminution of the productive rural population, was another problem, likely consequent in part on the processes enumerated above. "That the area of land under cultivation shrank considerably cannot be doubted. Abandoned lands (*agri deserti*) were a constant theme of imperial legislation from before Diocletian's time" (Jones 1964, 812).

Explanations for the population decline are varied. One possibility is the occurrence of plagues that began spreading through the Roman Empire in the second century A.D. (McNeill 1976, 103). Another is the exhaustion of the soil that appears to have occurred in some parts of the Mediterranean but not in most. Denuding of forests may be a more important source of decline in fertility and had by this time become a feature of the Mediterranean landscape. North Africa especially, but also Greece and portions of Italy had lost much of their forests. Loss of forest lands can accelerate soil degradation via loss of topsoil, not only in the denuded portion itself, but also as a consequence of rain waters that can now freely course through adjacent lands, in the absence of forests to control them.

Declining security also constitutes a possible explanation for the diminution of the rural population. Frontier provinces exposed to barbarian incursions were especially susceptible to the fleeing of the rural population or alternatively to the welcoming of barbarian tribes as protectors and the effective loss of Roman control over those provinces. Indeed in the later Empire, there were frequent arrangements made between "Roman" officials and barbarian chieftains allowing the tribes to settle within the boundaries of the empire (Goffart 1980; Whittaker 1994). The officials making these arrangements were themselves frequently of Germanic (i.e., barbarian) origins, especially among the military. Indeed, virtually the entire military by this time was populated by troops of Germanic origins.

In his final assessment of the causes of the fall of the Western Empire, A. H. M. Jones writes:

> Of the manifold weaknesses of the later Roman empire some, the increasing maldistribution of wealth, the corruption and extortion of the administration, the lack of public spirit and the general apathy of the population, were to a large extent due to internal causes. But some of the more serious of these weaknesses were the result, direct or indirect, of barbarian pressure. Above all the need to maintain a vastly increased army had far-reaching effects. It necessitated a rate of taxation so heavy as to cause a progressive decline in agriculture and indirectly a shrinkage of population. The effort to collect this heavy taxation required a great expansion of the civil service, and this expansion in turn imposed an additional burden on the economy and made administrative corruption and extortion more difficult to control. The oppressive weight of the taxation contributed to the general apathy. (1964, 1067)

It was the combination of the internal causes, headed in Jones's estimation by maldistribution of wealth (principally in the form of land), with the external pressure of the barbarian tribes and ever-escalating taxation that ultimately led to the demise of the Western portion of the empire. This, of course, was complicated by the *patrocinium*, a patronage system wherein a landowner's protection was extended over larger numbers of peasants and their lands, consequently removing these lands from the tax rolls and instituting higher taxation over the remaining lands. This incidentally is one distinguishing feature between the eastern and western halves of the empire that is suggestive of reasons for the survival of one and disappearance of the other, as will be examined shortly. According to Perry Anderson, "No Western Emperor ever attempted to check the spread of the *patrocinium*, despite the fact that it subtracted whole territorial areas from the surveillance of the agents of the State: but successive Eastern Emperors legislated against it, repeatedly, in the 4th century" (1974b, 99–100).

Inequality not only was endemic to the central Roman domains in Italy but extended to the provinces as well. In North Africa, for example, large estates were found, especially in the area that today is Tunisia, and fueled hatreds that were to appear in the Donatist violence against the Catholic authorities. "The religious hatreds of the 340s, feeding upon social inequality and rural poverty, had led to the rise of a new phenomenon: footloose bands of itinerant peasants, both men and women, who were fanatically devoted to the Donatist cause—and, it seemed, to freeing slaves and reversing the established order" (Raven 1993, 180). Landlords and usurers were the most hated social figures and were regularly attacked. Villas and churches associated with the Catholic cause were laid waste; debt collection, in particular, was impeded by those supporting the uprising.

Yet in one respect the explanation is incomplete, principally in the absence of an explanatory nexus among the growth of great estates, the corruption of the administration, and the barbarian presence—the first three causes listed by Jones. To be sure, we have seen important consequences of the large estates in the dominance of the civil service by large landholders, the increased burden of taxation on a serf-like peasantry tied to the estates, a concomitant population decline, and perhaps most important the tendency of lords of the large self-contained estates to make their own agreements with barbarian leaders and thus, piecemeal, diminish the boundaries of effective imperial control. But we also know that despite this tendency, there existed an army estimated at anywhere from 500,000 to 600,000 in size. Why could not this vast imperial force maintain control at the borders and prevent this continual attrition of the Roman boundaries? The barbarian armies were not terribly large at any given time (MacMullen 1988, 174), and even MacMullen's (1988, 41) estimate of 400,000 for the late imperial period still should have been large enough to operate effectively against small, less well-organized nomadic bands. (By suggesting an approximate size of 300,000 soldiers stationed at the *frontiers*, Whittaker [1994, 288] essentially agrees with MacMullen's estimate of the total.)

It is MacMullen who provides an answer to the question of military ineffectiveness, evidenced by a virtually uninterrupted string of battle losses beginning in the fourth century and ending with the disappearance of the Western half of the Roman Empire in the following century. The answer is corruption, which affected not only the civil service of the late imperial period but most especially the military. And this corruption was one important example of the impact of gross land inequality on the imperial decline.

We follow MacMullen in noting that decline is the appropriate description for the fall of Rome; no precipitous event led to its demise. Also, in noting the beginnings of decline, MacMullen is suggesting that the process began very early, likely around 250, requiring roughly only two centuries until the final events of the fall in the mid- to late fifth century. He adduces some rather startling, but decidedly heuristic, evidence concerning the sudden decline in the use of Latin texts around 250, but the continuation of Greek at approximately the same earlier levels. Given the rather glacial pace of social change in antiquity (short of outright conquest), this beginning of decline around 250 is consistent with the deleterious societal effects of extreme inequality in landholdings that began to be visible in the polity only several centuries later. In the first century,

Pliny remarks on the large estates ruining Italy, and we see the effects in the middle of the third. We must ask then, first, what are the specifics of the ruination process and, second, how do they relate to extreme inequality?

There appear to be numerous instances of corruption in the period after 250, and it was certainly not unknown earlier during the Republic and Principate. For example, MacMullen notes "In A.D. 14 reports came to Rome of officers virtually forcing their men to shake down the surrounding population for the money needed to buy security from 'the centurions' savagery,'" and, referring to a later incident in 270, "The troops pictured here represent a concentration of anarchic rapacity on the necessary scale, the scale of historical significance" (1988, 131). However, the numerous protests against such actions indicate that it was more the exception instead of the rule. But after 250 various corrupt practices became institutionalized, and protests diminished precisely because of the degree of institutionalization. Perhaps one of the more famous, or infamous, instances occurred while Caracalla was observing the chariot races; upset by the abusive epithets the crowds were shouting against his favorite, he ordered the soldiers to kill anyone who had participated in that behavior. The soldiers had difficulty in distinguishing between those who had and those who had not and "so they led away and killed anyone they caught, mercilessly, or barely spared only those *from whom they stripped all belongings, like a ransom*" (quoted in MacMullen 1988, 132; emphasis in original).

Incidents of this type and a general tendency toward extortion of the civilian population characterized the military during the later imperial period. Indeed, so extreme was their behavior that MacMullen concludes within the military higher officers

> profit from their own staff, some from regimental rations, where the men who have vanished live on, and they can feed off the names of the dead. These are great amounts; but there are even larger gold fields, of gold that should rightly remain in the men's hands but is transferred to their commanders. So the armed forces grow poor and dispirited, wearing mere bits of boots and ghosts of great-coats. Often it's the belly that must pay, and they lead off starving bodies to battle. (1988, 161)

It is no wonder that such a dispirited army, and one with little, if any, civilian support, would largely function as a guardian force behind city walls and rarely venture forth to do aggressive battle against even a moderately formidable enemy (MacMullen 1988, 176). As we shall see in the instance of the Arab conquests from Byzantium, similar behavior was documented there.

But why this extensive degree of corruption during the later imperial period? The answer is to be found in the growth of large estates as a vehicle for wealth, prestige, and influence that were now no longer available to the vast majority of aspirants. The imperial borders had ceased to expand, and the only area remaining open for aggrandizement was the government. The military was a traditional vehicle for advancement (MacMullen 1988, 81), as were various civil offices in the imperial administration. An indication of pressures on such offices was their vast increase. First, the number of provinces under Caracalla was increased by subdividing old departments of government and adding new ones. And after the earlier subdivisions, the existing provinces were themselves subdivided. "One total, however, is revealing. In the civil service of the late empire some thirty to thirty-five thousands were employed, to be set against perhaps three hundred career civil servants under Caracalla" (MacMullen 1988, 144). Although this astounding increase should be qualified by, for example, the replacement of slaves by soldiers and civilian administrators in the later empire, nevertheless, the vast increase in number of persons and especially the subdivision process are reminiscent of the pressure placed on a fixed quantity of land or other inelastic good, shown in Equation 2.1. But there is another inference we may draw from the existing evidence. That is the probable low salaries paid to government officials, whether in the military or in civilian administrations. We have already seen how the military fared poorly in this regard, and there is no reason to expect that civilian bureaucrats fared any better. Indeed the decline in the *curiae* in the towns is probably one clear indication. The *curiales* were actually obliged to support the local bureaucracy out of their own pockets. Thus, vast institutionalized corruption became a means of supplementing the meager, often nonexistent, salary from the state.

A final source of corruption may be found in envy of the extraordinary wealth and power of the great landowners, a socioeconomic status no longer available to outsiders in the later Empire, with all major avenues for social and economic advancement closed. Corruption became the only way that high civilian and military officials could even begin to approximate the social and political standing of the great landowners.

Here we see an important additional effect of the vast land inequalities. Not only did they allow the formation of virtually autonomous entities that could bargain with and come to a modus operandi with barbarian invaders, but even before this process became endemic, the limits on availability of land and envy of the fortunate landed few institutionalized corruption to a degree that seriously limited the effectiveness of both civilian and military administrations. As the barbarian pressure continued, even if sometimes only in small numbers, there was no one available to resist effectively, until a piecemeal dismantling of the Empire was effected.

Byzantium

We have observed Rome's fall from the perspective of the inequality formation developed here. But it must be kept in mind that this pertains only to the western half of the Empire, which fell in 476. We know that the eastern portion of the Empire survived and in fact flourished after its western counterpart disappeared completely as a political entity. What accounts for the difference? The answer turns out to be fairly complex, for it has several dimensions, not entirely independent of each other.

We turn to some of the more apparent differences between the two halves of the Roman Empire. The extent of barbarian pressure on the western half of the Empire was much greater than that on the east. Both the Danube and the Rhine presented long fronts that had to be guarded against ever-increasing pressure by barbarian tribes. In contrast, the only serious threat to the eastern half of the Empire was Persia, a civilized state that, between military engagements, generally observed its peace treaty commitments and therefore, in contrast to barbarian tribes that were inherently unpredictable, could be relied on to refrain from military activity in time of peace.

Another difference on which the majority of scholars of antiquity agree is the population differential between the two halves (Jones 1966, 363). The west was experiencing a depopulation of both cities and countryside, while in the east cities were flourishing. It is difficult for us to imagine the great topographic changes that have occurred since antiquity. Instead of vast areas of thinly populated near-desert, much of the Middle East and Northern Africa was verdant and capable of supporting large populations. Indeed, North Africa and Egypt were the bread-baskets of the Roman Empire, producing enough wheat to feed the entire Empire. In comparison, the densely populated urbanized areas of contemporary Western Europe were then largely forest, dotted with the occasional small villages (sometimes fortified), largely built by the Romans to support the imperial expansion.

The east also enjoyed greater political stability. Only five attempted usurpations occurred during the years between 284, the accession of Diocletian, and the death of Maurice in 602. In the west during the same period, there were eleven usurpations or open rebellions with heavy fighting and, after Valentinian III, a series of indifferent rulers.

But from our perspective the important distinguishing feature of the east was its economic structure. This was crucial in supporting a strong military response by the Byzantine Empire when threatened by the Muslim Arabs in the seventh century, a response that was not possible against similar threats to the west by the barbarians two centuries earlier.

Initially, however, the same weaknesses that had plagued the west were evident when the Muslims attacked. Walter Kaegi summarizes it well:

> What is so striking about the failure of Byzantine defenses of Palestine, Syria, and Mesopotamia is the similarity of many of its features to the weaknesses of Roman frontier defenses in earlier times. The soldiers' refusal to venture forth aggressively from fortified points to fight the invader, their inclination to stay behind the more comfortable fixed walls of towns, and the numerous gaps in defenses were dangerous features of Byzantine vulnerability that had revealed themselves in the east and the west in the fourth, fifth, and sixth centuries, long before the appearance of Islam. (1992, 274)

Thus the eastern half of the Roman Empire, ultimately to become the Byzantine Empire, was essentially no different from its western counterpart in the reluctance of its soldiers to emerge from fortified towns and the related disinclination or inability to defend the countryside itself. Why was this so? Kaegi touches on the reason when he mentions "the lack of identification of local population with the military leadership" and the fact that the Muslims were very successful in encouraging "local officials and populations, who were willing to sever ties with the former imperial authority and now switch over to recognize the authority of the Muslims, although not necessarily convert to Islam" (Kaegi 1992, 106, 239).

We can infer directly from these statements that the rural population was not eager to support the Byzantines when push came to shove. The probable reason of course is the same as in the West, namely the existence of large estates and the willingness to collaborate with any conqueror who seemed to offer decent treatment. The earlier depopulation of much of the Middle East as the result of revolts against Rome (66–70 and 132–35 in Judaea alone) or episodic warfare involving the Persians had led to the expansion of the existing estates on empty lands. In Egypt, as early as the Ptolemies, state-owned fallow land was assigned to private landowners who were obligated to cultivate it and to pay the corresponding taxes. This system came to be extended throughout the Roman Empire by the end of the third century (Ostrogorsky 1969, 41). In addition, the power of the landowning aristocracy was such that, if displaced by conquerors, they would be fully restored to their previous landholdings upon reconquest of those lands. This had happened in the middle of the sixth century when the Ostrogoths were defeated in Spain and the landowning aristocracy regained their lands (Ostrogorsky 1969, 71). As did the earlier Western Empire, the Byzantines apparently taxed the countryside and not the towns for support of the army. This we infer not only from Muslim practice, which apparently followed the Byzantine tradition in the conquered regions, but also from the policies of Justinian I, who made inhabitants of a particular countryside region responsible for support of the army stationed there (Kaegi 1992, 177).

We can now understand why so much of the Middle East fell so quickly to the Muslims. It was not so much holy war or superior military skill of the Muslim Arabs (they acknowledged as much by admitting to the superior technical skill of the Byzantines; Kaegi 1992, 261), but the social structure of the countryside that forced the Byzantines to fight from fortified towns and to rely little, if at all, on the rural population. Regarding the decisive battle of Yarmuk in 636, as a consequence of which Syria and Palestine were lost by the Byzantines, it was said that even most towns put up only a token resistance to the Muslims. "In fact Syria was lost less because of Yarmuk than as a result of the urban population failing to resist in the way they had previously resisted Persian invaders" (Nicolle 1994, 88). As Kaegi puts it, "the wonder is that there had not been some major debacle earlier.... It is unnecessary to ascribe the Byzantine collapse to a failure to wage or understand holy war" (1992, 275).

What saved the Byzantines from total collapse, as occurred in Rome under similar conditions? One factor, as we have seen, was the different geopolitics of the eastern half, which despite the losses to the Muslims, faced less of a threat on its remaining borders, in particular because of the territorial depth of Anatolia. The Muslims never devised an effective strategy to overcome the defenses established by the Byzantines at the Taurus Mountain passes (Kaegi 1992, 243). But why did this defense persist successfully against repeated Muslim thrusts into the Empire and even against aggressive Bulgars and Slavic tribes to the west? The answer lies in a change in social and military structure that clearly distinguishes Byzantium from Rome.

As early as Heraclius, during the time of the Muslim conquest, we begin to see development of the system of *themes* that was to do so much to save the Empire and even to lead to its expansion. Effectively, the system amounted to subordination of the civilian authority to the military commander in a given region. The Empire was divided into military regions or provinces, called themes, each headed by a *strategus*, or general. The army assigned to defend a province was also called a theme. Each provincial theme had a capital, which was the headquarters of the *strategus* (Treadgold 1988, 14–17).

Although Heraclius and his successors' organization and implementation of the theme system did much to defend the Empire, it was the accompanying socioeconomic transformation that reinvigorated the Empire.

Military estates, small in size and granted to individuals in return for military service, became the opening wedge in the formation of a new class of free peasant proprietors. The soldiers themselves constituted the nucleus of this class, but others gradually were added, for while the eldest son of a soldier inherited his father's plot together with the obligation of military service, the rest of the family were free to reclaim and cultivate the land that was vacant. The free peasants, cultivating their own land, paying the taxes, and, if necessary, serving in the army, came to constitute the dominant element in the agrarian society of Byzantium. They became a bulwark of the state, lent to it new vigor, and enabled it eventually to recover its position in the orient. By the end of the tenth century, Byzantium had become the most powerful state throughout the Christian-Moslem world. (Charanis 1967a, 171)

Essentially a new category of free peasants was created, very similar to that which existed some thousand years earlier in Rome. As the early expansion of Rome very much relied on the free peasant and his military contribution, so did first the defense and later the expansion of Byzantium depend on the soldier-peasant.

By 1025 and the death of Basil II, the Empire ranged from the Danube in the west to the Euphrates in the east and reached from the mountains of Armenia in the north to the Adriatic in the south. But the basis for future Byzantine success was found not only in a soldier-peasantry that was prepared to fight to protect its homes and property but also in a remarkable social and geographic mobility dating roughly from the eighth century. Although small, the upper class was quite varied in its origins. While the Empress Irene, who ruled in the late eighth century, was of Greek stock from Athens, Nicophorus I, who ruled immediately thereafter, was reportedly of Arab origin. Michael I apparently was of Slavic origin. Armenians were rapidly assimilated into the Empire and at times were highly favored by the ruling elite. Arabs and Slavs also were climbing to the top of Byzantine society. As early as 799, a descendant of Bulgar boyars was one of four patricians selected by Irene to lead the horses that drew her carriage (Treadgold 1988, 369). A Russian family appears to have entered the upper class at this time, because under Michael II, the Archbishop of Nicaea was a man named Inger (i.e., Igor). One descendant of his family was the wife of the Emperor Basil I and mother of Leo VI. As Warren Treadgold remarks: "The ruling class in the capital was so open to provincials and members of the lower class that our evidence reveals something about these groups in spite of itself" (1988, 371). It was mobility of this type that allowed Byzantine society to draw on the most talented of its Christian (i.e., Orthodox) citizens in defense and later expansion of its Empire.

However, as the theory suggests, it was the intensifying of inequalities through conquest and expansion that finally precipitated the decline in the eleventh century. It exacerbated tendencies already present in the early Byzantine period that were now to emerge in full force to hasten the decline of the Empire. Indeed, in regard to its predominant inequalities, the social structure that emerged was remarkably similar to that found in the western half of the Empire at the time of its fall, approximately a millennium earlier.

Although from its very beginning the large estate had been an element of Byzantium, it was only in the eleventh century that its rapid growth became corrosive to the Empire. During the tenth century, the great emperors of this period saw the dangers, especially in light of the opportunities offered by the expansion of the period. Emperors such as Romanus Lecapenus and Basil II issued novels (decrees) seeking to protect the free peasantry because, as Romanus Lecapenus put it:

It is not through hatred and envy of the rich that we take these measures, but for the protection of the small and the safety of the empire as a whole. . . . The extension of the power of the strong . . . will bring about the irreparable loss of the public good, if the present law does not bring a check to it. For it is the many, settled on the land, who provide for the general needs, who pay the taxes and furnish the army with its recruits. Everything falls when the many are wanting." (quoted in Charanis 1967b, 86)

These efforts largely failed, however, and the estates of the aristocracy grew larger. As George Ostrogorsky remarks, "The role of the military aristocracy promoted and favoured the great estates, particularly those of the laity. . . . It was laid down [in 1158] that grants of property could only be donated to those of senatorial rank or members of the *stratiotes* class, i.e., to pronoiars" (1969, 392).

The pronoiars are another element in the growth of the large estates. They were holders of military grants of land, rivers, or fisheries given by the emperors of the second half of the eleventh century to reward their partisans in the military. Most of the grants were in the form of land, which led to the enrichment of those who already occupied high military posts in the Empire. Indeed, so powerful had these military aristocrats become, that they emerged as a serious threat to the central government. Basil II had faced three dangerous revolts in the tenth century. When he was reconciled with one of the rebels sometime after 987, he was advised to exhaust the aristocracy by means of heavy taxation, lest they remain powerful and continue to be a threat to the central government (Charanis 1967b, 88).

In the eleventh century, there were serious efforts to decrease the power of the aristocracy, principally by lessening their hold on the military. Emperors of that time reduced the size of the army, thus eliminating many of the aristocracy's commands. They felt relatively safe in doing so because of the great victories of the preceding century, defeating both Arab and Bulgar alike, thus assuring a seeming perpetual security for the Empire. That they were wrong would be made strikingly clear at the famous battle of Manzikert (1071) when the Seljuk Turks defeated the Byzantines decisively and, by establishing a foothold in Anatolia, marked the beginning of Byzantium's long decline into extinction.

The process of decline was hastened not only by the *potential* danger to the state of the aristocracy, but by its *actual* reaction to the limitations imposed by the concerned emperors. A series of civil wars ensued in the wake of these attempted limitations and woefully weakened the Empire. One in particular, that of 1057, involving the imperial succession, was to especially undermine the empire in preparation for its fateful confrontation with the Seljuk Turks at Manzikert (Diehl 1967, 167). Even as late as the early fourteenth century, when the external threats were manifest, landowners opposed fiscal and military reform that could have strengthened both army and society (Bartusis 1992, 75).

One result was an army reduced not only in size but also in effectiveness. By the mid-eleventh century the army no longer had a majority of free native peasants, but

> was composed of Macedonians and Bulgarians and Varangians and other barbarians who happened to be about. There were gathered also those who were in Phrygia [the *theme* Anatolikon]. And what one saw in them [the enrolled soldiers of the *theme* Anatolikon] was something incredible. The renowned champions of the Romans who had reduced into subjection all of the East and the West now numbered only a few and these were bowed down by poverty and ill treatment. They lacked in weapons, swords, and other arms, such as javelins and scythes. . . . They lacked also in cavalry and other equipment, for the emperor had not taken the field for a long time. For this reason they were regarded as useless and unnecessary and their wages and maintenance were reduced. (Cedrenus, *Historiarum Compendium*, vol. 2, quoted in Charanis 1967b, 89; bracketed comments by Charanis)

Later in the eleventh century, the army came to be composed entirely of foreign mercenaries—Russians, Turks, Alans, Germans, Bulgarians, and others. Their interests often did not coincide with those of their emperors. As in the fall of Rome centuries earlier, the later armies were only a pale shadow of the determined masses of early free native peasants who understood that their own interests and those of the state were virtually coterminous.

The social structure of Byzantium was further weakened by the development of the *exkuseia*, whereby landowners and especially monasteries were excused from paying taxes (Charanis 1967b, 90). Although it appeared earlier, possibly developing out of the privileges granted to the Christian clergy in the fourth century, the widespread use of the *exkuseia* in the eleventh century and after insured that a significant portion of taxable land disappeared from the tax rolls, thus further burdening the peasantry. We see here a clear instance of the growth in power of certain institutions—in this case the military aristocracy and the church (Ostrogorsky 1969, 339)—during a post-conquest period, a growth that inevitably places additional burdens on the productive taxpayers. As the Empire is threatened, the army especially requires additional resources but at the same time, large sections of society have removed substantial portions of their estates from the tax rolls. The result is aptly described by Ostrogorsky: "The whole trend of the times, with the growth of the great estates, and the overburdening and impoverishment of the lower classes, made it inevitable that ever wider strata of the population were bartering their freedom to become, if not slaves, then at least serfs. In the end, the triumphant advance of feudal processes weakened the authority of the state and undermined the Byzantine polity's power of resistance" (1969, 393–94). It was simply a question of time as to exactly when the Byzantine Empire would cease to exist.

Rome and Byzantium illustrate consequences for the state of extreme inequalities manifested in inordinately large landholdings. Chinese history provides an illustration of the second of the three patterns in this chapter, namely a combination of small peasant holdings and larger fractal formations.

China

The question asked here is why did China persist while Rome fell? In some sense, this is an imprecisely phrased question, because the Chinese state fell several times, as did the Roman. However, the difference between the two instances resides in the finality of change. Whereas a unified China arose several times after serious disunity and at times virtual chaos, this did not happen in the case of Rome. When it fell in 476, there was never again a recognizable state existing within the approximate borders of the Roman Empire that could conceivably be called "Rome." It is to the salient features of Chinese history that illuminate this difference that we now turn. Not surprisingly, vastly different patterns of landholding, hence of inequalities and their associated consequences will emerge from the analysis. Specifically, the Chinese case will, as noted, illustrate our second pattern, that of a combined exponential subdivision of land among the peasants and larger fractal or EI formations held mostly by landlords, the patterned inequality associated with political violence, which will be discussed systematically in Chapter 8.

Decline and Fall of Empires and States / 111

In 1954, the great French scholar of Chinese civilization Etienne Balazs was able to predict with what appears to be considerable accuracy that our present "Russian-American century will be succeeded by a Chinese twenty-first century" (1964, 170, from an article originally published in 1954). With the third largest gross domestic product (GDP) in the world today (after the United States and Japan) and with a rapid growth rate, China is very likely to confirm this prediction. What accounts for Balazs's prescience?

For one, Balazs took a macro-view of Chinese history that encompasses many centuries of the development of Chinese civilization. As a consequence, he was able to suggest recurrent patterns of rebellion and regeneration throughout Chinese history. It will be useful to recount Balazs's understanding of these patterns before amplifying my own.

> Most dynasties fell as a result of agrarian crises. For instance—to name the most important—the Former [Western] Han dynasty perished in the anarchy created by the rebels who called themselves the "Red Eyebrows," and the Later [Eastern] Han went down in one of the bloodiest of all peasant wars, the revolt of the "Yellow Turbans," under its banner of the "Great Peace" (*T'ai-p'ing*). The T'ang fell under the blows of a rebel who combined in his own person all varieties of the humiliated and dispossessed: he was the son of a peasant, a candidate who had failed the examinations, and a smuggler. The Mongol conquerors were expelled by a movement that had at first a social and later a national character; its leader founded the Ming dynasty, which, in turn, was removed by a peasant rising, whereupon the vacant throne was occupied by the Manchu conquerors. This last dynasty never recovered from the blow dealt it by the T'ai-p'ing, those peasants who rose, inspired by a chiliastic faith half Taoist and half Christian, who ruled over the greater part of China for about a decade, and whose exploits have now become a favorite subject for study in present-day China. (Balazs 1964, 158–59)

Thus, peasant rebellion was closely tied into this pattern of dissolution and regeneration of the Chinese state, even into the mid-twentieth century. From the beginning, these rebellions were intimately connected with peasant landholdings. First, we note that the Chinese tradition of large families and the absence of primogeniture led first to the division and later the extensive subdivision of landholdings, until many were insufficient to support even the smallest family. Landlordism and tenant farming became endemic at various points in Chinese history. It was the Ch'in in the third century B.C. who led the transition from the old feudal system involving serfdom, championed by the Chou dynasty before it, to freehold farming that became the basis for land subdivision and later tenant farming. As China became unified under the Ch'in state, this pattern of freehold farming and its consequences were extended throughout the Chinese state (Hucker 1975, 41–43).

At the time of the formation of the Western Han dynasty in 202 B.C., agricultural production was deemed to be too low, and little grain was being stored. Agriculture was emphasized and commerce de-emphasized. This reliance on agriculture was to be a hallmark of Chinese civilization virtually until the late twentieth century. Approximately one century after the establishment of the Han dynasty the poor living conditions of the peasant became apparent. In 155 B.C. a farmer needed to pay only one thirteenth of the crop in taxes, but a generation or two later, conditions had deteriorated significantly, and many farmers had to sell their land to wealthy landowners while they themselves became tenants. In fact, according to Cho-yun Hsu, "the life of a tenant . . . was to be the fate of quite a large proportion of Han farmers"(1980, 16). Although Hsu also concludes that in the century from 119 to 17 B.C. the population doubled, there are few indications of demographic crisis and its accompanying phenomenon of vagrancy.

Nonetheless, by the time of the first century B.C. Emperor Wu, "The polarization between the rich and the landless farmers seems to have been so severe a problem that the government had to take measures to curtail the continuous deterioration of the society's structure" (Hsu 1980, 31). Lands over which no private ownership had been established and registered were granted—in actuality, lent—by the crown to those who had lost their own. These "grants" of land further implied that uncultivated land was no longer available to the farmer who required land.

As early as 7 B.C., when concerns about social structure become apparent, Shih Tan, a renowned Confucian scholar, made the first known suggestion of a true land redistribution that would return the empire to the ancient "well-field" (*ching-t'ien*) system, a legendary, perhaps mythical, part of the Confucian heritage that was to influence Chinese political and social philosophy for centuries to come. This system of equal holdings led to the suggestion that each adult male farmer should have at least 100 mu (4.764 acres) of land. This suggestion was shelved, but it represented official recognition that the uneven distribution of land was connected with the destabilizing polarization of rich and poor.

The final phase of landlordism was this polarization of agrarian society (Hsu 1980, 56). Tenants were so entirely subjected to the economic and political whims of the landlord that eventually imperial control of individuals collapsed. The tendency toward tenant farming was exacerbated by the existence of small scattered holdings that were bought up by landlords. Because these were geographically removed from each other, the only way to make them profitable was to rent each out individually to tenants. This situation set the stage for the "red eyebrows revolt" and the resultant anarchy in which the Western Han dynasty perished in A.D. 9.

The usurper Wang Mang attempted to solve the agrarian crisis by nationalizing all the land and reviving the well-field system. He ordered that any family whose land exceeded the average allowance of 900 mu per eight adult males should divide the excess among relatives and neighbors. The law was badly implemented, and private ownership was restored under the Eastern Han (A.D. 25–220). By 66, however, the new court ordered public lands everywhere in the empire given to the poor. Even so, under the Eastern Han there were nineteen major events (e.g., food riots) attributed to bands of vagrants roaming the countryside (Hsu 1980, 19). By this later period, population growth was placing a critical strain on the food supply. Per capita landholdings were low, and to complicate matters there was an uneven distribution of the population. Ultimately, the Eastern Han fell under the disastrous and bloody "Yellow Turbans," who amassed an army of 300,000 men (Gernet 1982, 694). A more detailed examination of the connection between type of landholding and location of these rebellions appears at the end of this section and will reveal much about the reasons for the longevity of Chinese civilization in comparison with that of Rome.

Recognizing that equality of holdings, or at least the avoidance of gross inequality, was essential to stability, the Later Wei (386–534) engaged in celebrated reforms proclaimed by Emperor Hsaio-Wen in 485 and 486 (Balazs 1964, 114). At this time, the ancient idea of equal distribution of land once more came to the fore. A certain amount of land was allotted in perpetuity to each family and to each individual was allotted a quota of arable land that had to be returned when the owner reached a certain age limit. The purpose here was not to pursue a utopian vision but to counteract existing inequalities. By the time of the Sui (581–618) however, despite the unification of the empire, it was difficult for an adult peasant to obtain even as little as 20 mu in those districts where the population density was greatest (Balazs 1964, 115).

The T'ang dynasty in 624 "aimed at providing each peasant family with enough land to support it and to enable it to pay its taxes. The 'method of equal distribution of land' (chün-t'ien-fa) adopted at this time was in fact indissolubly linked to the fiscal laws enacted in 619" (Gernet 1982, 246). Extant documents from the Wei through the eighth century T'ang confirm the relative absence of large landholders during this period (Huang 1990, 82). However two caveats are appropriate. First, statutory allocations of land were found only where land was plentiful, and it was during the early eighth century that large estates began to be prominent (Gernet 1982, 263). Officials in office had the right to "land owned in perpetuity" between 200 and 6,000 mu and to tax exemption. Monasteries (mostly Buddhist) were exempt from taxation. Mandarin farmers, retired officials, and their descendants (or those who claimed to be) also were exempt from taxation. In 754, just before the An Lu-shan rebellion that overthrew the empire, only 14.5 percent of the total population was eligible for taxation (Balazs 1964, 117).

Tenancy was on the rise because of the increasing indebtedness of the peasant. A decree of 752 contained the following language:

> Officials and rich families vie with each other in founding villas; they silently compete with each other as to who will swallow up the most land. They have no fear of the regulations; they all pretend to own waste land, and their fields are all cultivated.... As for lots for distribution, they buy and sell them against the rights of inheritance and against the law; or they change the titles in the registration lists; or they take the lots as pledge for debts. The result is that the common people no longer have any land of their own. Further, they get hold of men from other parts and hire them as agricultural laborers, and take possession of land belonging to local inhabitants. (Henri Maspero, quoted in Balazs 1964, 118)

At the end of the eighth century we witness the rise of manorial villas that take the place of much of the freehold farming. From the T'ang period onward through the Sung and the Mongol or Yuan dynasties, a class of tenant farmers and apprentice laborers existed that is much closer to that of our own period than to earlier epochs (Gernet 1982, 316). The peasantry was increasingly being reduced to "serflike status on the estates of large landlords" (Hucker 1975, 277). Reaction to the Mongols led to a new series of rebellions dominated by the Red Turbans, but the founder of the Ming dynasty, himself a peasant rebel, was the leader of a secondary rebellion that ultimately dominated the insurrection.

The new Ming empire, founded in 1368, was to restore many of the earlier yearnings for equality expressed in the equal-fields concept. The new system deliberately catered to the poor and humbled the rich. Large estates were confiscated and slavery was abolished. State-owned lands or those claimed by the state were rented out to the landless, and tax incentives were provided to resettle peasants in underpopulated areas. High tax rates were imposed on the rich (Hucker 1975).

But as before the relative equality of holdings achieved at the outset of this dynasty was undermined by growing land concentration between 1550 and 1650, particularly in the lower Yangtze, where it was said, "one man holds a hundred people's dwellings and one household occupies a hundred household's fields" (Wakeman 1975, 41). As before, tax privileges were used to purchase thousands of scattered plots, which then became the basis for tenancy. In 1644, when the rebellion against the Ming dynasty began, peasants flocked willingly to the rebels side. Tseng Ying-lin, a supervising secretary in the Ministry of War, wrote the emperor on February 24, 1644, stating:

> The gentry and the wealthy presently clothe themselves with rent and feed themselves with taxes, sitting at their leisure while they suck the bone marrow of the population. In peaceful times they manipulate trade so as to subordinate the people and monopolize vast profits. When there is trouble, ought we expect [the people] to share the vicissitudes of the gentry and the wealthy, putting forth efforts [on their behalf]? Indeed, the rich grow richer, invariably fleecing the people; and the poor grow poorer, until they are unable to survive at all. (quoted in Wakeman 1979, 45; bracketed comments are by Wakeman)

The rebels marched inexorably across Northern China, with Peking ultimately falling to the rebels on April 25, followed by Manchu troops on June 5. Thus began the Ch'ing dynasty, which was able to conquer China because of the successful prior rebellion.

Apparently, the local elite learned their lesson from that rebellion. A chastened mood appears to have set in. The blatant exploitation and excessive privilege so characteristic of the late Ming was lessened. The elite in the early Ch'ing period did not set themselves apart so arrogantly and so obviously from the local population (Beattie 1979, 264).

Down to our own time, we see strong echoes of the peasant uprising in connection with the fall of old regimes and the rise of the new ones. Balazs (1964, 167) interprets the rise of the Chinese Communists in this light, as does Ray Huang (1990, 143).

Balazs's identification of the persistent patterns of Chinese history is reinforced by the researches of Cho-yun Hsu, which provide evidence on the location of peasant uprisings in the Western and Eastern Han periods. Hsu (1980, 144-45) identified 45 such uprisings between the first century B.C. and the second century A.D. Hsu's initial expectation was that these disturbances would be found in the areas of greatest land concentration—those which had widespread latifundia—that also happened to be key economic areas and/or close to the capital city of Peking. In fact, just the opposite was found, with fully 42 of the 45 uprisings found outside of these areas, so that there exists "a mutual exclusion of uprisings and extreme land concentrations" (Hsu 1980, 143). These are indeed striking results.

Here we find one of the outstanding differences between China and Rome, which allowed the former to continue a relatively unbroken Chinese civilization while the latter had its language, culture, and civilization utterly transformed with the fall of the Roman state. Whereas the free Roman peasantry had virtually disappeared, especially after Diocletian's reforms tied the peasantry to the estates, this was hardly, if ever true of the Chinese peasantry. They persisted throughout Chinese history, even at times of the appearance of large numbers of latifundia; as Hsu states, it was the "free farmers who owned the greater part of the land" (1980, 66), with the number of tenants hardly more than 20 percent of the population. These peasants with their own small holdings were nonetheless aware of the existence of those with much larger holdings, even at some geographical distance, an awareness that fueled the resentment and increasing polarization of Chinese society at various historical intervals, as we have seen. At certain critical times, then, corresponding to those of simultaneous pauperization and extreme land concentration (the two processes, of course, not unrelated), a military revolt would occur or a famine or natural disaster would set loose bands of roaming vagabonds. There were ample numbers of peasants who felt that they had nothing to lose by joining these bands and attacking the government with its supporting landowning elite. This stands in bold contrast to the Roman instance where the last serious revolts were those of slaves, mostly foreign-born and captured in war. In the Roman Empire and the late Byzantine period, peasant uprisings were virtually unknown.

A major consequence of these rebellions was a persistent renewal of Chinese civilization or, in the instance of external conquest, such as by the Mongols or Manchus, a sinicization of the conquerors and their absorption, if at times incomplete, into Chinese society.

This pattern could not occur in Rome for the simple reason that an obverse process occurred. As we have seen, when the empire began to be pressed on its borders by the Germanic tribes, peasants as well as many latifundists were prepared to join the conquerors as a means of escaping the oppressive taxation (for both peasants and landlord) and oppressive social structure (for peasants). Instead of rebellion as in China, there were simply piecemeal or wholesale defections to the conquerors as they advanced. This is not to say that there were no defections in the Chinese case (there were; cf. Hsu 1965, 91), but the presence of domestic rebellion presented an alternative to the dissatisfied peasant, not available in the Roman instance, especially during the critical period of the later Empire. Thus China could persist through several transformations while Rome fell to foreign forces, never to be resurrected in anything like its earlier form.

Extreme land concentration had other consequences as well, for both China and Rome. In both instances such concentrations were associated with the absence of social mobility, a factor of considerable influence in solidifying the early Chinese state (Hsu 1965). Although the scholastic examinations for the civil service enhanced social mobility after their initiation during the Han period and their systematization in 669 (Gernet 1982, 257), at times of extreme land concentration, it was generally the wealthier landowning families that had greater access to the bureaucracy and a virtual lifetime sinecure. Only after the rebellions and institution of new government was this situation at least partially reversed. In the later Roman Empire, of course, there was little geographic mobility for the peasantry as the result of the laws of Diocletian and their aftermath, and of course virtually no social mobility. We might also note the contrast with early Byzantium, with its considerable social mobility and strong invigoration of the state.

The Maya

As a prime illustration of the third pattern, that of the instability and decay of a multipolar system of city-states, we turn to the Maya of the Late Classic, Terminal Classic, and beginning Postclassic periods, roughly from 600–1200. It was during this period that the major events surrounding the famous Maya "collapse" took place.

Why choose the Maya? After all there are other systems of city-states, such as that of Sumer, discussed in Chapter 3, or the Greek city-states before the Peloponnesian War or the Renaissance city-states of Northern Italy. I will, in fact, later compare these with the Maya. But the Maya demonstrate several advantages as an illustration of decline and fall. First, the apparent suddenness of the collapse distinguishes this instance from others. Within roughly one hundred years, from about 800 to 900, virtually all of the once flourishing polities in the Southern Lowlands were abandoned. A collective population of roughly 5,000,000 in these lowlands (Lowe 1985, 165; Sanders 1973) dropped swiftly to perhaps no more than several hundred thousand.

Second, the completeness of the collapse also distinguishes this case. In most other instances, such as those enumerated above in the Middle East or Southern Europe, there was a revival after collapse, even if in different form. Empires or larger states evolved in place of the earlier city-states. Here, there is no such transformation, especially in the Southern Lowlands; the cities are abandoned, never to be reestablished. Third, perhaps because of the fascination with suddenness and completeness, as well as major breakthroughs in deciphering the Maya language found on stone columns or stelae, we now know much of Maya history. There exists a veritable army of archaeologists and other social scientists working on Maya civilization. (There are nearly 1,500 bibliographical entries in Sharer 1994, with new knowledge accumulating at a very rapid rate.) Additionally, the Maya collapse is one of the few cases to have a seminar devoted specifically to this topic, which began in the late 1960s and resulted in the publication of a volume containing the preliminary findings of the seminar participants (Culbert 1973a). Many of the original group have continued their individual and collaborative efforts, leading to an accumulation of findings on the Maya collapse. Fortunately, we are therefore reasonably well-informed about the basic facts and likely patterns of dissolution pertaining to this collapse.

The Maya are also interesting because of the paradigm shift in understanding their civilization. Whereas earlier (cf. Morley 1946 [updated in Morley and Brainerd 1983] or Thompson 1954) they were viewed as a "peaceful theocracy dominated by priests" (Marcus 1992, 409) such is not the understanding at the present time. Since Tatiana Proskouriakoff (1960, 1963, 1964) recognized that designs on the stelae were not merely decorative but actually hieroglyphs amounting to a written language—the most developed pre-Columbian Mesoamerican writing system—we have enormous information on their history. The stelae in fact were monuments recording that history in the form of dynastic successions and many instances of warfare. The presumption of a peaceful theocracy in which war was virtually unknown and cities were repositories for temples and their priests gives way to the image of considerable warfare between city-states, perhaps at least as much as polities with a far greater reputation for war, such as the Aztecs (Marcus 1992).

A further contribution to our knowledge of Maya history comes from the *Books of Chilam Balam*, which contain a treasure trove of historical information covering the ancient Maya handed down over the generations. Although there were difficulties in their translation because the language is archaic, some of the chronology is obscure, and the books were written down only relatively recently, in the eighteenth or nineteenth century, it is generally acknowledged that they nevertheless reflect an authentic Maya sense of history and worldview (Sabloff 1990, 50).

The Maya collapse has been characterized in the following way by one of the participants in the 1973 meeting of the seminar on the collapse:

1. The failure of elite-class culture
    a. The abandonment of administrative and residential structures (palaces)
    b. Cessation of erection and refurbishment of funerary monuments and foci of ritual activities (temples)
    c. Cessation of manufacture of sculptured historical monuments and records (stelae)

Decline and Fall of Empires and States / 119

      d. Cessation of the manufacture of luxury items such as the finest polychrome pottery, fine stonework, and jade carving for the use of an elite class
      e. Cessation of the use of calendrical and writing systems, at least in Classic Period forms
      f. Cessation of nearly all behavioral patterns associated with the above and other elite-class-directed activity, for example, the ball game played in formal courts, the processionals, rituals, visits, and conferences characteristic of Maya elite-class life lapsed
      g. From the above, it follows that the Classic Period elite class ceased to exist
  2. The apparent rapid depopulation of the countryside and the ceremonial centers
  3. The relatively short period of occurrence—from 50 to 100 years (Adams 1973, 22)

Many explanations have been given for the collapse, some monocausal and, more recently, some multicausal. A few more sophisticated ones have had a causal sequence format.

Among the most prominent of the monocausal explanations have been those concerned with the Mayan environment. Simply put, the density of population had outrun the carrying capacity of the land. We know that population density was significantly increasing throughout the Preclassic and Classic eras, until it had reached approximately 600–700 persons per square kilometer (Culbert 1973b, 72; also see Cioffi-Revilla and Landman, 1996). Swidden agriculture, most probably utilized in the early period of Mayan settlement, gave way to raised-field agriculture, a far more intense form (Schele and Freidel 1990, 39). Related to that intensification of agriculture is the problem of soil erosion. Although pre-Hispanic populations attended to this problem in the Valley of Mexico, there is little evidence that the Maya were aware of it, even during the period of precipitous decline. In humid environments, the erosion rate is much less obvious because of the faster rate of weed growth, and so the problem could have become obscured (Sanders 1973, 338).

Evidence for ecological factors in the Maya decline is found in skeletal remains. Examining a skeletal series in Altar de Sacrificios, Guatemala, Frank Saul (1973) found evidence of nutritional deficiency in the skeletons for the Late to Postclassic periods. William Haviland (1967) found a statistically significant decline in stature among males from Early Classic to Late Classic times. Additionally, he found significant differences in stature between elite and non-elite tombs. This evidence is consistent with recent findings suggesting the onset of a major 200-year drought around 800, the most intense of any suffered by the region for 7,000 years ("Breakthroughs" 1995, 22).

Invasions also have been suggested as progenitors of the Maya collapse. Eric Thompson (1970) argued that Putun or Chontel Maya—rude cousins of the Classic Maya—expanded into the Maya Lowlands in the ninth or tenth centuries. Consistent with this suggestion, Jeremy Sabloff and Gordon Willey (1967) note an invasion by people from the Gulf Coast lowlands in the early ninth century. Evidence of "foreign" housewares and other detritus have been found at sites in the southwestern region. We will examine the role of foreign invasion shortly, in conjunction with the other explanatory elements to be examined here.

Disruption of trade is another explanation offered in connection with the collapse. Either in connection with foreign intrusions or as a result of internal difficulties, the removal of the lowlands from traditional Mesoamerican trade routes could have resulted in an elite collapse. No longer possessing obsidian or other Mesoamerican valuables, the Maya elite could no longer retain its position vis-à-vis the masses, and the entire hierarchy collapsed, resulting in depopulation.

Elite collapse also has been suggested to be a consequence of class conflict. Among the earliest hypotheses explaining the collapse has been that of peasant overthrow of the elite (Thompson 1954). Later, Robert Sharer (1977) suggested a gulf between elite and common beliefs that could have precipitated major class conflict. Finally, Robert Hamblin and B. L. Pitcher (1980) developed a mathematical model based on rates of change of monument construction and their demise that suggests to them a Maya mass rebellion. However, as John Lowe (1985, 108-9) points out, such conflict also could have been the result of interstate warfare or indeed of shifting economic fortunes or political conquest.

A major point of agreement among virtually all of the Mayanists is the growth of the elite during the Classic and Late Classic periods. Not only did the elite grow in number and power but so did the bureaucracy that they controlled (Sabloff 1990, 119). The Classic period witnessed an increasing number of "palaces" in comparison with temples, a sure indication of increased elite presence and secularization of Mayan society, but perhaps at a slower rate than other societies that evolved in this general way (e.g., Sumer).

A general explanation of the Maya collapse, as well as other such rapid declines, has been given by Joseph Tainter (1988). In his view, increased monument, temple, and palace construction has a decreasing marginal utility as the society matures. Increased ecological stresses (due perhaps to population density) and other stresses demand increased monument construction and other offerings to propitiate the gods and the apparently declining fortunes of the polity. It is this withdrawal of potentially productive labor from the agricultural sector that actually exacerbates the shortages, further necessitating monument construction, and a vicious cycle ensues.

This general emphasis on decreased marginal utility has counterparts in more specified causal sequences. Hosler, Sabloff, and Runge (1977) developed a simulation model that has food production suffering as a result of monument construction and the increased fraction of commoners involved in that work. Lowe further elaborates this type of model, emphasizing food production, regulatory capacity, elite population, food per capita, labor supply, and commoner population (1985, 192). Such models have the advantage of increased specificity vis-à-vis the earlier, more general explanation.

The explanation to be offered here does not exclude these models but emphasizes warfare as a consequence of other, prior variables. There is considerable agreement that warfare increased during the Classic and later periods. Despite the fact that much of the combat between Mayans likely was individually fought, hand-to-hand (Sabloff 1990, 88), evidence of defensive works has been found at Classic Maya sites. (For a list of references to these defensive works, see Marcus 1992, 412). Narrow artificial ridges, or parapets, have been found at Tikal and at Becan (Sabloff 1990, 84–87). More and more texts on warfare have been found, as have murals depicting warfare throughout the Classic Maya region (Marcus 1992, 412). And because raiding may have been a continual preoccupation of the Maya, aside from the more intense wars fought at less frequent intervals, much of that activity may not have been recorded (Sabloff 1990). Certainly the taking of captives for sacrifice at the many Mayan temples, a fairly common Mesoamerican practice, would have required an endemic low level of warfare. A number of scholars of the collapse have argued that increasing militarism and more especially escalating warfare between ceremonial centers was "an important contributing factor" (Cowgill, 1979, 51; also see Lowe 1985, 20).

But it is the less frequent but far more intense system-destroying type of war that we are concerned with. And for this there is increasing evidence, even in the Early Classic era. Linda Schele and David Freidel (1990) have been able to construct from the written record a war event that was system-transforming (by implication, also system-destroying), both in terms of the patterns of warfare and in terms of a resulting system dominance by Tikal. On January 16, 378, the forces of Tikal defeated those of its arch rival, the neighboring kingdom of Uaxactun. As a result, the king of Tikal ascended the throne of Uaxactun as well, ending the independence of that city-state. This however, was not the "traditional hand-to-hand combat of proud nobles struggling for personal glory and for captives to give to the gods. This was war on an entirely different scale, played by rules never before heard of and for stakes far higher than the reputations or lives of individuals. In this new warfare of death and conquest, the winner would gain the kingdom of the loser" (Schele and Freidel 1990, 145). The battle was "unlike anything the seasoned warriors on either side had ever experienced. And for the people of Uaxactun, it would be more devastating than their wildest imaginings" (Schele and Freidel 1990, 149).

The old ways of battle had been orderly, with limited strategic objectives. In the new style of battle, the gods of the defeated kingdom would be replaced, as would its political system, with that of the opposing kingdom; the expectation would be not the ransom of captured nobles, but their execution. Clouds of spears were used to kill masses of the opponents instead of the typical individualized combat (Hassig 1992, 76). This "total war" of imperial expansion by Tikal may have been influenced by Tikal's interaction with Teotihuacan, whose influence was then at its most extensive. There were large numbers of Teotihuacan traders in Tikal as part of the great web of trade in Mesoamerica innovated by that great city and a correspondingly equal number of Mayans traveled to the Valley of Mexico (Millon 1988, 115). On one stela, the conqueror of Uaxactun, Smoking-Frog, depicted himself in war regalia of the Teotihuacun style. It is likely that the Teotihuacan trade ambassadors intensified the already existing rivalry between Tikal and Uaxactun. Control of the trade network in the central Petén region of the lowlands would have been a prize worth fighting over. And it is possible that certain of the war tactics also were borrowed from the Teotihuacanos (Schele and Freidel 1990, 163).

As we now know, this war was only among the earlier of those to be fought among the Mayan city-states. The stelae at Caracol tell us that sometime between April 11, 556, and May 1, 562, Caracol had defeated Tikal in several serious battles. The absence of stelae at Tikal between September 17, 557, and March 18, 692, tells of the serious diminution of Tikal's status.

After the victory, Caracol chose Naranjo as its next target. Although Naranjo had been allied with Caracol (and Calakmul), it may have approached the defeated Tikal in friendship, thus incurring the enmity of Caracol. A series of victories by Caracol's forces ended on March 4, 636, with the total defeat of Naranjo.

When a city-state was defeated in this fashion, it was stripped of its king and its wealth. Worse was the forced cessation of monument construction—and worse still, the building of a monument to its own subjugation, as Naranjo was forced to build the Hieroglyphic Stairs as a record of defeat, in Naranjo itself. "When Caracol effaced the monuments of its enemies and impoverished them to the point where they could erect no others, it was taking away their most cherished possession—history" (Schele and Freidel 1990, 178). After the defeat of Tikal, for 130 years only one king left his name inscribed in the history of the kingdom. Some pottery and wood texts happen to have been deposited in his tomb; otherwise we might not even have this limited record.

Dos Pilas was the next city-state to embark on a path of conquest involving a series of wars that recorded the names of the captive kings but, as is the Maya custom, not necessarily the names of the city-states. The king of Dos Pilas involved himself in the increasingly complex political relations of the Petén kingdoms. He managed to insinuate himself in the affairs of Calakmul, a powerful kingdom in its own right and a nominal ally of Caracol but deadly enemy of Tikal and Naranjo. A pair of stelae show the participation of the king of Dos Pilas in the accession to the throne of the then monarch of Calakmul. And a scene painted on a pot shows the king of Calakmul kneeling in a subordinate position before the king of Dos Pilas. Naranjo proved to be the next target presented by the power vacuum created by the earlier defeats of Naranjo and Tikal. There, marriage to a noblewoman proved to be the avenue of influence.

Naranjo itself experienced a resurgence shortly thereafter, beginning a series of wars against the smaller allies of its hated enemy, Caracol. And here, in the seventh and eighth centuries, we see a quickening of the system-destroying wars that probably did much to insure the collapse of the Lowland Maya civilization. By the end of the eighth and beginning of the ninth centuries, the number of references in the Maya war record achieved its maximum. After this period, the number of stelae indicative of war diminished rapidly. In the last decade of the seventh century, the forces of Naranjo engaged those of Ucanal in battle several times, culminating in the defeat of February 1, 695. The subjugation of additional Caracol allies continued until finally there is a recorded cessation of hostilities on February 16, 713. Elegant strategies were used to maintain subject populations in check during the post-conquest period. For example, by keeping high-ranking captives alive for many years, the king of Naranjo was able to disrupt the lines of succession in the defeated cities, thus ensuring a fair degree of instability and chaos. As a result of all this, Caracol ceased to be a force to be reckoned with in the Petén. Finally, the king of Naranjo dismantled the hated Hieroglyphic Stairs that the victorious Caracol leaders had erected earlier.

At around the same time, Tikal began to experience a revival under a new leader who ascended to the throne in 682. He embarked on a new public works and building program that was to create the greatest temples and palaces the Mayan world had ever seen. In 695 he went to war against Calakmul, defeating it badly. In this fashion, the ally of Dos Pilas in the Petén was defeated while Naranjo, as we have seen, conquered the allies of Caracol, the other major enemy of both Tikal and Naranjo. These victorious kings of Tikal and Naranjo were succeeded by their sons, in the years 734 and 755, respectively.

These dates are significant because it is at the end of this period of warfare among city-states that monument construction virtually ceased, signaling the end of Lowland Maya expansion and the beginnings of decline. There are several indications of incipient decline during the middle of the eighth century. In 721, the number of monuments dedicated reached a maximum (Lowe 1985, 38). Several decades later, numerous small centers began to open throughout the Petén (Marcus 1976). A decentralization had begun, suggesting a concomitant decline of hierarchical control from large centers such as Tikal. By 785, the escalating death rate of sites themselves exceeded the rate of founding of new sites, suggesting that the collapse was now being felt. Prior to this time, new sites replaced older ones as soon as they dropped out, if not sooner (Lowe 1985, 39). As early as 750 (Rice 1986, 281), a decline in Petén influence had been found on the east coast of Yucatan, suggesting that the "Petén Corridor" transmitting trade and ideas to the Yucatan was being shut down. Evidence for a marked population increase on the west and north coasts of the peninsula about 770 has been found (Miller 1986, 203). This finding provides support to those who argue that the Putun Maya were invading the region, probably unopposed or only lightly opposed by the now weakened Classic civilization. The mid-to-late eighth century now began to witness the rapid decline of the Lowland Maya civilization.

To what process may we attribute the escalating warfare associated with the Maya decline? We have seen the ecological problems experienced by the Maya, but how might they be related to the escalating warfare? To answer this question we need to examine more closely the likely political structure of the Classic Maya.

As it may be surmised by now, the structure of the Lowland Maya was multipolar. There may be some disagreement as to the exact composition of the system, but the overall multipolar character is clear. For example, based on the use of emblem glyphs, Joyce Marcus (1973) points to at least four poles of the system, namely Palenque, Calakmul, Tikal and Copan. Two others, Yaxchilan and the Pentexbatun confederacy also might qualify (Marcus 1992, 184). Spaced around each of these main centers are five to eight secondary centers, such as Naranjo, which in itself may not qualify fully as a primary center despite the level of conflict with primary centers. (More on that later.) In Marcus's structure there are tertiary centers, which lack their own glyphs. Finally, there are quaternary centers, which lack inscriptions of any kind.

Another four-level hierarchical structure is given by Lowe (1985, 147) based on Guttman scale values of types and quantities of monument construction. Calakmul, Tikal, and Copan are once again found at the highest level with a second level consisting of centers such as Palenque, Naranjo, and Uxmal and two additional levels below that. Clearly such a hierarchy, including several primary and many (9) secondary centers that can conflict with primary centers and even numerous (15) tertiary centers, is multipolar in the extreme. In these schemes, or in another put forward by Norman Hammond (1974), the system is highly segmented into polar centers of power.

If one accepts Marcus's interpretations of many of the major conflicts among centers, it appears that serious warfare could occur between primary and secondary centers. In her interpretation of the evidence of conflict between Caracol and Tikal, for example, this was a war of independence of Caracol from its large neighbor. Many other wars among the city-states can also be accounted for in this fashion, such as those between Dos Pilas and Seibal (Marcus 1992, 429–30).

In addition to the many conflicts between Lowland Maya centers leading up to the beginnings of decline, we have other evidence for the importance of warfare as a progenitor of decline. This is indicated by the unique circumstances surrounding the rise of Chichen-Itza in the Northern Lowlands coterminous with the decline of the southern centers. Instead of the complete disappearance of Mayan civilization, as had once been thought, we now have evidence for the rise of great centers in the Puuc region to the north, just as the south was declining—a shift of population and politico-economic power from the south to the north (Sabloff 1990, 121). This does not mean that people fled directly from the collapsing south to the now thriving north (although this might be the case), but that either directly or in some stochastic fashion there was a transfer of power and civilization. The political structure of the most powerful state emergent in the Northern Lowlands suggests a salient reason for the southern decline and newfound northern robustness, As Schele and Freidel put it, "The key to success for the Chichén-Itzá lords lay in their redefinition of the political consequences of defeat in war. They turned away from the dynastic blood feuds of the past and moved toward effective alliance and consolidation. This consolidation would become the guiding principle of empire among the next great Mesoamerican civilization, the Culhua-Mexica" (1990, 375).

The Maya of Chichen-Itza did not glorify divine leadership but instead terminated the office of king and the principle of dynasty. Instead of monarchs of individual cities, the notion of alliance among kinsmen was propagated. A brotherhood of princes was founded as a kind of confederacy, in contrast to the earlier individual lines of descent. Apparently, there was a recognition of the deleterious consequences of the separate lines of kinship and these were now to be avoided. Chichen-Itza was extraordinarily successful by Maya standards, establishing a virtual hegemony over the Northern Lowlands after the defeat of the Puuc cities and Coba, its major competitors. Chichen-Itza's legacy extended into the Southern Lowlands, filling the vacuum left by the declining Classic polities of Tikal, Palenque, Calakmul, and the like.

Here we see the strong likelihood of a learning process that prevented the same mistakes occurring in the north as in the south. An avoidance of distinct monarchical lineages that could lead to exclusiveness and competition or warfare with rivals was the hallmark of Chichen-Itza and its empire. This political innovation very probably contributed strongly to the northern flourishing and the continued politico-economic health well after the virtual disappearance of the southern polities as viable entities. This effectively is a strong confirmation of the role of warfare among Southern Lowland city-states as progenitors of their decline, for by deliberately avoiding their sociopolitical pattern, the later polity of Chichen-Itza was able to grow and prosper.

Overall the explanation offered here for the decline in the Southern Lowlands based on incessant warfare dovetails nicely with that which emphasizes environmental degradation as the result of overpopulation and a consequent outrunning of the carrying capacity of the land. And this conclusion is in agreement with "the latest feeling among scholars . . . that the increasing militarism of Maya society may have undermined the ecological underpinnings of the economy" (Wilford 1991, C1). It is precisely under a condition of scarcity generated by overpopulation and its consequences that a strong inequality is predicted among the units comprising a multipolar system. That inequality, in turn, would generate envy and a competitiveness that easily could degenerate into repeated incidents of war. Such a process could be self-reinforcing, as warfare, in turn, absorbs more men from productive agricultural pursuits, lays waste more agricultural land, and further exacerbates the inequalities between most and least favored actors in a system, thus yielding more war.

Climatic effects could have further exacerbated this scenario. Stress points during the Early Classic and the Postclassic collapse are associated with late rains and droughts, most likely the result of global climate changes (Gunn, Folan, and Robichaux 1995). Joel Gunn and Richard Adams (1981) argue that the mid-range of global climatic variations (i.e., not too cold or too warm) is most favorable to domestic and wild species of plants and animals. It is interesting to note that these deleterious climatic conditions for the Maya coincide approximately with the Roman Climate Optimum of 300 B.C. to A.D. 300 (Crumley 1993; Greene 1986, 83), wherein global climatic changes had opposite impacts on both civilizations. Both events are precisely out of phase. "When the Maya flourish, Europe is in dire straits. When Europe is blossoming, the Mayans retire into subsistence agriculture" (Gunn 1994, 95).

A downward trajectory of ever steepening slope over time is the projected outcome of such a process. In fact, this is precisely what the rapidly changing curves in Figure 2.8 predict and thus provide an answer to the question posed at the outset, namely why the suddenness of the collapse. As the number of utiles or desiderata decreases, the inequality between most and least favored actors disproportionately increases, especially in the portion of the curve representing the greatest scarcity. This prediction is in agreement with the finding of "the remains of extensive fortifications seemingly erected in haste and other evidence that the character and scope of Maya warfare began to change in the seventh or eighth century. These signs of siege warfare, . . . indicate an escalation of militarism involving the general population in a desperate fight for survival" (Wilford 1991, C10). With greater inequality in a multipolar system and augmented insecurity from increased pressure on resources, there is greater likelihood of some major war with system-destroying consequences.

While it is unnecessary to recount in detail the decline of classical Greek civilizations under similar circumstances (see, e.g., Midlarsky 1988a), it is useful to indicate certain basic structural similarities. The rise of Athens and later Thebes to preeminence in the multipolar environment of the Greek city-states (Corinth, Sparta, Thebes, among others) parallels the early and later rise of Tikal and Palenque. Warfare was endemic in the Greek multipolar system, and most striking is the recent discovery of environmental degradation in Greece as early as 2500 B.C. (Runnels 1995, 99). Soil erosion in particular was found to be correlated with land clearing and deforestation associated with intensive human settlement. It is clear that the scarcity of good agricultural land associated with such overpopulation and soil erosion could have fed powerfully into the inequalities associated with multipolarity and the consequent warfare, much as we have seen in the Maya case.

Israel, Judah, and Ammon

The survival of a continuous Chinese civilization over the centuries in contrast to the virtual disappearance of the culture of the Maya elite and the near disappearance, or at least utter transformation, of that of the Romans raises general questions concerning the survival or disappearance of civilizations. One of the difficulties in comparing civilizations, however, is the vast cultural dissimilarity found among them. Although the diverse forms of inequality can be used as comparative foci, one might argue that other cultural and historical factors were decisive. A way to control for these influences would be to choose contiguous societies with common or at least similar cultures, including language, alphabet, and belief systems. (This necessarily entails choosing small societies.)

The societies chosen are ancient Israel and Judah, with some additional comments on Ammon, which have the requisite contiguities and cultural similarities but radically divergent histories. All existed together in that part of the Middle East occupying much of contemporary Israel and the West Bank (ancient Israel and Judah) and western Jordan (Ammon; the name for the Jordanian capital of Amman is derived directly from the ancient Ammonites). Indeed, all three were part of the combined kingdom of David and Solomon prior to the breakup of the united kingdom of Israel in 925 B.C. and the withdrawal of Ammon from the union at about that time. Ammonite script is very closely related to the Paleo-Hebrew script in use in Israel and Judah before the sixth century B.C. The language also is quite similar (L. G. Herr 1993, 30). Israel retained its independence until the Assyrian conquest of 722, and Judah until the Babylonian conquest of 586, while the Ammonites survived both invasions (Grant 1971, 10; Miller and Hayes 1986). Yet Ammon eventually disappeared, in ways that are still not clear to us. Israel too vanished from history, but Judah was recreated as a politically active province of the Persian Empire by the returnees from Babylon, beginning perhaps in 538 (Miller and Hayes 1986, 452). Work on reconstructing the temple in Jerusalem was begun in 520 by the returnees, together with some Jews who had remained in Judah, and was completed in 515.

The Kingdom of Judah was to persist in some form of independence or autonomy until the revolt against Rome of A.D. 66–70. The Jews of Judah and Babylon were to create the bases of Rabbinic Judaism that persists to this day and that additionally provided the theological bases for Christianity and Islam. Contemporary Israel, using a modern version of ancient Hebrew, is a political outgrowth of these earlier events. How do we account for these striking differences among the three kingdoms? Two disappeared into historical oblivion, while the civilization of the third was to survive if not flourish in one form or another until the present day. Some of the answers are to be found in the conditions obtaining at the time of their respective conquests and the earliest days thereafter. (This puzzle is made even more interesting by the fact that throughout their joint history, Israel was the larger and by far more powerful of the two Hebrew-speaking kingdoms. Judah often was subservient to and perhaps even a vassal of the kingdom of Israel. Ammon was at most a backwater kingdom, even smaller than Judah.)

One answer, given perhaps tongue in cheek or with some basis in the concept of national character, is that the Jews somehow became a "stiff-necked people" (*am kshe oref*), determined to persist, no matter the cost. But this answer begs the question of why the Judaic civilization survived but not the Israelite—or the Ammonite or even the Roman, the most powerful empire in the world at its height and surely governed by those who can be characterized as stubborn in the conviction of their own superiority. Another answer lies in the vagaries of chance, luck, or "fortuna" that found Israel conquered by the far more brutal Assyrians while Judah was ultimately conquered by the Babylonians. Presumably, according to this argument, the Assyrians would have been more destructive in their wholesale deportations of the Israelites and replacement by foreign peoples than the more "civilized" Babylonians. Yet we know now that the Assyrians were not nearly so brutal as poets such as Lord Byron portrayed them in the nineteenth-century Romantic era of exaggerated responses (Saggs 1989, 189). Moreover, we know that when Samaria and the Kingdom of Israel fell to Sargon II in 722, only 27,270 inhabitants were deported and the "remnants" of several little known and undoubtedly small tribes were settled in their place (Miller and Hayes 1986, 338). In contrast, in the later Assyrian attack on Judah in 701, Sennecharib claimed to have taken 200,150 prisoners (Miller and Hayes 1986, 164). Even allowing that this is an exaggerated figure, still the number of deportees must have at least exceeded that taken from Israel 21 years earlier, yet although it became a vassal state of Assyria in the process, Judah survived this attack.

The determination of Judah's capital, Jerusalem, to resist strongly must have been a factor in the withdrawal of the Assyrian forces from the environs of that city. When the Babylonians captured Jerusalem in 586, it required the destruction of the city walls and much of the city itself. Most of the population was deported by the Babylonians. And earlier evidence of Babylonian destructiveness is found in the virtually complete annihilation of the Philistine seaport of Ashkelon in 605 (Stager 1996, 58). "The massive destruction of Judah wrought by Nebuchadnezzar's forces is evident. The displacement of most of the population is indicated by the meager signs of occupation during the sixth century at excavated sites. Continued occupation seems to have occurred only in a handful of towns, mainly to the north.... The population by the close of the sixth century has been estimated at no more than twenty thousand" (Schoville 1978, 57).

In contrast, the walls of Samaria, the Israelite capital, were left intact by the

Assyrians after their conquest (Barkay 1992, 356; Negev 1986, 336), indicating a less intense battle for the city despite the three-year siege, hence perhaps a less determined resistance by the Israelite defenders. The location and construction of Samaria were deliberately designed by Omri, the Israelite king, for maximum defensibility against external attack (Miller and Hayes 1986, 267), yet the defense of the city does not appear to have been vigorous.

This seeming lack of vigor should be compared not only with the apparently successful defense of Jerusalem against the Assyrians by Judah in 701 B.C., but also with the remains of an extraordinarily intense battle before the destruction of Lachish by the Assyrians in that same war. Lachish was the capital of the Shephelah, one of the more important provinces of Judah, and was heavily fortified, as were so many of the cities in the land of Israel during this period (Iron Age II–III; see Barkay 1992, 344–45, 331). The discovery of a siege ramp put up by the Assyrians and a counter-ramp constructed by the defenders begins to suggest the intensity of the conflict: "It is the only siege ramp identified in the Iron Age anywhere in the Near East" (Barkay 1992, 345). Hundreds of arrowheads were found as were many spherical flint sling stones. The destruction was violent, and there is evidence of a great fire accompanying it.

After its fall, the Israelite nation disappeared into historical oblivion, never to return, leaving only the Samaritans, a mixed population of foreigners and descendants of the Israelites, who today number at most several hundred. Thus we have a determination to resist in the case of Judah, which appears as early as the Assyrian invasions of the late eighth century B.C., while the apparent level of resistance of the Israelites was lower. Moreover, many of the exiles from Judah to Babylon returned within roughly half a century after the destruction of Jerusalem. No such comparable return is found among the Israelites.

What were the social conditions that gave rise to these different levels of resistance and persistence among the populations of Israel and Judah? Fortunately we have a written record in the form of the Hebrew Bible. Although there are biases in the various historical accounts, nevertheless much of the basic historical record has been confirmed by Assyrian and Babylonian written records and stelae, as well as the writings of Greeks such as Herodotus and Romanized Jews such as Josephus.

What is striking about the Hebrew biblical accounts is the emergence of social prophecy surrounding the inequalities in ancient Israel prior to the Assyrian conquest (Coggins 1989, 176). Amos was a prophet who was born in Judah but preached in Israel (Miller and Hayes 1986, 312). This in itself is significant, for his preaching against gross inequalities of wealth and circumstance, not in his native land, but in the neighboring northern kingdom suggests that conditions must have been substantially worse in Israel. He preached against a wealthy upper class that was living idly and comfortably while so many of the population suffered in poverty.

> Woe to those who lie upon beds of ivory,
>   and stretch themselves upon their couches,
> and eat lambs from the flock,
>   and calves from the midst of the stall;
> who sing idle songs to the sound of the harp,
>   and like David invent for themselves instruments of music;
> who drink wine in bowls,
>   and anoint themselves with the finest oils,
> but are not grieved over the ruin of Joseph!
>   (Amos 6:4-6 as quoted in Miller and Hayes 1986, 312)

This was a radical departure from earlier prophecy, which was God-centered (e.g., Elijah or Elisha), and is further indication of the perceived importance of these social conditions in determining the fate of Israel. Amos also implies that practices of debt slavery and excessive taxation were rife. Government officials were accused of corrupting the judicial process and profiting thereby. Wealthy landowners appear to have acted in collusion with government officials to further oppress the poor, beyond the existence of the wealth inequalities themselves (Miller and Hayes 1986, 312).

Why were these conditions endemic to Israel but apparently not to Judah, certainly not to the same extent? Moreover, as Gabriel Barkay remarks, "From the end of the ninth century onward separate and independent material cultures crystallize in Israel and Judah. It becomes possible to distinguish between a northern culture and southern culture, especially in ceramic typology" (1992, 305). The answer to the question of differences appears to reside in certain distinguishing geographical, ecological, and socioeconomic characteristics. First, although both Israel and Judah sat astride the great commercial highways of the Near East, Israel was physically closer to the major highway linking Egypt and Mesopotamia, known later to the Romans as Via Maris (Grant 1971, 10; Negev 1986, 329). When Omri built Samaria and fortified it, apparently one factor in the choice of location was proximity to this coastal road linking the continents (Miller and Hayes 1986, 267; Negev 1986, 334). (This would not have been the first time that Israelites had engaged in major trade with foreign powers. The northern tribes of Dan and Zebulon had traded with the Phoenicians, and Solomon had simply built upon that trade in his program of expansion; Saggs 1989, 152). Thus, Israel, and Samaria in particular, would have benefited from this proximity to a major trade route. Barkay remarks on artifacts found in Judah that differed substantially from those found in Israel and notes that Judah's "maritime trade could hardly compare with that of Tyre [in Phoenicia] and Israel" (1992, 353).

Residents of Samaria and others in close proximity clearly would have benefited differentially, expanding the inequality gap between rich and poor. And this gap would have already been present, trade influences excluded, because of a high population density relative to Judah and Ammon. Examination of a distribution map of the highlands of Israel and Judah (Frick 1989, 89) indicates a much larger number of settlements in the Northern Highlands, where Israel was located, than in the Southern Highlands, where Judah was situated. This higher population density may have been a consequence of the greater rainfall in the north than the south (Grant 1971, 17) and thus, additionally, the somewhat diminished agricultural risk in the north (Frick 1989, 75). The higher agricultural density in the north (Israel) should yield greater land inequality relative to the south (Judah). Thus we have two sources of increased inequality: trade and agricultural density, both of which should reinforce each other in making for a substantial difference in domestic inequality between the two states.

This phenomenon is complicated by the presence of cults foreign to the YHWH belief system in both Israel and Judah, but probably exacerbated in Israel. Ahab's Phoenician wife, Jezebel, was a devotee of Baal, and he had an altar to Baal built for her. Although their children had names derivative of YHWH, indicating a probable adherence to that belief system, nevertheless a semiofficial sanction had been given to Baal worship. The Hebrew prophets consistently railed against idol worship in Israel to a greater extent than in Judah. It is likely that the Baal worshipers in the towns—especially in Samaria, sitting astride the major commercial route—also were wealthier as the result of their ease of interaction with Phoenician and other traders. They would have been the "cosmopolitans" of Israel relative to the more rustic believers in YHWH. Phoenician trade and culture were very important in the life of ancient Israel. As Barkay remarks:

> The [archaeological] discoveries reflect the Phoenician cultural influence of biblical fame, most pointedly expressed in the marriage ties between the dynasty of Omri and the Phoenician kings and in the influence of the cult of the Tyrian Baal. The Phoenician contacts are prominent in the magnificent ashlar masonry styles, in the ivories undoubtedly carved in Phoenician workshops, and even in the fine Samaria pottery, which is to be seen as a type of Phoenician pottery of the ninth and eighth centuries. (1992, 320)

When Assyria attacked and then deported many of the Israelites, it is possible that the gaps of wealth and culture of worship were simply too great to overcome in establishing a community that would survive either in the Assyrian diaspora or later in Samaria.

There is yet another source of the inequalities that Amos so decries. This is a probable consequence of the wars between the Arameans, especially at Damascus, and the Israelites. Around the middle of the ninth century B.C., intermittent warfare began between Damascus and Israel in the form of Syrian raids that the Israelites were powerless to defend against. This was a throwback to earlier defeats of Israel by Syria, often in alliance with Judah, at the end of the tenth century (Miller and Hayes 1986, 220; an archaeological record of one such likely defeat was just recently discovered and reported, the first ancient inscription discovered, outside of the Bible, that refers to the House of David [Wilford 1993b, C9]). Only after the accession of the Omrides (including especially Ahab) at the beginning of the ninth century did Israel emerge into international prominence and domestic prosperity, though this was somewhat eclipsed after the end of that dynasty in 843.

Around the end of the ninth century, the Israelites defeated the Syrian forces once again in their battles, thus ending this period of strong Syrian interference in the life of Israel (Miller and Hayes 1986, 300–302) and ushering in a period of revival in the life of Israel, usually associated with the reign of Jeroboam II (785–745). He "restored the border of Israel from the entrance of Hamath as far as the Sea of Arabath" (II Kings 19:25). In contemporary terms this would mean from the city of Dan in northern Israel of today to the Dead Sea. We also know that he restored Israelite control over portions of the Transjordan. Thus he expanded Israel's frontiers to approximately what they had been at their height after the breakup of the Solomonic kingdom. It was during the time of Jeroboam II that Amos preached.

We know that the earlier Syrian depredations had left many Israelites destitute. When a city resisted the Syrians and was placed under siege, inflation and extremely high prices followed (II Kings 6:24–25). It is unlikely that these people would have recovered substantially by the time of Jeroboam, but those who had benefited from the high prices and increased indebtedness would have been able to take financial advantage of the expansion under Jeroboam. This is a type of fractal formation during a period of expansion in which a very few benefit inordinately. Coming after a period of extreme stress for much of the population, this could only have made matters worse. In contrast, Syrian warfare against the somewhat more distant Judah was less intense, and the expansion of Judah after the defeat of the Syrians was correspondingly smaller. Shortly, we shall see certain similarities in the case of the decline of the Egyptian empire during the Twentieth Dynasty, the same period that witnessed the establishment of the Israelite tribes and the Philistines (Sea People) in Canaan as the result of the retreat from empire and the resulting power vacuum.

The factors examined so far have focused on the decline, fall, and disappearance of ancient Israel. The gross inequalities experienced by the Israelites made it unlikely that they could come together during their exile and possibly return, as did those from Judah after the Babylonian conquest. Differences in cultic worship likely reinforced the differences in wealth, thus minimizing the probability of cooperative behavior in exile.

In contrast, it is clear that the exiles in Babylon were organized into one or more communities. First, much of the major prophecy of the period emerges from the Babylonian exile. It is almost universally agreed that chapters 40–55 from Isaiah have a Babylonian background. Although there is some disagreement on the origins of Jeremiah, E. W. Nicholson (1970, 116–35) is confident of a Babylonian locus. And of course Ezekiel is easily located in Babylon by the opening verse that places him clearly among the exiles (Coggins 1989, 174). Second, there are references to the "elders of Judah/Israel" (Ezek. 8:1; 14:1; 20:1, 3), which connotes a level of community organization that would be possible only with a certain degree of cooperation among the exiles. The fact that there was open acknowledgment of these "elders" suggests the Babylonian community had already achieved a relatively coherent organization that foreshadows the later era of the synagogues in exile, after the destruction of the Second Temple. It was also sufficiently organized for Artaxerxes I to rely upon the community as an ally in allowing, if not encouraging, the return to Jerusalem by Nehemiah sometime around 445 B.C. (Miller and Hayes 1986, 470). We know from prior research (Deutsch 1985; Midlarsky 1985) that equality of circumstance is one of the most powerful progenitors of cooperation. (Witness the cooperative behavior of men at the front in war as they confront death in common, sometimes even across the lines of combat as occurred at times during World War I; Axelrod 1984.)[2]

Some sense of the ethic of this community can be gauged by Nehemiah's efforts to ameliorate the social inequality that had apparently grown up since the Babylonian conquest. Strong fractal patterns can occur when an area is depopulated. Those that remain in the area have an opportunity to expand their holdings considerably, generating substantial inequality vis-à-vis those who are not able to expand, or more to the point here, the returnees who would not have land of their own, at least not initially. Nehemiah went so far as to legislate against the amassing of wealth at the expense of the poor. He confronted the nobles and officials in a public assembly and demanded that interest on loans be forgiven and that property seized for the nonpayment of debts be returned.

He also had remitted taxes that previous governors had imposed for purposes of supporting themselves. He himself apparently was able to financially support the officials responsible for overseeing the reconstruction of Jerusalem's walls and the building of the temple (Miller and Hayes 1986, 470-71).

Nehemiah records the opposition of natives of Judah, as well as surrounding peoples, to the returnees and their efforts to rebuild both the city walls and the temple itself. Certainly those that had remained in Judah would have been upset by the activities of the returnees and their initially implied and later actualized efforts at increased equality (Miller and Hayes 1986, 470). These themes of equality and social justice were to animate the prophetic writings thereafter, as well as the cauldron of contending ideas in Judah around the time of the destruction of the Second Temple in A.D. 70. The strong influence of the returnees can be gauged, at least in part, by their ability to eventually supplant the older Paleo-Hebrew script then still in use in Judah with the Aramaic form imported by the returnees. Another change attributed to them was the replacement of the older Hebrew names for months of the year with Babylonian names.

Equality of circumstance, or at least the avoidance of gross inequalities, can be understood now as a factor distinguishing Judah from Israel, especially as reflected in the norms of Nehemiah and the returnees from Babylon. But what accounts for the survival of the Jews after the destruction of the Second Temple and the long Diaspora? Here, we are on much less secure ground, for we do not have the narrative flow of the Bible and supporting documents or the physical inscriptions of a people *in situ* in their own land. As Yosef Yerushalmi (1989, 16) observed, national memory in the form of written Jewish history ended with Josephus and the publication of his *Jewish Antiquities* in 93/94, some twenty years after the destruction of the Second Temple and less than a decade before the rabbis convened the council at Yavneh that would establish the bases of Rabbinic Judaism for both Judaea and the Disapora. Only in the nineteenth century would a self-conscious Jewish historiography emerge. In this long, near-two-millennium period, Jewish collective memory would be served by prayer and ritual, not the written history of the Bible, Josephus, or the nineteenth-century efforts of the German-Jewish "Verein für Kultur und Wissenschaft der Juden."

Yet despite the absence of written history during this period, various events set the stage for the resurrection of a modern national consciousness on a grand scale in the late nineteenth century. It was not only the persecution of Jews by tsarist Russia and later Nazi Germany that formed the political bases of modern Israel as a reconstruction of ancient Israel/Judah, but the memory of key national events in antiquity that would spur a national consciousness among

Jews. The modern Warsaw Ghetto revolt of 1943 had clear antecedents in the earlier, almost equally destructive rebellion of the Jews against Rome in 66-70. The ability to act collectively even in defeat against overwhelming odds and to make the rebellion endure—four years in the instance of Rome and one month in the instance of hopelessly outgunned men, women, and children in Warsaw—created a historical linkage of Jewish national life that would feed powerfully into the formation of modern Israel in 1948.[3] Other events, such as the Bar Kochbah rebellion of 132-35, which initially was even more successful than that of 66-70, were to feed into this collective sense of national identity when it was later required. The consecration of successful revolts, such as that of the Hasmoneans in 166-65 B.C. against the Seleucid Greeks, resulting in the holiday of Chanukah, or—in a variation on that theme—Purim, involving the defeat of an enemy of the Jews in Persia, amounted to a celebration of the victorious in Jewish life. The ancestor of all such remembered events, the Passover recounting of national revolt and rescue in the form of the Exodus from Egypt, provided a model for these later honorings of both victory and defeat of the Jews qua nation.

There are comparable elements with the Chinese experience. In contrast to the Roman Empire with its virtual absence of native Roman revolts, both Chinese and Jewish history are filled with either peasant- or religion-based rebellions that acted to solidify a national consciousness, even when couched in purely religious terms. The act of rebellion, both at the time of rebellion and later in its recounting, establishes a strongly cooperative relationship among the rebels and their descendants. At the time of rebellion, the definition of insider and outsider and the organization of the former into rebels, often requiring a long lead time and extreme preparations before the onset of violence, demands strongly cooperative behavior among those defined as participants in the rebellion. Similarly, descendants of the rebels also require a considerable degree of cooperation among themselves in the often elaborate celebrations of the earlier events. The Passover Seder is probably the quintessential illustration of such an event requiring considerable preparation.

It is not only in the cooperative behaviors that we find the national consciousness developed over time. Religious or secular forms of ideology can powerfully reinforce this consciousness. In the instance of the Jews, the incorporation of national events in religious celebration (Passover, Chanukah, Purim) is an obvious example. But a similar phenomenon is found in the case of China where ancient concepts of "equal fields" and Confucian forms of justice melded in the national consciousness at times of revolt.

Yet we must not lose sight of the salient difference between Israel and Judah

—the greater equality of circumstance within Judah that likely led to its survival, in contrast to the disappearance of ancient Israel. And this equality of circumstance was perpetuated over the centuries, not necessarily in the absence of economic and other inequalities among Jews, although their common experience of persecution probably had such a leveling effect, but in the periodic reminders of equality of circumstance in both victory and defeat signaled by the Jewish holidays. These not only are religious observances but also serve as common memories of national experience. It is precisely this common historical experience, especially if routinely commemorated, that lies at the root of the successful maintenance of community over a long period of time (Deutsch et al., 1957).

And what of the Ammonites, the people who were compared initially with ancient Israel and Judah? Without all of the formative vicissitudes of conquest, rebellion, national regeneration, and decline, followed by other rebellions, regeneration, and decline, they apparently passed peacefully into history, leaving only the archeological remains, inscriptions, and artifacts that have been found in the Jordanian desert (L. G. Herr 1993).

A Comparison with Ancient Egypt

One element identified in the fall of ancient Israel has a counterpart in the decline and fall of ancient Egypt, and interestingly in the instance of Byzantium prior to its fall, as well. This is a consequence of territorial expansion, in the form of inequalities between those who benefit by that expansion and those who do not. Particularly in the case of the Egyptian New Kingdom and Empire, we have the growth, not of the landed elite as in ancient Israel or in Byzantium consequent on war and expansion, but of an elite unique to a society without a deeply embedded sense of private property. Here we have the priesthood of the Theban god Amon benefiting enormously from the Egyptian imperial expansion, in comparison both with other temple elites and with other societal sectors.

The vast majority of the land was in the hands either of the state or of the priesthood (Erman 1971, 129) during much of the imperial period (approximately 1400–1100 B.C.). Because Thebes was the central capital of the Empire, the Theban god Amon would be chosen for special favor among many other competitors from the pantheon of Egyptian gods. As early as the beginning of the eighteenth dynasty (ca. 1500 B.C.) and the first Asiatic expansion that would lead to empire, there began a golden age of the temples. Indeed, "the entire economy of the New Kingdom was closely tied to the policy of conquest conducted by the pharaohs of the Eighteenth and Nineteenth dynasties" (Vinogradov 1991, 173). Adolf Erman (1971, 303) provides detailed lists of the temple revenues of Amon of Thebes, the sun-god of Heliopolis, and Ptah of Memphis during the twentieth dynasty, and summarizes by stating that Amon possessed at least five times as much property as the sun-god and ten times as much as Ptah. John Wilson (1951, 273) summarizes in tabular form the annual income of the temples of Amon, Re, and Ptah in the middle of the twentieth dynasty (about 1150) and finds Amon with at least 95 percent of the total income.

The political and economic power of the temples arose as a direct consequence of the imperial expansion of the New Kingdom. At the end of the seventeenth and beginning of the eighteenth dynasties a new social base was created consisting of soldiers and administrators involved in empire building. Although the older political and religious aristocracy cooperated with the newer soldiers and administrators, it was only during the common struggle against the foreign Hyksos domination that the coalition was solid. Once the enemy was repelled, the two elites, one old and the other new, began to conflict. The wars of conquest in Asia emanating from the effort to expel the Hyksos became necessary for two reasons. First, fertile lands of sufficient quantity to reward the new elite were no longer available in Egypt proper (Vinogradrov 1991, 176); only smaller parcels could be given. As a consequence, plunder, whether in the form of lands, prisoners, or wealth became necessary. Second, and perhaps more important, the temple elite increasingly began to oppose the newer empire-based administration in what appears to have been a classic power struggle. Funneling much of the imperial plunder toward the temples was an equally classic means of coopting a potentially dangerous foe.

The great monopolization of wealth by the Temple of Amon was reflected both in the political offices held by the priesthood and in its property holdings. Regarding the former, Wilson comments,

> The effective grip of the High Priest of Amon upon the civil affairs and finances of the state may be shown by the distribution of offices within one family. Ramses-nakht was the High Priest of Amon under Ramses IV. His father Meri-Barset had been Chief Taxmaster, and Ramses-nakht's sons were to hold two of the most potent offices in the land: Nes-Amon and Amen-hotep successively as High Priest of Amon, and User-maat-Re-nakht as Chief Tax-master and Manager of Pharaoh's Lands. Thus the priesthood of Amon could manage the finances of the state for its own benefit and withhold resources from the pharaoh as it desired. The divine king had become a prisoner of the temple or of the little clan which held the higher temple offices. (1951, 272–73)

This was a capture of the secular by the sacred, but for purely instrumental ends, economic and political power. A basis for this economic and political power was the enormous concentration of cereal wealth that could be stored by a major temple. As Barry Kemp puts it, "Grain was wealth. . . . Major temples were the reserve banks of the time" (1989, 195). The power of the purse was held not only by persons such as those beneficiaries of nepotism encountered in the earlier quotation, but also in the form of land. Counting workingmen in towns controlled by the Temple of Amon, Wilson (1951, 271) reaches the tentative conclusion that the Temple of Amon owned one person out of every fifteen and one acre out of every eleven. The temples as a whole owned approximately one person in every ten and one acre in every eight. All of this was heavily driven by empire, in the sense that so much of this wealth, and ultimately power, came from imperial expansion. There is evidence that the Temple of Amon was the chief beneficiary both of the imperial expansion and of much of the taxation (Gardiner 1961, 293, 298). As Wilson states:

under the Empire the temples of the gods became huge and acquired vast estates. Grateful pharaohs executed charters exempting the temples and the temple staffs from duties which fell upon other citizens. Egypt became top-heavy with priests and specially privileged temple holdings. This meant that the clergy of Egypt had invested in empire, and it was important to them that the domination of the foreigners by Egypt be pushed at all times. Ultimately the burden of maintaining such an effort was too great, and the nation gave up its empire and retired within its own boundaries. (1951, 185-86)

At the end of the twentieth dynasty, during the time of Rameses XI, we have evidence of a Theban theocracy founded by the High Priest of Amon, Herihor. He united all of the powers of the state—military, judicial, administrative, and sacerdotal—in his own person and handed them on to his descendants (Gardiner 1961, 305). The military aspect was especially important, given the threats to Egypt at this time, and efforts to expand or at least to restore the Empire to its former greatness. Retention by the High Priest of the title "great commander of the army" apparently continued well into the following period. His power was indicated further by the recourse to oracular decisions on virtually all important occasions (Gardiner 1961, 328, 321). As Nicolas Grimal observes, "The cornerstone of their [the later southern] regime was the temple estate of Amun, which was ultimately the only true beneficiary of the immense empire created by the Ramessid kings. By the end of the Twentieth Dynasty the temple of Amun had unquestionably become wealthier and more powerful than pharaoh himself" (1992, 292).

A similarity with the later Roman Empire is found in the presence of widespread corruption illustrated by the following papyrus:

Grave accusations [were made] against a number of persons, prominent among whom was a lay-priest of the temple of Chnūm charged with many thefts, acts of bribery, and sacrilege, not to mention the inevitable imputations of copulation with married women. Heinous offences against religion were his misappropriation and sale of sacred Mnēvis calves, his joining in the carrying of the god's statue while three of his ten days of purificatory natron-drinking were still to run, and his heaping of gifts upon the vizier's henchman to make them arrest his priestly accuser while the latter was only half-way through his month of ritual service. (Gardiner 1961, 296)

Although we have evidence of sacrilege in the form of tomb robbery and despoliation from the earliest dynasties, nevertheless, the extent of such corruption, if not its institutionalization, is found only during the later period of our concern here.

Here we have a dynamic for decline in some respects not terribly different from that of Rome (Kees 1961, 74). The great crown and temple domains—expanding in what was probably a fractal formation—were populated with prisoners of war and convicts. They were tied to the land in a manner not unlike that of the later Roman Empire. And also like the later Roman Empire, the Egyptian army now included many more foreigners: Sherdens, Libyans, Philistines, and others. The need to recruit these foreigners was exacerbated by the exemption of temple workers from military service, which required the drafting of one in every ten males (Vinogradov 1991, 191). This is but one more example of the generous gifts and privileges extended to the temples. Those who were not convicts or prisoners were exposed to high levels of taxation and requisition, especially in wartime (which was much of the imperial period). During the nineteenth dynasty, one official wrote: "Of the cultivators of the estate of Pharaoh which is under the authority of my lord, two have fled from the stable-master Neferhotpe as he beat them (probably when requisitioning). Now look! The fields now lie abandoned and there is no-one there to till them" (quoted in Kees 1977, 73; bracketed comment by Kees).

It is no wonder that there were flights from the land and a corresponding weakening of the agrarian—the most essential—basis of the empire. The government sought to ameliorate this problem by settling the land with priests, retired army officers, soldiers, and artisans, but the plan failed completely, probably because of the basic problem already identified, namely the monopoly of power held by a few families. The Pharaoh appears to have been under an obligation to placate these people, thus removing the fruits of empire from the vast majority of the Egyptian population. Frequent disturbances were a consequence of these practices, mainly in the form of hunger marches and sit-down strikes by workmen in the Necropolis (Kees 1977, 74).

But as argued here and in the case of Rome, the basic weakening of the state was not in the form of internal rebellion under such fractal formation, but of susceptibility to external conquest. Although not arguing from the formation of fractal-type inequalities, and hence lacking the kind of specificity suggested here, S. N. Eisenstadt nevertheless points to the general process of decline, giving ancient Egypt as an example: "Thus the centralized framework was preserved—but at the cost of aristocratization from within and conquest from without. The internal aristocratization resulted in concentrating economic productivity in semi-feudal units, shrinking internal trade activities, and incessantly withdrawing free resources from the central political institutions. These weakened the state until it was no longer able to withstand foreign invasion, and facilitated alliances between powers, war lords, and the invaders" (1963, 352).

This is one consequence of fractal-like expansion—benefit to the few—as the result of the concentration of economic activity in the hands of a small political or religious aristocracy and the consequent weakening of the state by the withdrawal of resources from it. In the case of Egypt, such weakening of the state resulted in a split of Lower Egypt from Upper Egypt at the end of the twentieth dynasty, ca. 1100 B.C. (Vinogradov 1991, 192). No longer would there be a unified Egypt. The ultimate consequence was a virtual colonial status for Egypt beginning with the Persian conquest of 525 B.C. and perpetuated through the Macedonian, Roman, Byzantine, Arab, Ottoman, and British periods of rule, until independence was once again achieved only in the mid-twentieth century. The culture and civilization of ancient Egypt, of course, have been long forgotten as ingredients of everyday life.

The Fall of the Aztecs and Incas

Although there would appear to be a serious disjunction between the sudden death of civilization by conquest exemplified by the Iberian conquests of the Americas and the preceding illustrations of this chapter, the differences may be more apparent than real. The dictum that Rome, Byzantium, or Egypt died a slow death via the political and socioeconomic processes detailed here while Cortés and Pizarro respectively, through superior military technology and native superstition, conquered and destroyed thriving Aztec and Inca civilizations establishes a false dichotomy that can be disproven. Certain of the same processes that yielded decline and fall in a gradual manner for Mesopotamian or Mediterranean civilizations also acted to weaken the indigenous American civilizations so that a mere handful of Spaniards could conquer empires with millions of residents.

The Aztecs present the less problematic case. Our concern with inequality and its consequences presents itself here, especially that inequality emergent from the likely fractal formation following rapid conquest that, in fact, we saw operative in the instances of Byzantium, Israel, and Egypt. The tragedy of the Aztecs (and the Incas as well) may have been the arrival of Cortés (and Pizarro) at a time when inequalities resulting from conquest were being institutionalized.

We know from the various written sources that the Aztec nobility gained considerable lands of their own upon expansion of the Aztec state (Conrad and Demarest 1984; N. Davies 1982; Soisson and Soisson 1987). It is likely that such expansion benefited the aristocracy disproportionately in comparison with other social classes. Indeed we have physical evidence of large preconquest holdings in the Valley of Oaxaca. As William Taylor notes, "The numerous pieces of land clearly owned by nobles without colonial grants and worked by hamlets of tenant farmers provide indirect evidence of the size and complexity of pre-Hispanic cacicazgos [noble holdings]. The serf-like status of entire barrios within the jurisdiction of a colonial cacique suggests that the residents were descendants of the *mayeques* (Indians of a subordinate class, below macehuales) who lived on these lands in pre-Hispanic times" (1972, 41).

At the same time, however, the hereditary landed nobility apparently did not have sufficient lands, even after the conquests, to satisfy the needs of their rapidly growing segment of the population, which multiplied exponentially as the result of the privilege of polygamy (Anawalt 1977, 1981). This population growth of the nobility was part of a general demographic expansion that witnessed an increase from 175,000 persons in the Early Aztec phase to nearly 1,000,000 in the Late Aztec period (Smith and Hodge 1994, 17). Their situation was complicated by another driving force for conquest, namely the need for captives for ritual slaughter at the temples of Tenochtitlan. An average of 15,000 persons were sacrificed each year in central Mexico, according to Sherburne Cook (1946). Many contemporary observers consider this figure to be conservative (Conrad and Demarest 1984, 47). The expanded number of priests, many from the lesser hereditary nobility, needed to prepare and sacrifice this large a number, became an "interest group" favoring imperial expansion in order to maintain and increase their sacrificial efforts. Thus there were strong expectations for expansion emanating from the nobility and priesthood. These expectations were reinforced by a more general population growth in the Valley of Mexico that required foodstuffs and other products to support the essentially nonproducing groups in Tenochtitlan (Conrad and Demarest 1984, 55). "The quest for wealth must be counted as a principal motive for the Aztec expansion. The desire to obtain enormous riches can clearly be seen on the tribute-lists and sumptuous costumes illustrated in the Codex Mendoza"

(Townsend 1992, 209). The constant search for riches represented a process of consumption with no end in sight. Captives and wealth had to be gained in war for sacrificial purposes of appeasing the gods and satisfying the needs of what Nigel Davies calls the "Potlatch state" (1980, 204). Vast amounts of tribute were given away at lavish ceremonies on frequent occasions. At the coronation of the great Aztec emperor Ahuitzotl, for example, a whole year's tribute was given away. Endless wars of conquest therefore had to be undertaken, with no instrumental purpose such as secure boundaries or ethnic commonality as justification. Yet it appears that the Aztec expansion under Moctezuma II had reached the limits of relatively easy expansion. The more readily conquered lands were now logistically too far away geographically to mount a relatively unencumbered campaign while the as yet unincorporated peoples near to Tenochtitlan were resisting mightily and successfully. One of these, the Tlaxcalans, were to later side with Hernando Cortés in his march on the Aztec cities.

A major response to this dilemma was for Moctezuma II to attempt to freeze the already existing inequality structures in favor of the hereditary nobility. Whereas under the previous emperor, Ahuitzotl, there had been a considerable degree of upward mobility of officials, warriors, and merchants who benefited from imperial expansion, now under a Moctezuma faced with the limits of such expansion, only the hereditary nobility would benefit. "Beginning at the top, his most sweeping (and unpopular) decrees purged the court of all counselors and leaders who were not of the highest birth. Some accounts even report that he executed all of the officials of his more socially liberal predecessor, Ahuitzotl. These 'reforms' were then extended downward into all levels of the administrative, military, and religious hierarchies" (Conrad and Demarest 1984, 66).

A rigid class structure resulted that had the likely consequence of easing the Spanish conquest of Central Mexico. Here one is reminded of Diocletian's reforms, which effectively ended geographic and social mobility in third-century Rome. Of course, one is also reminded of the freezing of the Venetian nobility. The hereditary nobility now simply wanted to maintain its holdings, while other social classes were strongly disaffected. Taylor tells us how nobles in areas such as the Valley of Oaxaca did not resist the Spaniards: "By submitting peacefully to the conquistador Francisco de Orozco in 1521, the Valley's Zapotec and Mixtec caciques [nobles] paved the way for special grants and rewards from the Spanish. Orozco himself is said to have promised to defend the caciques' traditional 'rights and prerogatives' in exchange for their support. Peaceful conquest spared the Valley of Oaxaca the loss of life and the grave social and psychological dislocations experienced by the Aztecs in the Valley of Mexico" (1972, 36).

The relative docility of many of the imperial nobility eased the Spanish conquest, in many ways reminiscent of the Roman elite as the Germanic tribes pressed on the borders of the Empire. This, along with the aid of opponents such as the Tlaxcalans, was to seal the fate of the Aztec Empire.

In the case of the Incas, the precise events of the Spanish conquest of course differ from those of the Aztecs in detail but still maintain a broad similarity not only to the destruction of the Aztec empire but, especially interestingly, to the decline and fall of Byzantium. The major differences between the fall of the two great empires of the Americas is the presence of a major civil war immediately preceding the arrival of Pizarro (as before the Byzantine defeat by the Seljuk Turks at Manzikert) and its absence prior to the arrival of Cortés. Yet the sources of this civil war reflect the same sorts of internal stresses in an expanding empire and one that is multi-ethnic, as was the case in Mesoamerica.

The civil war in the Inca empire arose in response to the problem of succession. Huáscar, the legal successor to the throne as the result of a sanctioned incestuous marriage, was challenged by the then emperor's favorite Atauhualpa, who did not have a legitimate claim to the throne. Sources on Inca history disagree as to Huáscar's fitness to rule, but generally agree on Atauhualpa's popularity with the army and his control of it (Conrad and Demarest 1984, 135). What further distinguished the two was Huáscar's apparent recognition that the limits of imperial expansion had been reached and that new resources for the empire had to come from internal sources. Geographically, the empire had apparently reached its limit, even with the excellent road network that had so surprised the Spaniards upon their arrival (Zuidema 1990). Marginal farmland was now being used in addition to the excellent land already farmed for centuries. In the more recent conquests before Pizarro's arrival, the Inca nobility had been seizing much of the conquered land, even as they dispersed the populations of these territories to other areas of the empire or settled them on their own estates (Metraux 1969, 93). This is the sort of scenario following expansion that we have seen in the instance of Rome, Byzantium, and the Aztec Empire.

Huáscar's solution, though, was unique to Inca civilization. He proposed to eliminate the immense drain on resources engendered by the maintenance of so much of the basic agricultural resources in the hands of dead rulers. Under the Inca system of split inheritance, the principal heir to the throne received the royal office and attendant rights and duties while other heirs received the dead monarch's person (mummified), possessions, and wealth to be tilled and guarded by his descendants in perpetuity (Conrad and Demarest 1984, 91). As noted in Chapter 3, the need for the new monarch to obtain his own resources constituted a major dynamic for imperial expansion. Many of the resources of the state were thus removed from cultivation and the tax rolls (generally in the form of the corvée), for they were now dedicated to the royal mummies in the form of care, rituals, and other types of labor. This was especially true of the overpopulated Cuzco region, the heart of the empire.

To understand this behavior, it is necessary to know that the Inca viewed their mummified kings as still alive, in the sense that their presence and rituals connected with them were required for the crops to grow and family life to proceed apace (Conrad and Demarest 1984, 11–17). One of the earliest accounts of the Incas, written by Father Bernabe Cobo, describes the accumulation of nonproductive wealth that this process incurred:

> The riches that were collected and gathered together just in the city of Cuzco, as the capital and court of the empire, were incredible; in it there were many important houses of the dead kings with all the treasure that each one had accumulated in his life. Since the one who ascended to the throne did not touch his predecessor's property and riches, which were given over to the *guaca* and service of the deceased, the new king had his own house built and acquired silver and gold and all the rest; thus the treasure in that city was immense, especially since each king tried to surpass all of his ancestors in having a richer, more illustrious and splendid house than they did. (Cobo 1979, 248)

Edward Hyams and George Ordish describe Huáscar's reaction to this accumulation: "He was disturbed—it is more likely to have been his accountants and the Apucama who were disturbed—by the drain on the state's resources of the increasingly important Cult of the Dead. The country had not only one living court to support; it had, grotesquely, the equally elaborate and costly 'dead' ones of Huayna Capac, Topa Yupanqui, Pachacuti, and possibly several others" (1963, 153).

Huáscar's position apparently struck at the heart of the nobility, for they were not only ideologically committed to the royal mummies, but derived much of their wealth through the care of these royal possessions. Thus they supported Atauhualpa in the civil war with Huáscar, so ensuring his defeat. Cobo's account suggests that even those who nominally supported Huáscar for reason of state or legitimacy of the succession deserted him because "he was lax in observing the veneration of the dead bodies of his ancestors and of the nobility that was to guard and serve these bodies; and for this reason his captains allowed themselves to be defeated by Atauhualpa and others came to Atauhualpa's side" (Cobo 1979, 166).

One of the first battles of the war was fought over the allegiance of the Cañaris, a people conquered by the previous emperor, Topa Yupanqui. They sided with Huáscar, thus provoking Atauhualpa's vengeance and the Cañaris's consequent support of the Spaniards in their war against the Incas under Atauhualpa and his successors (Conrad and Demarest 1984, 137). In this we see a similarity with the Aztec defeat—a powerful but temporarily vanquished people sides with the empire's opponents. A further similarity is the willingness of the native nobility to support the external conqueror for the sake of maintaining their holdings in both land and labor, as did the *curacas*, or elders, in Inca communities after the initial Spanish successes (Metraux 1970, 63).

A divided capital city also could not help but aid the Spanish. The feeble, perhaps nonexistent resistance of Cuzco to the Spaniards probably resulted not only from the hostile nobility but from the cruelties practiced by both sides in the civil war and its aftermath. "Huaman Poma [an early chronicler of the Incas] makes finally the revealing statement that the hatred for him [Huáscar] in Cuzco and the resulting disunity was so great that the city did not later defend itself adequately from the intruding Spaniards" (Brundage 1963, 276). Here we see a similarity with the apparent failure of the ancient Israelites to fiercely defend their capital city from the invading Assyrians, especially in contrast to Judah. This suggests the weakness of autocratic imperial rule, especially after a period of expansion and its consequent strain on resources, relations among classes, and incorporation of still hostile conquered peoples. As Geoffrey Conrad and Arthur Demarest put it in the case of the Incas,

> The Inca Empire of the early sixteenth century can be characterized as an impressive and highly ordered state, yet one increasingly pressed between internal problems and external limitations. Vast quantities of land and labor tied up in the hands of the dead, constant pressures for territorial growth, military disasters in the tropical forest, overextended lines of communication, provincial rebellions, increasing dependence on marginal land, governmental instability caused by friction between the emperor and high nobility, loss of traditional values, and a changing relationship between state and citizen—each would have been a serious difficulty in and of itself. In their combination and their interaction they were gutting Tawantinsuyu [the Inca name for the empire], destroying the substance beneath the glittering surface. By 1525, less than ninety years after Pachakuti's ascension, the situation had become critical. (1984, 133–34)

Unifying Themes and Differences

Here, in fact, is a broad similarity that covers not only the cases considered here, but extends beyond. Michael Doyle (1986, 217) for example, shows how the British imperial authorities made common cause with the landowning class in colonies such as Egypt. The willingness of landowners to support an external authority would appear to be for purposes of maintaining their holdings and labor supply. Similar arguments, but more from the perspective of caste, hold for the willingness of Hindu Brahmins to support the Muslim Moghul rulers (Menezes 1993) and the willingness of Slavic Christian landowners in Southeastern Europe conquered by the Ottoman Turks to convert to Islam in order to keep their holdings and thereby support an initially alien imperial rule.

If one seeks to emphasize the central theme of a majority of cases considered here, it is the growth of extreme inequality after an expansion that succeeds in benefiting only a small proportion of society—a particular economic, religious, or military sector expands at a differential rate, leaving others behind. Whether a similar process is currently happening in the United States and, even more broadly, in the industrialized West, is a matter to be considered in the concluding chapter. Yet the differences in processes of decline or regeneration also are apparent, as suggested by our examination of the three basic patterns of fractal formation and intense conflict in a multipolar setting. It is clear that there is no unique path of state destruction or dissolution, only certain predominant historical types.

Yet there may be one overarching mechanism through which inequality may affect the social fabric of all of these societies, as evidenced particularly by the population decline of the late Roman imperial period. Recently, it has been discovered that inequality is significantly related to health. Societies with more egalitarian income distributions tend to be healthier than those with greater income inequality. This finding has been demonstrated not only by means of comparisons between countries, but also within countries. For example a negative relationship has been found between income distribution and mortality within the fifty states of the United States (Wilkinson 1996, 79). Similarly, using a different unit of analysis, income and mortality demonstrate a negative degree of association among white U.S. males. Of course, life expectancies for blacks and whites are substantially different coincident with their differing levels of physical well-being (Wilkinson 1996, 99). Even individual communities demonstrate such an effect; for example, the immigrant town of Roseto, Pennsylvania, was noted for its low death rates during the earlier period of its founding by Italian-American migrants who experienced approximately the same level of occupation and income. The death rate from heart disease at that time was 40 percent lower than in neighboring communities, even when controlling for other possible causes. But as inequality inevitably increased, with the greater success of some persons in the first generation to be born into American society in comparison with others, the social fabric of the society began to erode and this distinct health advantage declined to the approximate level of the surrounding communities (Wilkinson 1996, 116–18).

PART III

Democracy

CHAPTER 5

The Timing of the "Social Problem" and Democratization

We turn now to an examination of democracy as a possible alternative to state collapse and in particular of the question why, along the path of state development, democracy was not chosen more frequently as a means of internal conflict resolution. After all, had not the early Roman Republic flirted with at least the forms of democratic governance, if not its substance? In this part of the book, we continue in Chapters 5, 6, and part of 7 the methods of comparative inquiry begun in Chapters 3 and 4, ending with a systematic analysis of the sources of democracy. History will then give way to systematic analyses of the contemporary period in the final part of Chapter 7.

Consider now the instance of Rome, a society that at one point at least, during the period of the Republic, appeared to be on the verge of democratization yet did not achieve it. There had been strong pressure from the plebeian class to open the political arena to increased participation from republican elements during the early third century B.C., yet this did not happen. As we know, Rome increasingly turned away from democracy, ultimately yielding the Empire (in Principate form), during the first century B.C. Let us examine the marked contrast between Rome and Athens, a polity that did indeed democratize and in fact provided a well-known model of democracy for Rome.

Athens and Rome

First, the early geopolitical circumstances differ strongly in the two instances. Whereas Athens found itself relatively isolated in the Attican peninsula (for a thorough treatment of the geography of Greece, see Tozer 1974), Rome was situated between two powerful nations. To the northwest were the

Etruscans, the rulers of Rome prior to the sixth century, and to the southeast, the Samnites. Even after the overthrow of the Etruscan Tarquin dynasty in 509 B.C., Etruria remained a considerable threat that required several wars to mitigate; especially lengthy was the subjugation of the powerful Etruscan city of Veii, ending in 396 B.C. In addition, Rome fought at least three wars with the Samnites between 343 and 290 B.C. before they were subjugated. Not only the Samnites but the other Latin cities of the peninsula required subduing—and much of this warfare followed the brief conquest of Rome by the Gauls in 390 B.C. Thus a virtually unbroken period of war preceded the critical stage of potential democratic development at the beginning of the third century. Athens, in its early period of democratic development, had nothing like Rome's combination of foreign rulers and repeated conflicts with extraordinarily dangerous opponents, one of which, the Gauls, destroyed almost the entire city.

During this period, the plebeians, who had now emerged as virtually a nation unto themselves within the Roman community, began to agitate for even greater political participation. The Concilium Plebis (council of plebeians) had in 287 B.C. received the right to legislate for the entire Roman people without consulting the Senate (Scullard 1991). Since the Roman Senate was the traditional policy-making body during the Republican period, this was a major change. Roman society seemed poised for a further breakthrough to complete representation or even direct democracy. But in 280 B.C. Pyrrhus, the great Hellenistic King of Epirus, attacked Rome, thinking to unite the Hellenistic cities in Italy and some indigenous Italian tribes in the interior. This was the first of several great wars, most famously the Punic Wars (264–202 B.C.). Thus the Senate, traditionally responsible for the financing and general conduct of war, was called upon to resume its prominent role. A renewal of the threat to Rome in the form of the most bloody and dangerous wars heretofore confronted effectively ended the drive toward democratization. By the time of the Imperial period, of course, it was much too late. Incessant warfare and the increasing power placed in the hands of the emperor in order to satisfy the needs of the Empire precluded any such efforts. After the civil wars of the first century B.C. a growing reliance on the military instead of the Senate also became a hallmark of the Principate and Imperial periods; the military increasingly became the arbiters of who should be emperor (Jones 1964, 1966).

The geopolitics of the steady Roman expansion and relative Athenian circumscription had clear societal ramifications. As M. I. Finley remarks:

In the first place, the regularity, scale, duration, and geographical spread of Roman campaigning were incomparable with Greek practice, and the differences were steadily magnified as the Romans moved relentlessly from subjugating their neighbours to the conquest of Italy and then of the inhabited world. Secondly, the Roman citizen-militia was totally integrated into the hierarchical structure of society, as the Athenian was not. It is necessary only to recall that command of the armies was automatically the duty of the consuls (or their surrogates when required), so that "consul" and "general" were synonyms, as was not the case in Greece, and the consul-generals had *imperium*, a power with sacral overtones that Polybius could not express because he had no Greek word that was suitable. And thirdly, *imperium* was but one expression of the central place of war in the religion, including the formal ritual system, of the Roman state. (1983, 129–30)

And there were specific direct political implications of this view. In Rome:

there was also no separation between the civil and the military departments of government. Not only was the army (though not usually the navy) a citizen's militia but the commanding officers were the ranking civilian officials. . . . The ten Athenian *strategoi* were elected annually and their roster in the fifth century includes the best known political leaders of the time, chosen to hold the highest military office because of their political influence, not the other way round. In Rome, Polybius tells us (6.19.4), no one could hold a political office until he had served in ten annual military campaigns. (Finley 1983, 58)

But the differential frequency of war is not the only critical variable here. Resolution of the "social problem," and more especially its timing in relation to war, is of key importance. And here we have an even more profound distinction between Athens and Rome. By the "social problem" I mean the pressures for reform resulting from existing massive societal inequalities. Small inequalities are tolerated in the vast majority of societies. Massive inequalities generally require some political interventions, if only to legitimize them by means of a religious or overtly political ideology. The strong theory of the divine right of kings of the pharaoh god-kings of ancient Egypt is a case in point. More recent theories of the divine right of kings or of fascism provide additional examples.

Failing an ideological justification for inequality, political and/or socioeconomic intervention may be required. In the case of the English peasantry, for example, the source of the pressure was slowly removed over time as the result of enclosures and an increasing commercialization of agriculture that led either to emigration or to an increased urban industrial population made up of the dispossessed peasantry (Moore 1966). In most instances, however, the source remains intact and prompts some form of direct political action. In Athens, the Solonic reforms relieved the debt burden of many, if not the majority, of farmers. The inequality of wealth between those with little or no land and the larger landowners with sizable farms diminished. This resolution of the social problem in the Athenian context was apparently sufficient to insure the absence of later demands for redistribution in Athens. As David Stockton puts it, "After Solon's day in the early sixth century, we can discern none of these moves to redistribute property or cancel debts which were so common elsewhere in other ancient states which were controlled by non-democratic governments" (1990, 55). It is also clear that this resolution of the social problem preceded the onset of serious occasions of war, at least serious enough to warrant building the city walls of Athens: according to Chester Starr, "Athens did not have a city wall until the days of Pisistratus, if then" (1991, 340). Pisistratus was a late-sixth-century B.C. tyrant who implemented an aggressive foreign policy, especially in the neighborhood of the Hellespont. Prior to that time the incidence of war apparently was not frequent and/or severe enough to warrant the building of fortifications to protect the city.

The point here of course is a resolution of the social problem *before* the serious incidence of war. For Rome on the other hand, the reverse was true, perpetuating oligarchic control.

In Rome, the particular oligarchic agency strengthened by war was the Senate, as we have seen, made stronger especially by its role in the Pyrrhic and Punic Wars. By the time the social problem was to be confronted, especially during the time of the Gracchi, the Senate had sufficient power that it could continue its oligarchic control despite the most serious opposition. In contrast, when Ephialtes sought to eliminate the important powers of the Athenian Areopagus, an elite council roughly equivalent to the Roman Senate, he was able to do so despite the prestige achieved by the Areopagus in directing the Athenian war efforts leading to the victory at Salamis in 467 B.C., some eighteen years earlier (Stockton 1990, 46).

The Gracchi sought to ameliorate the social ills that accompanied the indebtedness of large numbers of Roman farmers. In particular, as discussed in Chapter 4, there was rampant growth in large estates at the expense of those who held moderate or small holdings. Slavery became more widespread, especially on the large estates, and there was a concomitant decline in the number of those who could, as free citizens, serve in the army. The social problem as it evolved in Rome posed a threat to the security of the state not only because of the diminution in the core army size but because of slave revolts in Sicily and Asia Minor (ca. 133 B.C.). In the face of a similar pattern of slave revolts and decline in the number of citizen fighting men, the Spartans had redistributed land during the third century B.C. (Rostovtzeff 1960, 95–96). Tiberius Gracchus attempted to implement such a law (really only a reaffirmation of existing law that limited the size of land holdings). This effort polarized Rome, with the rich finding support among a majority of Senators, and the poor finding favor in the popular assembly. Ultimately Tiberius was murdered by partisans of the Senate. His brother, Gaius Gracchus, continued the efforts at reform, ultimately also to be killed by supporters of the Senate. This division in Roman society between rich and poor was to be continued for the most part in conflict between *populares*, or supporters of the people, and *optimates*, or supporters of the Senate. In the end, after much civil conflict, the Senate prevailed.

England

It is revealing to examine in some detail another instance, one where we have a detailed historical record. The case in point is that of England in the mid- to late seventeenth century, a critical period in the formation of English democracy, for it was during this time that Parliament rose to ascendancy as a major decision-making body and the monarchy was forced to accept additional limitations on its prerogatives that simply had not existed earlier. The current constitutional monarchy was built upon this foundation.

There are two major events in this period, the English Civil War(s) (or the Great Rebellion) of 1642-49 and the Glorious Revolution of 1688. Each was to make its own contribution to the parliamentary ascendancy. Especially crucial here is the emergence of this ascendancy *before* the great power wars of the late seventeenth and early eighteenth centuries, namely, the War of the League of Augsburg (1688-97) and the War of the Spanish Succession (1702-13). The latter was the most intense and devastating war of the times, and its influence on parliamentary authority was profound.

Interpretations of the origins of the English Civil War vary, but the outcome was certain. This was not merely parliamentary ascendancy, as was to result from the later Glorious Revolution, but parliamentary supremacy. The defeat of the royalist cause left parliament in command of the country, although the army under Oliver Cromwell was to emerge later as the arbiter of all important decision making until the death of the Lord Protector in 1658.

The question of the particular social problem addressed by the Civil War converges with the differing interpretations of origins. Richard Tawney, in a famous essay (1941, reprinted 1960), points to the rise of the wealthier gentry as a source of opposition to the crown. Following this insight, others, such as Hugh Trevor-Roper (1960), see the lower gentry as the major locus of opposition. J. H. Hexter (1960) finds fault with both formulations as too strongly rooted in the economic circumstances of both types of gentry. A review of these and others theories is found in Ashton 1978.

More recently, a consensus appears to have emerged concerning two points. First, there was a division between "Court" and "Country" concerning cultural and political mores and—most importantly—appropriate forms of government

(Briggs 1983). Certainly the Puritan ethic was firmly established in parts of the Country while the Court was deemed to be licentious in the extreme. Second, "divisions within the ruling class were more significant in generating political conflict than any struggles between it and other classes" (Speck 1985, 196).

If the traditional notions of class conflict do not apply, then what does? Here the factors of population growth, the emergence of dwarf holdings, and the impoverishment of the lesser gentry while the greater gentry grew more wealthy are relevant. As population grows, middle-sized holdings tend to diminish in number while both larger holdings (but not the very largest) and smaller ones increase in number. This is precisely what was found in studies of Chinese landholdings (see Table 4.1) and those of Cambridgeshire (Spufford 1974; 1976). Effectively, the wealthier among the gentry grow in both number and size of holdings as they buy the land given up by impoverished peasants, who then add to the number of landless peasants. Meanwhile, lesser gentry become impoverished. A divided society emerges, in Paul Slack's (1985) terms.

An indisputable consequence of all of this was the expansion of the gentry. They owned 25 percent of the land in the mid-fifteenth century but by the late seventeenth century they owned 45 percent, in part as a result of the dissolution of the monasteries, which benefited the gentry more than any other class (Slack 1985, 183). Their numbers expanded as well. Whereas "there were probably roughly 5,000 knights, esquires and gentlemen in the mid-fifteenth century: by 1625 there were more than twice as many" (Slack 1985, 183). The result was thus a much larger political and social elite.

During the period from the mid-sixteenth century to the 1640s, the general English population more than doubled. A consequence of this population growth was an increase in grain prices and inflationary pressure that drained some gentry fortunes. Population growth among the gentry was greater than that of the population as a whole (Hollingsworth 1965). As a consequence of this, combined with primogeniture, which sent many younger sons to the towns and to London, competitiveness grew among the gentry. According to Lawrence Stone, "The hostility of the majority of the peers to Charles I in 1640 can be ascribed in large measure to the failure of the King to multiply jobs to keep pace with the increase of titles, and to the restriction of the patronage system to a shrinking court coterie" (1965, 742–43). The increase in landless gentry led some to side with the king in the coming conflict, perhaps in hope of a future reward should he prevail in combat. As Alan Everitt notes, "The situation [in 1648] seems to have been aggravated by the remarkable surplus of landless younger sons in the king's armies, with no estate to root them in the countryside, no career but the army open to them, and little to support their pretensions to gentility" (1969, 49). Long-term rural unrest also was found to be associated with this demographic increase (Cornwall 1977).

More generally, as we saw in Chapter 1 and will examine in greater detail in Chapter 7, increased agricultural density and land inequality yield democracy. The question now is the particular way that this relationship plays out in the English context. If elements of the Country, as they emerged to greater land ownership, wealth, increased education (Wrightson 1982), and concern for public affairs, had been well received at the Court, then it is possible that the "Great Rebellion" might have been averted. Even the Solonic reforms as a major societal transformation in giving political weight to land ownership barely averted serious civil strife in Athens. But the English monarchy was inattentive to this divide between it and much of the countryside, and so the Civil War followed, from this and other sources that we shall discuss.

While the Civil War established parliamentary supremacy on a temporary basis, with the gentry pretty much in command, it was the Glorious Revolution of 1688 that was to make it permanent. The restoration of 1660 had to all appearances restored the full and perhaps even the divine right of monarchy. Yet when the first challenge to the culture and especially the religious mores of the nation came in the form of James II, the monarchy quickly gave way to the beginnings of the constitutional form we know today. James's intolerance, his attempt not only to gain equality for Catholics but, to all appearances, to slowly effect their supremacy was too much for the Anglican gentry. When a son was born to him in 1688, thus assuring a Catholic line of succession, the Anglican gentry joined with the landed aristocracy and invited William of Orange to come to England. This was the beginning of the end for James II, whose political life was to conclude finally at the battle of the Boyne in 1690 (Briggs 1983; Morrill 1988).

The Bill of Rights and the Act of Settlement constituted in effect a contract between king and people and paved the way for William's successor. They also most importantly established parliamentary supremacy (Morrill 1985, 204) or, as Paul Langford puts it, "the concept of a rightful king who owed his title to a *de facto* decision of Parliament, but not to the *de jure* ordinance of heaven" (1988, 401). The will of the nation expressed through Parliament was to be decisive in choosing the monarch and in limiting his or her decision-making power. Parliament's traditional control of the purse strings was reasserted. Extraparliamentary taxation was declared illegal, and the Bill of Rights explicitly required that Parliament must approve any peacetime standing army (Briggs 1983, 155). These provisions were to have important consequences in the years to follow. Parliament's role was emphasized again in the Triennial

Act of 1694, which specified that Parliament must meet regularly, at least once every three years.

Parliament was now established as the source of decision-making authority. And such authority was sorely required to fund the coming wars with Louis XIV. It was a fascinating concatenation of events that established parliamentary supremacy and at the same time set in motion the war-related process that would ultimately guarantee that supremacy. The invitation of William of Orange was the signal event that set off both processes. William accepted the throne, indeed fought James II for it, largely because he needed British resources to defend the Netherlands against Louis XIV, then Europe's most powerful monarch. He further was willing to accept limitations on that monarchy precisely in order to obtain the funds from Parliament that would be required to successfully prosecute the war against Louis. Here we now have the precise nexus between the establishment of ascendancy of a democratic institution *after* resolution of the social problem and its continued buttressing by war processes.

Basically a new concept arose, that of the national debt. The cost of the wars of the League of Augsburg and the Spanish Succession was approximately £150 million, compared to expenditures in peacetime of at most £2 million per year. Taxation was increased, but about one-third of the total sum required was met by borrowing. The level of borrowing during this period was so heavy that essentially a new infrastructure was required, in contrast to earlier times when sums could be obtained from the financial community on an ad hoc basis.

Thus the Bank of England was created in 1694. Everything depended on Parliamentary approval. The land-tax, the basic guarantee of the taxpayers' commitment to the national debt, was only cautiously voted for one year at a time. There was much debate and haggling over renewal of the customs and excise duties. Parliament was very jealous of its prerogatives in matters of finance. As Langford states:

The credit-worthiness of the new regime, based as it was on a parliamentary title, was negligible without clear understanding that the propertied classes would ultimately be prepared to foot the bill. Without a matching recognition on the part of the regime that it must closely collaborate with those classes and their representatives, no such understanding could exist. The National Debt and all it entailed was built on this essential nexus of interest linking an illegitimate dynasty, the financial world, and the taxpaying public. (1988, 404)

Parliament effectively constituted the institutional nexus that Langford refers to. As wars followed each other decade after decade, governments found it more and more difficult to avoid bureaucracy. At times, the main function of new taxation was simply to pay the interest charges on the debt. Parliament's role as the institutional embodiment of Britain's fledgling democracy was now secure. This outcome could have been effected only *after* resolution of the social problem and *before* British involvement in major warfare and its consequent national debt.

The history of democracy in the United States appears to have followed a similar route. This time, instead of Parliament, it was the Continental Congress that was jealous of its prerogatives. Of course, the United States did not inherit the social problems of the European states that grew out of serfdom and feudalism. But having no wish to exchange domination by king for that of any other single, commanding personage (in the form of George Washington, for example), Congress sought to assert its authority. It was successful in no small measure because of Washington's own willingness to support the Congress even when it was bankrupt (Schwartz 1983). Perhaps the legislative attitude toward the growing authority of a single individual is best exemplified by the commentary of the Provincial Congress of the Colony of New York, a few weeks after Washington's appointment as commander-in-chief: "[We] have the fullest assurances, that whenever this important contest shall be decided... you will cheerfully resign the important deposit committed into your hands, and reassume the character of our worthy citizen" (*Virginia Gazette*, July 15, 1775).

Clearly, it was the determination of colonial legislatures, especially Congress, to retain their authority that helped put American democracy on a firm foundation. The requirement for financial authorization by Congress likely strengthened the fledgling American democracy in its separation of powers and most importantly in its republican aspect.

France

Now we turn to one of the more interesting and hence perennial questions of comparative history, namely why France did not democratize at the same time that England did, especially given very similar sorts of historical trajectories and cultural influences emanating from Western Christianity and the tension between church and state. Our answer lies in the same sorts of considerations of the timing of resolution of the social problem in relation to war.

The dimensions of the social problem were more acute in the case of France for several reasons. First, population growth was having its effects on both nobility and peasantry. In Chapter 6 we will examine in some detail the processes of plot subdivision in Languedoc and a concomitant decline of the middle peasantry. According to Richard Bonney, the poorest peasants there had by

1653 become the "crushing majority (228 out of 262)" (1991, 384). This process must have been mirrored in the case of the nobility, for in the absence of primogeniture, noble holdings must also have diminished in size. As Bonney puts it, "Noble estates in France tended to fragment because there was no generalized law of entail. Primogeniture does not seem to have been generally practised even in the area of written law in the Midi, where inheritance arrangements favoured the unilateral settlement on one child" (1991, 380). Here we have one of the critical differences between England and France. Not only was the "peasant problem" ameliorated in England by the institution of enclosures and a consequent rapid urbanization and ultimately immigration as well, but the presence of primogeniture led to a secure noble class, at least for the first-born who inherited the large estates. To be sure, as a consequence, there were large numbers of landless nobility, as we have seen, but as England's cities grew and possibilities for emigration grew as well, they could be absorbed peacefully. Some, as we also have seen, entered the king's armies in the Civil War, a process that had its counterparts in the rise of France. But the central difference resides in the emergence of a secure landed nobility and gentry in England and its absence in of France.

An insecure and in many instances land-poor French elite combined with the presence of increasingly impoverished peasants had several consequences. First, as James Collins (1994) points out, there was the ever-present problem of order in Early Modern France. We know of frequent outbreaks of violence in taverns or riots over food distribution throughout rural France, especially at times of poor harvests (Bercé 1990). The disturbances of 1675 in Brittany constitute one such example. More serious than most, they contained elements of conflict between the old nobility—the *noblesse d'epée*—and the newer nobility, ensconced in their positions by the monarchy—the *noblesse de robe*, in which the former blamed the newer, judicial nobles for having instituted and supported the rebellion (Collins 1994, 207). A consequence of the violence, whether on smaller or larger scale, was the search by the nobility—of whatever background—for means of establishing order, in rural France and sometimes in urban France as well. For many who lacked the resources of large estates, either as refuge or as sources of funding to pay armed retainers, the only resort was the crown, which also had a vested interest in public order, if only for purposes of obtaining the *taille* or other forms of taxation and moneys to be granted the king (Collins 1994, 157).

Reliance on the crown by the nobility was not found only in the need for order common to both. The crown performed another extremely important function, by serving as the *source* of ennobling for those who sought to enter the aristocracy. During the period from 1515 to 1665, the number of offices in France increased from 4,000 to 46,000. A consequence of this vast increase was a concomitant increase in the *noblesse de robe* as the result of monarchical sale of these offices. Thus, a significant proportion of the nobility were not only indebted to the crown for their titles but also for the salaries that maintained their lifestyles (Bonney 1990, 340). One would expect therefore, a disproportionate increase in the *noblesse de robe* and a decrease in the older *noblesse d'epée*, as their estates were subdivided and those that could not support themselves went into the king's civil or military service. There were, in fact, "indications that the property holdings of the old established families in the Valentinois-Diois region stagnated or even declined" (Hickey 1986, 160). With the exception of the few older noble families that could maintain their estates (e.g., the de Chaulnes, Guémadeuc, and Lavardin families in Brittany) one would also expect an increasing absence of independence of the nobility. And this is precisely what we find, a "progressive weakening of noble institutions" (Hickey 1986, 152–53) beginning in the early seventeenth century, judging by meetings of the Council of the Nobility. Whether one can conclude that the "apparent decline in the legal apparatus of the second estate was indicative of a general demographic or economic crisis among the old nobles" (Hickey 1986, 153) is unclear. Nevertheless, the *institutions* of the nobility were unmistakably in decline, as further indicated by the increasing need for the nobility to meet with the clergy, since the nobles were incapable of operating as an independent body.

It was in the time of Louis XIV that the nobility (i.e., nobles as individuals) developed a secure grip on high clerical and governmental offices. As Perry Anderson states,

In the Church, all archbishops and bishops were of noble origin by the second half of the [eighteenth] century, and most abbacies, priories and canonries were controlled by the same class. In the Army, the top military commands were solidly occupied by grandees; purchase of companies by *roturiers* was banned in the 1760's, when it became necessary to have unambiguous noble descent in order to qualify for the rank of officer. The aristocratic class as a whole retained a rigorous late feudal statute: it was a legally defined order of some 250,000 persons, which was exempt from the bulk of taxation and enjoyed a monopoly of the highest echelons of the bureaucracy, judiciary, clergy and army. (1974a, 107–8)

One of the most important mechanisms for cementing relations between the state and the French nobility was the army. And, here the wars of Louis XIV were to play a most important role. From the Franco-Spanish War, which arose from the Thirty Years War and ended only in 1659, through the War of Devolution against Spain in 1667–68, the Dutch War of 1672–79, the War of the

League of Augsburg of 1688-97, and most importantly the War of the Spanish Succession (1702-13), France was hardly at peace during the latter half of the seventeenth century and the beginning of the eighteenth century. It was during this time that the military became a profession for the land-poor nobility. As J. Russell Major puts it, "Louis's numerous wars led him to increase the size of this army to 350,000 men during the course of his reign.... He managed to transform the half-feudal army of his predecessors into a well-organized, disciplined force commanded by loyal officers who owed their positions directly or indirectly to him. Its very size ensured employment for nobles who sought military adventure and removed the temptation of any magnate to raise the banner of revolt" (1980, 670). Indeed military affairs also became a reason for ennoblement (Hickey 1986, 158), thus further reinforcing the nexus between the military and the nobility and, of course, the crown itself, under whose auspices the military served.

It is clear that the problem of the crumbling in size of landholdings was not resolved effectively for either nobles or peasants prior to this full-scale entry of France into continental warfare, culminating in what was the most intense war of the eighteenth century—the War of the Spanish Succession (McKay and Scott 1983). Hence, in the instance of France, a difficult social problem affecting both nobility and peasantry had not been resolved prior to the onset of major warfare. And it was warfare that would solidify the nexus of dependency between crown and nobility, thus perpetuating the social problem until the upheaval of 1789 imposed its own unique form of resolution for crown, nobility, and peasantry alike.

Spain

Another instance in which war and militarism preceded resolution of the social problem is that of Spain. And here, as in Rome, we also witness the thwarting of democracy as the result of that militarism.

As expected, warfare is the avenue for the introduction of militarism. And because of the strength of the absolutist tradition in Spanish history, the possibilities for democracy appear much later than in Britain or France. First, Napoleonic control of Spain evolved into the Peninsular War (1801-14), pitting the French against the Spanish and their English supporters. A consequence of this warfare was the increased prestige of generals and their entrance into politics at the war's end. This increased influence was facilitated by the decay of the royal bureaucracy as the result of the Napoleonic occupations (R. Herr 1989).

Influence of the generals was further enhanced by the Carlist Wars that began in 1839. These conflicts pitted urban liberals against rural traditionalists, with the issue of the possible accession to the throne of Don Carlos, King Ferdinand VII's brother, the central point of contention. As in 1814-20, when the generals were able to force unwanted policies on Ferdinand, the generals again became the arbiters of politics. They were used as political swords by the main political groups—the *moderados*, upper-middle-class oligarchic liberals, and the *progresistas*, lower-middle-class politicians who were prepared to use the discontented urban masses for their own advantage. Finally, in 1854, a group of disaffected generals led by Leopoldo O'Donnell revolted, leading to the formation of a new government headed by the Duke of Victory (Livermore 1966, 380). This was to be only the first of several instances of instability, culminating in a restored constitutional monarchy in 1875.

The period 1875-98 was one of stability, but then two war-related events introduced difficulties for the monarchy. The first was the Spanish-American War, whose losses cast the monarchy in disrepute. The second was the deepening involvement of Spain in Morocco, leading to another disaster for Spanish arms, namely the defeat at Annual in 1921. Two years later Primo de Rivera staged his *pronunciamento* and took over the government. This was the beginning of overt right-wing ideology that of course culminated in the quasi-fascist government of Francisco Franco at the end of the Civil War in 1939. Thus the military was associated with increasingly right-wing ideological takeover of the government, despite the efforts at democracy by liberals and some socialists during this period.

What was the nature of the social problem in Spain? It was an agrarian problem that had its roots first in the *reconquista* and then in the *desamortizacion*. Both were to lead to a severe agrarian problem in southern Spain that it made it uniquely receptive to the rise of fascism.

The *reconquista*, or reconquest of Spain from the Moors by the Kingdoms of Castile and Aragon, proceeded in stages. Most rapid of all the stages was that which occurred between 1212 and 1250 (Malefakis 1970, 55), in which almost all of southern Spain was retaken. A consequence of this rapid conquest was (as our theory would suggest) the formation of large estates. The Castilian kings had placed themselves under obligation to military orders, so that when the conquest took place, the monarchy was obliged to yield much of that land to the military orders and individual nobles. Thus much of southern Spain became home to large estates, much larger and with greater land concentration than under the Moors.

The *desamortizacion* was to further aggravate this already large degree of land concentration. In the early nineteenth century, the landholdings of the

Church were put up for sale, and entail, the prohibition against the sale of noble landholdings, was lifted. The result was the vast increase in land concentration, again especially in the south of Spain. Speed of acquisition in this region is indicated by the fact that nine years after the sale of Church lands had begun in 1836, 65.6 percent of such land had been bought in the south, whereas only 49.9 percent had been purchased in the rest of Spain. The result was a region with vastly larger holdings than the remainder of the country (Malefakis 1970, 21). It was also a region that was to demonstrate some of the most severe agrarian problems, culminating in an eagerness of the landholding elite to welcome the invading armies (from North Africa) of Francisco Franco in the opening stages of the Civil War in 1936.

Spain had developed a unique form of peasant agitation associated with rural anarchosyndicalism. In the early twentieth century, before the formation of the republic, there was an extraordinary increase in membership of rural labor organizations. Around the turn of the century, the myth of the general strike and the apparent success of several institutional walkouts led to a wave of peasant unrest in 1903–4. After World War I, the Bolshevik Revolution in Russia and rumors of the possible redistribution of property influenced the even more intense agitation of 1918–20. The stage was now set for the rise of Primo de Rivera and shortly thereafter, Francisco Franco.

With these comparisons completed, we expand the historical purview to include civilizations that not only did not democratize, such as Rome, but also failed to form into coherent states at all, the Germano-Roman and Abbasid empires. Consideration of these failures should help considerably in understanding the further consequences of societal inequalities.

CHAPTER 6

Failures of State Formation and Democratization: The Germano-Roman and Abbasid Empires

Germany provides an excellent illustration of several processes detailed previously. Indeed if one were to seek an exemplar of early processes of state decay and hindrances to democratic development, one would be hard pressed to find a better case study. These failures occurred despite an extraordinarily promising beginning; Germany was the most powerful state in Europe between the tenth and twelfth centuries and appeared to be well on the way to solving its internal problems (Holborn 1959, 15). The early failure to develop into a unified German state will be considered first, followed by an examination of the rise of Prussia and the reasons for the death of early democratic institutions that under other circumstances could have flourished. The chapter concludes with an appraisal of the history of the Abbasid Empire.

Failure of State Formation West of the Elbe

German history illustrates the importance of the timing of fractal formation. If it occurs early, over a fairly continuous territorial space, as in the case of Prussia, then—if other conditions are also present (e.g., primogeniture)—there may be a good prognosis for state formation. If, on the other hand, the space is discontinuous, especially if the divisions follow ethnic or language lines, then the prognosis is less positive. As Hajo Holborn puts it, "Germany did not grow as did the Roman Empire, or medieval and modern France, from a single point, the city of Rome or the Île de France, around which in ever widening circles the realms expanded. Nature did not endow Germany with such unity" (1959, 12).

This poor prognosis is especially true if fractal expansions occur after only a weak state has been established (as in the instances of Egypt and Israel in their later expansions followed by decline). The absence of primogeniture will tend to augment state weakness considerably.

Both France and Germany were heirs to the Carolingian kingdom of the ninth and tenth centuries. As we know, France, despite a fitful start toward centralized monarchy, especially in comparison with England, achieved united statehood, whereas Germany west of the Elbe did not, until it was finally absorbed politically by Prussia in 1871. Even in Carolingian times, we see one element in particular that led to that outcome, an element we recognize from our earlier treatment of the decay of certain civilizations, especially the Egyptian. This is the early tendency to favor religious institutions at the expense of the state. We noted in Egypt the favoritism toward the Temple of Amon, which ultimately rendered the pharaohs politically dependent on that religious establishment. Indicative of that dependence was the granting of exemptions to the temple elite in the form of either taxes, military service, or both.

The Carolingian monarchs engaged in similar practices, which we also identified in the later Roman Empire (Western half). There, tax exemptions for the clergy and monasteries and further exemptions from military service placed both these burdens of state support on an increasingly impoverished peasantry. As a consequence, peasants fled the large Roman estates, sometimes joining the barbarian tribes at the edge of the empire. But the greater the number that fled, the heavier the burden on those who remained, thus increasing the incentives for the remainder to flee, ever further weakening the agrarian base of the imperial economy and increasing the proportion of Germans in the army in place of Romans.

It was under the later Saxon rulers of the German Kingdom that immunities and other exemptions became rife. As Geoffrey Barraclough remarks on the policies of the kings Otto I, II, and III (936–1002), "The basis of Ottonian policy towards the Church was the withdrawal of bishoprics and abbeys and their lands from the ordinary ambit of secular administration" (1984, 33). Under Otto I the grant of immunity became a general instrument of policy, motivated by the protection and support this generated from the Church. At the same time, royal control of the churches and monasteries also was assured, for in bringing the churches under royal administration, these monarchs withdrew them from the control of dukes and counts. Sometimes bishops and abbots were invested with the powers of counts, further involving the Church in the realm of the state. Landed wealth also was conferred on the Church, carrying with it immunities from taxation and other responsibilities. How deeply the concept of Church immunity was embedded in German rule of that period is revealed by the fact that after the death of Otto I in 973 "the privilege of immunity was so generally assumed that mention of it was frequently omitted in charters" (Barraclough 1984, 35). So interdependent had the German Church and Saxon rule become that 74 percent of the forces in Otto II's Italian campaign of 981 was supplied by German abbeys and bishoprics. And this not only symbolizes the reliance of the Saxon rulers on the Church but also foreshadows the future disaster that the Italian connection, with its strong sacerdotal overtones, would have for the German state.

A contrast between England and Germany proves useful here. "In England there were far more secular than ecclesiastical barons—the ratio was about four to one—whereas in Germany the ratio was about six to one the other way: the new estate of imperial princes comprised about ninety ecclesiastics and only sixteen lay princes, a figure which later rose to thirty" (Fuhrmann 1986, 173).

The Investiture Contest clearly demonstrated the consequences of this intimate reliance of the German state upon the Church, a reliance in which the balance began to shift to near dominance by the Church. It is not the province of this treatment to detail all of the issues involved in this critical controversy in German history, which involved the issue of lay investiture of church officials, hence the name given to it.[1] However, Henry III's reign was marked by his "deposition of three popes in 1046 and his installation of several Germans as bishops of Rome; of the seven Germans who have become pope, five reigned between 1046 and 1058" (Fuhrmann 1986, 43). But beginning in 1075, this controversy was to draw both Henry IV of Germany and Pope Gregory VII into a protracted conflict that proved to be extremely destructive for the German state. One of the bases of the conflict was the high level of control over the German Church under Henry II and Henry III. Essentially, the monarchy's early fostering of the Church and its claim to overlordship, now inherited by Henry IV, had become intolerable to the papacy; any further ambitions to connect crown and Church were intolerable. The connection between Germany and Italy became "funereal" (using Barraclough's term, 1984, 113) precisely because of the political incorporation of portions of Italy into the Frankish kingdom in Carolingian times, which was later reinforced by the conquest of the Italian kingdom by Otto I in 951 (Tabacco 1989, 165). Italy was now subordinated to Germany politically, but it was the religious controversy that was to so deeply embroil Germany in Italian affairs, much to her own ruin.

Gregory VII simply could not tolerate the emerging overlordship of the German state—now virtually a theocracy—over the German Church. Sacerdotal qualities claimed for the German monarchy—and more generally the divine right of kings—were under attack by the papacy, as Gregory came to support the concept of an elective monarchy. In this system, the real sources of authority in the kingdom would be the electors, namely the princes. A substantial, perhaps critical weakening of the German state would ensue as a result of the elimination of the hereditary claim to succession and with it the additional undermining of legitimacy by the withdrawal of divine right. The scale of warfare mirrored the importance of the issues. German church and lay society were split between supporters of king and pope. Marc Bloch, the great historian of feudalism put it well: "The very bitterness of the quarrel which thus divided the German kings and the Curia can, in its turn, only be explained by the fact that those kings were also emperors. While the popes could reproach other sovereigns only with the oppression of particular churches, they found in the successors of Augustus and Charlemagne rivals for the mastery of Rome, of the Holy See, and of Christendom" (1961, 2: 389).

This conflict between church and state was resolved finally through a compromise, the Concordat of Worms of 1122. But for understanding the trajectory of German history, the Investiture Contest had profound consequences that extended well beyond the contest itself.

A first consequence was the growth both of inequality within the nobility and of the feudal political structure that supported that inequality. "A great increase in the wealth and power of a few lords" has been noted (Barraclough 1984, 138). The civil wars associated with the Investiture Contest drove small nobles to larger ones for protection. Others, who had been dependent on the crown for protection, now also sought the protection of the stronger nobility. The result was a rapid structural differentiation (in itself promoting inequality; Midlarsky 1982) in the ranks of the aristocracy and a rapid growth of feudal structures. At the head of such structures stood the princes, who held not only great material wealth based on vast allodial estates but also political power over counts and lower-level freemen who had previously owed allegiance to the king. A vast hierarchichal structure now came into being, similar to that which already existed in France.

A consequence of this process, of course, was that while the princes gained, the crown lost. The royal government had been based on a large class of freemen, at the level of both the county and the nation, who were the principal source for the military; this was especially true of Saxony, where many of the early monarchs were born. The county organization was basically a group of freemen who would act at the king's behest in royal business under the count, the king's representative. All of this was drastically changed. Instead of direct access to a free population, the king had to deal with an extensive hierarchy with a prince at its head. An elective kingship, of course, augmented this power shift considerably. The Concordat of Worms formalized the power of princes, for it was they, in the form of a commission of twelve, six appointed by Henry IV and six by Gregory VII, who were to draw up the settlement.

Another far-reaching consequence of this extended conflict was the destruction and alienation of the crown lands. After seventeen years of civil war ended in 1092, the possessions of the crown had been reduced to shreds and patches. Henry IV had to grant large portions of his land to potential allies to insure their support during the Investiture Contest. The later monarchs did nothing to remedy this situation. As a consequence, "the weakening of the material foundations of the monarchy was, together with the strengthening of the electoral rights of the princes, a cardinal feature of the period 1106-1152" (Barraclough 1984, 159-60). This debility was to redound on the German state most notably during the reign of Frederick I (Barbarossa), who inherited the diminished material base of the monarchy. Outside of Swabia, where many of the Hohenstaufen lands were concentrated, Frederick lacked the territorial domains needed to solidify his position in Germany. Hence, he looked to Italy as a source of economic and political support for his rule. As Barraclough remarks,

> This change in the territorial balance of power is a fact of fundamental importance for the evaluation of his policy. It meant in the first place, that the Hohenstaufen dynasty, unlike earlier German rulers, could not count on an adequate material base for government within Germany itself. Hence from the very beginning of his reign Frederick's eye was on Italy and Burgundy. It was calculated in 1158 that a resumption of the usurped prerogatives of the crown in Italy would bring in approximately 30,000 talents annually. (1984, 173)

It was then that Frederick I's policy toward Italy and Burgundy was truly imperial. Between 1152 and 1157, he engaged in his first expedition to Italy, the beginning of his long conflict with Milan that was to occupy so much of his early reign. Frederick—and as a consequence, Germany—became involved in the complex politics of the balance of power in Italy. An alliance was formed among Sicily, the papacy, and Milan that had Frederick as its target. In 1167 the Lombard League was formed in opposition to Frederick; joining forces with the League of Verona, it forced the withdrawal of Frederick's forces from Italy (Tabacco 1989). This failure in northern Italy led to renewed efforts in Tuscany and central Italy that resulted in the consolidation of imperial rule in those regions and that was to embroil Germany in Italian affairs for generations to come. More damaging was the alliance by marriage between Henry VI, Frederick's son, and the Normans of Sicily, which led to Henry's direct involvement in Sicilian affairs. For sixty years, from 1190 onward, the Empire—now consisting of Germany, the central Italian holdings, and Sicily—was racked with the efforts to incorporate Sicily, where traditions, both political and religious, were vastly different from the remainder of the Empire. The conquest of Sicily in 1194 was followed by the revolt of 1197 and further warfare and drain on resources.

A principal consequence of the Sicilian involvement was the open antagonism of the papacy, beginning in 1198 with the accession of Innocent III to the papal throne. He was determined to recapture the temporal power lost to Frederick I and to remove the empire from central Italy and Sicily. He was not above resorting to international pressure on Germany, in the form of raising an anti-Hohenstaufen force under the leadership of Richard I of England. The French king, by contrast, supported his old allies, the Hohenstaufen. But French intervention was a mixed blessing, for it probably brought with it designs on territories that heretofore had been in imperial hands, such as Lorraine. A period of civil wars, chaos, and retrogression fell on Germany. Innocent supported the anti-king Otto of Brunswick, actually born in Normandy, against the traditional Hohenstaufen leadership. Although the legitimate dynasty was eventually restored, the drama of German involvement in Italy, with its implied fractal formation over a discontinuous space after only a weak state had been established, was not yet played out as the last of the Hohenstaufen, Frederick II, ascended the throne in 1215.

Frederick II was a Sicilian by birth, which meant that, simply put, Sicily and Italy came first. "For the first time, and on a grand scale, the Italian elements in imperial government were developed at the expense of the German" (Barraclough 1984, 219). This meant that Germany pretty much went its own way under the authority of territorial princes while Sicily and central Italy became the bulwarks of imperial government. Indeed early in his reign, Frederick had to make concessions to the princes to gain their general adherence to imperial policy, thus preventing more papal involvement and possibly civil war in Germany. Frederick undertook a reorganization of the Sicilian government and from 1225 onward engaged in an extremely destructive war with the Lombard League, which had thus far resisted the imperial orbit. Although he won the early battles, especially at Cortenuova in 1237, later the war turned against him. Pope Gregory IX sided with Frederick's enemies, securing the naval powers of Genoa, Venice, and Pisa in an alliance with the Lombard League for a consequent concerted attack on Sicily. Innocent IV continued the battle of the papacy against Frederick. Vilified by a council of the Church held in Lyons that was used to support the pope, Frederick was forced to make more concessions to the princes in Germany to maintain his position there. This was a particularly significant action, for in light of some later victories by Frederick in central Italy, Innocent realized that only by undermining Frederick in Germany could he attack him effectively. The pope accelerated his attacks on Frederick's position in Germany, prompting further concessions to the princes. Thus the German princes grew in power, and

> the powers which passed into their hands during Frederick II's reign remained in their hands for six centuries, surviving the dissolution of the Empire in 1806 and the creation of a new Empire in 1871; only in 1918 were the last vestiges swept away. The reign of Frederick II was thus a turning-point in German history; the resources which the crown had hitherto possessed, dissipated in the interests of Frederick's Italian policy, withered to a mere simulacrum of monarchy, and the reality of power was vested in the princes. The future lay with them and with the principalities. (Barraclough 1984, 233)

Perhaps most symptomatic of the fragile and underdeveloped bureaucratic condition of the German state was the absence of a fixed capital city for the court. Frederick II, as did emperors before and after him, simply took his court with him on his travels through various parts of the kingdom (Fuhrmann 1986, 167). The crown "bureaucracy," such as it was, was small enough to be transported.

The alienation of crown lands to gain adherents, which became more general after the death of Frederick II and the later accession of Conrad IV, was supplemented by the absence of primogeniture in Germany and indeed in much of continental Europe. There was thus a constant tendency toward partition that weakened the state considerably. As early as the death of Charlemagne in 814, the Frankish tradition of the division of inheritance among all heirs asserted itself. By the Treaty of Verdun in 843, the three sons of Louis the Pious, himself the son of Charlemagne, became heirs to three separate kingdoms: the west, containing Neustria, Aquitaine, and the Spanish march; the central lands of Frisia, Austrasia, Burgundy, Provence, and Italy; and finally, Franconia east of the Rhine, Bavaria, Swabia, Thuringia, and Saxony (Barraclough 1984, 12). This event, in effect, marked the end of the Carolingian empire.

This pattern continued in central Europe, and as Richard Bonney remarks, "the German principalities were weakened by the absence of any law of primogeniture applying within the Empire as a whole" (1991, 527). This, despite the Golden Bull of 1356 that not only reaffirmed the rights of certain German princes to elect the emperor but declared their principalities to be "indivisible and under the law of primogeniture" (Holborn 1959, 28). As late as 1688, the Great Elector of Prussia, Frederick William could endanger a whole life's work of state building by proposing to partition his lands among his four sons. Ultimately, the Hohenzollern of Prussia were more successful than the rulers of other German states because they refused to allow partition to weaken their control over their united lands. In contrast, for example, the landgrave Philip of Hesse had his lands partitioned among his four sons, and one of these divisions, between Hesse-Cassel and Hesse-Darmstadt, became permanent. Only in 1621 did the Austrian Habsburgs adopt the principle of primogeniture that was to aid their retention of a united governance, as did their soon-to-be-rivals, the Hohenzollerns (Bonney 1991, 528).

The contrast with England could not be more striking. William the Conqueror confiscated most of the lands of the Anglo-Saxons, giving lands to his Norman nobility and courtiers and doubling the holdings of the crown. Approximately one-fifth of England was in royal domain. "Nearly one-quarter of the land value in England was granted to ten men, most of them the king's relatives" (Nicholas 1992, 220). It has been estimated that only 8 percent of the country remained in Anglo-Saxon hands (Fuhrmann 1986, 50). The rapid assumption of primogeniture by the English crown and nobility did much to assure the continuity of both. For example, on one manor of Ely cathedral, the demesne constituted one quarter of the arable land in 1066. Twenty years later the demesne had doubled in area (Duby 1968, 194).

At the end of the Hohenstaufen dynasty the crown lands had been so reduced that they amounted in aggregate to only three-quarters of those of the Margrave of Brandenburg. Further, they were so widely scattered that they constituted a weak basis of political power compared with the resources of the wealthiest princes (Barraclough 1984, 246).

In part, as Norbert Elias reminds us, the problem of German state formation is a matter of scale: "Compared to the Germano-Roman Empire, the island territory that the Norman Duke William conquered in 1066 was quite small. It reminds us roughly of Prussia under the first kings" (1982, 102). Thus, ownership of a substantial proportion of the English lands by the king or his relatives occurred within a fairly compact area, which implied considerable control over that area. In contrast, given the primitive transportation and communications facilities of the day, the vast area of the Empire was administratively less subject to direct rule, even where lands were owned by the crown.

Formation of a Strong State in Prussia

Elias's comparison of England and Prussia is intriguing, because it suggests the fundamental commonality between them. At their respective times of initial consolidation, both were conquest states that suspended whatever political arrangements had existed earlier. The events of 1066 and their aftermath are well-known, and it is their marked contrast with the conditions we have observed in Germany that is of interest in the discussion of Prussia that follows. Indeed, the very points of comparison between Germany and England reveal what we need to know about England as a conquest state—the extension of the demesne, the majority of land in Norman possession, and much of that held by the crown and relatives of the king. In addition there was the essentially secular nature of the English state in comparison with that of Germany, as revealed by the reversal in ratio between secular and ecclesiastical barons.

In speaking of Germany, I have referred essentially to Germany west of the Elbe River. Until the thirteenth century Brandenburg and East Prussia remained outside the German orbit. It is to this chapter of conquest yielding essentially fractal formations in Prussia, as in England, that we now turn. By the tenth century, the Elbe and Saale rivers formed the eastern boundaries of Carolingian Saxony. But in the 960s, the frontier regions to the east were developed into several "marks," each under the authority of a margrave, or border count. The Nordmark was one such territory, stretching from the Elbe to the Oder in the east. Punitive raids against the Slavs were launched from Saxony until more secure settlements were established by immigrant Germans, but these efforts were set back by the great Slav uprising of 983 (Bartlett 1993, 311).

In the twelfth century this framework of German domination east of the Elbe was reestablished, this time with permanent consequences. The bishops of Brandenburg and Havelberg recovered their official seats, and new cathedrals were planned. In 1115 Albert the Bear of Saxony defeated a large raiding party of Slavs and began to lay the groundwork for what would become the principality of Brandenburg. Through the deft use of alliances with other nobility and with the support of Lothar, duke of Saxony, Albert was enfeoffed with the Nordmark. More important perhaps was the final capture in 1157 of the town of Brandenburg, which had been founded two centuries earlier by the Germans. After Albert, the Ascanians, as his family were called, ruled Brandenburg for seven generations and by 1319 they had extended the boundaries of their principality almost 200 miles to the east. They built castles and founded the cities of Berlin and Frankfurt an der Oder, among others. The religious dimension was not neglected, for they supported the Church and settled Dominicans, Franciscans, and Cistercians within their territories.

Robert Bartlett refers to these activities as those of an "expansionary aristocracy in a conquest principality" (1993, 35), for the settlement of agricultural lands, the building of castles, and the founding of towns took place at the expense of the native Slavs. Some were pushed eastward, but many tribes, in a combination of warfare and assimilation—both forced and voluntary—were killed or absorbed, ceasing to exist as separate peoples. Among those devastated in this fashion were the native Prussians, a Baltic people, whose name, ironically, was ultimately assumed by the conquerors.

Two points are noteworthy here. First, this is an aristocratic expansion based initially on military conquest. Only after the indigenous populations are subjugated or forced to flee by the knightly elements emerging out of Saxony do we have the makings of a principality. Second, the dynamics of this aristocratic expansion reveal much about fractal formation as a general process during this period. Although formulated initially to explain the Norman expansion, John Le Patourel's treatment of the general dynamics of expansion is useful here. He focuses on the "expansion inherent in a developing feudal society" (quoted in Bartlett 1993, 46). In the earliest stages of development, the lords seek vassals in order to gain political support and, most important, to acquire fighting men to defend their realms. In turn, the potential vassal seeks to be enfeoffed with land. This is a mutually reinforcing process with expansion as its outcome, for "the more land one had, the more knights one could enfeoff, and the more knights one had, the easier it was to conquer new lands" (Bartlett 1993, 47). And it was far easier to conquer those lands from thinly dispersed Slavic tribes in the east than from the already more densely populated lands west of the Elbe.

As mentioned earlier, the Church was intimately involved in the expansionary process. At the heart of this conquest across the Elbe was a "knightly-clerical-mercantile" consortium (Bartlett 1993, 208) that was moving ever eastward as the high medieval period dawned. The early crusades to the Middle East provided a model for an aristocratic militarization of Christianity, and the crusading military order was its consequence. The model order was that of the Knights Templar, founded around 1118 in order to protect pilgrims on their way to Jerusalem from the port of Jaffa. The Templars succeeded not only in this task but in others undertaken in the Mediterranean, and later in such far-flung places as Tempelhof in eastern Germany or Templo de Huesca in the Iberian Peninsula. They took vows of chastity, living an almost monkish existence, but eagerly took up arms against the pagans or members of competing faiths, such as Islam or Judaism. The Templars increased in number and in wealth, but most important for our purposes here provided a successful model for the later emergence of the Teutonic Knights in the Baltic region.

The first crusading presence in the Baltic region was the Swordbrothers, established by Bishop Albrecht of Livonia (comprising modern Estonia and part of Latvia) in 1202 and endowed with one-third of the lands of the new colony. This was, in effect, the first "order-state" in history. In return for these lands, the Swordbrothers, with their symbols of cross and sword, were to defend the Church against pagan attacks. The Teutonic Knights were founded in the 1190s in the Middle East and by 1230 were offered a base in Poland from which they could battle the pagan Prussians. In 1237 they absorbed the Swordbrothers. This combined force then emerged as the dominant power in the eastern Baltic littoral. "Particularly after 1280, the Teutonic Knights colonized the area with Germans with a severity that made even Henry the Lion [duke of Saxony and Bavaria] look tame by comparison. They deported many native Prussians and made serfs of the rest. They granted charters to their towns, several of which became prominent in the Hanse, the league of north German cities" (Nicholas 1992, 209–10). Justification for this behavior is found as early as 1008, when a Flemish cleric writing on behalf of the Archbishop of Magdeburg wrote, "The cruelest pagans have attacked us . . . men without mercy, who boast their inhumanity. . . . These [Slav] heathens are terrible men, but their land is rich in meat, honey, flour, birds, and if properly cultivated would be so fruitful that no other land could be compared to it" (Fuhrmann 1986, 123). Justification for crusading militancy against cruel pagans and economic opportunity are here neatly juxtaposed.

It was the secularization of the Teutonic Knights, combined with this knightly expansion, that was to ultimately distinguish Prussia from the western German principalities and allow it to later form the nucleus of a united Germany. In 1525, Albrecht von Hohenzollern, the last grandmaster, adopted Lutheranism and secularized the German Order of the Teutonic Knights, divorcing East Prussia from any Roman Catholic connection. Nevertheless, he paid homage to Sigismund I of Poland for his new duchy. In 1562, in order to gain the support of the principality of Brandenburg against certain Habsburg demands regarding Livonia, Sigismund II recognized the right of the Hohenzollerns in Brandenburg to virtually inherit the duchy of East Prussia at the end of their cousin's direct line. This event occurred in 1618, and John Casimir of Poland was forced to recognize the sovereignty of the Hohenzollerns over ducal Prussia in 1657 (Bonney 1991, 261, 272). The end result of Prussia's history as a conquest state emanating from the expansionist activities of a crusading aristocracy is revealed in the following statistics concerning land ownership: "In East Prussia at the end of the eighteenth century, out of some 10 million *morgen* in productive use, the state owned 65 percent, the nobility around 30 percent and cities 5 percent" (Blum 1978, 18). By way of contrast, in 1760 in Bavaria, one of the largest western principalities in Germany, the state owned 13 percent of the peasant holdings, the nobility 24 percent, and the Catholic church

56 percent (Blum 1978, 21). This pattern was a major factor in the dynamics of successful state-formation in the east in comparison with relative failure in the west.

Land Inequality and the Failure to Democratize

The absence of primogeniture during much of German history had consequences not only for state formation, as noted above, but also in the failure to provide the social and political bases of democracy. The middle group of the nobility was most affected by the division of lands, as we can infer from the Chinese case in Chapter 4 (Table 4.1), applied now to a different social class. The process of subdivision and diminution of the middle group suggested by the exponential distribution implies an increase in the number of impoverished nobles scarcely more wealthy now than the better-off peasantry. At the same time many of the lands sold off by the poorer nobility are bought by the wealthier nobles, so that a bifurcation emerges between rich and poor even within the nobility. In central Europe the richer nobles gravitated toward or actually became the princes of secular kingdoms or principalities.

This process of the decline of the middle group under conditions of partible inheritance is found in the agrarian conditions of both the nobility and the medieval peasantry. Commenting on a period before the effects of subdivision became apparent, Georges Duby remarks on the vitality of the middle group: "On the threshold of the fourteenth century we can see no weakness in the manorial economy. On the contrary, we can see everywhere revealed the vigour of medium-sized estates, controlled either by the petty nobility living on their ancestral lands, by the agents of prince or prelate, or increasingly by 'farmers', some of whom had risen from the village community" (1968, 280).

Mirroring the condition of the middle nobles, David Nicholas describes villages in areas of indivisible inheritance, which had an upper and lower class of peasants and "a middle group of prosperous householders who had enough land to support a family and provide some surplus for market"; they usually "constituted one-quarter to one-third of the inhabitants of the village" (1992, 292). And along similar lines, Rodney Hilton describes the "long period of the prosperity of the middle peasantry" in England (1990, 78).

Several centuries later, the situation had changed radically, especially in areas of partible inheritance. According to Richard Bonney, "At Lespignan in Languedoc, there were 53 middle-ranking peasant proprietors in 1492, but only 34 in 1653. Their share of the land went down from 51 percent to only 13 percent. Small-scale peasant proprietors had constituted just under half the total in 1492, but had become the crushing majority (228 out of 262 peasants) by 1653" (1991, 384). And the decline of the middle group of nobility would have grave consequences for the future of democracy in Germany, as we shall see now in the consequences of warfare for democracy in German lands.

As Duby tells us concerning the consequences of war for the nobility as a whole,

> But of course it was the lords' dwellings, more exposed because relatively richer, which suffered most, together with their appurtenances, mills, bakehouses, enclosures, orchards, in short all the luxury capital of the countryside. The fact that war struck the manorial economy harder is worth remembering. Damaging the rich more than the poor, it helped to level down the differences in rural wealth. At all events the capital losses it caused were very unequally distributed. (1968, 297)

However, not all of the nobility suffered equally.

> [The] manors belonging to princes and the great families, as well as those belonging to the church, suffered less. . . . As for the princely manors, they benefited first from the concentration of compulsory powers. This process protected them and also facilitated their restoration; the all-embracing taxation strengthened them by providing a constant stream of liquid funds and a part of this capital at least helped to stimulate the manorial economy. Lastly, the top ranks of the lay aristocracy were everywhere reduced in numbers and power lay in fewer hands. . . . The present state of research certainly shows that the most obvious signs of malaise revealed themselves in the middle ranks of manorial wealth." (Duby 1968, 316)

Thus the authority of princes was increased by war while that of the lower levels of nobility was decreased. This process was to have its most extreme consequences in virtually landlocked Germany, with its extraordinary experience of warfare in the sixteenth and seventeenth centuries.

Before the Reformation and the continual warfare associated with it, the princes of Germany and the various estates, including the nobility, had reached an accommodation. In the fourteenth century they shook off the superior control of the emperor and reduced the Empire to a collection of principalities. As early as the Investiture Contest, the princes had taken advantage of the weakness of the imperial authority and eliminated the counts who were agents of the direct royal administration (Holborn 1959, 20). By the fourteenth century, the individual princes acted to assert their authority over their subjects and destroy the privileges of the feudal classes (Barraclough 1984, 321). In this they were largely successful, having forced the estates, consisting of knights, cities, and often church prelates, to participate in States-General or territorial assemblies (*Landtage*) instead of the provincial ones. In this fashion, the authority of individual nobles was reduced, but the nobility as a whole, as well as the towns and elements of the church, still had to be consulted in matters of taxation by the princes governing a particular territory.

These States-General were not unlike the British Parliament in their financial roots but were also used to ventilate grievances and to begin reforming activity (Barraclough 1984, 350). The nobility, among other classes, were able to exert their influence in the various Landtage.[2] But the religious wars of the sixteenth century, followed by the Thirty Years War from 1618 to 1648, transformed German society. "The weakening of all classes in town and country, which was the inevitable consequence of generations of strife, the effect of war on commerce, industry and agriculture, brought about, with the religious changes, a further rise in the power of the princes, which ushered in the period of princely absolutism" (Barraclough 1984, 373).

The Reformation had the consequence of increasing the power of the princes as the result of Luther's need for their support in furthering the spread of Protestantism. In particular, the Peasants' War of 1524 frightened him and led to his increased support of princely power. This process was mirrored in the Counter-Reformation, in that Catholic princes also sought to tie the territorial church to the particular secular ruler. Hence religion was subordinated to the dictates of the princes. Afterward, however, as Barraclough observes, "Once they had bound the territorial churches to the secular power, the princes sought to drive home their advantage by attacking the nobility and the towns and freeing themselves from dependence on the States-General" (1984, 377).

As early as the sixteenth century, the Bavarian Landtag was in decline, and in Austria the Catholic rulers destroyed the power of the Landtage by driving out the nobility, the vast majority of whom were Protestant at the time. The principle of *cuius regio eius religio* emerging out of the Peace of Augsburg in 1555 and reinforced by the Peace of Westphalia in 1648 not only was a means of assuring religious uniformity between rulers and ruled, but was also a major step in the creation of German absolutism. Here in the German case, we see some of the dynamics by which the destruction of a nobility or at least of its political prerogatives results in the diminution of political rights. The failure to lay the foundations for a later democratic development may be dated from this time. In the following section, we will be exploring the relationship between church and state more directly.[3]

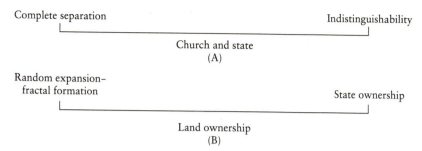

Figure 6.1. A thought experiment on church-state relations and landownership patterns.

The Abbasids

For a comparison with the preceding German illustration, it might prove useful to consider another example in a different geographical location, religio-cultural setting, and time period. The choice of civilization is suggested by a simple thought-experiment, or as the early-twentieth-century German physicists called it, a *Gedankenexperiment*.

Let us conceive of church-state relations as lying on a continuum (see Figure 6.1), with complete separation at one end and indistinguishability—where church and state are essentially one—at the other. Land ownership also can be conceptualized in this fashion. At one end, there exist fractal formations of private land ownership, often resulting from a slow and steady conquest. At the other end lies a state ownership or at least a state responsibility for the well-being of all important producing lands. If church and state are one (as on the right-hand side of part A, Figure 6.1), then the state may be seriously vulnerable, perhaps even more so than in the case of early Germany, in which the state dominated the church temporarily, but organizationally the two were distinct. And if, in addition, there is no landowning nobility (as on the right-hand side of part B, Figure 6.1), then there can be no external support for the monarchy in time of trouble. In such a case, state vulnerability is magnified and requires the support of other agencies, such as the military.

Of the several societies that are potential candidates for satisfying both criteria, the early Islamic is probably the most prominent. Church and state were virtually one and the same (Cahen 1970, 531). Indeed, as Bernard Lewis remarks, Islam and political power were deeply intertwined:

The true and sole sovereign in the Muslim view was God, from whose mandate the Prophet derived his authority and whose will, made known by revelation, was the sole source of law. The *umma* thus expressed from its inception the fusion of politics and religion characteristic of the later Islamic states.... In the Islamic world, therefore, there could be no conflict between Pope and Emperor, for the powers which these two represented were one and the same. (1987, xvi–xvii)

At the same time, the concept of individual land ownership so common in the west, especially during the feudal period, is largely absent. In part, this resulted from the tribal egalitarianism of the Arabs as they emerged from the Arabian peninsula. Certainly the nomadic patterns of these tribes diminished the importance of land ownership. But equally important was the essentially urban locus of the development of early Islam. Contrary to some popular beliefs, Mecca and even Yathrib (later to be called Medina) were thriving urban centers on trade routes in southwestern Arabia. Thus on the periphery of desert regions, "in contrast to the limits on expansion in agriculture, there seemed to be no limits on potential expansion in commerce" (Hodgson 1974a, 127). This pattern of urbanism was to be a hallmark of Islamic society from its inception.

These twin elements of the virtual union of church and state and the absence of a strong landed base for the monarchy had several important consequences. First, the monarch and his retinue were continually being scrutinized for their level of piety. Extensive displays of riches, opulence, or other deviations from the egalitarian and unadorned pietistic rigor of early Islam were to be condemned. Indeed this was one major source of the opposition to the Umayyads, the first dynasty of the Islamic empire. When added to factors including Arab intertribal rivalries, resentment directed at the Arab aristocracy, which at first resisted intermarriage with subject populations, and the later hostility of the Mawali (converts to Islam, often of mixed Arab–non-Arab marriages, who were excluded from the highest offices), the criticisms of pietistic groups were effective in mobilizing opposition to the Umayyads (Lewis 1993a, 69–74). Not only the Shiites, who had already expressed opposition to the Umayyads based on their support of direct descendants of Muhammed's family, but also the Khariji, a secessionist group of pietistic Muslims, began to openly oppose the Umayyad caliphate. Organized opposition among the Khariji manifested itself principally by guerrilla warfare (Hodgson 1974a, 215–21). By the time of the Marwanids, the last of the Umayyads, a general opposition to the caliphate arose under the rubric of what Marshall Hodgson calls the "piety-minded" (1974a, 252). Precisely because they were vulnerable to religious criticism, the Umayyads could be opposed successfully on those grounds, and this first Islamic dynasty, sometimes called the "Arab Kingdom," fell in 750 (Wellhausen 1927).

The Abbasids who succeeded them were equally vulnerable to such criticism, but unlike the Umayyads, they had agricultural and financial resources, inherited from the Sasanid Empire, which had been based in what is today Iran and eastern Iraq. This base also led them to move the capital from Damascus to Baghdad in what has been claimed to be a "Persianization" of the Empire (Humphreys 1991, 118).

Being the heirs to the Sasanid Empire carried both positive and negative effects for the Abbasids. On the positive side, the Tigris-Euphrates river valleys, with their sophisticated irrigation works, became a financial bulwark of the empire. The early Abbasids not only repaired and maintained these irrigation structures but also improved upon them (Cahen 1970, 532; Hourani 1991, 103). But by the time of the later Abbasids, in the late ninth and early tenth centuries, the financial return from these rich lands began to diminish. Meanwhile, political instability resulting from competing military factions was a major factor in the growing disruption of the irrigation works. For example, in 937, the Nahrawan canal was breached as the result of fighting, and it was not soon repaired (Hodgson 1974a, 495).

There were other reasons for the failure of the irrigation works in the Sawad, the great Mesopotamian agricultural region. One was geological change, a rise of the land in the vicinity of the Diyalah River that ultimately reduced the amount of land under cultivation. Excessive salinization—a consequence of the intense irrigation used here for centuries, if not millennia—diminished the productivity of the land, thus reducing the financial revenue for the state. By the early tenth century, the Sawad was returning a much smaller revenue than even during the preceding generation. The reduced revenue, in turn, increased turbulence among the military factions, because there was less money to pay the commanders and men, and fighting resulted in yet more damage to the irrigation works. The dependence of the Sawad on the cities instead of on local landowners increased the necessity for state intervention, for which there was less and less money available. As Marshall Hodgson notes:

> But once the political and social structure of the Sawad had become dependent on Baghdad and the other great cities, central intervention was necessary if the area was not to decline agriculturally even below the level which a more decentralized irrigation had maintained in pre-Sasanian times. Local initiative was no longer in a position to restore a more moderate prosperity, for the land was controlled from the cities; or else it readily fell into the hands of pastoralists, who alone had the tribal social structure and the nomadic alternative resources which would enable them to hold out against pressure from the cities. In the following centuries, the Sawad was eliminated as a primary source of centralized revenues in the region, giving the government that controlled it resources

to outlast rebellions and other disruptions elsewhere in the empire. But there was no visible alternative financial basis of the same order for a centralized bureaucratic empire. To survive, the empire would have to find a more general economic basis for continuity in its authority. *The problem of religious legitimacy was increasingly compounded by that of financial viability; and the political crisis of confidence, by interrupting and demoralizing central control, in turn hastened the economic troubles.* (1974a, 485; emphasis added)

Here, in Hodgson's words, we see the important interaction between religious legitimacy and a financial viability that was dependent on fertile and irrigated land, which, in turn, depended on the central government to maintain it. But how did this dependence of the land on the central government come about? We have noted the essential urbanism of early Islam, which interacted with the nomadic tribalism of the Arabs to diminish the emphasis on private land ownership. There were additional reasons for the absence of local care of the Sawad—which were, in fact, also inherited from the Sasanids.

At the end of the sixth century, before the Islamic conquest, the Sasanian Empire had just emerged from a revolutionary convulsion that had virtually eliminated the old quasi-feudal structure and replaced it with a military government and a mercenary army (Lewis 1993a, 48). In the second half of the fifth century the monarchy had sought to hobble the growing power of the nobility, essentially by supporting an egalitarian movement led by Mazdak, who advocated the reduction of landed privilege. Many nobles lost much of their property, and commoners were raised to positions of leadership. Later, there was some restoration of noble privileges but never to the same extent as earlier. At the time of the birth of Muhammad, a Sasanian leader by the name of Nushirvan developed a strong army consisting mainly of Arab tribesmen paid by revenues from taxation instead of special levies on the gentry. As a result, Nushirvan was free of constraints on his decision making; the Arab tribes were continually in a state of conflict with one another and so posed much less threat to the monarchy than did the nobility. As for the Sawad, much of it had become virtually a state farm in which the revenues were not allowed to go to private landowners (Hodgson 1974a, 143–44, 201). This was the centralized agricultural enterprise inherited by the Abbasids, and its diminished rate of return clearly would have implications for the later financial sustainability of Abbasid rule.

The vulnerability of the state to pietistic criticism when church and state are fused, coupled with the absence of a feudal landowning class to call upon for support in crucial times (or, alternatively, a friendly independent church), suggests the need for some additional source of state support. As we might infer from the thought experiment described earlier, such a regime will have to turn to the military for support at a very early stage in its development. And this is precisely what we find in the history of the Abbasid state.

Less than a century after the accession of the Abbasid caliphate, a civil war occurred between two claimants to the throne. There were religious issues, as well as those ordinarily faced in problems of succession, but in the end, "the civil war between al-Amīn and al-Ma'mūn had demonstrated the need for the caliph to have at his disposal an armed force which was completely loyal to him and which was outside religious quarrels. For this reason al-Mu'taṣim, even during the lifetime of al-Ma'mūn, and especially when he was appointed to important governorships, formed his own guard of 4,000 Turks of servile origin" (Sourdel 1970, 125). To an increasing extent then, commanders and guards began to gain more autonomy and eventually active power, as the caliphs gradually lost control. Many became tax farmers, who thus established their own sources of revenue independent of the central government. In 935, the office of "Commander of Commanders" was created in order to establish the primacy of the commander in the capital city of Baghdad over the remainder. In 945, the Iranian Buyeds, who already controlled the highlands above the capital occupied Baghdad. The chief Buyed captain assumed the title of "Commander of Commanders" and with it effective political control of much of the empire. The caliph was left with theoretical overlordship and a sizable local court, but real political power had passed out of the caliphate. The process of militarization was now complete (Hodgson 1974a, 495; Lewis 1993a, 105). It is rare that a functioning empire of such geographical scope and internal wealth would succumb to virtually complete militarization so quickly, but that is what our simple thought experiment predicts. Or, as Hodgson could surmise based on intimate knowledge of this period in Islamic history:

For when, as a result, no internally rooted social body could wield effective power, the solution could only be a military one. Without legitimized tenure, the lands tended to slip away from hereditary families of gentry, whose first base of power had been the land and who then had been soldiers as part of their responsibility as a gentry. The land was again and again distributed to men who were first of all soldiers, and held land only as a consequence of that—and held it only so long as they remained personally the best soldiers locally available. (1974b, 66)

At most, a "condominium of the army and the religious" (Cahen 1970, 537) could be expected, and this was to be a fairly common characteristic of Muslim countries.

Here we see a consequence for both state formation and state survivability of the unity of church and state and the absence of a strong landed gentry. The state itself is weak and ultimately disintegrates, as did the Abbasid Empire in 945. Moreover, the prospects for ultimate democratization are poor—although as we shall see in Chapter 7's analysis of the implications of the preceding chapters, not quite as poor as might be supposed.

CHAPTER 7

Sources of Democracy

We are now prepared to undertake a systematic analysis of certain of the major themes presented in the preceding chapters, aggregating them and testing their implications empirically. Of course, not all of our observations can be tested directly, because some of them emerge from prehistory or entail processes of state formation and decay many centuries old. However, it is possible to test certain of them, especially those pertaining to democracy. These fall into three categories: (1) land inequality; (2) environmental impacts, especially those connected to aridity and warfare; and (3) ideological impacts, such as that of Islam.

The first of these emerges from our repeated concern throughout these chapters with the consequences of inequality—especially land inequality—for elements of the polity. We have seen how continued plot subdivisions have their impact and how fractal formations have theirs. In this chapter we will examine more thoroughly the effect of land inequality on democracy. The environmental concerns of aridity and warfare have also been explored briefly in their impact on early democratic institutions. Now they will be examined systematically for their effects on political rights in a rudimentary form of democracy, on liberal democracy, and on democratic institutionalization as well. Finally, we saw that Islam entails an ideological unity of church and state that would make the evolution of political democracy extremely unlikely. Here we will explore the question of whether Islam and democracy are mutually exclusive.

Land Inequality

Our preceding illustrations have indicated that extreme land inequality, on the order of a system of latifundia and very small peasant plots, is not likely to lead to democratic development, if only because mass political violence is a more probable outcome, as we shall see in Chapter 8. However, there are reasons to suspect that moderate levels of inequality may be associated with democracy. Obversely, we saw in Chapter 6 that the diminution of the lesser nobility, with a consequent strong increase in inequality, was an important factor in the disappearance of representative institutions and the rise of autocracy in Europe. A more direct example, to be examined more closely in this chapter, lies in the origins of democracy in ancient Athens precisely in legislation that mandated a graduated land inequality as a basis for representation.

In the following treatment, the origins of democracy in agrarian society will be informed, initially, by this Athenian experience. This instance is chosen not only because of the justly achieved fame of Athenian democracy as a prototype but also because, when early Athens is compared with other areas of the ancient Aegean, "here, and perhaps here alone, there was [a] firm, unbroken continuity of existence which, while not spectacular in these Dark Ages, was never moribund either" (Warren 1989, 136). Indeed, Anthony Snodgrass goes so far as to assert that "The Greeks' espousal of a small-scale polity in which the community of citizens could act in concert, later so resonant in the pages of Plato's *Republic* and *Laws* and Aristotle's *Politics*, appears to have been a strong factor from the very start" (1986, 58). Thus there is opportunity here to observe the long-term societal processes that, in the end, may yield mature political democracy from beginnings that, in their essentials, were not terribly different from those of nondemocratic societies.

The following account of early Athenian political development draws principally, although not exclusively, from some of the more recent writings of M. I. Finley, the eminent classicist. Although in *Early Greece* (1981) he does not theorize directly on the reasons for the rise of democracy in Athens, he does present a concise summary of the distinctive features of Athenian society.[1] Finley distinguishes especially between the pattern of societal development in Athens and those of other Greek city-states, setting forth the salient features of Athenian society that will yield the outlines for a model of the early stages of democratic development in agrarian societies.

Beyond an investigation of the analytic origins of democracy per se, our analysis will yield several other dividends. First, in contrast to other studies that do not find significant associations for the *level* of democracy, this analysis will specify variables most closely associated with three different levels of political rights as operational forms of democracy. Second, a particular form of inequality, land inequality, will demonstrate a robust positive relationship with all three measures of democracy in a somewhat counterintuitive, but nevertheless straightforward, theoretical development. This type of inequality will prove to be related positively to political rights, but in ways not foreshadowed by the hypothesized negative association between income inequality and political democracy (Bollen and Jackman 1985; E. N. Muller 1988; Rubinson and Quinlan 1977). Indeed, in contrast to the prevailing wisdom concerning the requirement of economic equality for democratic functioning, the broad assertion here states that the rise of democracy requires some differentials in observable wealth for the process to take hold. Although *maintenance* of the democratic polity when fully formed may require a degree of economic equality, the *initiation* of democracy in agrarian society seems to demand an inequality in land possession.

Essentially, this argument is about the rise of nonascriptive elites whose influence is a function of some form of material achievement in place of tribal, hereditary, or other closed systems of ascription. It is worth noting that the successful transition from communism—a form of ascriptive influence based on ideological (and in many cases familial) associations—to capitalism and democracy, as expressions and representations of material achievement, may require processes similar to those outlined here.

Ancient Athens

Ancient Athens can be identified by three main features. First, Athens differed from the remaining Greek city-states by not participating in the colonization process. While other city-states, largely as the result of overpopulation, generated colonies in the Mediterranean basin and even as far as the Black Sea, as Finley observes, Athens "took no part in the colonization movement. Though individual Athenians may have migrated, the city as such, unlike Sparta, had not even one Taras to her credit" (1981, 117).[2] Yet we also know that population density must have been high in Athens because of the large number of indebted farmers who formed the impetus for the Solonic reforms of the sixth century B.C. (ca. 594–93). Archaeological evidence for a rapid population growth during the prior two centuries is given in Snodgrass 1977 and Morris 1987. Only through an emerging land scarcity that resulted from a growing population (as in all of Greece during this period) could such a large number of farmers have become indebted to their neighbors or other larger landowners. The heart of the Solonic reforms is the cancellation of this debt or the "shaking off of burdens" (Finley 1981, 119).

This major reform—the second defining feature of Athens—eliminated the gross sorts of land inequality that had existed until that time and replaced them with a no less visible, but nevertheless more moderate form. As John Fine describes it, "By the removal of the *horoi* [markers for the encumbrance of land due to debt] and the elimination of the class of *hektemors* [tenants on the fields of the rich], the wealthy lost control over all the land on which the *hektemors* had toiled as tenants, but their own estates remained intact" (1983, 199). Thus, debt was canceled, restoring control of the land to the farmer (peasant) owners, but there remained substantial land inequality, because lands originally owned by the wealthy were not affected. (Later we shall note another important element of the Solonic reforms that is also critical to our understanding of the origins of democracy.)

These two factors lead us to the first variable to be introduced, that of population density in relation to agricultural land. This choice not only is the consequence of the critical importance of agrarian density already implicit in Finley's account, but also emerges from the nature of the Greek city-state itself. In contrast to our contemporary understanding of a clear difference between urban and rural environments, such a distinction was not found in ancient Greece. Again, we allow Finley to speak, "Plato and Aristotle did not write nonsense; they took city and hinterland, town and country, together as a unit, not as distinct variables in competition or conflict, actual or potential. Even those farmers who lived outside the town were integrally *in* the *polis*. . . . Discussions of property and property ownership are only about land" (1982, 5). Thus, politics in Athens depended as much on the farmer as on any other citizen.

The final distinctive feature of early Athens singled out by Finley is trade. He points to "the remarkable upsurge in Athenian fine painted pottery, which about the middle of the sixth century rapidly acquired a virtual monopoly among Greek pottery exports to the other cities of Greece, to the western colonies, and to the Etruscans" (1981, 124). Here the wisdom of Solon's reforms stands out once again, for it was he who guided the Athenian economy away from its reliance on growing grain in the relatively poor Attican soil and toward an emphasis on olive oil and wine for export that, in turn, would produce more than enough money to purchase high-quality grain abroad (H. J. Muller 1961, 179). Trade will later be measured by the ratio of trade to gross national product (GNP) to control for the overall size of the economy.

Theoretical Development

Despite the example of the Athenian model, the importance of agricultural density requires theoretical development. Why should agricultural density be related to democracy—or to political rights, which we shall later use as a measure of democracy? There are three possible mechanisms for the impact of agricultural density.

The first of these is the most direct and stipulates the connection between agricultural density and land inequality. Increased density yields increased inequality as the result of the increased scarcity of land attendant on the population increase. (Chapter 2 and Appendix A demonstrate the theoretical/mathematical connection between the two variables using a formal model.)

In descriptive terms, this model may be understood in the following manner. One assumes a relatively equal distribution of land parcels at some early point in time. As population grows, there is a geometric subdivision of the land, so that at a later point in time, an exponential distribution describes the landholdings. The greater the scarcity of land, due either to circumscription or to population growth (or both), the steeper the exponential curve and the greater the inequality in holdings.

Land inequality implies gradation in wealth that would make some persons more likely to influence the political process than others. In traditional or tribal societies, of which ancient Athens was an example, the political division initially is based largely on tribal affiliation. It was a major element of the Solonic reforms not only to stabilize patterns of landholding but to transform the tribal basis of Athenian politics to one based on wealth. Four categories of citizens were created, with a formalized gradation of influence on the political process based on the wealth of each group (Finley 1973, 1981; Grant 1987). Each of these groups had differing rights and responsibilities, varying from eligibility for the highest offices for those in the wealthiest category to election to a new council of state, the Boule, for members of the next two categories to rights to attend and vote in the assembly for those in the last category.

Two points are worthy of emphasis. First, as Finley observes, "The citizen-body was divided into four classes according to wealth, measured, it is essential to stress, not in money but in agricultural yield" (1981, 120). Thus land inequality (and its use, of course) are the sole bases for political participation. Second, without the emergence of this land inequality as the result of population density, there would have been no basis for the assignment of political rights other than the traditional tribal, hereditary, and/or clan affiliations.[3]

Although the Solonic reforms clearly did not establish a democracy in the modern sense, they did lay the foundation for the later introduction of democracy per se by Cleisthenes. As Finley comments, "Later Athenians looked back to Solon as the man who set them on the road to democracy" (1981, 125). Evidence for this comes not only from the literary sources that are the basis of Finley's judgment, but from Attican grave sites, which reveal a steady democratization (less regard to rank) in burial practices during the century after the Solonic reforms (Morris 1987). In this first model, then, agricultural density leads to land inequality that in turn leads to increased political rights.

In England and Sweden as two prototypical modern democracies we see similar processes at work. As Athens was among the first to unite relatively heterogeneous elements under one governmental framework in Attica, so too were England and Sweden among the first to establish centralized, large-scale polities in the European context. Further, we can now concentrate on the stable institutional manifestations of democracy (Huntington 1968)—the English Parliament and the Swedish Riksdag—and their growth in relation to the landowning sector of society.

In England, for example, "by the mid-fifteenth century . . . only the peers of Parliament . . . were universally regarded as noble. . . . At these levels of late medieval society, the possession of landed wealth was a *sine qua non* of entry and of survival" (Harvey 1985, 132). By the end of the English Civil War,

> the abolition of institutions like the Court of Wards (founded in 1540), "that great bridle of feudality" . . . has been described as "probably the most important single event in the history of English landowning." Landowners were now free not only from the burdens of feudal service but from monetary substitutes for it and by the end of the century, *when all barriers to hereditary title* had disappeared, the claims of private property, and of the large estates in particular, were more firmly established than they had been at the beginning of it. (Briggs 1983, 136; emphasis added)

With the abolition of essential elements of feudalism and hereditary requirements for landowning nobility, English politics could take its fitful steps into an embedded institutional democracy. Just as Solon abolished exclusive hereditary entitlement to political influence in Athens, so too did the English abolish such exclusivity as the result of the Civil War and the Glorious Revolution of 1688, while still emphasizing the role of landownership in relation to representation in Parliament. In the eighteenth century, the parliamentary system became also a two-party system. "The majority of both parties defended the rights of private property and sustained an hierarchical social order in which precedence was given to the great landowners" (Dickinson 1985, 207). The nineteenth century witnessed the continued dominance of the landowning aristocracy in Parliament, but now with an expanded franchise as a result of pressures for reform (Matthew 1988, 546–47). It was in this fashion that British democracy evolved into its contemporary popular form.

In Sweden, the process was similar but with an interesting historical fillip that placed nonnoble landowning at the center of the evolution toward democracy. Whereas the removal of the requirement of hereditary entitlement took place only in late seventeenth-century England, in a sense it was always absent in Sweden. Landownership was required for membership in the Swedish Riksdag, but not a hereditary title. From its inception then, commoners were represented in the Riksdag. Referring to the parliamentary consolidation of the fifteenth and early sixteenth centuries, Franklin Scott remarks, "The nobility [landowners], the clergy and the burghers (in that order) were the influential elements, but a full *riksdag* also had to have representation from the commonality.... This was not yet democracy, but it was a step in the slow progress toward democracy" (1988, 112). In 1617, a Riksdag ordinance established six estates for representation (Scott 1988, 185). Two of these never really materialized (princes and army officers), leaving the nobility, the clergy, burghers, and landowning farmers as the bases for Riksdag representation. The landowning nobility was still the dominant group, and they actually increased their power over time, as their landholdings increased and they mounted further challenges to royal power. By the early eighteenth century, however, the power of the nobility had been somewhat reduced and "the unique body in the *riksdag* was the farmer Estate, incorporating in the governmental machinery representatives of the large class of landholding farmers, the *bönder*. And this Estate grew in significance as the century advanced.... The *riksdag* met once every three years. The council, composed entirely of nobles, had been the 'king's council' under Karl XI; after 1719 it became the 'council of the kingdom' " (Scott 1988, 243).

Of course, the combination of noble and farmer landholdings on the one hand and an increasing number of very small holdings and the resultant class of landless and tenant farmers on the other contributed to a substantial degree of land inequality as the eighteenth century progressed. Eventual large-scale emigration, primarily to the United States, was the result (Samuelsson 1968). As of the late eighteenth century, "commoners and nobility were given equal access to most governmental positions as well as to the ownership of any class of property except the most highly privileged holdings, which were still reserved for the nobility. Furthermore, the peasants' unrestricted right to dispose of their holdings as they saw fit was formally recognized" (I. Anderson 1958, 92).

Another theoretical perspective proceeds from a different premise: that political violence is the midwife of democracy. Certainly the English, French, and American revolutions lend credence to this view. Barrington Moore (1966) is perhaps the most prominent exponent of this nexus between political violence and democracy. From Aristotle to Marx, the connection between inequalities of various sorts and political violence has been asserted and confirmed in a variety of studies, although of course, not without controversy. Some of these are Midlarsky 1988b; Muller and Seligson 1987; Muller, Seligson, Fu, and Midlarsky 1989; and Perotti 1996. The seminal treatment of land inequality in relation to political violence is Russett 1964, while that for general relative deprivation and violence is found in Gurr 1970. Controversial aspects of these findings are highlighted in Weede 1986 and 1987 and in the detailed argumentation found in Lichbach 1989 and 1990.

In this second view, land inequality results in political violence, which in turn leads to democratic reforms, either directly as a response to the violence or through a more complex revolutionary process and its aftermath (e.g., the French Revolution).

Interestingly, the American Revolution may represent the thwarting of the Athenian model and the emergence of political violence. With population growth over time and a consequent increased agricultural density, land inequality increased. As Richard Wilkinson observes of pre-Revolutionary New England, "Under the pressure of population growth, land holdings were subdivided, and within a few generations there were signs of a land shortage and a concomitant appearance of increasing numbers of landless poor" (1973, 149).

In this interpretation of the American Revolution, an affluent, expansionist, landowning, and merchant elite (Egnal 1988), who had emerged at the fortunate end of this land inequality, sought to break through the hereditary and, in many respects, "tribal" governance of the colonies by crown and Parliament. Essentially, a new colonial landowning hierarchy had been established and was becoming increasingly assertive politically as the eighteenth century progressed. Had the British government been responsive to the desire for increased political rights by the affluent colonists (or at least a formal voice in the making of tax and trade policy), then it is possible that the American Revolution would not have occurred and the attainment of democracy and independence would have had a far more evolutionary cast, as in the Canadian instance—and that the process of increased political rights, or democracy, would have conformed to the Athenian model. Failing that responsiveness by Westminster, political violence did indeed erupt in the form of the American Revolution.

It is noteworthy that the threat of political violence, although not its actual occurrence, may facilitate the Athenian model. Referring to the time of Solon, Andrew Lintott remarks that "the grievances of the Athenians in this period are important as evidence of incipient civil strife, which did not come immediately to fruition" (1982, 43).

There is a third perspective that is the most complex yet reasonably straightforward. High population density and the resultant land scarcity and inequality are sufficient to propel the landless or other rural poor to the cities, thus increasing urbanization.[4] Both ancient Athens and England in the seventeenth-century preindustrial era experienced this process (Morrill 1988; Wrightson 1982). Technological developments in both the city and the countryside increase trade and economic development in response to this ecological challenge (Wilkinson 1973), even as we saw in the Athenian illustration. In turn, economic development leads to political democracy by the arguments found in such seminal works as Lipset 1959, Lenski 1966, and Dahl 1971.

Environmental Influences

The second major theoretical emphasis of this chapter is that of environmental influences on democracy. This has venerable antecedents in the theories of Alfred Mahan (1890) and Halford Mackinder (1919) on the respective macro-influences of sea and land on national power. And Harold and Margaret Sprout (1962) later developed a coherent theory of environmental influences on international relations. A nexus between environmental change and violent conflict is found in the recent work of Homer-Dixon, Boutwell, and Rathjens (1993). However, there are still few outstanding general theories on the impact of environmental change on societal conditions.

One of the few theorists to have offered a general theory of environmental influences on domestic societal concerns was Karl Wittfogel (1957). Although often interpreted as a theory of the origins of the state (Haas 1982, 146), his was actually a theory of the rise of Eastern autocracy. This section will empirically examine his theory of hydraulic civilization, a process that presumably gave rise to autocracies in such civilizations as ancient Mesopotamia. This treatment also will "reverse the causal arrow" in examining the effects of war on democracy instead of the converse, as has been done recently. In doing so, it will reveal an important environmental influence on democracy, that of sea borders.

Because Wittfogel's theory is well known, it will not receive extensive presentation here, beyond the elements needed to advance the argument. By contrast, the effects of war on democracy are little known and so will receive a more developed exposition. As we shall see, aridity and the threat of war implied by many land borders constitute twin environmental threats to human civilization that historically have led to rigid controls in the form of political autocracy. But we shall also see that sufficient rainfall and a certain maximum number of sea borders can minimize the environmental threat and allow the growth of democracy without the need for despotic control of irrigation systems, food distribution, or the mobilization of sedentary populations to confront invading hostile forces.

Hydraulic Civilization

Karl Wittfogel enjoyed enormous influence on social-scientific treatments of the origins of the state. Researchers such as William Sanders and Barbara Price (1968) and even theorists such as Robert Carneiro (1970, 1987) based much of their earlier thinking on Wittfogel's theory. Briefly, the theory stipulates that early autocracies arose as a result of the human need to manage irrigation waters in arid zones. A bureaucratic-despotic organization was needed to manage the water diverted from rivers and streams—hence the term "hydraulic civilization," coined by Wittfogel, and its intimate connection with autocracy.

As Wittfogel puts it, "The fact that work on the public fields was usually shared by all corviable adult males indicates the power of the hydraulic leadership to make everyone contribute to its support. The establishment of a money economy goes hand in hand with greater differentiations in property, class structure, and national revenue. . . . Comparison shows that in this respect it was much stronger than the governments of other agrarian societies" (1957, 70). Or elsewhere, "Demonstrative and total submission is the only prudent response to total power. Manifestly, such behavior does not gain a superior's respect; but other ways of proceeding invite disaster. Where power is polarized, as it is in hydraulic society, human relations are equally polarized. Those who have no control over their government quite reasonably fear that they will be crushed in any conflict with its masters" (1957, 154).

Although several studies have disputed the relevance of Wittfogel's theory to the origins of the state (R. McC. Adams 1966; Chang 1986), none to my knowledge has in a systematic way empirically addressed the issue of hydraulic civilization in relation to autocracy or its logical and empirical obverse, democracy.[5] Perhaps one reason for this failure to test Wittfogel's hypothesis in relation to autocracy or democracy is its overused and misinterpreted application to the origins of the state per se. Another may be the difficulty in statistically analyzing the small number of historic hydraulic civilizations, but this problem may be solved by viewing it from an obverse standpoint. Rainfall and the need for hydraulic agriculture can be seen as flip sides of the same coin or as mirror images. As we have seen, aridity, as well as sources of irrigation, is required for a hydraulic civilization. Zones of sufficient rainfall (as in Northern Europe), by definition, are not arid and also do not require irrigation. Wittfogel himself recognizes this duality when he states that "the stimulating contradiction inherent in a potentially hydraulic landscape is manifest. Such a landscape has an insufficient rainfall or none at all; but it possesses other accessible sources of water supply. If man decides to utilize them, he may transform dry lands into fertile fields and gardens" (1957, 15–16). Further, we can examine the effect of rainfall on autocracy as well as democracy by using as the dependent variable a scale that reflects a continuum of political rights from the most complete to the most restricted. This scale will be introduced shortly.

Interestingly, the connection between hydraulic civilization and autocracy is not found only in ancient civilizations. Contemporary arid landscapes that have sources of water supply can also furnish illustrations. Spain, for example, has many arid regions that require irrigation for successful agriculture. And it was the Spanish dictator in the 1920's, Primo de Rivera, the precursor of later Spanish fascism, who made the most concentrated efforts up to that time to emphasize hydraulic agriculture. Indeed, according to Edward Malefakis, "Primo de Rivera . . . emulated Mussolini in deriving the maximum publicity from his hydraulic projects" (1970, 284).

There is another reason to identify rainfall as a relevant factor in the rise of democracy or diminution of autocracy, the need for centralized distribution systems in arid climates. Just as a bureaucratic-despotic regime can arise as a consequence of the need for centralized irrigation control, so too the need to store food and redistribute it in times of frequent drought-induced famine can lead to a centralized autocracy. Food and water are functionally interchangeable in this context. Bureaucracies necessary to administer the distribution of water in arid zones would be equally necessary to store and distribute food in time of drought. Decisions to distribute each of these commodities require centralized political control.

Spain offers another illustration of centralized decision making in response to aridity, this time for food redistribution. As in many other countries with arid climates, the monarchy took it upon itself to require the storage of food and its redistribution in times of scarcity. As Richard Herr remarks on such activities in eighteenth-century Spain, "The first response of the crown to the growing threat of grain shortages was to expand an institution long familiar in Spain. Beginning in the Middle Ages, Spanish authorities had established public granaries (pósitos) as a defense against bad harvests" (1989, 32). Clearly a central authority, and one likely given to autocratic methods in response to desperate human need, would be required. Wittfogel's comment on the polarization of power in hydraulic societies cited above applies to the instance of food redistribution as well as to irrigation. In extreme cases of aridity and drought, warlordism, an extreme form of despotism, can arise or be intensified, as we have recently seen in Somalia.

A third reason for identifying rainfall as a potential source of democracy is the ability of individual persons to escape from a despotic authority and begin to establish a more egalitarian and democratic society. In arid climates dependent on bureaucratically managed irrigation or food redistribution, people would not have that option. The desert in Egypt or Mesopotamia could not support large numbers of human beings if they chose to dissent from the prevailing despotic authority. (As we saw in Chapter 3, Carneiro (1970) identifies this situation as "circumscription" and ties it to the origins of the state.) In zones with large amounts of rainfall, on the other hand, escape to "open" villages, as in England, offered a reprieve, respite, and a potential source of opposition to the regime. These were areas that were not clearly tied into the dominant British political or social system and hence could serve as breeding grounds for dissent of various types and a further democratization of British society. Keith Wrightson, describes these areas in the following way: "As for the inhabitants of the 'open' parishes, certainly they were often poor and they were not immune from government, but the different conditions of their existence and the more egalitarian structure of their communities helped preserve to them what their social superiors saw as a worrying degree of independence of spirit which they did not trouble to hide" (1982, 171–72).

In general, rainfall is an *enduring* feature of the environmental landscape (as are sea borders, to be introduced shortly), in contrast to the vicissitudes of personal despotisms, which can vary considerably over time. Environmental variables of this type provide a constant backdrop to the political arena and constrain it to move in one or another direction.

Warfare and Democracy

Our second environmental concern emerges from the process of warfare. Just as bureaucratic-despotic political organizations can arise in response to the twin needs for irrigation and food redistribution as the result of limited rainfall, so too can they arise in response to the threat of war. Indeed, Wittfogel was concerned with the problem of war, but primarily in the form of conquest and expansion by hydraulic civilizations as a consequence of the control exercised over large, submissive populations. As he put it, "Organized control over the bulk of the population in times of peace gives the government extraordinary opportunities for coordinated mass action also in times of war" (1957, 59). Here, however, we are concerned with the *origins* of despotism, not its consequences for success in war and territorial expansion. As a result, the theoretical orientation differs from that of Wittfogel and in fact emerges from a different literature concerned with war and democracy.

In recent years, the relationship between democracy and war has begun to receive full exploration. The early philosophical development of the concept of "perpetual peace" by Kant has been expanded by scholars such as Michael Doyle (1983). Direct empirical examination of this relationship has led to the generally accepted conclusion that democracies seldom, if ever, fight each other (Rummel 1983; Chan 1984 and 1997; Maoz and Abdolali 1989; Morgan and Campbell 1991; Bremer 1992; Ember, Ember, and Russett 1992; Schweller 1992; Dixon 1993; Maoz and Russett 1993; Mintz and Geva 1993; Russett 1993; Ray 1995; Russett and Starr, forthcoming).[6] This chapter asks a different but ultimately related question, namely, what happens when the causal arrow is reversed? What is the impact of war on democracies, especially in their earliest stage of development, when they are still embryonic and clearly vulnerable? This question is of obvious importance in light of the large number of new democracies emerging from the former Soviet Union as well as those in Latin America and now, increasingly, Africa. To answer this question, we will need to turn to the early history of state-formation to discover the impact of warfare on early democracies, or at least societies that exhibited evidence of political rights for their residents. This analysis will set the stage for more systematic analyses of the modern period.

In fundamental ways, this treatment differs from that of Charles Tilly (1990, 16-28). Whereas Tilly points to the role of accumulated coercion and capital formation within states as a path to war, the analysis here emphasizes extreme threats to societies (states, chiefdoms, or other organized social forms) that may lead to autocracy as a mobilized response to the external threat. Early democracy can be easily vitiated in this fashion.

Three elements of democracy are emphasized here. First, in any democratic polity, or even one that has retained only the vestiges of democracy, there are limitations on executive or monarchical authority. Of course, this was the basis of English democracy as expressed initially in the Magna Carta and carried forward in history until the present. Second is the matter of representation, in which societal units of whatever form (congressional districts or Chinese *kan*, which were described in Chapter 4 and to which we shall return below) are represented within the governing unit(s). Finally, and perhaps most important in the modern period, is free and open elections as a basis for fair and impartial selection of the representatives who will govern.

This last requirement, although critical in contemporary history, especially in light of the political depredations of the twentieth century, is less salient for early societies. The massive size of modern political units themselves, compared with their early predecessors, requires a fair method of selection among so many potential candidates. In early city-states, however, the population was small enough so that all free men (and in some instances women) could participate in the assembly. Additionally, in ancient societies smaller groupings such as lineages likely had standard methods (e.g., age) for selecting among relatively few possible candidates, so that the issue of selection itself was not of central concern. As we shall see, political representation and limitations on monarchies will be found in one form or another in virtually all of the cases in prehistory considered here. Later, in the systematic analysis for the modern period, we will use the political rights index as a measure of early democracy, based principally on freedom of election.

Early Developments

Four ancient societies will be examined for whatever evidence they may offer on the nexus between democracy and war—ancient Sumer, Mesoamerica, China, and Crete. All have been discussed in Chapter 3, but the emphasis here is on the impact of war on early democratic forms rather than on state formation in general. As we saw in Chapter 3, the first three are generally acknowledged by anthropologists and archaeologists to be "pristine" states, meaning that they arose *spontaneously* and not through any external influence from earlier established polities (Fried 1967). Crete is not considered pristine, having been exposed to some Near Eastern influences and having been influenced by Egypt as well. But as I argued earlier, the coercive state as it developed in later Mesopotamia and Egypt was a model, not to be emulated, but to be escaped from. As such it would not likely be imitated by observers. In any event, Colin Renfrew (1972), a preeminent analyst and chronicler of the ancient Aegean, and Kwang-chih Chang (1986), perhaps the dean of American archaeologists of China, argue respectively that in both instances, the continuous development of indigenous cultures overshadowed any external influences. These influences also appeared well after the native civilizations had taken their unique forms. We also examine these societies well *before* increased population density led to the widespread use of centralized irrigation systems and a consequent autocracy. Certain elements of these societies discussed earlier in Chapter 3 (including potentially heterarchical ones; see Crumley 1995) will now be expanded upon in explaining the nexus between the threat of war and increased autocratic rule.

Sumer. Evidence for the early development of what has been called "primitive democracy" (Jacobsen 1943) comes from one of the earliest written documents, the Gilgamesh epic. Perhaps it is best to allow Samuel Kramer to summarize:

In early days, political power lay in the hands of these free citizens and a city-governor known as *ensi*, who was no more than a peer among peers. In case of decisions vital to the city as a whole, these free citizens met in a bicameral assembly consisting of an upper house of "elders" and a lower house of "men." As the struggle between the city-states grew more violent and bitter, and as the pressures from the barbaric peoples to the east and west of Sumer increased, military leadership became a pressing need, and the king, or as he is known in Sumerian, the "big man," came to hold a superior place. At first he was probably selected and appointed by the assembly at a critical moment for a specific military task. But gradually kingship with all its privileges and prerogatives became a hereditary institution and was considered the very hallmark of civilization." (1963, 74)

Elsewhere, Kramer (1981, 30–35) refers to a bicameral "congress" consisting of a "senate" of elders and an "assembly" of fighting men. Recently disclosed archaeological evidence from Mashkan-shapir in Mesopotamia supports this view. As Elizabeth Stone and Paul Zimansky put it, "The overall organization of Mashkan-shapir suggests that textual sources have not misled us about the broad involvement of Mesopotamian city dwellers in shaping their local power relationships" (1995, 123).

Supporting evidence has recently been found in an ancient Hurrian city, Urkesh, a contemporary of the Sumerian cities (ca. 2300 B.C.), located in northeastern Syria. An unexpected gender equality emerges in which the queen, Uqnitum, apparently had at least equal, if not superior, power to the king. Most of the official seals discovered were hers, not his, and "she appears as a property owner in her own right, as distinct from the king. . . . She could exercise direct control at least over that part of the storehouse where her goods were being kept" (Buccellati and Kelly-Buccellati, quoted in Wilford 1995, C5).

Here, in a nutshell, is the basic argument. The early state evolves in a democratic or quasi-democratic fashion, including, as in this instance, bicameralism, but the threat of war intervenes in the form of hostile city-states or predatory nomadic herdsmen. The influence of the latter on early state-formation has been singled out especially by Ronald Cohen (1978). The "big man" becomes necessary to confront the danger of these external threats by his or her (cf. the Biblical heroine Deborah) examples of bravery or organizational skills. When the threat of war persists, as it frequently does, the temporary military leader can, over time, easily become the hereditary monarch.

As late as the Old Babylonian period (early second millennium B.C.), the office of *rabianum* or "mayor" of a small city rotated every year among the "elders." By this time, the assembly had been reduced to an organ of local administration but it "could nevertheless write letters to the King, make legal decisions, sell real estate, and assume corporate responsibility for robbery or murder committed within its jurisdiction" (Oates 1977, 476). Even the later Mesopotamian city, according to A. Leo Oppenheim is characterized by a "lack of status stratification" (1977, 11), suggesting the continuation of the earlier essentially egalitarian and democratic practices.

In the Epic of Gilgamesh we even have a record of a likely transition from the earlier democratic period to the later monarchical one. Gilgamesh himself very probably was a ruler of Uruk in the Early Dynastic I period (mid-third millennium B.C.). At the beginning of the poem, Gilgamesh tells how he had to suppress the people of the city in order to build a city wall (Nissen 1988, 95). Here we have the nexus between the necessity for fortifications to counter the threat of war and coercive action against the population that is characteristic of the end of democracy and the rise of autocratic rule. Additional evidence for the gradual emergence of autocratic leadership, likely stemming from temporary war leadership, is given by Harriet Crawford (1991, 170).

The transition from democracy in our other instances is less clear. Nevertheless there is evidence of what I call vestigial democracy in all three.

Mesoamerica. As we have seen, the Maya were a literate people that left various records in the form of glyphs and stone carvings. Although they were exposed to other Mesoamerican cultures, probably the Olmec and certainly Teotihuacan, again whatever influences were decisive occurred well after the Formative period and the consolidation of the indigenous culture. A sequence of events occurring between 200 B.C. and A.D. 200 basically transformed the culture (R. E. W. Adams 1991, 128).

An explicit model for rotation of political and religious offices by early Maya leaders has been put forward by Evon Vogt (1971). Theoretically, every man in Maya society was eligible for such offices. Successful fulfillment of lesser political and religious offices qualified one for higher offices, which rotated among the eligible persons. Although Vogt suggests that the model may even extend to the Classic period, Richard Adams argues that "the model might well fit the Middle and late Formative societal picture but not the later Classic period," because of the "increasingly aristocratic principle" (1991, 189) that developed later and was associated with considerable warfare among the Mayan city-states or regional polities (Hammond 1988). This warfare, as we have seen in Chapter 4, along with other factors, probably led to the Maya collapse, at least in the lowlands (see also Culbert 1973a).

Warfare also very likely intensified elite control of Mayan society. We know that the Maya aristocracy must have gained increasing control, not only by evidence of the increasing distance between elite and commoner (Sabloff 1990, 143), but also by the spurt in Maya construction by the elite, especially at

Tikal during the Terminal Classic period before the collapse (Blanton et al. 1981, 208). Such large-scale construction must have required the mobilization of significant numbers of commoners, probably by force or at least the threat of severe sanctions. The democratic or quasi-democratic practices suggested by Vogt would have had to give way to the increasingly emergent aristocracy, as competition and warfare became prevalent in the Maya civilization.

An interesting perspective is provided by research on the island of Cozumel off the Yucatan coast. The island began to flourish in the Terminal Classic period and continued through the Late Postclassic, well after the heyday of the Lowland Maya and their frequent internecine wars. The island may have escaped much of that warfare by virtue of both its temporal development and its island status. Many sites have been found inland, suggesting the avoidance of raids by tribesmen and others from the mainland. Of greatest interest is the large number of sites and the dense population of the island along with evidence of an increasing egalitarianism in the holding of goods by the commoners in the population (Sabloff 1990, 133–34). This possible association between increasing density of agricultural population and their increased political rights, in the absence of war, will have strong echoes in the subsequent analysis.

Evidence of a vestigial nature also comes from another, somewhat unexpected area of Mesoamerica, Teotihuacan. Long thought of as an absolutist theocracy, recent research has suggested a decentralized element of its rule. As noted in Chapter 3, George Cowgill (1983) has focused on the Ciudadela, a great structure in Teotihuacan that is generally believed to have been the residence of the rulers of that city-state. The basic question that he raises is why, in light of the monumental aspects of that structure, the apartments within it cover so small an area. Centralization of political authority would require much larger space. As Cowgill puts it, "the most important point is that the Ciudadela does not seem to provide enough facilities for much of the day-to-day government of either the city or the state of Teotihuacan" (1983, 331). He then identifies several possible political loci outside of the Ciudadela that could have fulfilled administrative functions. The importance of this structure apparently resides in its symbolic significance as a home of the political elite. The building of it likely "represents the relatively orderly intensification of long-term trends" (336) of increased autocracy. If so, then there should exist earlier periods of outright decentralized rule, if not a rudimentary democracy, that gradually came under greater centralized and autocratic control. It is noteworthy that the Ciudadela remained pretty much as it had been constructed for approximately 350 years, with changes in its architecture occurring only at a time close to the fall of the city. High-level centralized political management may have been required at the time of external threat to the city, consistent with the hypothesized relationship between increasing external threat and autocratic rule.

Crete. The evidence in the case of Crete is not abundant, partly because there is no translation of Linear A, the apparent language of Minoan Crete. Linear B, an early ancestor of classical Greek, also was discovered on the island and has been translated. It is likely that the Linear B script was introduced after the Mycenaen conquest of Crete from the Greek mainland (after 1400 B.C.; Graham 1987). Nevertheless, there is evidence for at least a vestigial democracy in Minoan Crete, which likely occurred in the absence of war, because prior to the Mycenaen conflict there is no evidence of fortifications on the island. This remarkable lack of fortification distinguishes Minoan society from the remainder of the ancient Aegean and even from the vast majority of the world (Branigan 1970; Cadogan 1976; Finley 1981; Matz 1973; Renfrew 1972; and Willetts 1965). Let us now examine the kinds of political arrangements that attended the growth of this island civilization.

Initially, the society was egalitarian, as suggested by the undifferentiated status of individuals interred in the Early Minoan tombs (Branigan 1970). Later, as in most other societies, stratification occurred, but the consequences for leadership tenure appear to differ from the hereditary status of leadership that developed in societies in which warfare, or at least the threat of war, is prominent. As Keith Branigan tells it

> In Early Minoan II and Early Minoan III as overseas trade grew and towns began to emerge from villages, the importance of the man who produced and controlled the main commodities of trade would increase greatly. Such men would naturally rise to prominence and be elected to office. It seems not unlikely that the period of tenure would be eight years. The legends which relate the octennial offering of Athenian youths to the Minotaur and the octennial departure of Minos to converse with Zeus are thought to indicate that this was the period of tenure during the palatial era and such an important tradition would very probably have its roots in the origins of the system, which seem to be in the Early Bronze Age. (1970, 119)

Thus, leadership tenure apparently was limited. This is consistent with another limitation that also distinguishes Crete from other ancient societies. In comparison with other cultures of the same period, there is little that is royal or majestic abut the political presence in the palaces. As we saw in Chapter 3, even the throne is not especially impressive in the largest palace at Knossos. No pictures exist that depict historical events or "which reveal administrative or judicial activity or any other manifestation of political power in action" (Finley 1981, 41). Finley (42) associates this absence of monumentality with the absence of war, but it could also easily be associated with the absence of hereditary monarchs who would seek to augment their own status as did the pharaohs of Egypt and other leaders of that period.

China. There is also evidence in China suggestive of an early vestigial democracy. I rely here on Chang's (1980) analysis, for it is the most complete study in English of the Shang, the first Chinese civilization for which we have written records, particularly in the form of a king list. Other studies in English exist (e.g., Keightley 1983), but the majority of analyses are in Chinese and indeed many of them are reviewed by Chang (1980, 1986).

Members of the ruling clan actively involved with the kingship were segmented into ten categories, called *kan* units, which had both ritual and political significance. In turn, *kan* units were affiliated with two divisions, A and B, that constituted two large aggregate groupings. As described in Chapter 3, there were two rules of succession for the kingship: "First, it could not stay within the same *kan* unit and second, when the kingship stayed within division A or B, it had to be assumed by an heir from another *kan* unit from within the same generation as the former king, but if it went over to the other division, it had to go to an heir of the next generation" (Chang 1980, 180-81). Put another way, when the kingship passed to another generation, it was forced to move to the opposite division. An alternation in power between two political groupings, not terribly dissimilar to that of a two-party system, is found here. Further, the king's principal official advisor was the chief of a *kan* unit from the opposite division. Thus, no individual *kan* unit was allowed to dominate politically, in addition to the alternations between divisions A and B.

Certainly these rules do not constitute democracy, but they do establish political rights for other political and religious units in Shang society. And this vestigial form of democracy, expressed as political rights, existed well after warfare became fairly endemic, both within the more civilized portion of China and between the settled villages and invading nomads from the north and west that in fact necessitated the building of the Great Wall of China during the first dynasty to unify China, the Ch'in (Hucker 1975, 44). Without such incursions, it is possible that an earlier, possibly more egalitarian form would have persisted, instead of the more vestigial version that we find in Shang society.

One pattern emerges clearly: the increasing aristocratic control of these ancient societies, usually associated with increasing incidence of war. From this we can infer the existence of early, less autocratic, or more democratic control, at least in the form of representational arrangements for clans, kinship groups, and the like.

The Impact of Ideology: The Huntington Paradigm

The third strain of theory in our analysis is concerned with ideology, specifically Islam in its relation to democracy. In the summer of 1993, Samuel P. Huntington published a now famous article in *Foreign Affairs* (1993a) suggesting the strong likelihood of civilizational conflict in the foreseeable future. This suggestion did not go without challenge, and a subsequent issue of *Foreign Affairs* contained several critiques (among others, Ajami 1993; Bartley 1993) and a still later issue presented Huntington's response (1993b). A more detailed development of his ideas is found in Huntington 1996.[7] It is my purpose to test empirically and systematically at least one central implication of Huntington's formulation, an enterprise that has not previously been accomplished, despite the considerable publicity generated by his writings. Among the results of this test is a reflection on the necessity for this additional level of analysis for understanding international conflict.

I should begin by clarifying several features of Huntington's position as well as the nature of the empirical test. First, although in his original article Huntington did not assert that his "clash of civilizations" was paradigmatic, he did do so in response to his critics. As he put it, "The Clash of Civilizations is an effort to lay out elements of a Post-Cold War paradigm" (1993b, 187). Like the Cold War paradigm it replaces, this "Clash of Civilizations" is essentially descriptive, but at the same time contains intimations of an explanatory paradigm for future international conflict. Second, my test of the paradigm is only partial, although as we shall see, it is concerned with a critical aspect of his formulation. It is extraordinarily difficult to test directly the whole of a current state of affairs that, it is presumed, will in the future burgeon into a full-fledged set of international divisions reflecting a state of extreme tension, if not outright violence. Thus, selecting one key feature of that paradigm, democracy, and testing it is a far more manageable way to proceed and, as we shall see, will pay dividends beyond that of examining the Huntington paradigm itself. The test is partial in a second sense, in that only one of the civilizations mentioned by him will be examined, but that civilization, Islam, occupies the lion's share of his attention and so is deserving of emphasis here.

Findings that emerge from this analysis will reflect not only on the relationship between democracy and Islam, with implications for the future occurrence of civilizational conflict, if any, but also on three different forms of democracy—a basic freedom-of-election index, one more associated with liberal democracy, and a third index, more explicitly associated with institutional forms. These measures will be shown to have divergent structures of explanation, with important consequences for understanding the sources of democracy in differing contexts. They also may yield different conclusions concerning the likelihood of war between democracies when employed in future research. The culture of democracy will be evident in predicting to two of the measures, but not to the same extent to the remaining one, which is better explained by environmental and socioeconomic variables.

Huntington's formulation asserts the primacy of civilization as the current salient basis of human organization that will likely evolve into future civilizational conflict. As he puts it, "Civilization identity will be increasingly important in the future, and the world will be shaped in large measure by the interactions among seven or eight major civilizations. These include Western, Confucian, Japanese, Islamic, Hindu, Slavic-Orthodox, Latin American, and possibly African civilization. The most important conflicts of the future will occur along the cultural fault lines separating these civilizations from one another" (1993a, 25). The reasons for this conflict are straightforward. Again in Huntington's words:

Civilizations are differentiated from each other by history, language, culture, tradition and, most important, religion. The people of different civilizations have different views on the relations between God and man, the individual and the group, the citizen and the state, parents and children, husband and wife, as well as differing views of the relative importance of rights and responsibilities, liberty and authority, equality and hierarchy. These differences are the product of centuries. They will not soon disappear. They are far more fundamental than differences among political ideologies and political regimes. (25)

But of the civilizations enumerated by Huntington, one is singled out above all of the others as the basis for future conflict with the West, namely Islam. A fault line is suggested to exist between Western and Islamic civilizations that has persisted for 1,300 years. Further, "On both sides the interaction between Islam and the West is seen as a clash of civilizations" (32). After several quotations supporting this view and an enumeration of current conflicts between Muslims and other groups such as Orthodox Serbs, Jews in Israel, and Hindus in India, he concludes that "Islam has bloody borders" (39). Further, "the next world war, if there is one, will be a war between civilizations" (39).

It is clear to Huntington that there are salient features of Western society that distinguish it from others. "Western concepts differ fundamentally from those prevalent in other civilizations. Western ideas of individualism, liberalism, constitutionalism, human rights, equality, liberty, the rule of law, democracy, free markets, the separation of church and state, often have little resonance in Islamic, Confucian," and other civilizations (40). It is these features that suggest a test of the Huntington paradigm, for if they are indeed distinct from Islam, with no hope of a mutual incorporation, then Huntington is probably correct in his prognosis of future civilizational conflict. If, on the other hand, Islam is shown to have certain compatibilities with the characteristics enumerated by Huntington, or at least no strong enduring constraints against them that could not be rectified by other societal means, then a significant portion of Huntington's paradigm is put into serious question.

What do these characteristics of Western civilizations have in common? It is clear that they all converge on democracy or its strong form, liberal democracy. Each of the features enumerated by Huntington, whether it be liberalism, constitutionalism, human rights, liberty, or democracy itself, has some association with modern democratic governance. Thus, it is democracy and its variants that we should examine to see the extent to which Islam may demonstrate compatibilities.

Huntington is not alone in his concern for the potential conflict between Islam and the West, or, more specifically, the relationship between democracy and Islam. An entire issue of *Current History* is devoted to the question of whether or not democracy and Islam are mutually exclusive (see, e.g., Norton 1995). An issue of *Foreign Affairs* places four articles under the rubric of "the Islamic Cauldron" (including Shirley 1995 and Viorst 1995). This current concern is not without antecedents, for it has been generally acknowledged that the relationship between the Islamic faith and government in predominantly Muslim societies is more intimate than most. In the words of Bernard Lewis, previously quoted in Chapter 6,

The true and sole sovereign in the Muslim view was God, from whose mandate the Prophet derived his authority and whose will, made known by revelation, was the sole source of law. The *umma* thus expressed from its inception the fusion of politics and religion characteristic of the later Islamic states.... In the Islamic world, therefore, there could be no conflict between Pope and Emperor, for the powers which these two represented were one and the same." (1987, xvi–xvii)

More recently, Lewis affirmed the unity of Islam as a civilization, for, as he put it, "It is a political identity and allegiance, transcending all others" (1993b, 4–5). In such a fusion or even near fusion of politics and religion, it is difficult to envision the evolution of political democracy as we have come to know it in the West.

Observers of the actual practice of democracy in Islamic societies tend to agree. For example, after a comprehensive examination of democratic practices or their absence in six Islamic societies (Algeria, Egypt, Iran, Malaysia,

Pakistan, and Sudan), John Esposito and John Voll (1996) observe that "In these debates, it is clear that Muslims are not willing simply to adopt Western democratic models. The period of unquestioningly borrowing techniques and concepts from Western experience has passed (if it ever took place), and now the effort is to establish authentically Islamic democratic systems." Analysts of Islamic societies in other regions such as the former Soviet Central Asia tend to agree (Haghayeghi 1996).

In addition to its centrality in Huntington's paradigm and a more general scholarly and societal concern, there is another compelling reason for examining the relationship between democracy and Islam. This is the now often confirmed finding that democracies seldom, if ever, fight each other, certainly not in the modern period. Thus, if Islamic states can democratize, even to some extent, then the likelihood of conflict both among themselves (e.g., Iran-Iraq, Egypt-Libya) and between them and Western states would be vastly diminished.[8]

The Model

The Dependent Variable: Democracy

Huntington's separate listing of *liberalism* and *democracy* in his enumeration of the salient characteristics of Western civilization reveals an important distinction. Whereas *democracy* itself can emphasize basic political rights, such as freedom of election, *liberal democracy*, which is more closely identified with Western forms, tends also to include other freedoms (of belief, assembly, or political opposition) and an effective legislature.[9] A third measure of democracy—an explicit emphasis on institutional forms—has also been used. Indeed there exist three data sets with just such differing emphases. The first, that of Raymond Gastil (1988), is called the political rights index, which emphasizes free elections and has been used in the explanation of more rudimentary forms of democracy (Midlarsky, 1992a; 1995). The second, explicitly called an index of liberal democracy, was developed more recently by Kenneth Bollen (1993). It includes, in addition to the emphasis on basic political rights, two other components, the existence of a free political opposition and an effective legislative body. Bollen's index was built upon an analysis of several other indexes of democracy, including Gastil's, which he found to have the highest "validity" of any of the existing indexes examined, the lowest systematic or "method" error, and no random error associated with it (Bollen 1993, 1220). The index of liberal democracy is especially useful here because of its inherent Western cultural content, to be examined in relation to the strong cultural elements in political Islam. This sets the stage for a potential contrast with the less culturally oriented political rights index. Finally, a measure that has been used extensively in recent analyses of democracy is the Polity III index (Jaggers and Gurr 1995), in which the scale reflects such institutions of democracy as competition among contending groups, constraints on the exercise of political power, and the openness and competitiveness of executive recruitment to serve within the major political institutions.

These indexes offer three variations of our dependent variable of analysis, reflecting different emphases in measuring democracy. For the purposes of the later multivariate statistical test I have averaged Gastil's political rights index for the fifteen-year period between 1973 and 1987, effectively an updating of Charles Taylor and David Jodice's averaging of Gastil's published index for 1973–79 (Taylor and Jodice 1983, 1: 58–61). The averaging was done (1) to allow for the correction of errors if they crept in for an earlier year, (2) to give a fairly long "window" of measurement in contrast to virtually all other measures of this type, which are given for one year only, (3) to allow for greater variability in the dependent variable by adding a decimal point to yearly data, which in the data source are given only in single-digit form (a scale of 1 to 7), and (4) to provide a median year that is comparable to Bollen's (1993) data. Averaging also minimizes the possibility of systematic error found by Bollen. Random error proved to be nonexistent in the Gastil data set for 1980 and the validity was found to be 93 percent, the highest of all the data sets examined by Bollen, but that still leaves 7 percent for "method" or systematic error (Bollen 1993, 1220). If judges' ratings leading to the scale scores of Gastil's index tend toward bias in one year or two, then it is possible that averaging over a fifteen-year period may minimize such method bias. On the whole, the scores tend toward consistency for most countries during this period, and fluctuations, where found, are not extreme. A parallel analysis using only the 1980 data (the median year) yielded virtually identical conclusions, but without the clarity of findings and increased percentages of the variance explained made possible by the averaging process. The creation of a sensitive political rights index is especially important here, because, as we shall see, this index is, of the three, inherently the least intimately associated with the variable Islam; for theoretical reasons, every opportunity should be generated to maximize the negative association between Islam and this measure of democracy.

Because the averaging process for the dependent variable yields 1980 as the median year, and the most complete data for the independent variables, which we will discuss below, are circa 1970 and 1975, a desirable five-to-ten-year lag is effectively introduced to allow for the impact of the societal variables on political rights. The average scores, as noted, are from 1 to 7, taken to one decimal place, thus effectively yielding a scale from 10 to 70 (10 = most political rights, 70 = least political rights), comparable although certainly not identical in range and precision to that of Bollen. The scale criteria are given in Gastil (1988, 29-35).

Bollen's liberal democracy index (1993) is scored from 1 to 100 and is an equal weighting of Arthur Banks's (1971; 1979) political opposition and legislative effectiveness measures and Gastil's (1988) political-rights index. The data are given only for 1980, the same year as the median year for the political-rights index examined separately here. The Polity III democracy scores, chosen for 1980, comprise eleven-point scales constructed from codings on the competitiveness of political participation, competitiveness of executive recruitment, openness of executive recruitment, and constraints on the chief executive (Jaggers and Gurr 1995, 471).

The Independent Variables and Data Sources

With the dependent variable in place, we can specify the independent variables in a straightforward manner. Countries included in this analysis were those with market economies during the period 1973-87 (see listing in Appendix B), in keeping with the basic strategy of obtaining as many cases as possible, consistent with the time span of the political-rights index and a time lag between independent and dependent variables. As noted above, this time lag was considered necessary to allow some time for the socioeconomic variables to affect the measure of democracy, especially more "remote" variables such as agricultural density and land inequality. Thus, most of the data for these variables center on 1970, whereas those with perhaps some more immediate impact, such as economic development, are circa 1975, allowing for an approximate five-to-ten-year lag for most variables until the median year of 1980 for the dependent variable. The actual lag is not crucial, as these variables do not change rapidly in time.

Agricultural density is reported for the year 1970 in Taylor and Jodice (1983, 1: 102-4), whereas for the Gini index of *land inequality*, circa 1970, the data in Muller and Seligson (1987, 445-47) were used, because this is perhaps the most comprehensive recent list of such data available. *Age of the polity* (logged to control for outliers so that they will not unduly influence the findings) is introduced as the year of independence to control for maturation of democratic processes and is found for most countries in Taylor and Hudson (1972, 26-28); where necessary this is supplemented by values from Lye and Carpenter (1987).

Two economic indicators also are included as variables. Economic development is measured by *GDP per capita* to allow for the impact of purely domestic processes and is found in Summers and Heston 1984 for the year 1975. This makes it consistent with the second economic variable, the *trade/GNP ratio* for 1975 (Taylor and Jodice 1983, 1: 226–28), which is included to examine the impact of external commercial contacts while controlling for the overall size of the economy. In this case the entire economy, not just its domestic component, should be controlled in relation to the international variable, trade.

The variable *deaths per capita due to political violence* was drawn from the numerical listing of the 1948 to 1977 series found in Taylor and Jodice (1983, 2: 48–51) and divided by population size. Data for later years (1976 and 1977) were deemed to be part of the entire political violence process and so were included.

Our two environmental variables for empirical testing are *precipitation* and *minimization of the threat of war*. Average precipitation for a country is measured by the annual average experienced by all major cities in that country for the period 1931–60 (Bair 1992).[10] The use of all major cities is simply a means of obtaining a geographical dispersion for a country. Smaller countries, of course, have a smaller number of cities associated with this measure.

The minimized-threat variable is also to be understood within an environmental context, namely the *number of sea borders*. This connection may require some explanation. First, except for Crete, all of the preceding illustrations of eventual autocratic empires—Mesopotamia, Mesoamerica, and China—were land-based. And Crete, as we have seen, never really evolved into an autocratic empire comparable to the others. Second, we know that several studies have found a significant positive relationship between the number of land borders a country has and that country's war experience (Richardson 1960; Starr and Most 1978). Thus, the number of sea borders constitutes one element of a country's minimization of the threat of war.

This measure also does not suffer from difficulties in interpretation that a direct measure of war experience would incur. Whereas it is clear that democracy cannot cause geography in the form of sea borders, no such certainty exists in the case of autocracy and actual war experience. Autocracies may begin more wars, as is implied by much of the earlier research cited. On the other hand, autocracies may be a consequence of wars, as I have suggested here. Correlations, even within a multivariate setting as will be done shortly, cannot distinguish between these two possible interpretations. There is another problem that is equally troublesome, namely, that the available war data during the past several centuries do not reflect the earlier experiences of nation-states that may have laid the foundations for democratic development many centuries ago, as in the instances of England and Iceland. Minimization of the threat of war and especially of invasion from abroad may have occurred in early national history, thus allowing for a slow democratic development not hindered by a constant military preparedness. The existence of a large military establishment, of course, increases the probability of military intervention against democratic rule, as the Costa Ricans understood nearly a half century ago.

Democracy in ancient Athens, in fact, may be a consequence of the minimization of external threat resulting from a peninsular setting. We know that Athens is one of the few ancient Greek city-states that was distinguished by continuity even through the dark ages (Warren 1989), perhaps as a result of its semi-protected position on the Attican peninsula. Equally to the point is the evolution of democracy in portions of the Cyclades and other islands in the Aegean not far from Attica off the Greek coast. Renfrew (1982) emphasizes the interaction among various Aegean polities that likely led to the spread of democracy among the Ionian-dominated islands. It is probable that geographic protection from war among these islands and peninsulas allowed for a continued democratic development which simply was not experienced by communities in the interior, subject to the threat and actuality of war.

Another argument for use of the sea borders variable emerges from an exacting test of an earlier model of democracy (Midlarsky 1992b). In an examination of residuals from prediction, those countries whose values were least well explained by domestic variables were those that were either islands or peninsulas. Sri Lanka, Papua New Guinea, Jamaica, Malaysia, Ireland, Dominican Republic, and Greece were underpredicted by the model, having in fact levels of democracy that were simply too great to be explained by the variables then constituting the model. These countries also had levels of international violence that were very low or nonexistent relative to the international norm.

As a final assessment of the validity of sea borders as a measure of minimum threat, it was correlated with *change in the size of military force*. Clearly force size alone is a function of many domestic and international factors, not the least of which may be political and bureaucratic inertia stemming from earlier historical experiences. (Both Austria and Hungary had officers with the rank of admiral in their military establishments during the interwar period, when both countries were landlocked.) But changes in such force sizes, even in the short term, can reveal feelings of security or insecurity associated with geographical position. The sea borders variable (0–4) was constructed by assigning 0 to countries with no sea borders, 1 to those with one sea border, and so on through islands, defined as having four sea borders. The source was Lye and Carpenter (1987).

Change in the size of military force itself is measured by increase, decrease, or no change in the number of military personnel per thousand working-age persons between 1965 and 1975 (Taylor and Jodice 1983, 1: 37–39).[11] A reduction or no change between the two years was coded as 1, while an increase was coded as 0. The number of sea borders and change in military personnel size correlated $r = .35$ ($N = 113$, $p < .001$), suggesting a highly significant relationship between them. Given the many reasons for changes in military force size, including purely bureaucratic ones, this relationship between a large number of sea borders, reflecting a fair degree of security, and decline or no change in military personnel size over a ten-year period is noteworthy. Later we will see that the geographical variable performs better in explaining democracy than changes in military force size, probably because of additional extraneous influences (e.g., bureaucratic) on those changes.

Islam, as we have noted, is predicted to be negatively related to democracy. This variable is measured by the percentage of the population who are Muslim, circa 1980. This measure was chosen because the greater the proportion of the population that is Muslim, the more probable it is that Islamic laws will govern the society, at least in part. Within a predominantly Muslim society, an identification between state and society can occur in which Islam is the only religion that has governmental sanction (Turan 1991). Most any government that allows revealed truth to be its guiding ideation tends to be more autocratic. Moreover, Islamist movements generally seek an "authentic" Islam. To the extent that such movements emphasize the particularistic elements of Islamic culture, thereby denying the universalistic elements associated with liberal humanism, they tend to be undemocratic.

At the same time, using the percentage of the population that is Muslim allows for the possibility of large Muslim populations *not* opting to be governed by political Islam (as in Morocco and Tunisia) and also avoids conflating Islam and *political* Islam in its current fundamentalist manifestation. Further arguments concerning the use of this measure are found in Midlarsky 1998.

Standard references such as *The World in Figures* (1988) and *Statesman's Yearbook* (1983, 1990, 1991) were consulted. An earlier, "pilot" study used a dummy variable based on whether the government was Muslim-dominated or not, but this dichotomous variable yielded smaller proportions of the variance explained, hence lower predictive validity than did the continuous one used here.

Two more variables are included—*British colonial heritage* and *European location*—that principally reflect the strong cultural content of Western forms of democracy. Many of the islands that have democratized, such as Sri Lanka, Jamaica, and Ireland, were British colonies and so, to avoid an artifact of democratic rule simply as the result of diffusion originally at the hands of the British navy, conquering territories that later established parliamentary forms of government, British colonial heritage (0, 1) is included.[12] A similar argument holds for the inclusion of European location as a variable (0, 1). The possibility of a diffusion of democracy there, especially under the impetus of the European Community/European Union, should be controlled. The culture of democracy (Putnam 1993) may have originated and then been reinforced in Europe. A possible artifact of precipitation associated with democracy because of a European locus (more precipitation obviating the necessity for irrigation works and their implied association with autocracy), but not elsewhere, also should be controlled.

Finally, *population size* is included, for two reasons. First, island countries tend to be small in size and therefore potentially limited in population, and this could introduce an artifact of size. Second, smaller countries may be more easily governed democratically, as suggested by Robert Dahl and Edward Tufte (1973). Population size for 1975 (Taylor and Jodice 1983, 1: 91–94), logged to control for outliers, is used to control for these possibilities.

Testing the Model

For our first test of the model, presented in Table 7.1, it is informative to examine the bivariate and multivariate impact of the independent variables, especially Islam, on the three dependent variables—political rights, liberal democracy, and the Polity III index—in the absence of the environmental variables. Tables 7.2 and 7.3 then present a sequence of added variables and assess their overall effect. This process will allow us to include the maximum number of cases in the analysis at each stage, until we reach land inequality in the last table, for which data are not plentiful. In each of the three tables, then, there are three rows of values for each of the independent variables, one for each of the forms of the dependent variable: the political rights index in the first row, the liberal democracy index in the second, and the Polity III index in the third. Zero order—bivariate correlations examining the effect of one independent variable on the dependent variable without controlling for other factors—and partial correlations are included to examine the changes that occur when additional variables are introduced into the equations. Effectively, a partial correlation reports the impact of a single independent variable with the effects of all others in the equation controlled. The numbers in these two columns, varying between −1 and +1, provide degrees of association, negative or positive, between the independent and dependent variables.

Tolerances were examined as measures of the extent of collinearity, but in the interests of brevity and continuity of presentation are not included. (The tolerance is defined as $1 - R_i^2$ where R_i^2 is the maximum explained variation in one independent variable by all of the others.) Another measure of collinearity, the Variance Inflation Factor (VIF), sometimes is used and is the reciprocal of the tolerance, thus containing precisely the same information (Kleinbaum, Kupper, and Muller 1988). A t test of significance for each of the regression coefficients, another measure of controlled association for each independent variable, is shown in the final column.

As expected, Islam is strongly negatively associated with all three indexes in Table 7.1, and GDP per capita is positively associated. Both the bivariate and partial correlations are high, and the regression coefficients (b) are highly significant, as shown by the t tests in the final column. Interestingly, even after introduction of the remaining variables in the equation for political rights, Islam has the second-highest partial correlation. In the remainder of the table each of the equations—for political rights, liberal democracy, and Polity III— will be discussed separately, for the findings at this point diverge. First, regarding political rights, British colonial heritage is significant in the predicted direction, but agricultural density is significant in the opposite (negative) direction, a matter that will be treated in the following discussion. Both the age of the polity and population size are significant, as is the trade/GNP ratio; shortly all of these elements will prove to be nonsignificant. The proportion of explained variance, R^2, is substantial, as is the proportion of explained variance adjusted for specifics of the analysis, R_a^2. Tolerances, as noted earlier, are not included here but are high, uniformly above .40, suggesting that multicollinearity (an excessive degree of association between two or more independent variables) overall is not a problem here, although agricultural density and the trade/GNP ratio will shortly be shown to demonstrate a collinear bias.

In the second row for each of the variables, the analysis of the liberal democracy index, we see certain similarities with the findings reported in the first, but fundamental differences as well. Islam, GDP per capita, and British colonial heritage still are significant, but now European location also is significant, as shown by the high t values in the final column. This theme of cultural influences on liberal democracy recurs throughout the various analyses. The only other significant variable is population size; the proportions of explained vari-

TABLE 7.1.
Regression of the Political Rights, Liberal Democracy,
and Polity III Indexes on the Initial Explanatory Variables

Variable	Bivariate correlation (r)	Partial correlation	Regression coefficient (b)	t value[b]
Islam	−.43[a]	−.33	−.01	−3.26***
	−.44	−.37	−.26	−3.64***
	−.44	−.35	−.03	−3.46***
British colonial heritage	.08	.26	.77	2.52**
	.20	.36	20.84	3.54***
	.19	.40	2.72	4.06***
European location	.60	.13	.57	1.26
	.59	.27	22.17	2.56**
	.60	.27	2.52	2.55**
Economic development (GDP per capita)	.79	.54	.001	5.93***
	.73	.46	.01	4.85***
	.75	.50	.001	5.26***
Agricultural density	.01	−.21	−.0001	−1.97*
	.02	−.14	−.002	−1.33
	−.02	−.20	−.0003	−1.85*
Age of the polity (log)	.51	.20	8.14	1.88*
	.36	.02	16.12	.19
	.38	.09	8.38	.87
Deaths per capita due to political violence	−.21	−.15	−.04	−1.43
	−.07	.01	.06	.11
	−.06	.11	.06	.98
Population size (log)	.20	.21	.25	2.00*
	.22	.22	4.92	2.06*
	.13	.07	.17	.64
Trade/GNP ratio	.06	.22	.01	2.09*
	.04	.13	.15	1.20
	.06	.13	.02	1.17
Constant			53.17	1.62
			94.96	.15
			61.57	.84

$R^2 = .72$, $R_a^2 = .69$, $N = 97$[a]
$R^2 = .68$, $R_a^2 = .64$, $N = 96$
$R^2 = .70$, $R_a^2 = .67$, $N = 95$

NOTE: Positive signs (implied by no indication of sign) denote positive impact on the measures of democracy while negative signs denote a negative impact.

[a] For each variable and for the squared multiple correlations at the bottom of the table, values given in the first row are for the political rights index, those in the second row are for the liberal democracy index, while those in the third row are for the Polity III index.

[b] These are one-tailed tests because of the directional hypotheses tested here; * = $p < .05$, ** = $p < .01$, *** = $p < .001$.

ance, R^2 and R_a^2, are less than those found in the explanation of the political rights index. This probably reflects the greater random error found in the liberal democracy index, with its measures from Banks, which, as noted above, Bollen found to contain more random error than Gastil's political rights index. Turning now to the Polity III index analyzed in the third row for each variable, the principal findings are similar to those for the liberal democracy index. Here too, the cultural dimension appears to be emphasized, but with an institutional orientation, as the partial correlation for British colonial heritage is second in size only to that for economic development.

Adding the two environmental variables to the analysis in Table 7.2 provides a very different picture, at least for purposes of explaining the political rights index. The number of sea borders is highly significant in the explanation of political rights, and precipitation is also significant, as are GDP per capita, British colonial heritage, and European location. Age of the polity and agricultural density (to be treated shortly) also are significant, as they were in the political rights rows of Table 7.1. For the first time, however, we confront the statistical nonsignificance of Islam—the addition of the environmental variables has rendered Islam nonsignificant as an explanation of political rights. Whereas in Table 7.1, the addition of the remaining independent variables in the multivariate analysis only moderately depressed the size of the bivariate correlation for Islam to that of the partial, here in Table 7.2, the change is a marked one, from −.46 to −.18 in the analysis of political rights. In understanding the origins of political rights as a more rudimentary form of democracy, then, the environmental conditions of such a democratic emergence supersede Islam as a contributing factor. The significant constant suggests the possibility of incomplete model specification because the significant variation represented by the constant is not explained by the independent variables included here. This potential difficulty will be remedied in the following analysis.

This pattern does not hold for the analysis of the liberal democracy index. Sea borders still is significant, precipitation is not, and Islam is significant now, as it was in Table 7.1. Nevertheless, the size of the partial correlation and level of significance are diminished compared to Table 7.1. Along with the significance of Islam, a major continuity between the liberal democracy index rows of Tables 7.1 and 7.2 is the high level of significance of British colonial heritage and European location. Thus, whereas the structure of explanation of the political rights index is substantially altered by the introduction of the environmental variables, that of the liberal democracy index is changed much less. Note that in Table 7.2, population size is not significant, nor will this variable prove to be significant in the later analysis.

TABLE 7.2.
Regression of the Political Rights, Liberal Democracy, and
Polity III Indexes on the Initial Explanatory plus Environmental Variables

Variable	Bivariate correlation (r)	Partial correlation	Regression coefficient (b)	t value[b]
Islam	−.46[a]	−.18	−.01	−1.60
	−.46	−.28	−.20	−2.59**
	−.47	−.29	−.02	−2.63**
British colonial heritage	.06	.22	.58	2.01*
	.19	.33	17.87	3.07**
	.18	.37	2.39	3.55***
European location	.58	.19	.72	1.69*
	.58	.30	24.09	2.80**
	.59	.28	2.60	2.61**
Number of sea borders	.49	.38	.40	3.72***
	.46	.30	6.16	2.86**
	.40	.26	.59	2.35**
Precipitation	.001	.19	.01	1.69*
	−.03	.05	.04	.47
	−.07	.03	.003	.24
Economic development (GDP per capita)	.79	.54	.001	5.78***
	.72	.43	.01	4.27***
	.74	.46	.001	4.63***
Agricultural density	.002	−.19	−.0001	−1.69*
	.01	−.10	−.001	−.87
	−.03	−.16	−.0002	−1.42
Age of the polity (log)	.50	.23	8.66	2.11*
	.35	.04	30.37	.37
	.37	.12	9.87	1.02
Deaths per capita due to political violence	−.14	−.07	−.02	−.63
	.003	.14	.76	1.22
	.01	.19	.13	1.74*
Population size (log)	.18	.04	.04	.33
	.20	.07	1.56	.60
	.10	−.07	−.18	−.60
Trade/GNP ratio	.02	.08	.01	.69
	.01	.01	.01	.04
	.03	.02	.003	.18
Constant			58.41	1.87*
			229.02	.36
			75.87	1.03

$R^2 = .76, R_a^2 = .73, N = 92$[a]

$R^2 = .70, R_a^2 = .67, N = 92$

$R^2 = .72, R_a^2 = .67, N = 90$

NOTE: Positive signs (implied by no indication of sign) denote positive impact on the measures of democracy while negative signs have a corresponding interpretation.

[a] For each variable and for the squared multiple correlations at the bottom of the table, values given in the first row are for the political rights index, those in the second row are for the liberal democracy index, while those in the third row are for the Polity III index.

[b] These are one-tailed tests because of the directional hypotheses tested here; * = $p < .05$, ** = $p < .01$, *** = $p < .001$.

Once again, the Polity III index behaves pretty much as does the liberal democracy measure, with British colonial heritage standing out in the value of its partial correlation. Consistent with the institutional emphasis of the Polity III index, sea borders has the lowest partial correlation of any of the three indexes. Interestingly, for the first time, deaths per capita due to political violence is now significant, thus providing some support for Moore's (1966) argument for the positive relationship between political violence and the emergence of democratic institutions. In the analysis of Table 7.3, this variable and its possible theoretical linkages with democracy will be explored in greater detail.

In Table 7.3, as a validation procedure, size of military personnel replaces sea borders as a more proximal but not necessarily better measure of threat, and land inequality is introduced. Once again in the analysis of the political rights index, Islam is not significant, but military personnel size, precipitation, and especially land inequality are significant in their relationships with this measure of democracy. Indeed, land inequality has the second highest partial correlation, second only to economic development. The constant term is not significant in all three multiple regression equations, suggesting more complete model specification.

The contrast between the structure of explanation of the political rights index and that for the other two measures is enhanced. Whereas military personnel size and precipitation are significant in the analysis of the political rights index, they are not for liberal democracy and Polity III. British colonial heritage and European location are both significant in the explanation of the latter two measures of democracy, but only European location is significant in its association with political rights, thus reinforcing the cultural dimension underlying liberal democracy and institutional forms. A consistent element among all three measures is the significant influence of land inequality, suggesting its importance even for more complex forms of democracy beyond that of basic political rights. In the Polity III index the significance of land inequality combined with the nonsignificance of political violence, in contrast to Table 7.2, suggests potential complex relationships between land inequality and democracy. Land inequality may lead directly to democracy by the processes we have examined earlier, but political violence also could be an intervening variable between land inequality and democracy. This tentative conclusion is supported by the substantial reduction in the tolerance values for political violence when land inequality is introduced in Table 7.3 (from .86 to .59). Further research may yield more definitive conclusions.

As a result of the additional variables, Islam is nonsignificant now only in the instance of the political rights index. Note also that in contrast to the pattern reported in Tables 7.1 and 7.2, that for Table 7.3 shows agricultural den-

TABLE 7.3.
Regression of the Political Rights, Liberal Democracy, and Polity III Indexes on the Explanatory Variables, Adding Land Inequality and Substituting Size of Military Personnel

Variable	Bivariate correlation (r)	Partial correlation	Regression coefficient (b)	t value[b]
Islam	−.46[a]	−.19	−.007	−1.42
	−.45	−.29	−.24	−2.18*
	−.45	−.24	−.02	−1.76*
British colonial heritage	.12	.22	.58	1.62
	.23	.38	22.99	2.99**
	.19	.31	2.22	2.31*
European location	.57	.42	1.52	3.36***
	.58	.43	33.73	3.45***
	.58	.40	3.85	3.17**
Size of military personnel	.51	.35	.82	2.78**
	.39	.13	6.30	.99
	.40	.17	1.00	1.24
Precipitation	−.11	.32	.01	2.50**
	−.18	.09	.07	.66
	−.20	.13	.01	.95
Economic development (GDP per capita)	.78	.61	.001	5.59***
	.72	.42	.01	3.43***
	.74	.49	.001	4.00***
Land inequality	.22	.43	.03	3.49***
	.13	.28	.40	2.15*
	.11	.30	.05	2.29*
Agricultural density	.19	.22	.001	1.68*
	.18	.22	.02	1.63
	.11	.13	.001	.92
Age of the polity (log)	.53	.01	.59	.10
	.41	−.02	−16.48	−.13
	−.40	−.04	−4.82	−.32
Deaths per capita due to political violence	−.27	−.03	−.04	−.24
	−.25	.06	1.39	.45
	−.28	.003	.01	−.02
Population size (log)	.19	−.01	−.01	−.09
	.19	.02	.49	.16
	.08	−.07	−.19	−.51
Trade/GNP ratio	−.01	−.04	−.002	−.26
	−.03	−.08	−.09	−.59
	.02	−.04	−.01	−.31
Constant			−3.55	−.08
			−129.21	−.14
			−37.79	−.32

$R^2 = .82, R_a^2 = .78, N = 67$[a]
$R^2 = .73, R_a^2 = .67, N = 67$
$R^2 = .73, R_a^2 = .67, N = 65$

NOTE: Positive signs (implied by no indication of sign) denote positive impact on the measures of democracy while negative signs have a corresponding interpretation.

[a] For each variable and for the squared multiple correlations at the bottom of the table, values given in the first row are for the political rights index, those in the second row are for the liberal democracy index, while those in the third row are for the Polity III index.

[b] These are one-tailed tests because of the directional hypotheses tested here. * = $p < .05$ ** = $p < .01$ *** = $p < .001$

sity positively related to democracy, as expected theoretically.[13] This finding resulted from the removal of Singapore from the data set because of the absence of data for military personnel size for 1965. Singapore, with by far the highest value of agricultural density, also had the highest value for trade/GNP ratio, thus contributing a positive collinear bias that is now removed ($r = .66$ reduced to $r = .11$ between the two variables). The tolerances for agricultural density demonstrate a dramatic increase in Table 7.3, also because of the removal of this case.

In the analysis of the political rights index, age of the polity is no longer significant, though it was in Tables 7.1 and 7.2, suggesting the influence of substantive societal variables now introduced into the analysis. Partial dependence of political rights on polity age, but total absence of same for liberal democracy or institutional forms, suggests the probable evolutionary path of political rights over time, and the dependence of contemporary liberal democracy and related institutions on more directly proactive cultural influences. Consistent with the preceding tables, the proportions of variance explained in Table 7.3 for the liberal democracy index and Polity III are less than that for the political rights index, as shown by the values of R^2 and R_a^2.

A striking difference between the findings for the political rights index and those for liberal democracy in Table 7.3 is seen in their relationship to economic development. (This result is somewhat less dramatic for the Polity III index, suggesting a possible intermediate position for it between the political rights and liberal democracy indexes.) Whereas the bivariate correlation between GDP per capita and the measure of liberal democracy is reduced considerably to the partial correlation by the remaining variables (.72 to .42), that between GDP per capita and the political rights measure is reduced far less (.78 to .61). The net effect of economic development on basic political rights appears to be much greater than on liberal democracy. Indeed, the partial for the cultural variable, European location, is larger than that for economic development in the liberal democracy row of Table 7.3 but this is not true for the top row, wherein the partial for economic development is by far the largest of all the explanatory variables. The remaining tables also demonstrate the relative robustness of economic development in its relation to political rights but less so in its association with liberal democracy. This finding has implications for the influence of economic development on the generation of a basic democracy in Muslim societies, but suggests that liberal democracy is less likely to be a result.

Implications for the Future

Now we can see an explanation for the rapid failure of democracy in Eastern and Central Europe after World War I. As land-locked countries, or nearly so, these newly independent nations were prone to the threat of war. In addition, at the end of the war, each had large numbers of militarily trained and combat-experienced personnel and, of special significance, a military leadership that had served in the armed forces of the former empires, Austria-Hungary, Russia, and Germany. The existence of both a rank-and-file cohort and a leadership prone to autocratic or at least hierarchical military control likely made it far easier to assume military control, as did Marshal Pilsudski in Poland in 1926, than if such war experience were absent.

On the other hand, the prognosis for democracy in many of these countries is somewhat better today. Although they are still subject to the threat of war, the absence of very recent experience in major armed struggles using large numbers of armed personnel may make it more difficult for current military establishments to intervene. There is, however, a probable covariation between the increasing tendency toward military violence in Eastern Europe and the threat to democratic development. The more that communal conflicts in those countries fester, the greater the likelihood of political intervention by military personnel accustomed to autocratic methods of resolving political disputes.

Of course, failures of economic development also are suggested as potential pitfalls for these new democracies, as suggested by the high correlation of GDP per capita and democratic development.

Agricultural density demonstrated a significant relationship with political rights, apart from any connection with land inequality, as shown in Table 7.3 when collinearity effects were minimized. This finding suggests an independent effect for agricultural density that is consistent with the findings of Edward Crenshaw (1992, 1995, 1997), whose work has emphasized the role of agricultural density as a progenitor of social and institutional complexity that, in turn, generates democracy as an end-product. Greater density yields greater social and structural differentiation; political democracy is surely one illustration of such complexity. Thus, as density on the land increases, the likelihood of democracy increases. Currently, some of the least democratic countries also have some of the lowest population densities, as in the Middle East. With rapidly growing populations, this situation is likely to change quickly, if it has not already done so.

The importance of land inequality has been reinforced over and above earlier findings (Midlarsky 1992a) as a result of the introduction and control of variables such as European location, which had the effect of comparing Latin America with much of Africa and parts of the Middle East. A major difference, of course, is that Latin American countries were conquest states in which a conquering elite not only ruled the subject population for centuries but, in the process, seized much of the land, generating a considerable inequality. (England, as we have seen, is a much earlier case in point.) In Africa, by contrast, the colonial conquest was not so thorough and of much shorter duration. As a result, there was no homogenizing influence of a long-term conquest elite and little land inequality that could be used as a secure basis of economic and political control to allow a gradual introduction of more political rights at a later time. Rather there was a continuation of tribal politics that limited democracy and in many cases led to tribal warfare that limited even state governance itself, let alone democracy.

This is a fundamental reason for the difference in findings between Rueschemeyer, Stephens, and Stephens (1992) and the present study. That study, although nonquantitative, is still based on a careful examination of advanced capitalist societies and Latin America; African countries are excluded. Yet it is precisely in the comparison between African and Latin American countries that we can see the differences in early democratic development dependent on emergent inequalities that can provide leadership independent of tribe or heredity. Clearly, African democracies have foundered on tribal animosities at least as much as on any other cause. In much of Latin America, it is probably the very gradually liberalizing consequence of a fairly secure long-term conquering elite, unchallenged by any serious competitor and therefore less likely to block rudimentary (hence unthreatening) democratic development that is captured by the land inequality variable. Alas, it is difficult to institutionalize such a process, if that is even desirable, and so limitations on democracy in Africa can be expected for the foreseeable future.

The institutionalization and diffusion of democracy in Europe, however, appear to be robust. European location is significant in all of the analyses, suggesting the important role of the European Community (EC) and later the European Union (EU) in providing a carrot-and-stick approach to democratization emanating from the core countries of the older European Economic Community (EEC). Those countries that will not democratize will not be allowed the benefits of membership—which is becoming increasingly desirable. At the same time, a successful model for stable government is provided by the core countries.

Although the salience of the number of sea borders for the development of democracy might seem discouraging, since geography is a "given" of international life, it is the threat of war and its minimization that we are directly concerned with, and here, of course, much can be done. A major change in the international political climate can yield dramatic results, as, for example, in the instances of three conflict-prone countries, Afghanistan, a land-locked country, and Syria and Egypt, with at least two land borders each. The economic and political strains of the Soviet Union and its impending collapse forced its withdrawal from Afghanistan and the removal of that country from major international conflict. Syria and Egypt were moved to modify their stances considerably on several key Middle East issues by the new U.S. diplomatic inroads into the Middle East after the 1973 Yom Kippur War. Other countries with many land borders can be affected in a similar fashion, as the United States and the European Union powers have been attempting to do in the case of the former Yugoslavia, especially Bosnia. Thus, although environmental factors such as the number of sea borders may provide broad limits to what can be done, in no sense are they deterministic.

Precipitation also does not exert a deterministic influence on democracy, as we have seen from the findings reported in Tables 7.2–7.3. Yet, in contrast to sea borders, future changes in this environmental variable are possible. Global warming may increase rainfall in some parts of the world and diminish it in others. To the extent that this process yields increased aridity in some countries, the prospects for democratic development may diminish. African countries have thus far demonstrated the strongest tendencies toward drought and famine with a concomitant increase in warlordism as a form of centralized control within regions. Somalia, of course, is a particular case in point.

Conclusions from Testing the Model

The independent impact of land inequality on all three measures of democracy has demonstrated a robustness under varying analytic conditions, which, in turn, supports the Athenian model of the origins of democracy in agrarian societies.

It may be useful for the moment to dwell on reasons for the importance of land inequality beyond those immediately articulated in the Athenian and developmental models. This importance does not likely reside in land scarcity alone or in its ecological imperatives for political rights, but more generally in its implications for the accumulation of wealth in society. It is the accumulated wealth that supports the political rights of certain persons beyond the hereditary or tribal entitlements of others. Accumulated wealth in the bourgeois period of eighteenth- and nineteenth-century England may have performed a role in the development of English democracy similar to that of land inequality in the Athenian. Any form of wealth, not just land per se, may have similar consequences in breaking down the barriers of family or tribe in gaining access to the political process. As Huntington puts it, democracy "is as likely to be the product of oligarchy as of protest against oligarchy" (1984, 212). Here the oligarchy exists in the form of a landed elite empowered to make political decisions in place of a traditional closed hereditary counterpart. This initial expansion of the process of decision making can be the basis for the next widening of political participation.

At the same time, other mechanisms may be operative. As we saw in the analyses of Tables 7.2 and 7.3, complex relationships between land inequality and political violence may lead ultimately to democracy. Alternatively, instead of violence, increased urbanization as the result of mass migration from the countryside to the city as a consequence of extreme land inequality may, through the increased density of interpersonal interactions, lead to increased democracy (Crenshaw 1997).

Another major contribution of this model is to emphasize the important influence of environmental factors on the genesis and sustainability of early democracy. Hostile environments can generate autocratic responses, either subverting an early democratic development or preventing its organization altogether. As we have seen, Wittfogel singled out one such threatening source in the form of aridity and a bureaucratic-despotic response in the form of hydraulic civilization. This theory has been generalized to include the influence of precipitation on democracy and has found empirical support.

The second environmental threat takes the form of invasion by hostile peoples and the consequent need for military preparedness that can lead to autocracy in countries with many land borders. In contrast, countries with many sea borders, while not immune from such threats, nevertheless enjoy at least a modicum of security. In this sense, both aridity and many land borders share a common dimension—a threatening environment for human populations that can give rise to rigid controls in the form of despotic political organization.

A contribution of this chapter has been to emphasize an international dimension in understanding the origins and survivability of early democracy. The international venue is robust when compared with other antecedents of democracy such as precipitation, economic development, and land inequality. Minimization of the threat of war is an important condition for the emergence of a durable democracy, as indicated by the evidence pertaining to four ancient societies and the systematic analysis of the modern period.

Although not directly examined here, it is likely that there is a reciprocal and, over time, reinforcing influence between the threat and actuality of war and democracy. A portion of the literature cited earlier strongly suggests the inhibiting effect of democracy on war between democracies. This, combined with the finding here that minimizing the threat of war enhances democracy's chances of survival, strongly suggests this reciprocal relationship. Over time, the continued absence of first the threat and then the actuality of war reinforces the burgeoning democracy, and in turn this even stronger democracy further inhibits the likelihood of war, at least with other democracies.

These findings also explain a historical anomaly. Why have democracies apparently been so rare in recorded human history? It clearly does not require a modern economy to initiate and maintain democratic practices, as the ancient Athenians so clearly demonstrated. Why then was prototypical modern democracy confined to this and, later, a relatively few others, such as the English, Icelandic, and American examples in the Medieval and Early Modern periods? Two answers, as we have just seen, are insufficient rainfall and the ubiquity of warfare in countries with many land borders. But the relative isolation of polities with many sea borders—islands and peninsulas—may itself be a factor in the limited spread of democracy. Only the nearby Cyclades and the Ionian polities on the Anatolian coast could be directly influenced by Athens, and only an offshoot such as the American colonies could be strongly influenced by the English model. While well protected from the threat of war, Athens and England were also somewhat limited in their day-to-day interactions with other polities, interactions that might have encouraged the spread of democracy to additional political units. (Interestingly, another isolated instance, Switzerland, protected not by the sea but by the mountains, also evolved as an early democratic polity.)

What of the ideological influences on democracy, especially that of Islam? Democracy and Islam are not mutually exclusive, certainly not if democracy is measured by the more rudimentary political rights index. With the introduction of environmental variables, as shown in Tables 7.2 and 7.3, Islam is not significant in any of the multivariate regressions using the political rights index as the dependent variable. This finding suggests possibilities for the initiation of democracy based upon the appropriate responses to environmental constraints. For example, the threat of war can be ameliorated by international guarantees, if not forms of integration, as perhaps is occurring now in relations between Israel and Jordan. Minimal rainfall can be countered by adequate food distribution, perhaps insured by international agents, either in the form of other nation-states or international organizations.

The same cannot be said for the liberal democracy index. Here Islam is significant in all of the analyses, suggesting, as we have seen, the strong cultural dependence of liberal democracy. (The role of economic development or modernization should nonetheless not be minimized, for it can play a potential role in the generation of political rights, if not liberal democracy.) Liberal democracy can probably evolve over time, but its more rapid contemporary genesis is probably a result of strong cultural influences, either from within the society or from international pressure. In contiguous societies with some common cultural heritage, such pressure can yield positive results, as we have seen in the spread of democracy throughout Europe since the end of World War II (the Balkans excepted). However, in more insular cases, such as many of the Islamic countries, international pressure could be counterproductive, thus leaving only the more rudimentary political rights form as the one serious possibility for change in the direction of democracy.

All of this suggests that democracy is not to be viewed unidimensionally, either as a concept or in its measurement. As we have seen, the environmental variables tended to have far stronger impact on the more rudimentary political rights index and the cultural variables on the liberal democracy index, with the Polity III index occupying a somewhat intermediate position. However, land inequality was common to the explanation of all three, suggesting that the origins of democracy in differential land-holdings breaking through hereditary or tribal entitlements on the path to democracy may have contemporary relevance—as we have seen in the contrast between the political histories of Latin America and Africa. The culture of democracy may not be immune from the need for a strong state to guide it through the difficulties engendered by strongly conflictual competing interests.

Differences in explaining the democracy indexes may also have implications for the burgeoning literature on democracy and war. In particular, recent challenges to the now widely accepted findings that democracies do not fight each other (see, e.g., Layne 1994) rely on a somewhat more relaxed definition of democracy, perhaps more akin to the political rights index. The claim, for example, that Wilhelmine Germany was a democracy, yet fought Britain and France and later the United States, depends on the basic rejection of the notion that democracy always must be defined as liberal democracy (Owen 1994). More use of measures such as the political rights index may shed light on this growing controversy and in particular, on when, if ever, more primitive democracies may go to war with each other. Given a continuum of democracy ranging from rudimentary political rights to liberal democracy, with institutional forms somewhere between the two, equally important could be the discovery of where on this continuum the democracy-peace relationship "kicks in," as it were.[14] This research agenda also could simultaneously answer the question of whether *democracy* alone is sufficient to sustain the democratic peace or whether, as Kant long ago suggested, it is *liberalism*, at least in its current democratic manifestation, that is required.

There is another somewhat unexpected outcome of the analysis. The sequence on the continuum discovered here—political rights, institutional articulation, and liberal democracy—suggests a possible pathway that states may have to adopt in order to ultimately achieve stable liberal democracy. First, political rights in the form of basic electoral freedoms would be achieved, followed by the establishment of strong institutions, and then the granting of civil liberties associated with liberal democracy. It is interesting to reflect on the early U.S. experience in first achieving basic political rights in the revolution against Britain, followed by agreement on the structures of potentially strong institutions at the Constitutional Convention, and only after that the formulation of the Bill of Rights as the basis for an evolving liberal democracy. Prior experience with colonial representative institutions may have imbued the founders of the American polity with the necessity for this sequential ordering.

Finally, we return to the question of whether civilizational conflict is probable, thus requiring a new meta-level of analysis. Results of this study suggest that such conflict is not likely in the foreseeable future, if only because there are certain compatibilities between democracy and Islam that deny the mutual-exclusivity hypothesis. Civilizational conflict probably requires a level of disjunction severe enough to motivate at least one side to engage in such an intense confrontation. The Crusades or the many intense wars between European Christians and Muslim Ottomans come to mind. An Islamic version of democracy that entails certain differences with Western forms but still allows basic political rights likely would not sufficiently motivate such an endeavor on either side. This is especially true if liberal democracy is not demanded as the sine qua non of democracy, but less exacting forms such as basic political rights are given their due. Economic development can influence the generation of political rights, as we saw, but Islamic societies still face a conundrum. If increased political rights in the form of free elections are used by fundamentalist parties to establish totalitarian states, then the role of economic development as a generator of political rights could be Pyrrhic in its consequences. Care must be exercised, if at all possible, to avoid this outcome. The rapid development of strong institutions suggested by the sequence identified above may be one way to prevent such early failure. For the foreseeable future, the state will be the focus of political efforts either to democratize or to amplify an already existing authoritarian tendency.[15] To the extent that states democratize, they may provide the basis for a more peaceful future, both within civilizational entities such as Islam and between them and potential competitors such as the West.

Yet, as we saw, the culture of democracy may not be immune from the need for a strong state to guide it through the difficulties engendered by strongly conflictual competing interests. This surmise will establish the bases for one of several paradoxes of democracy to be considered in the concluding chapter. Before reaching that discussion, we will need to consider the consequences of patterned inequality for violence and of equality for cooperation in the following two chapters.

PART IV

Violence and Cooperation

CHAPTER 8

Inequality and Political Violence

Our investigations of inequality have thus far concerned the rise and decline of states and influences on the development of democracy. We have also touched on, especially in the case of China, the role of violence in the transformation of society. Earlier arguments implied that two separate distributions of holdings might create divergent views of society and in particular of the state of justice within it.

Here I will take a position somewhat different from that of other researchers' previous efforts. First, I will assume that the relationship between inequality and political violence is context-specific. By that I mean that different regions of the world may yield different sorts of relationships between these variables because of large-scale historical and geographical differences. The term *context* also has an additional meaning pertaining to the *pattern* of inequalities. I hasten to add that the assumption of context specificity does not automatically imply that the relationship between inequality and political violence is not of universal validity, although it may not be. It merely suggests that different world regions could have different empirical *expressions* of inequality, which in the end yield political violence.

The theoretical structure upon which this study is based also will depart somewhat from others' efforts, particularly in the choice of intellectual tradition. It emerges from a concern for social and, in particular, distributive justice that is really as old as Aristotle, but that has modern exponents.

A modern theorist of justice approaches this problem from the need for a requirement for justice that it also be stabilizing—the requirement by John Rawls (1971, 302) that each gain to the most advantaged in society be accompanied by a gain to the least advantaged. This "difference principle," as articulated by Rawls, is stated to ensure that whatever inequalities are the result of differences in talent or inheritance are not perpetuated to the point of generating really severe societal inequalities. An expanding economic scenario can foster a minimal sort of identification between the wealthy and the worst-off, for both are gaining from the newly created largesse.

However, this positive form of the difference principle, in which all gain as the result of economic expansion, should be complemented by the negative form, in which all lose as the result of economic contraction.[1] In the event of a depression or some other social or natural calamity, the declines of both rich and poor should be evident. It is the identification between rich and poor simultaneously losing that may have prevented mass political violence from occurring in many instances. The image of rich investors leaping from tall buildings in the 1929 Wall Street crash may have done much to establish the common sense of identity between haves and have-nots in the United States that would forestall any serious efforts at massive political change which might in turn have resulted in mass political violence. In contrast, in two recent instances of mass political violence, in Nicaragua and in Iran, such mutual identification was absent. Immediately after the earthquake of 1972, the Somozas of Nicaragua were perceived as gaining in wealth from the Red Cross aid while many, mostly the poor, suffered (Midlarsky and Roberts 1985; Roberts and Midlarsky 1986). In Iran, the severe decline in economic activity, especially in the building trades in Tehran, differentially affected rulers and ruled; the shah and his family were hardly affected at all, while unemployment increased dramatically and the poor were still further impoverished (Nejad 1986).

Identification between rulers and ruled is the intellectual anchor of Part IV of this book. This identification does not have to be uniform or complete, but means only that, in a Rawlsian sense, if one societal sector is increasing in wealth or at least holding its own while another, poorer sector is declining, then identification between ruler and ruled is virtually nonexistent. Successful leadership often is heavily dependent on the development of identity. As Harvard psychologist Howard Gardner puts it,

A leader is an individual who creates a story—a mental representation—that significantly affects the thoughts, behaviours, and feelings—the mental representations—of a significant number of persons (termed followers). Since followers invariably know many stories, a leader can only be effective if his or her story is powerful, if it can compete successfully for influence with already prevalent stories. *The most powerful stories turn out to be ones about identity: stories that help individuals discover who they are, where they are coming from, where they are, or should be, headed.* (1995, 15; emphasis added)

If the development of such identity between rulers and ruled fails to occur and if the absence of identification, combined with continued impoverishment of the population relative to the ruling sector, continues for long, then large-scale political violence becomes more likely. In the societies to be examined below, landed elites generally have constituted the ruling oligarchies, which, if not directly in control of governments, at least have exercised considerable influence from a short distance. Land distributions in such societies can become potent indicators of bifurcation between rulers and ruled if the appropriate models are applied to reveal those bifurcations.

There is an interesting confluence between this perspective and one that was recently put forward by Roberto Perotti (1996). He developed a measure of income inequality that specifically associates the proportion of the middle sector of the income distribution with the degree of equality. Using an index of sociopolitical instability composed of assassinations, deaths due to political violence, and both successful and unsuccessful coups, he finds significant negative associations between this index and the proportion of the income distribution garnered by the middle class, while controlling for other variables such as GDP per capita. Clearly the emphasis on bifurcations and their positive associations with political violence adopted here and Perotti's on the proportion of the middle sector of the income distribution and its negative association with political instability are but two sides of the same coin.

As will become apparent in the empirical analysis, I am dealing here with patterned instead of generalized inequalities, as measured by the Gini index of land inequality. By *patterned inequality* I mean a systematic distinction in the pattern of holdings of one societal sector relative to the pattern of holdings of another. Here I will be measuring the pattern of landholdings although, in principle, any societal good can be treated in this fashion. Intrinsic to this analysis is the assumption that human beings are pattern recognizers par excellence. It may even be our ability to recognize the pattern of an environment and react to it successfully that accounts for our evolutionary success as a species (Pagels 1982, 110). The peasant is in a unique position to observe and assess the environment, for the peasant spends much time in the fields and is keenly aware of his or her holdings relative to others'. It is not that the peasant is expected to accept or reject a mathematical model at some probability level, as I shall do shortly, but that the constant exposure to the agricultural environment, along with family and village histories passed down from one generation to the next, make of the peasant, even if illiterate, an acute observer and interpreter of the environment.[2]

Empirical Foundations

The empirical results on the relationship between inequality and political violence certainly are not uniform and typically suggest only a weak level of significance. Sometimes the relationship is above the level of significance (generally $p < .05$; E. N. Muller 1985; Nagel 1976; Parvin 1973; Russett 1964; Sigelman and Simpson 1977; Tanter and Midlarsky 1967), sometimes below it (Hardy 1979; Nagel 1974; Weede 1981, 1987); but rarely is there a robust relationship discovered between the two variables. Equally rarely does the relationship plunge into the black hole of nonsignificance. Moreover, most of these studies (with the obvious exceptions of Nagel 1976, Russett 1964, and Tanter and Midlarsky 1967) have emphasized income inequality as opposed to land inequality. Several recent exceptions emphasize population growth and an attendant land inequality as progenitors of the French, Russian (Skocpol 1979), Chinese (Midlarsky 1982), English (Goldstone 1983), and Salvadoran (Midlarsky and Roberts 1985) revolutions.

In the last of these studies, the coalition-based insurgency against the Somozas in Nicaragua is contrasted with the largely rural-class-based insurrection in El Salvador. With increased population growth and no change in the amount of arable land, an exponential distribution of landholdings would be predicted as land becomes scarce relative to population size. That was found to have occurred in El Salvador but not in Nicaragua, suggesting land scarcity and inequality were not present there to the degree found in El Salvador. And, as noted, a broad-based coalition of business, banking, and urban groups as well as peasants participated in the Nicaraguan revolution, not terribly dissimilar to that which developed earlier in Cuba (Dominguez 1978) under conditions of similar dictatorship. A general conclusion of these analyses was that rural-class-based revolutions are more likely where the land is scarce and the exponential distribution is an adequate descriptor, as in El Salvador. Where the land is less scarce, as in Nicaragua or Cuba, other types of revolutionary behaviors can arise, and broad-based revolutionary coalitions are more likely.

Theoretical Expectations

The analysis now proceeds according to the following expectations: Where there exists scarcity of agricultural land for the peasantry, the exponential is expected to be the theoretical model for the lower portion of the land distribution. This should be so not only because of the prior finding of the applicability of this distribution to the Chinese and Salvadoran cases at the time of the outbreak of their revolutions but because of the reasoning invoked earlier. The peasantry situated on fixed plots of land would reproduce over time and divide their holdings among their children, thus leading in the limit to the exponential distribution of small but roughly equal land holdings at the lower end. At the upper end of that distribution, however, the process should be a fractal (EI) distribution. The tendency for primogeniture to prevail at this societal level, or simply the financial ability to send younger sons to the city or abroad, would leave most of these landholdings largely intact. Any subdivision that did occur would likely be at a much slower rate than for the peasantry, who ordinarily have larger families (often necessary for working the land) and are unable to help male offspring financially other than by the process of land subdivision and inheritance.

These expectations for the distributions of land at the upper and lower portions of the curve are the limiting equilibrium statistical distributions that evolve after a relatively long time period. The peasants' sense of common identity, the feeling that the large landowner as a human being is essentially no different from them, can be eroded by extreme envy, and this may ultimately even lead to violence if the land distributions are vastly different and the differences are in fact worsening. The "limited good" theory of the peasant environment leading to extreme envy has been developed by George Foster (1967) and further amplified into a theory of the "tunnel effect" by Albert Hirschman (1981), who argues that societies will tolerate extreme inequalities only for a certain time after they are instituted, after which revolutionary behavior is expected if benefits do not accrue to the worst-off in society. A dichotomized agricultural universe would also more likely lead to a radicalized peasant response than a more graduated environment with inherently more options available.[3] As we have suggested and shall soon see in greater detail, El Salvador, with the history of the most intense recent conflict in Latin America, has a classic bifurcated distribution between rulers and ruled.

Empirical Tests

Ideally, of course, one would want to have a cross-national test across as many country units as possible. Yet the preceding arguments constrain the boundaries of the country universe. First, the distribution of land must be relevant to at least some significant proportion of the population, else the theoretical connection with political violence is virtually meaningless. The numbers of persons affected by land distributions must be large enough to have at least some influence on social turmoil. This requirement effectively excludes the United States, Canada, and the European countries, as well as Japan, Australia, and New Zealand, for all of these cluster at the low end of the data on the percentage of the labor force in agriculture (Taylor and Jodice 1983, 1: 208-10).

Second, the sequential acquisition process must have had some chance of operating, usually in colonial contexts within recent history, in order to generate a bifurcated distribution. This too would exclude the European countries and, interestingly, several African countries, largely governed by the French in colonial times. Cameroon, Chad, Congo, and Gabon are examples of countries that simply do not have a distribution at the upper end that could conform to the fractal (EI) (Food and Agriculture Organization 1981, 36), probably because of the absence of large-scale European settlement. Another reason for excluding Africa—in addition to the heterogeneity of historical experience, language, religion, and ethnicity—is its differential experience of anticolonial activity. Whereas most of the African countries had a peaceful transition to independence, others, including Algeria, Kenya, Angola, and Mozambique, underwent violent revolutions against the colonial authorities (or their immediate legacies, as in Zaire or Nigeria with its bloody civil war), thus introducing a large domestic violence component that was mostly independent of recent land distributions. In addition, the majority of data available for African countries are found in the results of the *1970 World Census of Agriculture* (Food and Agriculture Organization 1981, 33-38), which, for the most part, do not reflect the colonial experience.

A test of the theory, therefore, requires a set of countries that can at least potentially meet the preceding requirements. Latin American countries, being for the most part agrarian and having been settled by Iberian colonists, would be suitable, because the land distributions of these countries would satisfy the requirement of sequential acquisition.[4] The fair degree of cultural homogeneity (relative to other regions of the world) also facilitates comparisons. Incidence of mass political violence is frequent enough to provide considerable numbers of instances of such violence and, more importantly, variation on the dependent variable, deaths due to political violence, 1948-77 (Taylor and Jodice 1983, 2: 48-51).[5] Land distribution data for Latin American countries during almost the entire post–World War II period are found in the *Statistical Abstract of Latin America* (Wilkie and Perkal 1986).

In one sense at least, the following should be viewed as a cross-national test of the theory and not as just an examination of the details of Latin American politics. For I am concerned only with the validity of the proposed relationship in *any* context that would prove to be suitable, as Latin America proved to be

TABLE 8.1
Tests of the Exponential and EI Models of Landholdings in El Salvador, 1960

Size of holdings (in hectares)[a]	Number of holdings	Observed percentage of holdings	Predicted percentage of holdings
Lower portion (exponential)			
0.00–0.99	107,054	55.38	52.54
1.00–1.99	48,501	25.09	25.71
2.00–2.99	22,038	11.40	12.58
3.00–3.99	8,527	4.40	6.16
4.00–4.99	7,178	3.71	3.01
$k = .7147, A(k) = .7511$			
$\chi^2 = .945, df = 3, p < .90$			
Upper portion (EI)			
50.00–99.99	2,214	51.16	54.80
100.00–199.99	1,121	25.90	26.80
200.00–499.99	713	16.47	11.18
500.00–999.99	189	4.37	5.09
1,000.00–2,499.99	91	2.10	2.12
$k_1 = 1.0319, A_1(k_1) = 47.1698$			
$\chi^2 = 2.877, df = 3, p < .50$			

SOURCE: Wilkie and Perkal 1986, 36.
[a]Category ranges are the same as those presented in Wilkie and Perkal. Data are for 1960, the last year such differentiated data are available. Values of x_i were estimated by the midpoints of each category of the size of holding.

in its recent history of sequential acquisition and certain other properties. Any other area of the world with a similar historical experience would be equally acceptable.

The case of El Salvador is instructive, for it is the country that has experienced the most intense class-related conflict in recent years and at the same time demonstrates one of the most clearly bifurcated distributions of any Latin American country. Table 8.1 gives the most recent detailed land distribution for El Salvador. The predicted values for the lower portion of the distribution[6] are given by the exponential distribution of Equation 2.1,

$$p_i = A(k)e^{-kx_i} \qquad k > 0, \ 0 \leq x_i < \infty, \ i = 1, 2, 3, \ldots.$$

The fractal (EI) model for the upper portion is given by Equation 2.3,

$$P_i^1 = A_1(k_1) e^{-k_1 \log_e x_i} \qquad k_1 > 0, \ 1 \leq x_i < \infty, \ i = 1, 2, 3, \ldots.$$

The theoretical (predicted) values in Table 8.1 are calculated by first linearizing the probability distributions as a consequence of taking logarithms of both sides of equations 2.1 and 2.3.[7] This leads to

$$\log_e p_i = \log_e A(k) - kx_i$$

for the exponential and

$$\log_e p_i^1 = \log_e A_1(k_1) - k_1 \log_e x_i$$

for the fractal (EI) distribution. The values of k and k_1 are estimated by regressing $\log_e p_i$ and $\log_e p_i^1$ on the independent variables, and the regression coefficients serve as least squares estimates. The values of $A(k)$ and $A_1(k_1)$ are chosen to normalize the equations so that the sum of proportions equals unity, or

$$A(k) = \frac{1}{\sum_{i=1}^{n} e^{-kx_i}}$$

and

$$A_{-1}(k_{-1}) = \frac{1}{\sum_{i=1}^{n} e^{-k_1 \log_e x_i}} .$$

Predicted and observed distributions are compared by means of the chi-square goodness-of-fit statistic. A higher probability value for the chi-square statistic implies a better fit between observation and prediction while a lower value implies a poorer fit. In order to adopt a conservative policy on acceptance of either model (Equation 2.1 or 2.3), a model will be rejected at $p < .20$ (instead of the usual $p < .05$), which indicates of course that any probability levels higher than .20 imply acceptance of the model. Acceptance or rejection will be modified in one instance to allow for the introduction of approximations to continua that are probably better reflective of social reality.

Chi-square values for both the upper and the lower distributions in El Salvador are well above the chosen probability level and in fact indicate an excellent fit between observation and prediction. This is but one illustration; however, it does suggest the value of performing a general systematic analysis of the relationship between patterned inequality, as defined by the two segments of land distribution, and mass political violence in Latin America.

Note that the observed distributions in Table 8.1 are aggregations of landholdings of similar sizes, in the ranges specified, from all parts of a single country. Thus, it is probable that a single hacienda or other large holding will be surrounded by much smaller holdings. It is possible to imagine the declining degree of identification between the large and small landowner, if it ever existed in significant measure, as the small holdings subdivide over time while the large holding nearby remains mostly intact.

Table 8.2 lists the results of the chi-square goodness-of-fit tests between the theoretical distributions and the observed values for landholdings in twenty

TABLE 8.2
Results of the Exponential and EI Analyses
of Land Distribution in Twenty Latin American Countries

	Upper portion of landholdings (EI)			Lower portion of landholdings (exponential)		
	χ^{2a}	df	$p <$	χ^2	df	$p <$
Argentina (1960)	4.433	3	.30			
Bolivia (1950)[b]	4.381	4	.50	3.584	2	.20
Brazil (1960)[c]	3.815	3	.30			
Chile (1950)[d]	3.126	3	.50	1.310	3	.80
Colombia (1960)	2.862	3	.50	4.086	4	.50
Costa Rica (1960)	4.167	2	.20			
Cuba (1952)	0.120	3	.99			
Dominican Republic (1950)[e]	1.717	3	.70			
Ecuador (1954)	1.205	3	.80			
El Salvador (1960)	2.877	3	.50	0.945	3	.90
Guatemala (1950)	2.737	2	.30			
Haiti (1970)[f]	1.672	3	.70			
Honduras (1960)	1.021	3	.80			
Mexico (1960)	2.696	5	.80			
Nicaragua (1960)	3.712	3	.30			
Panama (1960)	0.302	2	.90			
Paraguay (1960)	6.230	6	.50			
Peru (1961)[g]	1.186	3	.80	3.057	2	.30
Uruguay (1960)	5.680	3	.20			
Venezuela (1960)	1.287	3	.80			

SOURCE: Wilkie and Perkal 1986, except as noted.
[a] Where the expected value was below 1.5, adjacent categories were combined for the chi-square test until that figure was obtained, as suggested in Gibbons 1971, 72.
[b] Heath, Erasmus, and Buechler 1969, 35.
[c] Roberts and Kohda 1967.
[d] Lower portion fractal (EI).
[e] Food and Agriculture Organization 1955.
[f] Upper portion exponential.
[g] Food and Agriculture Organization 1966–70.

Latin American countries, first for the upper portion of the distributions and then for the lower. The year for each distribution was chosen based on the availability of the most detailed information for that distribution. Where the amount of information given was equal for two years, the earlier one was chosen to allow the maximum amount of time for the possible development and mobilization (generally slow) of antiregime organizations. Only a few countries are listed for the lower portion because so many can be rejected simply by inspection; they are not montonically decreasing as demanded by the exponential distribution but rise to a given peak and then fall. Most of the cases, however, do conform to the fractal (EI) for the upper portion, as suggested by the theory of sequential acquisition.

Five distinct patterns emerge from the table: instances (1) where both fractal (EI) and exponential models can be rejected, (2) where only the exponential model is applicable to the upper portion, (3) where only the fractal (EI) is applicable to the upper, (4) where the fractal (EI) is applicable to the upper and there is a near applicability (to be defined) of the exponential to the lower portion, and (5) where the models are applicable respectively to their theoretically suggested domains. Effectively, an incremental procedure is used to accommodate the variation in fit of these models to the data in order to begin to approximate a continuum of applicability. Five categories of potential for political violence are now suggested for the examination of the proposed relationship, based on these five groupings and increasing in potential from (1) to (5).

With regard to the near fit in category (4), this can be accomplished in one of two ways. First, there can be doubt as to whether the exponential or some other distribution, such as the fractal (EI), fits the data for the lower portion. The second way a land distribution can be included in this category is by obtaining $p < .20$ for the exponential distribution in the lower portion along with a precise fit of the fractal to the upper—a near overall fit but not precisely meeting the adopted criterion.

Deaths from political violence (Taylor and Jodice 1983 2: 48–51) is treated in a similar fashion. The range for the same twenty Latin American countries is segmented into quintiles with four countries in each. This variable is chosen because it can reflect the experience of instability from various sources. There is no necessity for the agrarian structure described here to lead to any one type of instability. A variety of either anomic or organized, violent activities can occur, simply based on the availability of a large number of persons with severe disaffection from the prevailing authority structure. An additional element in favor of the deaths from political violence variable is the fact that reporting of deaths tends to be more accurate than other measures of instability (Weede 1981).[8]

Table 8.3 lists the cross tabulation of deaths due to political violence by the five patterns that emerged from Table 8.2. The value of tau-b, a measure of association for ordinal data, is significant at $p < .005$, as can be seen in the table. In addition, the value of gamma, another such measure that is conditional on a distribution of this type without tied ranks, is fairly robust at .70. These values should be compared with those between the values of the Gini index of land inequality itself (Taylor and Hudson 1972, 267–68, in order to maximize the number of cases) and the same violence variable with tau-b equal to .36 ($N = 15$, significant at $p < .05$) and a value of gamma equal to .43. When compared with the results of the analysis of Table 8.3, there is a tenfold increase in significance level for the patterned inequality variable and its relationship to political violence over and above the Gini index. Note that a difference in

TABLE 8.3
Association Between Patterned Inequality and
Political Violence for Twenty Latin American Countries

Deaths from political violence (by quintile)	Patterned inequality (by quintile)				
	1 (Both models rejected)	2 (Exponential model for upper portion)	3 (EI model for upper portion)	4 (Near fit of models for both portions)	5 (EI model for upper; exponential for lower)
5			Argentina Nicaragua		Colombia El Salvador
4			Cuba Dominican Republic Venezuela	Bolivia	
3			Guatemala Mexico	Chile	Peru
2		Haiti	Brazil Ecuador Paraguay		
1	Costa Rica Uruguay		Honduras Panama		

NOTE: $\tau_b = .51, p < .005, \Gamma = .70$.

significance levels does not translate directly into an estimate of the likelihood of political violence, only a difference in probability levels of obtaining certain values of inferential statistics.

It is further instructive to consider the relationship between patterned inequality and the Gini index. A value of tau-b equal to .27 ($N = 15$, not significant at $p < .05$) was calculated with an associated value of gamma equal to .40. These statistics suggest a low level of association between the two measures of inequality. They further suggest that generalized land inequality, at least as measured by the Gini index in the Latin American context, either is more heavily influenced by random factors or is tapping a somewhat different dimension than is the patterned inequality variable.

We should note here that the finding of a significant relationship at $p < .05$ between the Gini index and political violence is thoroughly consistent with earlier findings of either a barely significant relationship, just nonsignificant, or just about at the significance level as was found here (actually $p = .048$). This suggests that this finding conforms to the majority of studies undertaken thus far, and perhaps even implies some degree of generalizability of these findings beyond the strict confines of Latin America. What distinguishes the present analysis from these earlier ones using the Gini index is the substantially improved degree of association between patterned inequality and political violence.

There is an additional aspect of Table 8.3 to be noted. This is the commonality of experience of the countries in the fourth and fifth quintiles for patterned inequality. All of them—Chile, Peru, Bolivia, Colombia, and El Salvador—experienced either intense political violence or redistributive governments.

In the case of Chile, a Marxist-redistributive government—that of Salvador Allende—received a plurality of votes in 1970 (and even earlier in 1964), leading to a government whose policies were sufficiently antithetical to the preferences of the military to lead to the coup of 1973 and the subsequent repression. In Peru, the 1968 coup by the military completed the work begun by the 1964 agrarian act and a major land redistribution was undertaken. Bolivia experienced a successful revolution in 1952, with its associated violence in overthrowing the military government and inaugurating a thorough-going land redistribution. Colombia and El Salvador, where both models are entirely applicable (cell no. 5,5 in Table 8.3), of course, have experienced intense violence, with Colombia's La Violencia stretching approximately from 1948 through its gradual decline in the late 1950's and denouement in 1964 (Dix 1967; Hamby 1986; Oquist 1980). It is of interest that the land redistribution of 1961, which was not insubstantial (Wilkie and Perkal 1986, 39), apparently was instrumental in ending La Violencia several years later. In El Salvador, of course, violence had been extremely intense. At the other end of the diagonal of Table 8.3, we have Uruguay and Costa Rica, which in most respects have been among the least prone to larger-scale rural violence of any of the Latin American countries and to which both theoretical distributions do not apply.

Variation in political violence among the countries with the same pattern of holdings in the middle column suggests the invariance properties of the EI—which is also known as the Pareto-Lévy distribution, one of the only two types of distribution (the other being the Gaussian) that are invariant upon the addition of other random variables (Mandelbrot 1960; 1961). Thus it would be expected that once the pattern of the EI distribution has formed, only serious institutionalized efforts at redistribution would be capable of breaking it, and we find this to be the case in the conformity of so many of these countries to this model in the upper portion of the distribution.

The Urban Disorders of the 1960s

One can also see the effect of the contrast between the exponential and EI distributions on the urban disorders of the 1960s in the United States. It is not my purpose to carry out a major reanalysis of these disorders, but I do want to suggest a perspective that in fact is consistent with more recent evidence concerning the conditions of African-Americans at that time. (For reviews of the earlier literature, see, e.g., Miller, Bolce, and Halligan 1977; Midlarsky 1978).

For American blacks the period from the end of World War II to the disorders of the mid-1960s was one of enormous demographic changes. Chief among them was the transformation from a principally rural population to a mainly urban one. Between the census enumerations of 1940 and 1970, the percentage of blacks living in urban centers increased from 49 to 81 (Jaynes and Williams 1989, 279). From the perspective of political violence, the early period of this transformation was fairly uneventful, but by the mid-1960s political violence had become widespread.[9]

What light can be shed on these events through the use of the distributions we have been describing? First, consider a basic assumption underlying the use of the exponential distribution—the assumption of scarcity, which typically does not apply to income, because, historically, incomes have tended to expand in industrial society. However, there is much information to suggest that it might indeed be applicable to the income of African-Americans in the early 1960s. One measure of scarcity conditions is the increase, decrease, or constancy of jobs for which most blacks would have been qualified, given their recent arrival in the cities. These tended to be jobs in industry for which less than a high school education was required. Especially in the North, where most of the violence took place, there was a reduction in the number of those jobs between 1959 and 1970 in cities such as New York (-9 percent) Philadelphia (-36 percent) or Boston (-1 percent) (Kasarda 1988, 177). As Nicholas Lemann put it, "the jobs that had drawn blacks to the North in the first place dried up. From 1960 to 1964, manufacturing employment increased noticeably by 3 per cent but fell in New York, Chicago, Los Angeles, Philadelphia and Detroit" (1991, 201). These were precisely the cities that would experience the most intense disturbances during this period. But after the mid-1960s new opportunities arose under Lyndon Johnson's Great Society programs, which made government jobs available to blacks at both the local and federal levels. These programs had not yet been created or had not yet begun to be operative in a substantial way at the time of the greatest intensity and diffusion of the disorders. Thus the window for which scarcity conditions should be operative for urban African-Americans, especially in large Northern cities, was precisely during the early to mid-1960s. Does the exponential distribution apply to this period of time?

Figure 8.1 plots the chi-square goodness-of-fit statistics for the exponential distribution applied to the incomes of African-Americans during the years

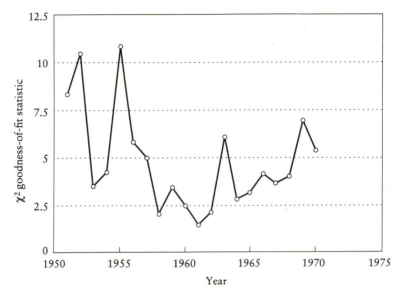

Figure 8.1. Goodness of fit of the exponential distribution to income levels of African-Americans, 1950–70 (data from *Historical Statistics of the United States* 1975).

1950–70. Despite fluctuations in the chi-square values, the minimum and therefore best fit is found in the early 1960s, just prior to the onset of the disorders. Hence, the scarcity-inequality nexus described by the exponential distribution is operative during this time. One would expect some time lag between the onset of economic scarcity conditions, in the loss of both jobs and future prospects, and the onset of specific responses in the form of the disorders.

One must also take into account another form of scarcity operative at the time, namely the physical environment of the ghetto. Before the open-housing legislation that was soon to be passed into law, the overcrowded, mostly slum-infested black ghettos of Northern cities must have seemed to be physical incarnations of the economic scarcity operative in the marketplace. This would have been especially salient to younger black males with little hope of either physical movement outside of the ghetto or jobs in a manufacturing sector that was beginning a precipitous decline. This physical form of scarcity supplemented and reinforced the economic form.

Comparison with white America of course reveals its very different circumstances. Indeed the upper tail of the income distribution is distinctly fractal in appearance, as Vilfredo Pareto (1935) demonstrated decades ago for most income distributions. Income distributions for black and white Americans are compared in appropriate fashion by Gerald D. Jaynes and Robin M. Williams, Jr. (1989, 278-81).

In their summary analyses of the status of African-Americans in American society for the National Research Council, Jaynes and Williams provide relative black/white odds of being in poverty for the period 1939-84, with special emphasis on the latter portion of this time interval. Although there is a general decline in the odds (relative to a white family) of a black family being in poverty beginning in 1939, that decline is temporarily reversed in the mid- to late 1960s. When the data are disaggregated by gender of head of household, the findings are even more pronounced. While the resurgence of the odds of being in poverty is relatively mild for households headed by women, it is very strong in the mid- to late 1960s for households headed by men, as shown in Figure 8.2 (Jaynes and Williams 1989, 280-81). When young black males see their older counterparts suddenly out of work or unable to find it after migrating from the South, then their own prospects appear to worsen dramatically, leading to an increased probability of striking out at the system when the opportunity arises. This is probably the scenario that was played out during many of the riots of 1965-68.

The increased applicability of the exponential distribution during the early 1960s combined with the later dramatic rise in the relative black/white odds of being in poverty (the actual condition of poverty should come shortly after the first significant experience of scarcity) suggest a fairly strong confluence of two analytic sources and their complementarity in helping to explain the onset of the disorders. Further light is shed here on the prevalence of disorders in the Northern cities, with far fewer instances in the South. Cities such as Atlanta and Houston actually experienced an increase in the number of manufacturing jobs between 1959 and 1970, in comparison with the decline in cities such as New York and Philadelphia (Kasarda 1988, 177).

It is useful to compare the results emerging from this perspective with those of one of the most recent studies of the urban disorders (Olzak, Shanahan, and McEneaney 1996). Consistent with earlier findings, non-white poverty and unemployment were not found to be associated with the disorders. In this study, as in earlier ones, a cross-sectional design is used, which estimates unemployment and non-white poverty at one point in time (1960 and 1959, respectively). In contrast, we have explicitly compared the odds of being in poverty for the non-white population to that of the white, as a trend over time (see Figure 8.2). Similarly, we have also examined the applicability of the chi-square goodness-of-fit of the exponential distribution over time (Figure 8.1).

Interestingly, despite the differences between their cross-sectional design and the essentially longitudinal approach here, there is a theoretical overlap.

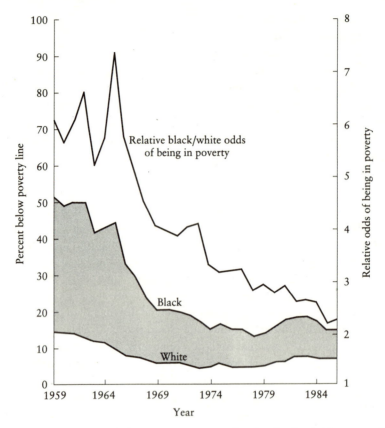

Figure 8.2. Poverty rates of African-American and white families headed by men and odds of being in poverty by household type, 1959–86. (Adapted with permission from Jaynes and Williams, *A Common Destiny: Blacks and American Society*, 280–81. Copyright 1989 by the National Academy of Sciences. Couretsy of the National Academy Press, Washington, D.C.)

One of the principal findings of Olzak, Shanahan, and McEneaney is that a dissimilarity index which essentially measures extent of segregation of the black population from the white is significantly associated with the disorders. In the present study, scarcity for the black population is suggested not only to be income-related but also to be reflected in the increasingly segregated ghetto life of this period, coincident with applicability of the exponential distribution to non-white incomes. Only later were these conditions ameliorated by open-housing legislation.

Support for a longitudinal approach also emerges from a recent study of the relation between income inequality and criminal behavior. For both blacks and whites, increased income inequality was positively associated with increased arrest rates, but income inequality was the only uniformly significant explanatory variable for the black population (LaFree and Drass 1996). Although one can not deem all of the behaviors during the disorders to be criminal, nevertheless a significant subset of them were, as indicated by the high arrest rate (*Riots, Civil and Criminal Disorders* 1967), the dependent variable in the LaFree and Drass study.

It is here that we see the consequences of the absence of mutual identification in life circumstances—both in the Latin American land distributions that form the basis of peasant existence and in income levels as well as in living conditions for African-Americans in the early to mid-1960s. What happens when there is the obverse, namely equality and a mutual identification between societal groups? Cooperation may well be the outcome, in contrast to violence, and that is precisely what we find in Chapter 9's analysis of cooperation and helping of Jews by non-Jews during the Holocaust.

CHAPTER 9

Equality and Cooperation or Helping

In order to reflect on the implications of the preceding analysis of mutual identification and violence, it is useful to consider the obverse in an instance of an extreme form of cooperation—helping under conditions of considerable stress. Such an environment was found during World War II when, under conditions of extreme danger, non-Jews helped save Jews from certain death. Until recently, this dimension of the Holocaust has received undeservedly little attention. Perhaps this is not merely because incidents of this type were all too few, given the terrible magnitude of the slaughter (although Yad Vashem in Israel has in recent years documented a growing number of such cases). Instead, much of this neglect, at least on the part of social scientists, may derive from the absence of frameworks for the understanding of behaviors of this type. Recently, however, more serious efforts to acknowledge and study these acts have been made by scholars such as Samuel Oliner and Pearl Oliner (1988), Mordecai Paldiel (1993), and Eva Fogelman (1994). Still, certain basic questions need to be answered. Why were certain communities saved from the Nazis, especially as the result of the concerted efforts of non-Jews, and others not? More specifically, what distinguishes the non-Jewish helper of Jews during the Holocaust from those who behaved as indifferent observers or, in severe cases, served as active participants in the mass murder?

Negative-Sum Outcomes Avoided by MAD

A first clue is provided by the recent Cold-War process of MAD (mutually assured destruction), which is another instance of potential mass murder, albeit under different circumstances. Each of the nuclear powers targets the other's cities and virtually all other targetable population centers for destruction in the event of nuclear war. In effect, each side holds the other's population hostage.

As a result there can exist a mutual identification between populations in affected societies.

MAD is a means of creating a mutual identification—if only in suffering and death. Before MAD, the various combatants, both military and civilian, could indulge in the illusion that there were fundamental and irreconcilable distinctions between sides. This increasingly was the case as the propaganda mills of each side dehumanized the other in World War I. In the extreme, a coarse dehumanization occurred in World War II with Jews considered "Untermenschen," or little better than animals, by the Nazis. The infamous use by the SS of dogs ordered to kill Jewish inmates in concentration camps with the cry "Man, kill that dog" is a horrifying case in point.

The introduction of nuclear weapons into international conflicts by both sides makes this kind of scenario extremely difficult to sustain. It is not merely that each side can retaliate against the other and that both now have extremely destructive capabilities. Rather, more central to the MAD process is the likely commonality in death of all human beings participating in such a war. The racial, religious, ethnic, and national differences, so blatantly visible to the national or racial dogmatist, now are blurred by the charred bodies, skeletal remains, and other perceived horrific outcomes of a nuclear war. This perception of commonality in extremis may be one of the sources of mutual identification among antagonists in the nuclear era.

A common identification between affected populations can avoid the negative-sum consequences of a nuclear war. A more positive case can be found in the example of a successful Japanese firm, where we can see that one basis for the absence of strikes and the ability to maintain consistent quality control is a form of identification between management and labor. Managers often are paid little more than labor, have offices on the factory floor, and even dress in shirtsleeves or other forms of attire that differ little from those of the worker. The need for a common effort to enhance the firm's (and Japan's export) market position is strongly emphasized in both labor and management. Such forms of mutual identification can be credited, at least in part, with the avoidance of intense conflict between labor and management.

Equality and Identification Between Rescuer and Victim

The concept of mutual identification can thus be one important means of avoiding overt conflict. The context of rescue or altruistic behavior in the Holocaust is similar. Under conditions of an extreme identification between the Jewish victim and the potential rescuer, the initially defined negative outcome for the Jew also has strong negative implications for the helper. A morally or religiously generated identification ("I am my brother's keeper"; "the Jew is my brother") simply may yield too many negative implications for the helper to allow Jews to go unaided to their deaths. The possibility of rescuing the Jew and thereby removing both persons from the negative-sum condition then is an appealing outcome.

Other, less extreme, but nevertheless important types of identification also exist. There can occur a class identification between Jews and non-Jews of similar socioeconomic positions. It is no accident that many wealthy or well-known Jews in business, education, or the arts and sciences were rescued before World War II. It is not merely that such persons may have been more wealthy and therefore could have used their wealth to escape; more salient is the fact that many non-Jews of a similar socioeconomic status bent every effort to help their Jewish counterparts. (An interesting and tragic story is that of a famous Polish-Jewish Professor Mehring who, rather than agreeing to be hidden outside the ghetto by his admiring non-Jewish colleagues, chose to remain with his people in the Lodz ghetto and from there to be taken to his death in Treblinka; Steiner 1967, 170–71).

A form of identification can also occur in which non-Jews who see themselves equally marginal to society's mainstream as are the Jews or who themselves experienced persecution as did the Jews, tend to act disproportionately as helpers. French Protestants, or Huguenots, who were slaughtered after the revocation of the Edict of Nantes in 1685 and thereafter remained outside the center of French religious thought and practice, were outstanding as sources of help to French Jewry in World War II (Hallie 1979).

Certain of these modes of identification were actually found to be central in identifying rescuers in one of the few systematic studies of this kind (London 1970). Oliner and Oliner (1988, 191–92) also report on the role of identification in the helping of Jews, but more episodically and less systematically. However, they confirm the importance of equality and, indirectly, identification as major sources of the helping of Jews. An "egalitarian" factor was found to be one among four that had the highest predictive power in distinguishing between helpers on the one hand and nonhelpers and bystanders on the other. (The Oliners' other three factors are strong family attachments, having Jewish friends, and having broad social commitments.) One of the highest positive factor loadings on the egalitarian dimension was for findings of similarity between the helper and victim, while ethnocentrism had one of the highest negative loadings (312, 322–24). Rescuers of Jews tended to be socially marginal and also had an intense identification with a parental model of moral conduct.

These findings tend to support the importance of various types of identification for altruistic behavior.

At this point, it will be useful to define the meaning of the term *identification* as it is used here. Within the context of this chapter, identification means a perceived similarity between the giver and receiver of help. The perception of similarity should not be of a superficial nature but rather one that also has existential implications. Thus, although the theory predicts that common life circumstances (e.g., middle-class origin) should be associated with helping during the Holocaust, that is not the entirety of the identification. The common humanity of the rescuer and victim should also be part of the perception. At the very least, there should exist the recognition that if the human being who happens to be labeled a Jew can be deported and murdered, then the rescuer himself also could be at risk at some time in the future.

Identification here is *not* taken to mean a personal liking for the victim by the rescuer or to imply identification in the sense of modeling behavior, such as we encounter the parent-child forms of identification found in Freud (1953) and reviewed by Urie Bronfenbrenner (1960) and Elizabeth Midlarsky and William Suda (1978). In most, if not all of these writings, there exists an emotional tie between the actors. This does not have to be the case between rescuer and victim. Nor does there have to exist on the part of the rescuer a desire to be in some sense "equivalent" to the victim. Emotional ties or modeling in the sense of personal equivalence are omitted from our definition of identification.

We turn now to an examination of the implications of the present theory. Does the evidence available thus far (in addition to that in London 1970) support the concept of identification as an explanation of rescue during the Holocaust? Although the evidence is meager at this time, two strategies can be adopted. The first will be a comparison of extreme behaviors. Two countries with thoroughly opposite rescue behaviors toward Jews will be compared for their general characteristics. The second strategy will be to analyze altruistic or rescue behaviors in one country for which some systematic data exists, namely Germany.

The Cases of Denmark and Lithuania

The two countries selected are Denmark and Lithuania, both small countries situated on the periphery of much larger powers.[1] The former is generally acknowledged as the country with the most concerted and complete rescue of Jews during the Holocaust. Ninety-six percent of Danish Jewry were rescued from the Nazis, and most of the remaining Jews incarcerated by the Nazis survived, largely because of Danish expressions of concern and interventions, even with concentration camp administrators (Flender 1963; P. Friedman 1957). Lithuania has been singled out as the country with perhaps the most abysmal record of help to the Jews. It also had one of the lowest survival rates for Jews. According to one estimate, the total "number of Jews rescued by, or with the help of, Lithuanians does not even reach one-half of one percent of the Jewish population" (Neshamit 1977, 329).

There are certain obvious differences. Lithuania was in the zone of direct SS control from very early on (Fein 1979), whereas Denmark was not under the SS until August 1943. And for Denmark there was a sympathetic neutral nation nearby, Sweden, willing to accept the Danish Jews. (It is worth noting that Bulgaria, which did not have the fortunate circumstance of such a neighbor, also managed to save the vast majority of its Jews).

More fundamental differences, however, are found in the matter of identifications, or their absence, between the majority of non-Jews and the Jewish minority. In the case of Denmark, at the time of the proposed *Aktion* against the Jews by the Nazis, strong identifications of the non-Jewish Danes with the Jews had already developed. In the early stages of the occupation of Denmark by Germany after April 1940, a considerable degree of autonomy was allowed the Danes. They had not resisted the Nazi occupation and were therefore, because of the German perception of an "Aryan similarity," viewed as a model protectorate. In the absence of a strategic imperative, wherein Denmark until 1944 was remote from the important European fighting, there was no necessity for a direct occupation. Denmark actually had a self-governing status until November 1942, when Hitler, dissatisfied with the absence of enthusiasm for Nazi goals by the German political and military representatives in Denmark, appointed a General Plenipotentiary in November 1942. Even then, substantial Danish autonomy existed, as evidenced by the ability to hold a parliamentary election in 1943 in which the local Nazi party and the Danish fascist party (Bondepartiet) together received only 3 percent of the vote (Fein 1979, 145).

Resistance to the Nazis, however, rose during late 1942, culminating in a dock strike in August 1943, along with other strikes, riots, and sabotage. The government effectively was forced to resign in that month, and the Germans assumed direct military command. It is not the function of this chapter to trace all the developments leading to the rescue of Danish Jewry to safety in Sweden, but certain of the highlights should be noted. Shortly after the assumption of direct command by the Nazis, a raid was planned against the Jews. As the result of warnings received from a German shipping official in Copenhagen and relayed to the Jews by the leadership of the Danish Social Democratic Party, the

Chief Rabbi publicly warned the community just before the start of the Jewish New Year. Warnings were spread by Social Democrats, priests, politicians, and others. As a result, when the first raid was carried out on October 1–2, 1943, very few Jews were found at home. The vast majority were in hiding, ready to be ferried to Sweden in fishing boats. Even many of the 475 who were seized were saved from death in Theresienstadt by the constant intercession of Danish officials, shipments of food parcels from Denmark, and other expressions of concern.

In Lithuania, there was no such effort. Indeed, a group of anti-Soviet "partisans" apparently killed approximately 5,000 Jews even before the German invasion of Lithuania was complete, as the Soviets were fleeing. In contrast to Denmark, where antisemitism was almost unknown, Lithuania was seething with anti-Jewish feeling. On the eve of World War II, students staged antisemitic riots at Kovno University. By the end of the 1930s, almost all Jewish officials had been removed from government offices, municipal institutions, and the Lithuanian army. From July 2, 1941, shortly after the invasion of Lithuania, until December 1, 1941, mobile machine gun units in Lithuania murdered 133,346 Jews, nearly one-half of the 250,000 Jews estimated to have been living in Lithuania at that time (Neshamit 1977, 293). Only eight to ten German soldiers were required in these units; all the rest were Lithuanians. Acts of torture and sadism accompanied these killings: rabbis were burned alive, people were thrown in pits that contained boiling plaster, and water was pumped into people's mouths until they burst. According to one observer, a Lithuanian doctor:

With the exception of a few individuals, all the Lithuanians, and especially the intelligentsia who lost their positions during the Soviet regime, hate the Jews. . . . The coarse Lithuanian mob, as opposed to the total apathy of the intelligentsia (who in all likelihood agree with them), acted with such beastly cruelty that by comparison, the Russian pogroms seemed like humanitarian deeds. . . . I cannot believe my eyes and ears. I am totally shaken up by the force of blind hatred which they cultivate to satisfy the most base instincts. (Quoted in Neshamit 1977, 294)

Only a very few individual Lithuanians were found to have helped the Jews. Among them were a farmer who saved a total of 22 Jews, the librarian of the Lithuanian University in Vilna, a few priests, and an illiterate would-be monk who wished "the world would know that there were some decent people among the Lithuanians" (Neshamit 1977, 315–16).

Several Correlates of Victimization

How do we account for these astonishing differences? First, I should like to review some of the findings of one of the major systematic studies of the Holocaust (Fein 1979) and relate them to the Danish and Lithuanian cases. The variable with the strongest correlation with Jewish victimization during the Holocaust ($r = .92$; Fein 1979, 355) was the extent of Jewish isolation, as the result either of segregation efforts by the Germans or of the enforced restriction of Jews to their already existing Jewish neighborhoods. Here we see a powerful difference between the conditions of Danish and Lithuanian Jewry. The Jews of Denmark were interspersed and integrated throughout Danish society. The Jews of Lithuania manifestly were not. Not only were their modes of dress and appearance different from Lithuanian non-Jews, especially for religious Jews, but the Jews generally resided in their own villages or in clearly demarcated neighborhoods within larger cities. Moreover, the majority of non-Jewish Lithuanians were rural, while almost the entire Jewish population of Lithuania was urban. The geographical differences were manifest and distinct. This level of distinctiveness made it easier for Lithuanians to define their own nationalism in opposition to the Jews, as we shall see momentarily.

A second variable with strong correlation with rescue of Jews was the presence of church protest of the slaughter ($r = -.63$ with victimization; Fein 1979, 355). Here the differences also are profound. Whereas the Danish clergy throughout the war period openly expressed its antipathy to anti-Jewish measures, there was a thorough absence of such protest in Lithuania. As early as 1940, a young theologian at the University of Copenhagen gave a series of public lectures that emphasized right and justice for the Jews as inextricably linked with justice and freedom in Danish life (Fein 1979, 146). The Danish national Lutheran Church frequently came out in support of the Jews. At the time of the raids against Jews in Denmark, Bishop Fuglsang-Damgaard of Copenhagen expressed the relationship between Jews and non-Jews in this way:

Whenever persecutions are undertaken for racial or religious reasons against the Jews, it is the duty of the Christian Church to raise a protest against it for the following reasons:
1. Because we shall never be able to forget that the Lord of the Church, Jesus Christ, was born in Bethlehem, of the Virgin Mary into Israel, the people of His possession, according to the promise of God. The history of the Jewish people up to the birth of Christ includes the preparation for the salvation which God has prepared in Christ of all men. This is also expressed in the fact that the Old Testament is part of our Bible . . . (Quoted in Fein 1979, 114)

The bishop had expressed such thoughts as early as 1938, denouncing the persecution of German Jews after Kristallnacht. At a conference at the University of Copenhagen in December 1941, Lutheran theologians agreed to protest publicly the onset of any discrimination against the Jews. In early 1943, before the beginning of activity against the Jews, the Bishop of Copenhagen once again deplored racial hatred (Fein 1979, 115). (The Metropolitan Stefan of Sophia took a similar public stand against Jew-hatred in Bulgaria, where so much of the Jewish community was saved.)

In Lithuania, according to the most authoritative sources (e.g., Neshamit 1977), not a single document has been found indicating even one public appeal by Lithuanian clergy to help the Jews. Instead, the Archbishop Juozas Skvireckas and his assistant Bishop Vincentas Brizgys signed a cable congratulating Hitler for liberating Lithuania from the Soviet yoke. A report of the German SD (the intelligence service of the SS) on the activities of Bishop Brizgys stated that he issued a pastoral letter in 1941 at the height of the massacres, forbidding priests to help Jews. According to the report:

The stand adopted by the clergy on the Jewish question is generally clear-cut. In addition, Bishop Brizgys forbade the priests to help Jews in any way whatsoever. The requests of Jewish representatives who visited him personally and asked for his intervention with the German institutions were refused. In the future, he will not even allow Jews to approach him. . . .

There still have not been any cases of Jews converting to Catholicism. The Catholic clergy will oppose such conversions as they believe that the Jews would never convert out of faith, but rather for supposed benefits which they would receive. (Quoted in Neshamit 1977, 314)

After 1943 when it became clear that the Allies could win the war, more of the Lithuanian Catholic clergy were willing to help Jews. But this was after the vast majority of Lithuanian Jewry had been destroyed, and it has been argued that at least some of that help may have been given to curry favor with the victorious Allies after the war's end.

Political Identification

Yet another variable with a strong negative relationship ($r = -.57$) with Jewish victimization is "state age since 1830" (Fein 1979, 355). Here the forces of contemporary nationalism come into play. Whereas Denmark is one of the oldest and most socially integrated of the European states, Lithuania was one of the youngest, having become independent in 1918 largely as the result of the then extraordinary weakness of the Soviet Union following World War I and the Bolshevik revolution. Indeed, one can argue that Lithuania's statehood and its supportive nationalistic base were among the most fragile in Europe. Not only had Lithuania been independent for only 22 years when the Soviets annexed it in 1940, but its prior history of statehood had also been deeply involved with the early history of Poland, in the "Personal Union" of the Polish and Lithuanian ruling dynasties in 1385 and the more formal joining of the two nations in the Lublin Union of 1569 (Harrison 1928, 30). Thereafter, Lithuania was ruled either indirectly by Poles or directly by Russians until 1918.

It is no accident, therefore, that "the devil and the noble (local Polish landowner)" were joined with the Jews in an infamous trinity, and after the German invasion it was said that the "Jews, Burlokai [Russian peasants] . . . and Polish imperialists and refugees are mushrooms on the body of the Lithuanian people and they must be destroyed as quickly as possible" (P. Staras, quoted in Neshamit 1977, 290–91).

We can understand Lithuanian nationalism, then, as defined in opposition to Jews, Poles, and Russians. Even the contemporary capital of Lithuania, Vilnius, then called Vilna, was situated within the boundaries of prewar Poland and had large Polish and Jewish populations. The recency and fragility of the Lithuanian nationalistic base took as its principal target the most helpless and legally sanctioned (by the Germans) scapegoat, the Jews. The Soviet annexation in 1940 and consequent deposing of the native political and intellectual elite of course only inflamed matters further, for it emphasized the extraordinarily fragile and possibly transient nature of Lithuanian independence.

These factors now enable us to define more precisely the differences between Denmark and Lithuania, in particular the various forms of identification or their absence. It is clear from recent Lithuanian history that Lithuanian self-identification as a nation-state relied on opposition to the Jews, among others. Only older, more mature societies such as Denmark have experienced sufficiently long, relatively peaceful histories as independent states that they do not require such external negative referents. Thus non-Jewish Danes had the opportunity to identify with the Jews in Denmark, whereas quite the opposite situation existed in Lithuania. A negative identification of nationalism in opposition to several groups, Jews foremost among them, had developed during the nineteenth century (both the left and clerical right included notorious antisemites), culminating in the state supported antisemitism of the 1930s, followed by the massacre of Jews during World War II. In contrast, a political identification had developed between Jewish and non-Jewish Danes such that, as Leni Yahil describes it:

For two or three weeks, the Danes, identifying the Jews' fate with their own, became totally involved in the rescue operations. They viewed the rescue of the Jews as a manifestation of their national revolt against the Germans, and thus the rare situation was created in which it was not the Jews who were asked or sought to prove their identification with the host country, but rather it was the Danes who proved by their response and actions how great the identification was between their national interests and the fate of the Jews. (1977, 620-21)

Moral-Religious Identification

Another form of identification is moral and/or religious and once again, we see stark differences between our cases. By publicly declaring that discrimination against Jews must be opposed and that Christ himself was a Jew, the Bishop of Copenhagen established a firm basis for religious identification. In addition, those Danes who were initially inclined to help on moral grounds would have been spurred to even greater lengths by declarations of this kind. In Lithuania, this certainly was not the case. The Catholic clergy, with few exceptions, defined their religion in apposition, and in many cases in opposition, to that of the Jews. No public declaration of any kind was made by the Lithuanian clergy in support of the Jews. As we have seen, there is evidence of an explicit injunction to priests against giving help to Jews. Priests were active in bands of "partisans" who killed Jews, and some were even associated with Lithuanian police battalions who murdered Jews in Belorussia and in the camps of Treblinka and Majdanek (Neshamit 1977, 312).

Socioeconomic Equality and Identification

There was also far more opportunity for socioeconomic identification among Danish Jews and non-Jews than among their counterparts in Lithuania. The majority of Danish Jews were middle class, boasting among their number scientists of world renown such as Niels Bohr, who having one Jewish parent, was listed by the Nazis as a Jew. The Danes of Copenhagen, especially those who were initially involved in the organization of the rescue, also were predominantly middle class. The socioeconomic and geographic integration of Jews into Danish life was virtually complete, especially in Copenhagen.

We have already seen that this was hardly the case in Lithuania. The largely rural Lithuanians held almost nothing in common with the more urban, more middle-class, geographically segregated, and far more intellectualized Jewish population of cities such as Vilna and Kovno. Indeed the former city was known as the "Jerusalem of Lithuania," connoting its intellectual preeminence in the history of Eastern European Jewish thought. Incidentally, this was likely the reason for the very early onslaught against Lithuanian Jewry; its striking intellectual history made it the prime candidate for extinction by the Nazis.

We can, however, say more about the role of socioeconomic identification between rescuer or helper and victim. Here, data on Nazi Germany, first presented by Sarah Gordon (1984), are very helpful, for they suggest findings that defy the conventional wisdom concerning the sources of Nazi support. The present theoretical framework, on the other hand, would predict these findings.

The theory of identification offered here suggests an increase in aiding of Jews would follow from an increase in identifications of various sorts, particularly political, moral-religious, and socioeconomic. Given the middle-class nature of German Jewry in the period from the formation of the German Empire in 1871 to the rise of the Nazis, one would expect a predominance of helping of Jews, or at least active opposition to the Nazis, among the German middle class. Equality of circumstance here is predicted to promote cooperation or helping (Deutsch 1985; Leventhal, Karuza, and Fry 1980). And this is what Gordon's data generally demonstrate.

In an exhaustive analysis of archives from the Nazi period, Gordon extracted data on opponents to Nazism found in the Gestapo files of the Governmental District of Düsseldorf. There were "203 Gestapo files on individuals who aided Jews, 42 files on critics of racial persecution, and 30 files on individuals suspected of aiding Jews. The archive also holds 137 files on Germans who had sexual relations with Jews, 40 files on persons who were suspected of having sexual relations with Jews. . . ." (1984, 211).

The Nazis labeled those who gave direct help as Judenfreunde (friends of Jews), while those who had sexual relations with Jews were termed Rassenschänder (disgracers of the race). Sexual relations with Jews were forbidden to Germans by the Nüremberg Laws and therefore involved at least an element of risk, if not outright opposition to the regime. In the statistics to be quoted from Gordon, she does not differentiate between the two categories in overt class-based opposition. However, in a comparison between Judenfreunde and Rassenschänder as to percentages in each category during the different phases of persecution (1933-34, 1935-37, 1938-39, 1940-44), there were no substantial differences between the two categories (Gordon 1984, 216).

The statistics of greatest interest in Gordon's study are presented in Table 9.1. Percentages of Jews in Germany in 1933 in the various occupational categories are compared with percentages of Jews in the Rhine province to establish

TABLE 9.1
Occupational Distribution of Jews and Opponents of Antisemitism in Germany, the Rhine Province, and the Governmental District of Düsseldorf (in percentages)

	Jews in Germany, 1933	Jews in Rhine Province, 1933	Jews in Germany, 1939	Opponents of antisemitism in the Governmental District of Düsseldorf, 1933–44
Independents (professional and self-employed)	51.7	53.4	16.2	33.6
Civil servants	1.1	1.0	00.0	6.6
White-collar	37.5	35.6	25.5	44.4
Blue-collar	9.8	9.9	58.3	15.3

SOURCE: After Gordon 1984, 227, who cites the following: for the occupational distribution of Jews in 1933, see *Statistik des Deutschen Reichs*, vol. 470 (1937), no. 1: 8; for 1939, see vol. 552 (1944), no. 4: 74; for the occupational distribution of Jews in the Rhine Province in 1933, see *Statistik des Deutschen Reichs*, vol. 455 (1936), no. 16: 60. For the occupational distribution of opponents of antisemitism, see Gordon 1984, appendix B, 324–25.

that there are no visible differences of serious magnitude between the two data sets. This lack of difference suggests that the percentages of opponents in the Governmental District of Düsseldorf are likely (but not certain) to be representative of the pattern of opposition throughout Germany. It is clear that white-collar middle-class opponents of the Nazis are vastly overrepresented relative to the remaining classes. This is all the more surprising because for a substantial portion of this period, 1939–44, the Jews remaining in Germany were mainly blue-collar. Thus, the opportunity for a blue-collar Christian to help the blue-collar Jewish colleague would have been greater than for a middle-class one.

This finding concerning the predominance of white-collar opponents of the Nazi racial policies is even more surprising given the conventional wisdom of middle-class electoral support for the Nazis. One would expect, therefore, a diminution of middle-class helping of Jews and perhaps a predominance of blue-collar support of Jews, especially in light of Communist opposition to the Nazi regime. Yet such is not the case. The theory of equality and identification, on the other hand, predicts this finding of greater helping by white-collar Germans, based on perceptions of similarity between middle-class Germans and their Jewish counterparts and, perhaps at some level, common fate. This outcome is supported in the data.

In this chapter we have developed a theory of identification for helping under conditions of extreme potential cost to the helper, or negative-sum conditions. This is the obverse of the lack of identification, the patterned inequality of

Chapter 8, that is associated with political violence. Several different types of identification have been isolated, namely, political, moral-religious, and socioeconomic. Behavior toward the Jews during the Holocaust, in the contrasting cases of Denmark and Lithuania and in a study of German helpers of Jews, supports the applicability of the theory. The concluding chapter now will reflect on several implications of these findings for the functioning of a democratic polity.

PART V

Conclusion

CHAPTER 10

Paradoxes of Democracy and State Survivability

It is time now to draw the various threads of the analysis into a tighter skein. We began with a close consideration of various types of inequality. Following the various logics of inequality in regard to state formation and dissolution, state failure, failures to democratize, and the sources of democracy, we examined the relationship between inequality and violence and then the relationship between equality and cooperation.

Sometimes one's own effort can be clarified and strengthened through a comparison with a parallel work, one with certain similarities but also key differences. Here a work by anthropologist Marvin Harris, *America Now: The Anthropology of a Changing Culture* (1981), brought to my attention after I had written the first draft of this book, provides such a parallel, not in relation to states and their rise and fall, but in relation to corporations and their effect on national life. Writing from the perspective of the emergence of oligopoly in the American economy, Harris observes correctly that just a few large corporations tend to dominate any market, following the expansion of some and the contraction or disappearance of others. This, of course, parallels the fractal formation resulting from the expansion of small feudal principalities or states until there emerge only a few dominant powers. Harris also points to the subsequent emergence of inefficiencies, bloated bureaucracies, shoddy manufactures, and insulated executives at the top of the largest corporations. Such weakness can invite only decay, which as we have seen in the case of the state, leads to dissolution, most often as the result of conquest from without, but sometimes through catastrophic collapse from within. Many of the smaller corporations disappeared, conquered not by force of arms or dynastic marriages, but by corporate takeovers of various sorts. Harris prescribes a decentralization of the economy to yield a larger number of smaller corporations, which has, in fact, occurred to a certain extent, especially in newer industries, since the writing of his book.

But a major consequence, not foreseen by Harris, has been the "leaner and meaner" look of corporations that have been restored to profitability principally as the result of downsizing and the introduction of greater efficiencies. Neglecting the ethical implications of this process for the moment, because they apply far less to the dismissal of corrupt officials, the parallel with certain state trajectories is important, for it suggests a process that declining states might have adopted in order to stave off collapse. In particular, had Rome adopted an approach that encouraged decentralization of elements of the Empire beyond the administrative division between East and West (acknowledging or even formalizing the increasing autonomy of the growing latifundia) as well as greater efficiency in its governing bodies, the outcome might have been very different. Shorn of the burden of the increasingly corrupt tax collectors, both the towns and the latifundia might have tamed their vigor and retained a Roman patriotism that, as we saw, diminished greatly during the later Empire. Seen from this perspective, Diocletian's centralizing reforms that both tied the towns and estates closer to the imperial administration and increased the bureaucracy and taxation ultimately had to have disastrous consequences, after the temporary reinvigoration that they provided.

After the passing of the Merovingian and Carolingian monarchies as remote successors to the Empire, only the Roman Catholic Church remained as a direct lineal descendant of Rome. But as a fundamentally ecclesiastical enterprise and one that retained many hierarchical characteristics inherited from the Empire, it could not become the successful loosely organized imperial framework that would have dispensed with gross inefficiencies and excessive taxation in order to command the secular loyalties of the towns and estates. Indeed, in late antiquity there were serious efforts by the Church and other societal agencies to mobilize hierarchical forms of authority, possibly in anticipation of the weakening of the imperial authority (Lim 1995). In contrast, Byzantium, in resorting to the system of themes, essentially took advantage of the autonomy and relative efficiency of these uniquely military administrative units in successfully combating the Muslim invaders and survived for another thousand years beyond the fall of Rome in the West.

From the perspective of liberal democracy perhaps the two most disturbing elements of our study are, first, the inevitability of inequality under conditions of scarce desiderata and, second, the robust relationship discovered between land inequality and three measures of democracy, including liberal democracy and institutional forms. Moreover, this finding of the relationship of land inequality to all three measures of democracy occurred despite strong differences in their structures of explanation; the cultural variables had far greater impact on liberal democracy and institutional forms. The inevitability of inequality is even more disturbing than may be apparent at first reading because it does not rely on the sequential acquisitions of fractal formation but can even occur under conditions of random allocation. Hence, it is not surprising that virtually all democracies are to varying extents redistributive, not only because all voters, including the poorest, have access to the political process, but also because of the continual effort needed to overcome both the more obvious inequalities induced by sequential arrivals and the more insidious types that evolve simply from scarcities imposed upon random allocation. Both the appearance and the actuality of gross inequalities can be destabilizing and feed into the process of state dissolution, as we saw in Chapter 4. These inequalities and other elements of our analysis give rise to five paradoxes of democracy—namely, those of inequality, cooperation, corruption, environmental influence, and ideology.

The Paradox of Inequality

The first of our paradoxes of democracy is that a certain degree of inequality may be required for the initiation and maintenance of democracy, yet if inequality is extreme and patterned, it can result in political violence. We have also seen that some degree of equality—and its concomitant sense of identification—is conducive to cooperation among different groups, yet the repudiation of all inequality could undermine the bases of democracy. How do we resolve this seeming paradox?

At the outset, it must be emphasized that the robust findings of positive relationships between land inequality and the three measures of democracy probably signify an element of historical state strength or at least elite security. In older, more mature conquest civilizations (England is perhaps the best example), a long-established and secure class of landed elites without serious challenge to their authority could eventually yield limited political rights that eventually would mushroom into more encompassing ones. Thus elite security as measured by land inequality may be the operative variable.[1] Nevertheless, this response still begs the question, for to maintain a secure elite, by definition, some inequalities must exist between the elite and the mass of the population, and so the paradox persists.

If, on the other hand, we take the view that there may be more complex relationships between inequality and democracy than simply positive or negative monotonic variants, then the paradox may lend itself to resolution. Consider the possibility of an inverted U function for the relationship between inequality and democracy, shown in Figure 10.1. To generalize the variable across

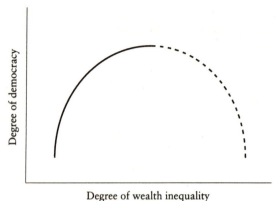

Figure 10.1. Relationship between inequality and democracy.

time beyond land inequality and to avoid conflating with income inequality, which likely has different correlates (Midlarsky 1992a), let this variable be inequality in wealth. Large differentials in wealth generally result from patterns of ownership of the principal modes of production—in the preindustrial era this meant land—and so this is an appropriate, albeit approximate generalization. Although only the left portion of the curve, denoted by a solid line, received empirical confirmation in our analyses, it is more than likely that the dotted portion to the right, not confirmed empirically here, held sway during much of historical time prior to the contemporary period. Centralized monarchies, feudal monarchies, and other strongly hierarchical political schemata clearly limited the political rights of their citizenry. Thus on the right-hand portion of the curve, the greater the inequality, the smaller the extent of democracy.

Still, even in the face of the passing of absolutist monarchies, there should be some evidence of the negative impact of inequality on democracy implied by the right-hand portion of the curve, if only in the residues of inordinately larger landholdings by the *ancien* elite. Until the dawn of the modern period, this certainly would have been true. Since the end of World War II, however, there have been considerable efforts at land reform in many of the world's countries. Even England, which did not undergo an explicit land reform, effectively experienced one as the result of the postwar Labor government's redistributive policies and the impoverishment of the old nobility. In many cases however, these land reforms either have been incomplete (witness Iran's under the Shah) or have been vitiated by a later burgeoning population growth that resulted in land impoverishment and an emergent tenant class on larger holdings, effectively undermining the earlier efforts (as in Egypt, for example). Thus, contemporary holdings in many of the world's countries are far from egalitarian, but still not at the pre-twentieth-century levels of extraordinary inequality. Only Communist countries, which were not examined in Chapter 7, had thoroughgoing land reforms (excepting Poland) that effectively were maintained until Communism's collapse.

The Paradox of Cooperation

As we have seen in Chapter 9 and in the comparison of the differing fates of Israel and Judah in Chapter 4, equality of circumstance fosters mutual identification and cooperation, yet a certain degree of inequality appears to be necessary for a functioning democracy. At the same time, democracy relies on cooperation, at least to the extent of avoiding overt competitions that can lead to violence. In the extreme case, such violence can sunder the polity in civil war. Although related to the first paradox of inequality, it is not easily resolvable by the positing of a relationship as in Figure 10.1. The difficulty here is that the choice of a point on the curve that maximizes democracy would not guarantee the cooperation needed to maintain a functioning democracy. As Robert Putnam (1993, 170) concluded in his comparison between the civic regions of Italy that functioned best democratically and those that functioned least well, such as Naples: "Cooperation is often required—between legislature and executive, between workers and managers, among political parties, between the government and private groups, among small firms, and so on."

In a multicultural society, even small economic differences between groups can minimize cooperation. The recent disclosures of deep discontent among the African-American middle class (Cose 1993), even when confronted with only small economic and social differences, is a case in point. Such discontent can appear in deeply divergent views on the guilt of an alleged murderer, such as O. J. Simpson, and be manifested overtly in an unwillingness to cooperate politically with whites to the same extent as with blacks. Of course, the more massive sorts of inequalities between the ghetto underclass and the remainder of society have given rise to a willingness among some of the impoverished to engage in social deviance of various types. That, in the long run can be equally corrosive to societal cooperation and so also to democracy.

The Paradox of Corruption

The third paradox of democracy, that of corruption, may also not easily present an analytic resolution. Contemporary democracies tend to have leaders who, if not actually corrupt, do engage in practices that can be considered ethically dubious. The recent peccadillos of President Clinton, especially the Whitewater matter and later allegations of the use of the Oval Office for "extracurricular" sexual activities, the financial dealings of former Vice President Spiro Agnew, and especially the nefarious activities of former President Nixon in the Watergate affair, suggest a pattern.[2] Clearly one can condemn the moral climate of modern American life as a source of the corruption, but that is too facile an explanation. Alternatively, one can point to the seemingly increasing public corruption as an artifact of the growth of media interest in what Manuel Castells (1997, 338–41) calls "scandal politics." More to the point, however, is an implication of the present analysis that modern leaders lack the influence that comes with large landholdings or other accouterments of wealth. Without the large-scale material bases of influence, modern democratic leaders—or indeed modern leaders generally—must resort to other methods of influence. Charisma, identified earlier by Max Weber, is of course one such method, and organizational skill another. Interestingly, Leon Trotsky and Joseph Stalin, respectively, employed these methods of influence. Stalin, as we know, was extraordinarily successful in his organizational efforts, and it is possible that if Trotsky had exerted his charisma more judiciously—for example, at Lenin's funeral, at which he failed to appear—the outcome of his conflict with Stalin might have been very different.

Soviet history provides a model in extremis of the basic argument, for here we have virtually no land inequality or other manifest distinguishing features among citizens of the polity and, at the same time, no democracy. Lacking the oratorical skills of a Trotsky or the organizational abilities of a Stalin, the ordinary *apparatchik* had to resort to other, often more nefarious methods to insure his continued influence. Hence, corruption was a continued fact of life in Communist bureaucratic systems, beyond the first blush of utopian visions in the 1920s.

Must modern democratic (and other) systems turn a blind eye to corrupt practices as the price of an increased egalitarianism in the modern age? This question has more than ethical significance, although that of course is important in itself, and touches on two areas of performance in democracies. First, there is the connection between corruption and the decline of the state, as we saw in the history of the later Roman Empire in Chapter 4. To be sure, in contrast to Rome, corrupt leaders in a democracy can be cast out of office, but if the culture of corruption is widespread, then the incumbent corrupt leader will simply be replaced by another of equally corrupt tendencies. Here corruption can imperil the very existence of the state, for in the extreme instance major portions of the economy and society can simply be sold off to the highest or most threatening bidder. It is unlikely that barbarian armies will lay siege to the American polity, ultimately bringing it down as happened in the case of Rome. Instead, various officials responsible for the health of the polity (including immigration policy) could simply be bought off so that they would no longer effectively guard the best interests of the people of the United States. Aldrich Ames, the Soviet spy in the CIA, may be a case in point, for with large amounts of money as inducement, he was perfectly willing to sell the most closely guarded secrets to the Soviet Union, thus leading to the deaths of many American agents.

Second is the likely diminution of cooperation under conditions of even moderately widespread corruption. Only the corrupted would cooperate with each other, and then only so long as mutual benefit persists. "In-groups" and "out-groups" would be defined by the criterion of who benefits from the corruption, with cooperation extending only to those within the in-group. And as we have seen, a fairly widespread sense of cooperation is essential for effective democratic functioning.

The Paradox of Environmental Influence

It is indeed paradoxical that the practice of democracy, which appears to be the quintessentially volitional mode of governance, is subject to ofttimes unyielding environmental constraints. Democracy is action oriented; it involves repeated choices and an ongoing participation by the electorate. Without the continual aggregation of individual choices, by whatever means (representative or participatory), democracy will simply cease to exist. It is no accident that the Greek polis was conceptualized essentially as a political community involving extreme cooperation, at least in political matters, and the continuing capacity to make public choices. As Cynthia Farrar puts it, "One reason why the polis is so important is that it can foster this capacity for interpretation and self-control, thereby increasing the likelihood of its own survival, and thus the survival and continued well-being of its citizens" (1988, 155). Yet the analysis of Chapter 7 tells us that the threat of war can minimize democracy, and as we know, Athens, the prototype of the polis, succumbed to the threat and actuality of war, never to regain its political autonomy and local democracy. The most volitional democratic polities are circumscribed by environmental conditions of various sorts. Perhaps the most dangerous of these is the threat and actuality of war, which can destroy the democratic polity. This lesson for state survivability will be pursued later in this chapter.

The Paradox of Ideology

Democratic thinking is one of the oldest of political philosophies, dating from the Sumerians and the ancient Greeks, yet in its genesis it is perhaps independent of any specified ideation. In the absence of any particular environmental constraints such as the threat of war, it may be perfectly natural for small communities to engage in collective decision making that approximates a rudimentary participatory democracy. The philosophy or ideology of democracy may not be at all necessary for such a process to begin. Liberal democracy, on the other hand, as we saw in Chapter 7, may require a culture of democracy that is indeed reliant on an analytically developed justification for democratic rule. Thus, the origins of democracy are not to be found in any sort of explicit democratic thinking or ideation, but in the absence of environmental constraints in unique cases that allowed the more primitive forms of democracy, common in many societies, to continue in several of them. Later, of course, many writings emerged arguing for and justifying democracy; the culture of liberal democracy is an even more recent development.

One could interpret this sequence of ideation built upon an earlier material base as akin to the Marxian ideological superstructure built upon the economic base, but despite a superficial similarity, there is a fundamental difference. The Marxian view assumes that modification of the economic base (e.g., achieving a more equitable distribution of goods and services) will yield a more just and harmonious society, even to the point of approximating an infinite perfectibility of human beings. (Hence, we witnessed the Soviet reluctance to release crime statistics.) The environment, on the other hand, unlike the economic base of Marx, admits of no facile tinkering or even major restructuring. Land borders and aridity can be accommodated by various political schemes, often autocratic, but cannot be readily changed, even by draconian revolutionary methods. This is a far more pessimistic view and has a paradoxical core. A political ideology of public choice, such as democracy, may in the final analysis be conditional, at least in its origins, on constraints admitting little choice.

Although the paradox of ideology is analytically distinct from the paradox of the environment, there are certain areas of overlap. The paradox of ideology asserts the independence of early democracy from any ideological source, whereas that of the environment emphasizes the particular material influences on early democracy. Nevertheless, they are effectively two sides of the same coin. Given an absence of ideology in the development of early democracy, democratic practices must have emerged from some source or at least from the absence of constraint, which we have specified as environmental, in two particular forms—rainfall and sea borders.

State Survivability

The Role of Democracy

Clearly an underlying theme of this book has been the sustainability of democracy in the face of processes both of state dissolution and of political violence. As we saw in Chapter 5, in both England and ancient Athens resolution of the "social problem" before the incidence of serious war dampened the probability of later political violence and aided the eventual emergence of democracy. Certainly democratic Athens, and indeed the entire presumed prehistorical democratic period, dissolved into the historical mists. Yet in the case of Athens, as we know, and in the early instances of prehistory as suggested by the theory and findings of Chapter 7, it was warfare that did so much to undermine the bases of democracy. The Peloponnesian War began the process of eroding Athenian power to the point where it ultimately could not remain independent as a democratic polity. And there is evidence from the Epic of Gilgamesh in Sumer and in ancient China, Mesoamerica, and Crete that early democracy existed, albeit not in the representative form most familiar to us in the very late twentieth century.

Warfare is probably the greatest danger to democracies, because of either conquest from without or the limitation of political rights from within. Interestingly, apart from Athens, few democracies have succumbed to the vagaries of war. This seeming anomaly is itself probably the result of one of the initial conditions for democracy, namely an island setting or at least a large number of sea borders to insulate the fledgling democracy. (Perhaps George Washington understood this principle well when he counseled against foreign entanglements for the fledgling U.S. democracy, separated from Europe by the expanse of the Atlantic.) Democracies so protected are less likely to be invaded by hostile forces; hence the historical record is not likely to be replete with such instances.

More good news for democracies emerges from the findings of Chapters 3 and 7 concerning the probable existence of rudimentary democracies in prehistorical times. Only the threat of war, a spreading aridity, or some other environmental threat appears to have diminished their numbers or transformed them into temporary or more often permanent autocracies. And as we saw in Chapter 7, environmental conditions—in particular, sea borders or abundant rainfall, both of which mitigate the threat of war and enhance democratic development—actually can supersede the influence of a strong ideational variable such as Islam in its negative influence on democracy. Turkey, Malaysia, and Indonesia, with many sea borders, tend to be more democratic than most other Islamic countries. We also found, in Chapter 3, that warfare is not necessary for state formation, as has often been claimed (e.g., Carneiro 1970). Warfare and the state are not inextricably linked, and so the continued existence of states does not imply the continued existence of war. The state can serve beneficent functions for its citizens without serving as a vehicle for enhancing the probability of war. If the states in question are democracies, then according to the burgeoning literature reviewed in Chapter 7, the probability of war among them should be small indeed.

Democracies also are less likely to disintegrate as a result of domestic violence. The electoral process, combined with the capabilities of interest groups to influence the government, allows for the possibility of redress of grievances, which is not so easily available in autocracies. Possibilities for the redistribution of wealth are amplified, as is the satisfaction of specific grievances by incumbent officials interested in reelection.

Yet in one key respect democracies are challenged today almost as never before. Although far more advantaged in this regard than, say, Rome during the later Empire, democracies are still being faced with the prospect of integrating large numbers of culturally dissimilar people into the polity. Hardly a Western democracy exists today that does not have large immigrant populations which may present an internal threat to the state, much as the Germanic tribes provided a basis for the later conquest of Rome by other Germanic tribes—or in fact by members of the same tribe. This is an illustration of what Arnold Toynbee (1946) calls the "internal" and "external" proletariats (in the sense of a subordinate class) who combine, even unwittingly, to undermine the threatened state. The comparison with Rome may be even more appropriate, because the internal Germanic "proletariat" was reasonably well integrated with the population at the frontiers of the state and many served Rome as soldiers in its armies. A recently arrived immigrant population may appear to be well assimilated, yet share certain cultural commonalities and values with hostile external forces. Whether they will openly collaborate with these forces is, of course, another question.

The Role of Inequality

This condition clearly can be exacerbated by extreme inequalities, as we saw in Chapter 4. If the newly arrived population experiences strong inequalities vis-à-vis the indigenous elite—and continues to experience them over several generations—then there clearly can be a basis for social discord and perhaps even political violence. Again, however, the presence of democratic procedures, the possibility of electing representatives from the new immigrant groups, and other mechanisms of redress distinguish these more contemporary instances from that of Rome.

It is also unlikely that neighboring countries would be seriously threatening to the world's democracies, partly because of location, as in Europe, where each democracy is virtually surrounded by other democracies. The economic and military power that can be brought to bear by major powers, such as the United States and Japan, also protects them from external threat.

Probably a more realistic danger is that of an ethical corrosion from within, wherein stark inequalities fuel corrupt practices on the part of disadvantaged populations. This is the Roman scenario of Chapter 4, without necessarily the end of state dissolution. Stark inequalities fuel the desire for gain by the disadvantaged by whatever means, including corruption, thereby augmenting whatever tendencies toward corruption already existed. Under these circumstances, the armed forces of such a state might be weakened considerably, as was the case in Rome, where in the long run borders could not be defended effectively. A more immediate danger might be the inability to project military power out of fear that the armed forces, weakened by corruption, might not be up to the task. The experience of the Soviet armed forces in Afghanistan may have been such a precursor of eventual state dissolution.

On the other hand, it may be argued, as in Chapter 4, that corruption arose in Rome in part because of the growth of large estates and the withdrawal of the elite to these virtually autonomous entities, leaving the remainder of society to cope as best it could, which included reliance on corrupt practices. At first glance, we might argue that surely this does not apply to Western societies, especially the United States, with its more egalitarian social structure. Yet despite the presumed and very likely real American egalitarianism in comparison with that of Rome, certain similarities of elite withdrawal have been noted. As Christopher Lasch puts it:

> To an alarming extent the privileged classes . . . have made themselves independent not only of crumbling industrial cities but of public services in general. They send their chil-

dren to private schools, insure themselves against medical emergencies by enrolling in company-supported plans, and hire private security guards to protect themselves against the mounting violence against them. In effect, they have removed themselves from the common life. It is not just that they see no point in paying for public services they no longer use. *Many of them have ceased to think of themselves as Americans in any important sense, implicated in America's destiny for better or for worse.* Their ties to an international culture of work and leisure—of business, entertainment, information, and "information retrieval"—make many of them deeply indifferent to the prospect of American national decline. (1995, 45; emphasis added)

This orientation away from the state, emphasized in the quotation, is eerily reminiscent of the later Roman Empire. The commonalities of ethnicity and language between the "internal" and "external" Germanic elements, combined with political collusion by large landowners, are here replaced by commonalities of workplace, work "language," and ultimately shared values of this internationalized privileged class.

In addition to corruption as an immediate danger to Western democracy, especially the United States, there exists a longer-term danger that is shared with the historical experiences of Venice, Rome, China, Germany, and perhaps other instances as well. This is the decline of a middle group, whether it be lesser nobility in the instances of Venice and Rome, middle peasantry in the case of China, or lesser nobility and a consequent decline of the *Landtage* in Germany. Clearly, the consequences of such a decline depend on the context. Whether it be large-scale fractal formation and weakening of the state in the face of external pressure in Venice and Rome or political violence in China or decline of representative institutions in Germany, the overall consequence is a danger to the polity that, without strenuous efforts at renewal (as in China, for example), can lead ultimately to disintegration.

There is evidence that such processes are occurring today in the United States. In addition to the contemporary decline of the middle class, other long-term trends are even less encouraging harbingers of the future. The recent techno-economic expansion in the United States may be functionally equivalent to the expansions of ancient Israel, Egypt, Byzantium, and the Aztecs, in which a small elite benefited disproportionately prior to the decline and fall of the state.

Consider the comments of Felix Rohatyn, a preeminent analyst of financial affairs and senior partner of Lazard Frères, quoted at length in a *New York Times* column by A. M. Rosenthal. It is worthwhile including the quote in its entirety, for it touches not only on the processes themselves, but also on some basic social mechanisms of importance.

The big beneficiaries of our economic expansion have been the owners of financial assets and a new class of highly compensated technicians working for companies where profit-sharing and stock ownership was widely spread. What is occurring is a huge transfer of wealth from lower-skilled middle-class American workers to the owners of capital assets and to the new technological aristocracy.

As a result, the institutional relationship created by the *mutual loyalty of employees and employers in most American businesses* has been badly frayed.... These relationships have been replaced by a combination of fear for the future and a cynicism for the present as a broad proportion of working people see themselves as simply temporary assets to be hired or fired to protect the bottom line and create "shareholder value." (Rosenthal 1995, A21; emphasis added)

Rohatyn mentions the undermining of mutual loyalty between employees and employers, which easily translates into the analytic lexicon of this book, namely the destruction of identification between rulers and ruled. We saw the absence of such identification in a patterned inequality and the onset of political violence and witnessed its presence in the instance of cooperation and helping during the Holocaust. The elimination of a middle group in society effectively destroys the avenue or "ladder" of identification. It is extraordinarily difficult for an inner-city black youth to identify with a white corporate executive in a far suburb, but far easier to identify with a black middle-level manager living in the city or near suburb. The middle group of society establishes that ladder or conduit of identification between the upper and lower levels. Without such a middle group, the gap between elite and mass is so wide that any number of consequences may follow, including political violence or societal ennui and ultimately decay. Contrast the social mobility of early Byzantium and the dynamic aspects of that state with the moribund condition of late Byzantine society.

And here we engage one of the more important yet problematic—and at this point in history undecidable—issues, namely, whether the fundamental desiderata of the contemporary period are elastic or not. Historically, the transition from land as the basic means of production to industry entailed, after the initial socioeconomic dislocations, a general rise in the standard of living, contrary to the expectations of Marx and Engels (see Chapter 1). As the economy grew, so did the average wage, so that the poor grew less poor as the rich got richer, albeit at disproportionate rates. Zero-sum gains between upper and lower classes were avoided. In a real sense, the debate between Julian Simon (1990) and Paul Ehrlich (Ehrlich, Ehrlich, and Holdren 1977) is whether such expansive and positive-sum processes will continue. Simon claims that human technology and ingenuity will overcome any stresses imposed by the scarcity of inelastic commodities, whereas Ehrlich asserts that unremitting population pressures render such roseate predictions obsolete. Interestingly, several years ago Simon won a 10-year-old bet he had made with Ehrlich (Tierney 1990), correctly predicting declines in the prices of certain metals. Simon and Ehrlich present one dimension of the issue of elasticity, namely, which of the two is correct (or more nearly correct) concerning the consequences of scarcities of various types for both democratic and international politics. (In the international realm this debate is more fully developed in Midlarsky and Hopf 1993.)

The second dimension is even more contentious, for it concerns not mineral or other nonhuman resources, but human capabilities. Without judging the merits of the debate over the claims of *The Bell Curve* (Herrnstein and Murray 1994)—and they have been contentious, even vitriolic in the extreme[3]—I will address only one of the issues raised in that debate and in a fairly restricted domain. This is the question of how widespread are the genetic capabilities to master the technology of the information age. If, as Richard Herrnstein and Charles Murray claim, the low birth rate of the educated elite *and* the relative technical incapacity of welfare classes widen the existing gap between the two, then this limited (artificially, due to birth rate) "smart" genetic pool effectively constitutes a scarcity of an important desideratum. This scarcity in fact underlies elements of the quotations from Lasch and Rohatyn, for only in the event of a restricted or scarce desideratum can one even have an elite. On the other hand, if virtually all people are educable in modern technical matters, then this scarcity does not exist, and we do indeed have a genuine elasticity of this human commodity. Thus the debate between Ehrlich and Simon concerning nonhuman resources and that over *The Bell Curve* concerning human resources have strong implications for the presence and extent, if any, of future massive inequalities.

One harbinger of an affirmative response to the question of whether there will be future large-scale inequalities is the current low, relatively flat rate of wage increases as the U.S. economy expands. Traditionally, in the industrial era, wage increases kept pace with the rate of economic expansion, thus benefiting virtually all societal sectors. The recent pattern, with its major benefits confined mostly to a better-off minority of the population (Bernstein 1995; Thurow 1995), or to the lowest deciles of the national income distribution principally through minimum wage increases (Uchitelle 1998), has been, at least until now, quite exceptional. This question will not have a definitive answer until serious efforts have been made to utilize both human and nonhuman resources in the most efficient manner possible. Widespread efforts in education are required in the former instance.

In the final analysis, democracy is no guarantee of state survival, only one important avenue for a dialogue between rulers and ruled that can maximize the possibilities for state continuance. Even representative democracies can make decisions that shorten their life spans, as is perhaps occurring now in the United States in matters regarding the separation of church and state. Historically, strong states have tended toward increased secularization, as we saw in early Sumer, but states have tended to weaken when the church gains a strong foothold within the operations of the state. The ancient Egyptian, the Germano-Roman, and the Abbasid empires are cases in point, as we saw in Chapters 4 and 6. This problem assumes a contemporary form when states with Muslim majorities are confronted with Islamist movements that seek to create theocratic governments.

Another illustration may be found in the history of tsarist Russia, never a really strong state, in which the Russian Orthodox Church was actually a department of the state. One may hazard a similar observation on the Soviet Union in which the latter-day "church" of Communism was not only inextricably linked with the state but provided the ideological raison d'etre for the state itself and very likely hastened its dissolution. As the influence on the peace process of the Jewish religious establishment in Israel, especially its more fundamentalist wing, was minimized during the recent Labor Party regime, the economy and other elements related to state strength concomitantly increased. In recent years, the increased influence of the religious right and the slowing of the peace process have led to a decline in the rate of economic expansion.

We have demonstrated the influence of climate on politics in the form of rainfall enhancing democratic development. But there may be additional climatological effects beyond those addressed in Chapter 7, and these may go directly to the issue of state survivability. As we saw in Chapter 4, the Maya downfall may have been initiated by a severe 200-year drought beginning about A.D. 800, which apparently left the region drier than it had been for approximately 7,000 years. The new massive scarcity may have exacerbated inequality and accelerated conflict both between and within the city-states ("Breakthroughs" 1995, 22). And we also now know that the collapse of the earliest known empire, Aggad, which conquered the Sumerian city-states around 2300 B.C., also may have been the result of drought. Aggadian cities were abandoned all across the northern plain as the result of a 300-year drought that began only about 100 years after the rise of the empire. A warm, dry period may have contributed to the collapse of several of the Middle Eastern empires at the end of the third millennium B.C. (Issar 1995, 354; Weiss et al. 1993). As Harvey Weiss put it, "This is the first time an abrupt climate change has been directly linked to the collapse of a thriving civilization" (quoted in Wilford 1993a, C1). There may be discoveries of additional impacts of climate on civilizations as archaeology grows ever more sophisticated in its analytical armory.

Drought, of course, is hardly unknown today, as we have seen recently in East Africa. And the effects of ozone depletion and, perhaps most important, global warming also are largely unknown, although recent evidence thus far is consistent with earlier predictions of a global warming and its consequences (Löfstedt 1995), and 1997 was recently named the hottest year on record (Kerr 1998). Additionally, recent evidence indicates that our century is the warmest in 600 years (Stevens 1998). The preliminary observed phenomena of continental warming in the interior combined with coastal rainfall and flooding, may have consequences that are as yet unfathomed—and that require close examination for their potential impacts on politics.

Inequality and State Survival

What questions have been answered concerning the evolution of inequality in relation to state survival? First, the analysis of Chapter 2 suggests that under conditions of scarcity, inequality is *always* evolving in the direction of greater inequality. Even in the most affluent societies such as the United States, strong evidence for growing inequalities in the absence of active redistribution has emerged (Holmes 1996, A1; Peterson 1994). And if the scarcity of valued commodities increases, then inequality increases. Thus, in the interest of stability or merely to avoid the increasing rigidification and moribund state of society under conditions of extreme inequality as occurred during the later Roman Empire, some redistribution is virtually essential. Second, even as inequality diminishes through redistribution, it continues to be associated with democracy, at least in the form of land inequality, perhaps indicative of the prerequisite of a strong state and a secure elite. To attempt to eliminate all vestiges of such inequality is probably to invite the consequences of extreme egalitarianism as was attempted in the Communist world. If state collapse does not ensue, then such a world still is surely as uncreative and moribund[4] as is one with extreme inequalities. It is perhaps no accident that the Soviet Union, at one end of a continuum of equality and Rome at another, did not disappear as the result of a sudden conquest. Instead, both experienced fairly long processes of decay (relative to the pace of social change in their respective periods) until the final collapse came from relatively small external pressure. It is entirely possible that in denying human possibilities for growth and development, both extraordinarily egalitarian societies and those with extreme inequalities experience similar consequences.

And what of the "seed" of predictability contained within the analysis alluded to at the end of the Introduction? Clearly, given the nonlinearities of the functions developed in Chapter 2 and Appendix A, and the perhaps even chaotic behavior of processes of state dissolution, micro-prediction of time and place may be impossible. Nevertheless, macro-prediction of overall tendencies, if not the precise timelines of the trajectories of these tendencies, may be possible. The key is to be found in the nature of human adaptation to processes outlined in the preceding chapters, whether planned or unplanned. The comparison between China and Rome is once again apt, for in China the process of political violence and consequent regeneration, albeit at times in very different form, constituted an unplanned adaptive process. The Roman or indeed even the Aztec response was not an adaptation but an acceleration of already existing tendencies that rigidified the social order. Thus, the response was essentially a maladaptive and accelerated continuation of already existing societal tendencies. In contrast, early Byzantium represents a planned adaptive response to the Muslim threat, principally in the form of themes as a military and political innovation, but also in almost deliberate fashion, an encouragement of social mobility for those of non-Greek origin who demonstrated skills useful to the state.

The timing of adaptation and whether it is in fact maladaptive may be critical for state survivability. In Byzantium, the structure of themes and encouragement of social mobility for the talented occurred not long after the Muslim threat appeared in Mesopotamia and with it the consequent threat to Byzantium in Anatolia. In contrast, Diocletian's reforms, which came late in Roman history, simply accelerated existing tendencies and intensified social rigidification long after processes of corruption deeply inimical to the health of the state and especially its army had already set in. The Aztecs' belated response to the threat of disruption was a similar rigidification of noble status. Large-scale building programs of the Maya during the Terminal Classic period, designed perhaps to appease the gods and relieve environmental stress, might, if undertaken earlier—say at Chichen Itza—have had the consequence of yielding another Teotihuacan, a great religio-cultural and trade center in the Maya lowlands.

Given the large-scale tendencies toward gross inequalities in tandem with rigidification, either as the result of maladaptive reform or some other societal dynamic detailed in the preceding chapters, one can engage in the macro-prediction of an end to state or empire, but certainly not the precise timing of collapse or the exact catalyst for the state's demise. The Soviet Union experienced such rigidification, and despite an overall egalitarian income structure there was a growing inequality between the small Communist elite and the remainder of the population. The "more of the same" philosophy carried on through the Brezhnev era, consistent with that of the later Roman Empire, suggested a likely extinction of that state.

Can one make such predictions for democracies given the fairly continual process of adaptation undertaken by representative assemblies such as the U.S. Congress? There is, of course, no guarantee that responses to stress will be adaptive if undertaken by the assembly, but if in fact a maladaptation occurs, then there is the possibility for redress in the form of future elections. Certainly, single-member districts or first-past-the-post systems are stable, but the question remains whether they are sufficiently sensitive to counter an earlier maladaptive response. Whether recent Republican congressional efforts that will very likely have the consequence of increasing inequality will prove to be adaptive or maladaptive in response to current societal stresses is as yet an open question. Certainly democracies have the built-in mechanisms for continual adaptation that make prediction virtually impossible. Indeed, this may be one of the great strengths and resiliencies of democracies, that they contain within themselves adaptation mechanisms that on a fairly regular basis can react to the stimuli and stresses of political life. Whether these mechanisms will be used wisely by the democratic populace and its representatives is, of course, another open question.

Yet in another sense, as suggested in the introductory chapter, predictability is possible. I refer not to the prediction of specific events at some points $t + n$ number of years in the future, but to the findings of aspects of society not immediately evident. For example, in the present framework, increased inequality is related positively to increased scarcity, suggesting that societies with minimal scarcity should experience greater equality among all groups, including those related to gender. We saw that process operating in New Kingdom Egypt, where the shift of the political and societal center of the country northward to the agricultural abundance of the Delta region (not to mention the growth of empire in Asia) was associated with the emergence of a rather spectacular gender equality, especially in comparison with neighboring societies of that period. Similarly, we would predict that ancient nomadic societies existing prior to the emergence of ideologies (sacred or secular) of male primacy would experience a substantial gender equality over and above sedentary agricultural societies, which are subject to the scarcities of arable land, especially after substantial population growth. And this is precisely what was found recently in archeological excavations in Kazakhstan at the Russian border. The burial mounds of Indo-European-speaking herders who lived on the steppes in the sixth to second centuries B.C. revealed significant evidence of women buried with weaponry such as bronze arrowheads and iron daggers, indicating warrior status. Other graves of women contained luxury goods and stone altars suggesting upper-class status or the role of priestess. Such findings of warrior, priestess, and high social rank for women are almost never found simultaneously in excavations of agricultural societies. Although these archeological findings were excavated only within the past four years (Wilford 1997), they could have been readily predicted by the theoretical framework that guided the present inquiry.

Appendixes

APPENDIX A

Mathematical Derivations of the Equations for the Exponential and Fractal (EI) Distributions

This appendix presents the mathematical derivations of Equations 2.1 and 2.3, respectively the exponential and fractal (EI) distributions.

The Exponential Distribution

To begin, let us posit an equal opportunity scenario wherein each person has an equal opportunity of achieving any one of r societal categories. These categories may constitute quantities of income, wealth, or some other valued commodity such as land ownership. The value of r might then be in acres—or hectares or mu (the Chinese unit of agricultural land area). It is easy to show that under these circumstances, the most probable scenario is the one in which all categories have the same number of persons. This can be seen by finding the number of ways N persons can be distributed among r categories. This distribution, M, is given by

$$M = \frac{N!}{n_1! n_2! \ldots n_r!} \qquad \sum_{i=1}^{r} n_i = N,$$

where n_1 is the number of persons in the first category; n_2, the number of persons in the second; and n_r, the number in the rth category, which is simply the multinomial expression for the distribution of N objects into r categories (Feller 1968). To find the most probable state, we must maximize the quantity M since it gives us precisely the number of ways in which a particular configuration can be obtained.

To carry out this maximization procedure, standard methods of calculus are used in which the maximum value or peak of the distribution occurs when its rate of change is equal to zero. The solution to the initial problem of finding the most probable distribution (Dutta 1966; Good 1963; Jaynes 1957; Midlarsky 1979) requires that

$$\log_e \frac{n_i}{n_r} = 0,$$

where n_i and n_r are, respectively, the numbers of persons in the ith and r^{th} categories and the logarithm is taken to the base e. As a result

$$\log_e n_i - \log_e n_r = 0,$$

and

$$n_1 = n_2 \ldots = n_r. \tag{A.1}$$

Thus, the number of persons in each of the various categories is the same, and as a result the most likely state resulting from the maximization process is one in which all of the classifications or categories have equal numbers of persons. This condition is shown as the horizontal dashed line of Figure 2.1, labeled "infinite abundance," to signify the absence of any and all constraints on the amount of the valued commodity.

This consequence, of course, agrees with our intuition that the numbers in each of the categories should be the same as a result of the initial postulate of equality of opportunity for all persons. Note what happens now if we add the constraint of scarcity in some valued commodity such as land, income, or natural resources. This can be done for multiple functions, but for the sake of simplicity only one function of scarcity will be treated at a time. When one additional constraint is now added in the form of some quantity C being conserved, we can write that

$$C = \sum_{i=1}^{r} n_i x_i,$$

indicating that each person in any one of the r categories possesses some quantity x_i, all of which must sum over the r categories to equal the total number A. When this constraint is introduced into the system, we arrive at the equation (Jaynes 1957)

$$\log_e n_i + \hat{k} + k x_i = 0,$$

where k and $\hat{k}$ are constants. This equation can be rewritten as

$$n_i = e^{-\hat{k}} e^{-kx_i},$$

and since $e^{-\hat{k}}$ is a constant, when we divide both sides of the equation by N, we have

$$p_i = Ae^{-kx_i}, \qquad (A.2)$$

where $p_i = n_i/N$ and A is another constant, which is equal to $e^{-\hat{k}}/N$. This is Equation 2.1, with the constant A yet to be defined in relation to the normalization requirement that the sum of the probabilities equals unity.

Equation 2.1 thus states that there exists a negative exponential relationship between the value of the scarce quantity and the probability of its attainment, and this is illustrated as the scarcity condition of Figure 2.1. This conclusion stands in contrast to that found in Equation A.1, which stipulates the relatively egalitarian condition of equal numbers of persons in each of the categories as shown in the figure. The scale of increasing value on the horizontal axis is non-specific, of course, but for our purposes may be interpreted as units of land area owned, such as hectares or mu. Not only is there now an inequality among the persons in the several categories in regard to their possession of the valued item, but the decrease in numbers in a category as value increases is not simply a proportional effect or linear decrease, but is disproportionately decreasing or curvilinear—that is, exponential.

To illustrate two different conditions of finite resources, in contrast to the infinite state, the comparison between the exponential conditions of extreme scarcity and relative abundance is shown in Figure 2.2 with k arbitrarily set at .8 ($A = 3.954$) in the instance of scarcity and at .1 ($A = .3503$) in the instance of relative abundance. The value of k is estimated as the reciprocal of the mean as a maximum likelihood estimator (Derman, Gleser, and Olkin 1973, 361) and the value of A is that number for which the sum of the probabilities equals unity, that is

$$A(k) = \frac{1}{\sum_{i=1}^{r} e^{-kx_i}}.$$

In the instance of relative abundance, the mean $\bar{x}$ is large, but not infinite as in Figure 2.1, and much larger than in the scarcity condition. As a result, the value of k is substantially smaller in the case of relative abundance than in the scarcity condition. This smaller value of k appears in the much smaller slope or decline of the relative abundance curve in comparison with the scarcity curve as the scale of increasing value progresses to larger numbers.

If the value of k as the reciprocal of the mean is varied from zero in the infinite abundance condition to larger values such as .8 or .9, it can be shown that the Gini index as a measure of inequality (the area between the Lorenz curve, which plots the actual proportion of holdings [land or wealth] owned by the corresponding proportion of the population, and the line of perfect equality) increases monotonically, but as the value of .8 or .9 is reached, the Gini index declines. This is a condition of equality in extremis under conditions of extreme scarcity, where almost everyone has very small holdings on the left portion of the scarcity curves in the figures, in contrast to the very few on the right.

The Fractal (EI) Distribution

Now we turn to the mathematical basis of the fractal distribution of extreme inequality. In place of the equiprobability of access, suppose that there is a programmed inequality. Instead of each of the early landholdings being approximately equal in size and the subdivision process over time inducing inequality, the inequality is inherent in the distribution at the outset. There are processes that exhibit such severe inequalities. Any sequestering of a scarce resource that also requires a surrounding "cushion" or margin of safety is a case in point. Those who come later to the process must defer to the earlier arrivals who already have established their control, with the accompanying margin of safety to ensure continued control. An example might be the founder of a corporation who takes all the reins of power required to operate effectively and at the same time remain in that position indefinitely. Those who come later to the corporation clearly will receive only some proportion of the resources initially allocated to himself by the founder. Or consider the colonial process, wherein the early colonial powers will arrogate to themselves as much territory and population as is required to ensure continued political and economic control over the chosen colony. Frequently, this means including the extra margin of safety to prevent other colonial powers from competing effectively or the indigenous population from revolting effectively.

Access to resources (e.g., water, as in rivers) and an infrastructure of political and economic control also may require such expanded sovereignty over a large territory. The history of the British in India expanding to the Northwest Frontier is a case in point. Later the French in Asia could colonize only on the fringes of the large British holdings. Still later the Germans, especially in Africa, could colonize only on the fringes of the British and French holdings. In successive stages, each of the arrivals determines the smaller proportionate share of the later arrivals, in contrast to the equiprobability of initial access assumed in deriving the exponential distribution.

Land distribution is another variable likely to be modeled successfully by this sequential process. As in the sequence of colonial acquisitions, the first arrivals to a sparsely settled area will have first choice, or at least will be in the best position to oust the indigenous population. Proximal land with required resources such as water also will likely be taken by the first arrivals. Later arrivals will be able to take only some (smaller) proportion of the remaining area. Land distribution in Latin America as territory settled by the Iberian arrivals after the fifteenth century is one case in point.

An Expository Geometric Approach to the Fractal (EI or Pareto-Lévy) Distribution

The following derivation represents sequential arrivals of conquerors or acquisitors of various kinds, in which inequality is explicit at the outset. An actor arrives and by successful competition, war, or other aggressive behavior takes some large (random) proportion of what is available. In turn, the next arrival (e.g., a loser in the first round) takes a large random proportion of what is left. This procedure is repeated with the sequential arrival of M actors until even a large proportion what remains is not worth taking. Although each proportion taken is random, one can, as for any random variable, calculate a mean or some other measure of central tendency as a descriptor of the proportion taken in the overall process.

Sequential processes of this type can be modeled geometrically in the following manner. This treatment is not intended to contribute anything new mathematically; it is intended to be virtually a pictorial account of the generation of a distribution of extreme inequality. The following is an expository geometric derivation in order to impart the particular flavor of the sequential sequestering of resources and also to emphasize the initial scarcity assumption, which, to my knowledge, is never explicitly introduced in other derivations of the Pareto (also known as the Pareto-Lévy) distribution.

Consider a variation on the Koch curve used by Benoit Mandelbrot (1982, 34-45) as a basis for the generation of infinite sets and as a further basis for his theory of fractals. We consider first a straight-line segment as in Stage 1 of Figure A.1. The middle third of the segment is then replaced by two pieces, each as long as the middle third, which are joined together as two sides in an equilateral triangle. This is shown as Stage 2. Now for the two remaining line segments on each side of the triangle, again the middle third is removed from each, and two new equilateral triangles are formed on each side of the original, but of course encompassing a much smaller area, as shown in Stage 3.

290 / APPENDIX A

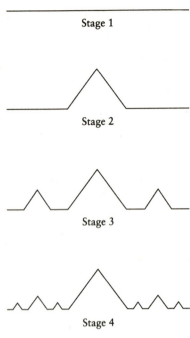

Figure A.1. Fractal formation on a straight-line segment.

(In a non-modified Koch curve, the sides of the original triangle also would have their middle thirds removed and replaced by equilateral triangles, but for reasons that will become clear in a moment, only the remaining straight-line segments are treated here in this fashion.)

We continue this process of removing the middle thirds of remaining straight-line segments and replacing them with equilateral triangles for as long as we please. Of course this process can be infinite, for there is no limit to the number of straight-line segments remaining at each stage of the procedure. Indeed, the generation of infinite Cantor sets often is the main purpose of such processes (Rucker 1982, 8; Sparrow 1982, 36); here the intention is quite different, as suggested by the use of triangle areas to model land area or other ultimately finite resource acquisitions.

It is intuitively clear that the area of each of the smaller triangles is some proportion of the larger ones, since the removal of the middle third of one segment for the formation of one triangle leaves two proportionately much smaller segments on each side for the construction of two additional smaller triangles. It can be shown exactly that the area of each of the new triangles is 1/9 the area of its immediate predecessor. Given the original line segment (Stage 1) as three unit lengths, with the middle third now of unit length, the area of the resulting triangle in Stage 2 is equal to 0.4332 units squared. Each of the two smaller triangles constructed in Stage 3 is equal to 0.0482, while those formed in Stage 4 are equal to 5.348×10^{-3}. (All of these direct calculations of triangle areas are subject to rounding errors.)

It is also clear that the number of each of these triangles increases geometrically upon each new segmentation. The number of new triangles at each stage is equal to exactly twice the number constructed at the previous stage. Thus, one triangle is formed at Stage 2, two at Stage 3, four at Stage 4, eight at Stage 5, sixteen at Stage 6, and so on. This is a geometric progression with parameter 2; the sequence of numbers of triangles $N(S_n, 2)$, with area x_n at iteration n and parameter 2, is

$$N(x_n, 2) = (2)^0_{x_0}, (2)_{x_1}, (2\cdot 2)_{x_2}, (2\cdot 2\cdot 2)_{x_3}, (2\cdot 2\cdot 2\cdot 2)_{x_4},$$
$$(2\cdot 2\cdot 2\cdot 2\cdot 2)_{x_5}, \ldots, (2)^r_{x_r}, \qquad n = 0, 1, 2, \ldots, r.$$

Let $x_1, x_2, \ldots, x_r$ denote the r distinct triangle areas in increasing order; therefore the size of each triangle constructed at the ith stage is $x_{(r-i+1)}$. Also let $S = \sum_{i=1}^{r} 2^{i-1}$ denote the total number of triangles after all r stages have been completed. In addition, let the area of the triangle obtained by a particular person be represented by the random variable X.

If we assume that each person has an equal chance of obtaining any one of the S triangles (as if he/she was selecting one at random), we then arrive at the probability distribution for X:

$$P(X = x_n) = \frac{2^{r-n}}{S} \qquad \text{for } x_n \in (x_1, x_2, \ldots, x_r) \qquad (A.3)$$

$$= \frac{2^{r-1}}{S} \left(\frac{1}{2}\right)^{n-1} \qquad \text{for } x_n \in (x_1, x_2, \ldots, x_r).$$

More generally, where $y = \theta(X)$ is an as-of-yet undefined one-to-one function of the randomly acquired triangle area, we get the following probability distribution:

$$P(y = y) = \frac{2^{r-1}}{S}\left(\frac{1}{2}\right)^{n-1} \qquad \text{for } y = [\theta(x_1), \theta(x_2), \ldots, \theta(x_r)].$$

If $\theta(x_i) = i$, y is a truncated geometric random variable.

Or, more generally still for numbers, q_1, q_2, and triangle area x_n (with r stages to the sequence), we have by induction:

$$P(Y = y) = q_1(1 - q_2)^{n-1} \qquad \text{for } y \in [\theta(x_1), \theta(x_2), \ldots, \theta(x_r)]. \qquad (A.4)$$

In Equation A.3 we see that the probabilities of obtaining a triangle of a given size decrease by powers of ½ as the size increases. It would be the case that X is a linear function of a (truncated) geometric random variable if its possible values were equally spaced; that is, if they differed by some additive increment ξ. Unfortunately, the values are not additive but multiplicative; it is straightforward to show that each particular area is exactly ⅑ the size of the next largest (see Figure A.1). Thus, if x_r is the area of the largest triangle then $x_{r-1} = x_r/9$ is the area of the second largest, and so forth. The possible values for X are therefore:

$$\left(\frac{1}{9}\right)^{r-1} x_r, \left(\frac{1}{9}\right)^{r-2} x_r, \ldots, \left(\frac{1}{9}\right) x_r, x_r.$$

Consider then the random variable $Y = \theta(X) = \log_e X$. Taking the logarithm (base e) of each value in the above sequence, we get the possible values for Y:

$$(r-1)\log_e\left(\frac{1}{9}\right) + \log_e x_r, (r-2)\log_e\left(\frac{1}{9}\right) + \log_e x_r, \ldots,$$

$$\log_e\left(\frac{1}{9}\right) + \log_e x_r, \log_e x_r.$$

Here we see that the values are equally spaced; in fact, they differ by increments of $\log_e(⅑)$. It is then the case that Y *is* a linear function of a random variable with probabilities as in Equation A.3 for the possible values $1, 2, \ldots, r$. This is exactly what we want.

Passing to the exponential form as the continuous analogue of the geometric distribution (Feller 1968, 458), and one that is more tractable in the analysis and computation, we have

$$f(x) = A_1(k_1) e^{-k_1 \log_e x} \qquad k_1 > 0, \ 1 \leq x < \infty, \qquad (A.5)$$

where k_1 is a constant and $A_1(k_1)$ is a normalization constant designed to make the sum of the probabilities equal unity. In turn, the function $\log_e x$ transforms the ordinary exponential distribution into the Pareto distribution[1] (Gumbel 1958, 151; Johnson and Kotz 1970, 240):

$$f(x) = Bx^{-\eta-1} \qquad \eta > 0, \ 1 \leq x < \infty. \qquad (A.6)$$

Equations A.5 and A.6, with the appropriate equality of constants, are identical. This identity can easily be seen by taking logarithms of both sides of equations A.5 and A.6 and setting the appropriate constants equal to each other. The constant η here is the familiar Paretian exponent, α.

This geometric derivation emphasizes the scarcity condition, in that only the line segment in Figure A.1 and the area above it are allowed to be acquired. It also shows explicitly the connection with the ordinary exponential as a distribution representing inequality derived from scarcity. Most important, the logarithmic function emphasizes the extreme inequality derived from the sequential nature of resource acquisitions modeled directly in this geometric representation.

It is instructive to compare this geometric approach with that of D. G. Champernowne (1953), who also derived the Pareto distribution exactly, but from analytic considerations based on a Markov chain defined on a logarithmic scale of income classes, u. Here the Markovian assumption is

$$x_s(t+1) = \sum_{u=-\alpha}^{s} x_{s-u}(t) \, p_{s-u,s}(t), \tag{A.7}$$

where $x_s(t)$ is the number of income earners in the logarithmic range s in year t, and the $p_{s-u,s}(t)$ are the transition probabilities for income earners going from one income range to the next at time t. If it is assumed that transitions are possible only in the range between $-n$ and $+1$, and the income distribution reaches an equilibrium, then equation A.7 reduces to

$$x_s = \sum_{u=-n}^{1} p_{u,s} \qquad s > 0. \tag{A.8}$$

Note that this is precisely the same assumption as in the preceding geometric derivation. In that instance, each succeeding area is some constant proportion of the previous one or

$$x_{n+1} = \hat{C} x_n \qquad \hat{C} > 0, \tag{A.9}$$

where $\hat{C}$ is a constant—in fact equal to $1/9$ in the preceding numerical treatment. Each state of the system is linearly dependent only on the immediately preceding one, which of course, is a first-order Markov process. The Markovian assumption is never made explicit in the geometric representation; it emerges nevertheless as a consequence of the unfolding of the geometric process.

A nontrivial solution of the difference of equation A.8 requires that the expectation of possible transitions is negative, or a shrinkage of income or $p_1 < p_{-1}$. This assumption leads directly to a geometric distribution of the form (Champernowne 1953, 326; Steindl 1965, 35)

$$x_s = N(1-b)\,b^s \qquad 0 < b < 1, \; s = 1, 2, 3, \ldots$$

where N is the total number of incomes. Pareto's law then follows directly.[2]

Note that in Champernowne's formulation, the logarithmic scale had to be explicitly introduced; in the geometric derivation, it emerged directly from the initial Koch curve construction. The mathematical expectation of shrinking income as time increases also had to be an explicit assumption by Champernowne (to some, this is a controversial assumption; see Steindl 1965, 361). Again, in the geometric derivation it emerged as a direct consequence of the Koch curve and the initial scarcity assumption—never made explicit in the Champernowne formulation.

There exists here a convergence with the work of Carl Futia (1982) who demonstrated that a Markovian operator, as in equations A.8 and A.9, converges at a geometric rate to yield an invariant distribution. This of course is also consistent with Mandelbrot's (1960) singling out of the weak Pareto distribution as the only one (aside from the Gaussian) that is invariant upon the addition of several random variables of similar form. This finding further suggests that distribution A.5 or A.6 will emerge on the simultaneous occurrence of several processes of the type outlined in Figure A.1. There can be any number of such simultaneously occurring processes in, say, different regions of a country, all of which together will yield distributions A.5 and A.6.

The Pareto distribution has been found to be applicable to the upper tail of income distributions among other random variables (see Chipman 1976 and Sahota 1978 for excellent reviews). The applicability of this distribution to the tail of income distributions can be understood as follows. If there is some finite resource (it does not have to be scarce at the outset), such as the number of cities requiring railway connections between them in the nineteenth century, the first to exploit this societal need will take the lion's share—in this case, connections between the largest cities. After this has been done (say, by the Harrimans in the United States), railroads between smaller cities, probably a less profitable venture, will then need to be built, and the initial entrepreneurs in this second-round activity will take the lion's share of that undertaking. We are left with still smaller and less profitable rail connections, and the process is once again repeated. In this fashion, a process quite similar to that detailed in Figure A.1 takes place sequentially, with each arrival getting a disproportionately smaller share of the total resources. Income will be proportional to the possession of these resources, hence the Pareto distribution will be applicable (Chipman 1976, 150). Note that the same persons or their descendants do not have to be in possession of the resources. All that is required is that there exists a hierarchical structure of resource possession along the lines of the preceding geometric argument, occupied by some persons who will receive incomes proportional to their holdings.

APPENDIX B

Countries Included in the Analysis of Chapter 7

	For Table 7.1	For Table 7.2	For Table 7.3
Afghanistan	X	X	
Algeria	X	X	X
Angola	X	X	
Argentina	X	X	X
Australia	X	X	X
Austria	X	X	X
Bangladesh	X	X	
Belgium	X		
Bolivia	X	X	
Brazil	X	X	X
Burma (Myanmar)	X	X	
Burundi	X		
Cameroon	X	X	X
Canada	X	X	X
Central African Republic	X	X	X
Chad[a]	X	X	X
Chile	X	X	
Colombia	X	X	X
Congo	X	X	X
Costa Rica	X	X	X
Denmark	X	X	X
Dominican Republic	X	X	X

296 / APPENDIX B

	For Table 7.1	For Table 7.2	For Table 7.3
Ecuador	X	X	X
Egypt	X	X	X
El Salvador[b]	X	X	X
Ethiopia	X	X	
Finland	X	X	X
France	X	X	X
Germany, West	X	X	X
Ghana	X	X	X
Greece	X	X	X
Guatemala	X	X	X
Haiti	X	X	X
Honduras	X	X	X
India	X	X	X
Indonesia	X	X	X
Iran	X	X	X
Iraq	X	X	X
Ireland	X	X	X
Israel	X	X	X
Italy	X	X	X
Ivory Coast	X	X	X
Jamaica	X	X	X
Japan	X	X	X
Jordan	X	X	
Kenya	X	X	X
Korea, South	X	X	X
Liberia	X	X	X
Madagascar	X	X	
Malawi	X	X	X
Malaysia	X	X	X
Mali	X	X	X
Mauritania	X	X	
Mexico	X	X	X
Morocco	X	X	
Mozambique	X	X	

Countries Included in the Analysis of Chapter 7 / 297

	For Table 7.1	For Table 7.2	For Table 7.3
Nepal	X	X	X
Netherlands	X	X	X
New Zealand	X	X	X
Nicaragua	X		
Niger	X	X	
Nigeria	X	X	
Norway	X	X	X
Pakistan	X	X	
Panama	X		
Papua New Guinea	X	X	
Paraguay	X	X	
Peru	X	X	X
Philippines	X	X	X
Portugal	X	X	X
Rwanda[c]	X		
Senegal	X	X	
Sierra Leone	X	X	X
Singapore	X	X	
Somalia	X	X	
South Africa	X	X	X
Spain	X	X	X
Sri Lanka	X	X	X
Sudan	X	X	
Sweden	X	X	X
Switzerland	X	X	X
Syria	X	X	X
Tanzania	X	X	X
Thailand	X	X	X
Togo	X	X	X
Trinidad and Tobago	X	X	X
Tunisia	X	X	
Turkey	X	X	X
Uganda	X	X	
United Kingdom	X	X	X

	For Table 7.1	For Table 7.2	For Table 7.3
United States	X	X	X
Upper Volta (Burkina Faso)	X	X	
Uruguay	X	X	X
Venezuela	X	X	X
Zaire	X	X	X
Zambia	X	X	X
Zimbabwe	X	X	

[a] Data not available for the Polity III index because Chad was coded in an interregnum condition in 1980.

[b] Data not available for the Polity III index because El Salvador was coded as transitional in 1980.

[c] Data available for the political rights and Polity III indexes but not for the liberal democracy index.

Reference Matter

NOTES

Chapter 1 / Theoretical Overview

1. As will become clear in Chapters 3 and 4 the state is something more than a chiefdom operating within the small confines of a city-state. Morton Fried got it right when he asserted that the "state is better viewed as the complex of institutions by means of which the power of the society is organized on a basis superior to kinship" (1967, 229). The important operative phrase here is "superior to kinship," for a clan-based or kinship-based chiefdom would not constitute a state in any developed meaning of the term.

2. Joseph Strayer actually reverses the causal arrow between warfare and earlier state formation in his comment, "The success of thirteenth-century rulers in building states had made fourteenth-century wars necessary and possible" (1970, 61).

3. See Crumley (1987b, 252) for a clear depiction of this population loss, at least in France, the locus of so much early feudal expansion.

4. Although the concept of a pristine state probably is not essential to the argument, especially in light of the discussion to follow in Chapter 3 concerning peer polity interaction (Renfrew and Cherry 1986), nevertheless this concept is useful to consider when examining the origins of stratification and its later impact on state formation.

5. This growing inequality is probably a good argument for redistribution, in addition to those made from a Rawlsian perspective by Mancur Olson (1987). The argument here though, as it will be developed in the Conclusion, is based far more on the direct political consequences of such inequality.

6. An interesting variant on equality and cooperation is given by Elias Canetti in his association between equality and crowds. As he puts it, "It is for the sake of this equality that people become a crowd and they tend to overlook anything which might detract from it" (1973, 32).

7. In the words of Mark Lichbach, "An empirical standard for evaluation is the predictability of particular outbreaks and aggregate levels of collective dissent. CA [collective action] theories, it turns out, do not yield a general theoretical statement of the etiology of conflict. They cannot be used to forecast protest and rebellion" (1995, 30–31).

8. In a conference paper initially presented in December 1993 (Midlarsky 1997), I predicted that a mobilization war would follow in the Balkans consequent upon the structural war that had already occurred. (Structural wars occur largely as the result of systemic considerations such as alliances—e.g., the Peloponnesian Wars, World War I— and mobilization wars follow upon the mobilization for war of a participant in the earlier structural conflict—e.g., Macedonian War, World War II; Midlarsky 1988a, chap. 7). It was difficult to predict exactly which entity would mobilize for war (in this case it was principally Croatia, in its successful attack on Serb-held Krajina in August 1995), but some such war was extremely likely.

9. As a personal anecdote, when my daughter, a recent graduate of the University of Wisconsin, Madison in International Affairs opined that the social sciences were incapable of prediction, at first I was nonplused. I had difficulty thinking of an answer. Suddenly it struck me that prediction is possible in several obvious areas. For example, it is possible to predict that, excluding the case of family reunion, countries with a high gross domestic product (GDP) per capita (that allowed immigration) would be the targets of third-world immigration, with countries having a low GDP per capita in far less demand. It would be difficult to predict exactly which would be the country of choice for a particular immigrant, but certainly the United States would stand high on the list of preferences—with Myanmar much lower on that scale. The more systematic illustrations cited above also then came to mind.

Chapter 2 / Scarcity and Inequality

1. Probably the best-known recent exponent of relative deprivation as a source of political violence is Ted Gurr (1970), while rapidly declining economic circumstances as progenitors of instability are found in James C. Davies (1962). Scarcities and consequent inequalities in the etiology of revolution are explored in Midlarsky 1982 and Midlarsky and Roberts 1985.

2. Raymond Aron, for example, asserted that "The interstate order has always been anarchical and oligarchical: anarchical because of the absence of a monopoly of legitimate violence, oligarchical (or hierarchic) in that, without civil society, rights depend largely on might" (1968, 160). On the other hand, theorists of the long cycle, such as George Modelski (1983), assert that there are periods of global order with a hegemonic power at the head of the hierarchy. Robert Gilpin (1981) argues for the existence of hegemonies and the periodicity of hegemonic wars.

3. This distribution is given for precisely this type of problem in Johnson and Kotz 1977, 114. Also see Feller 1968, 35.

4. For the use of such a measure, see Chenery and Syrquin 1975. For a general review of measures of inequality, see Sen 1997.

Chapter 3 / Warfare and the Origins of the State

1. Barry Schwartz (1983) points to this quality of George Washington, namely his willingness to step down after his victory as military head of the revolutionary forces, as a basis for his later extreme popularity as president.

2. According to Colin Renfrew, "The specific state is legitimised in the eyes of its citizens by the existence of other states which patently do function along comparable lines" (quoted in Cherry and Renfrew 1986, 153).

3. Heterarchy has been used in a variety of ways, including "(1) an array of independent, homogeneous elements . . . (2) the membership of elements in many different unranked interaction systems with participation in each system determined by the needs of each element . . . (3) the membership of elements in many different systems of rank-

ing where the same element occupies a different rank in the different systems . . . (4) the existence of two or more functionally discrete but unranked systems that interact as equals . . . (5) the existence of two or more discrete hierarchies that interact as equals" (Brumfiel 1995, 125).

4. However, if the trade is in prestige goods, then the hierarchy actually can be reinforced, as noted by Earle (1997) and, in a somewhat different context, by Chase-Dunn and Hall (1997, 141).

Chapter 4 / Decline and Fall of Empires and States

1. We also know that other tribal, if not imperial, expansions occurred as the result of "surplus" children who could not be supported under the prevailing socioeconomic system. Male Celts (the Gauls of Roman history) could not marry if they did not own property; hence they continually expanded their tribal domains (Mallory 1989). And, as we have seen, the Incas considered the peasants and property of dead kings inalienable, thus precipitating a constant search for new lands by later Inca rulers (Conrad and Demarest 1984).

2. One of the possible sources of the early absence of cooperation among Jews forced into ghettos during World War II was their inequality of circumstance prior to the war. Only after they began to appreciate their commonality in confronting death, as did men at the front, did they cooperate effectively in opposing the Germans, as in the Warsaw Ghetto uprising of 1943.

3. Interestingly, from a different perspective, Benedict Anderson (1991, 205) also makes the connection between the Warsaw Ghetto uprising and the formation of modern Israel. In the development here, issues of equality or inequality of circumstance lead to feelings of identification or their absence. Anderson argues that such identification is achieved through imagined communities that can yield affective connections across historical time and across space.

Chapter 6 / Failures of State Formation and Democracy

1. For an intensive treatment of the investiture controversy, see Blumenthal 1988.

2. A history of representative institutions in one central European country, Austria, is found in Brunner 1992.

3. Recall that the fall of the Aztecs was precipitated in part by the continual consumptive, hence virtually limitless, search for sacrificial captives and riches for potlatch-type ceremonies, which essentially united politics and religion (N. Davies 1980, 203).

Chapter 7 / Sources of Democracy

1. For broader treatments of Athenian democracy, including the later, classical period, see Finley 1983; Jones 1986; Ober 1989; and Stockton 1990.

2. These colonies as offshoots of Greek city-state populations are to be distinguished

from the later allies and political satellites to be found in quasi-imperial organizations such as the Delian League.

3. As L. H. Jeffrey remarks on this shift away from hereditary rule, "But always the original shift away from the monopoly of ruling power, once made, went on increasing, for peers in an aristocracy were apt to quarrel, and in these breaches *rich and ambitious men* whose families were outside the closed ring of government might make their resentment heard, and so the widening process continued. . . . Gradually through the seventh century the oligarchies became less exclusive, and below the heights of the high office-holders the ordinary citizens too could look for increased rights" (1976, 41; emphasis added).

4. Initially, I included urbanization in an earlier analysis, but collinearity problems dictated its removal; see Midlarsky 1992a, 470.

5. Michael Mann (1986, 94-98) cogently argues against Wittfogel's proposed connection between hydraulic agriculture and despotism, but provides no systematic evidence for his position. Recently, Landes (1998) also revives Wittfogel's arguments.

6. After completing the analysis of the impact of external threats on early democracy for its first presentation at the 1992 American Political Science Association meetings, under the title of "Reversing the Causal Arrow" (Midlarsky 1992b), I became aware of Brian Downing's (1992) treatment of a similar theme concerning the decline of representative institutions in central Europe as the result of war during the Early Modern period. Of course, a major difference between the two treatments, among others, is the much longer time span and geographical scope incorporated here. A similar distinction is found between the present treatment and that of Bruce Porter (1994).

7. While the book is a more reasoned and in certain respects a more balanced presentation (see especially chapters 4-6), the original article has the advantage of presenting the argument boldly and succinctly and so will be emphasized here.

8. Robert Bartley (1993), one of Huntington's critics, suggests that economic development will lead to greater democratization, which, in turn, should yield greater global integration of political values.

9. For an emphasis on liberalism as a key component of democracy, especially in relation to war, see Doyle 1983, which builds on Kant's early emphasis on liberalism and international peace. Also see Owen 1994.

10. This is the period for which reliable time series data exist, as given in the latest edition of the data source (Bair 1992). For our purposes here, the fairly substantial time lag between the independent variable, precipitation, and democracy is an advantage, for it is clear that an environmental variable such as aridity or precipitation existing as a societal backdrop would require a long time to affect the structure of politics.

11. James Payne (1989) uses a similar force ratio. Additionally, he finds no relationship between "political freedom" and his military-force ratio (182), but his causal arrow is reversed from that hypothesized here. Whereas his dependent variable is his military-force ratio, that employed here is the measure of democracy.

12. The variable of British colonial heritage controls for countries such as Australia,

New Zealand, India, Nigeria, and others that would have been directly affected by the European experience with democracy.

13. Agricultural density appears to have an independent positive influence on democracy, as suggested in the techno-ecological framework of Edward Crenshaw (1992, 1995, 1997). Crenshaw 1992 finds a negative relationship between agricultural density and income inequality. Because prior studies have found a negative association between income inequality and democracy (e.g., Midlarsky 1992a, 468), one can infer a positive association between agricultural density and democracy—as, in fact, is found in Crenshaw 1997.

14. Mansfield and Snyder (1995) warn of the dangers of war in time of regime transition toward either democracy or autocracy, which can make the transition toward democracy somewhat perilous for interstate relations.

15. Fouad Ajami, in his critique of Huntington, argues that states are still the building blocks of international relations: "The solitude of states continues; the disorder in the contemporary world has rendered that solitude more pronounced" (1993, 9). Also see Sisk (1992).

Chapter 8 / Inequality and Political Violence

1. This point is developed at greater length in Midlarsky 1983, 195-99.

2. As Finley remarked in connection with Mycenaean peasants, "Illiterate peoples, even rather primitive ones, are capable of considerable feats of memory in the ordinary routines of living. They transmit their mythologies and genealogies, they sort out rather complicated kinship patterns, they know exactly where their hunting and agricultural lands are located, and what the precise status of obligation is at any moment in potlatch or bridewealth arrangements—all without any records whatsoever. To them it would be accepted as a matter of course that Eumaeus, without consulting documents, could say to a stranger: 'My master is so rich that not twenty men together have so much wealth. I will enumerate it for you: twelve herds of cattle on the mainland, twelve of sheep, twelve of swine, and so on'" (1982, 214).

3. Evidence has emerged from another cultural context (Poland) that suggests a political radicalization, especially in the egalitarian direction, of those who perceive a dichotomous social universe (Zaborowski 1986, 117).

4. Although two Latin American countries, Argentina and Uruguay, rank just above the European countries in percentage of the labor force in agriculture (Taylor and Jodice 1983, 1: 209-10), it was decided not to exclude them from this study. In the first place, it is desirable to have the country universe complete. But more importantly, in contrast to the European countries and Japan, the sequential acquisition process occurred much more recently in the Latin American countries. The political residues of such an agrarian bifurcation could still affect contemporary social turmoil, even as the country moves away from dependence on the agrarian sector. It has been estimated that at least 70 years are required to establish a stable party system (Converse 1969), and an equal time is likely required to reverse the remains of earlier political conflict.

5. In order to update the dependent variable, more recent (until 1982) data on deaths from domestic violence were obtained from the Interuniversity Consortium on Political and Social Research. However, very little difference was observed between these data and the published data (until 1977), even for countries, such as El Salvador and Nicaragua, that are known to have experienced intensive violence after 1977. Walter LaFeber (1983, 239) for example estimates the dead in Nicaragua during this period to be on the order of tens of thousands, which would place Nicaragua in the first quintile of deaths. As a result, both Nicaragua and El Salvador were placed in the upper quintile; no other changes were effected in the 1977 data.

6. The point at which the exponential was chosen to end and the fractal (EI) to begin was selected by inspection. As a result, the degrees of freedom will vary from case to case, in addition to the differences in reporting of landholdings by various countries. In many instances, the point was fairly clear, as shown in Table 8.1, with, in most cases, the middle of the distribution omitted because of mixing of the two models (exponential and EI) over time. Where there was doubt about the accuracy of the point selected, at least one point below and one above were also selected for additional calculations to ensure that the reported findings represent the best possible fit between model and data.

7. In Chapter 2, the maximum likelihood method was used to establish the value of k for Malta and Gozo. This method of estimation could be used in that instance because, by inspection, the estimated value appeared to give a good fit between observation and prediction. More generally, however, ordinary least-squares methods tend to give a better fit. Of course, the specific method of estimation is purely an empirical matter; the theoretical applicability of one distribution or another is indifferent to the empirics of the estimation procedure.

8. In Chapter 7, deaths per capita was used as a measure of political violence, whereas here, the absolute number of deaths is used. The issue of using absolute numbers instead of deaths per unit population is a matter of analytic preference and varies especially according to the theoretical orientation of the analyst. Using death rate as the dependent variable entails the hidden but important assumption of a proportional or linear relationship between the likelihood of deaths due to political violence and population size. This assumption is frequently unwarranted. But if one assumes, as I do, that potentially long-term revolutionary processes—not isolated periodic disturbances—are the likely outcome of patterned inequality and that such processes are driven by a frequently nonlinear dynamic, then population size is much less relevant and may even mask important relationships. On the other hand, as an independent variable in its influence on democracy in Chapter 7, the assumption of a proportional linear relationship with population size is justified by the long-term lower level of deaths associated with democratic revolutions such as the American or even the ancient Athenian. In any event, the use of absolute numbers of deaths in the analysis of that chapter made no significant difference in the impact of the political violence variable.

9. Lewis Lapham (1988, 191) implies that disparities in income distribution in the

United States might lead to future widespread violence even more extreme than that experienced in the 1960s.

Chapter 9 / Equality and Cooperation or Helping

1. One can also compare Denmark with Holland, in which the Jews suffered an 80 percent victimization rate. Despite certain similarities between the two countries, such as relatively small size, a long history of national independence, and prior hospitable treatment of Jews, these similarities turn out to be only superficial. First, the existence of relatively homogeneous and easily identifiable Jewish neighborhoods in Holland, especially in Amsterdam, where most Jews lived, distinguishes the two cases. This made it easier for the SS to isolate the Jews and then begin the systematic process of destruction. Second, and most important, the Dutch very early in this process exhibited a distinct absence of identification with the Jews. As B. A. Sijes remarks about the early Dutch complicity with Nazi rule in 1940, "The Dutch authorities, and in particular the Secretaries-General, who had been invested with governmental authority by the departing Dutch Government, were the first who must bear part of the responsibility for separating Jews and non-Jews by implementing laws which were completely contrary to existing Dutch law. This was the starting point for the development of a barrier between the two groups" (1977, 552).

Only later, in 1944, when the Dutch themselves were experiencing difficulties with the German occupation, especially labor conscription, did resistance movements develop that were of some help to the Jews. As Helen Fein suggests, "Why did a movement to aid people in hiding emerge almost a year after it would have been of most benefit to the Jews hunted for extermination? One answer, advanced by de Jong, cites the belated development of identification with Jews and the ambivalence or antipathy among the founders of this movement, who came from different social classes and regions than did most Jews" (1979, 287).

When one adds to this the fact that of all the occupied countries Holland gave the largest number of volunteers per capita to the Nazi-sponsored Dutch version of the SS, then possibilities for an early identification with the fate of the Jews were remote indeed.

Chapter 10 / Paradoxes of Democracy and State Survivability

1. Another process leading from land inequality to democracy may have occurred and in fact may be complementary to the first discussed in the text. The enlargement of estates in populated settings generally proceeds by means of the absorption of peasant holdings that, as a result of population increase and subdivision, are too small to be economically viable. The displaced peasant often moves to the city, where large concentrations of such peasants then either organize politically or, more frequently, engage in protests or civil disorders that lead to concessions by the political authorities in the form of greater political rights. Thus, an increase in land inequality may have the second

consequence of increasing urbanization, which then leads to increased political participation and democracy. Alternatively, economic development may result from urbanization, which, as we have seen, is strongly related to democracy.

2. Nixon also sought to maximize his political advantage vis-à-vis other more traditionally entrenched groups. His choice of Henry Kissinger as National Security Advisor and later Secretary of State, for example, proceeded at least in part, from the realization that as a German-born Jew Kissinger would have little if any political support in a State Department bureaucracy dominated by a non-Jewish elite often educated at the most expensive and exclusive private academies. Thus, Kissinger would be reliant directly on Nixon and not on any other base of political support.

3. A thoughtful review of *The Bell Curve*, among other books dealing with this subject, is found in Browne 1994. Strong critiques of *The Bell Curve* are found in Gates 1994, Glazer 1994, and Hacker 1994, among others in response to an article by Murray and Herrnstein (1994) in a special issue of *The New Republic* devoted to the debate over *The Bell Curve*. For additional critiques, see *The Black Scholar* 1995 and Fischer et al. 1996.

4. As John Keep puts it in a review of Walter Laqueur's *The Dream that Failed: Reflections on the Soviet Union*, "One is almost tempted to say that the Soviet elite bored itself to death" (1995, 8).

Appendix A / Derivation of Exponential and Fractal Distributions

1. This is the most frequently encountered form of the Pareto distribution. For two other variations, see Johnson and Kotz 1970, 234.

2. Suppose that the proportionate income range is 10^h (the logarithmic assumption) and that the lowest income is Y_{min}; x_s is then the number of incomes in the range s whose lower bound is given by $Y_s = 10^{sh} Y_{min}$, $\log_{10} Y_s = sh + \log_{10} Y_{min}$. The number of incomes exceeding Y_s is $F(Y_s) = Nb^s$, $\log_{10} F(Y_s) = \log_{10} N + s \log_{10} b$. If we put $\alpha = -(1/h) \log_{10} b$; $\gamma = \log_{10} N + \alpha \log_{10} Y_{min}$, we obtain Pareto's law in its logarithmic form: $\log_{10} F(Y_s) = \gamma - \alpha \log_{10} Y_s$.

BIBLIOGRAPHY

Adams, Richard E. W. 1973. "The Collapse of Maya Civilization: A Review of Previous Theories." In *The Classic Maya Collapse*, ed. T. Patrick Culbert. Albuquerque: University of New Mexico Press.

———. 1991. *Prehistoric Mesoamerica*, rev. ed. Norman: University of Oklahoma Press.

Adams, Robert McC. 1966. *The Evolution of Urban Society: Early Mesopotamia and Prehispanic Mexico*. Chicago: Aldine.

Ajami, Fouad. 1993. "The Summoning." *Foreign Affairs* 72 (Sept.-Oct.): 2-9.

Allbaugh, Leland G. 1953. *Crete: A Case Study of an Underdeveloped Area*. Princeton, N.J.: Princeton University Press.

Anawalt, Patricia R. 1977. "What Price Aztec Pageantry?" *Archaeology* 30: 226-33.

———. 1981. *Indian Clothing Before Cortés: Mesoamerican Costumes from the Codices*. Norman: University of Oklahoma Press.

Anderson, Benedict. 1991. *Imagined Communities: Reflections on the Origin and Spread of Nationalism*, rev. ed. London: Verso.

Anderson, Ingvar. 1958. "Early Democratic Traditions in Scandinavia." In *Scandinavian Democracy*, ed. J. A. Lauwerys. Copenhagen: The Danish, Norwegian, and Swedish Institutes.

Anderson, Perry. 1974a. *Lineages of the Absolutist State*. London: Verso.

———. 1974b. *Passages From Antiquity to Feudalism*. London: Verso

Angell, Norman. 1911. *The Great Illusion: A Study of the Relation of Military Power in Nations to their Economic and Social Advantage*, 3rd ed. New York: G. P. Putnam.

Applebome, Peter. 1991. "Scandals Casting Shadows over Public Life in South Carolina." *New York Times*, 12 May, L16.

Aron, Raymond. 1968. *Progress and Disillusion: The Dialectics of Modern Society*. New York: Praeger.

Ashton, Robert. 1978. *The English Civil War: Conservatism and Revolution 1603-1649*. London: Weidenfeld and Nicolson.

Atkinson, A. B. 1996. "Promise and Performance: Why We Need an Official Poverty Report." In *Living as Equals*, ed. Paul Barker. Oxford, Eng.: Oxford University Press.

Axelrod, Robert. 1984. *The Evolution of Cooperation*. New York: Basic Books.

Bair, Frank E. 1992. *The Weather Almanac*, 6th ed. Detroit: Gale Research.

Balazs, Etienne. 1964. *Chinese Civilization and Bureaucracy: Variations on a Theme*. Ed. Arthur F. Wright. Trans. H. M. Wright. New Haven, Conn.: Yale University Press.

Ball, R. C., M. J. Blunt, and O. Rath Spivack. 1989. "Diffusion-Controlled Growth." In *Fractals in the Natural Sciences*, ed. M. Fleischmann, D. J. Tildesley, and R. C. Ball. Princeton, N.J.: Princeton University Press.

Banks, Arthur S. 1971. *Cross-Polity Time-Series Data*. Cambridge, Mass.: MIT Press.

———. 1979. *Cross-National Time-Series Data Archive User's Manual.* Binghamton: State University of New York at Binghamton.
Barkay, Gabriel. 1992. "The Iron Age II-III." In *The Archaeology of Ancient Israel,* ed. Amnon Ben-Tor. Trans. R. Greenberg. New Haven, Conn.: Yale University Press.
Barraclough, Geoffrey. 1984. *The Origins of Modern Germany.* New York: W. W. Norton.
Bartlett, Robert. 1993. *The Making of Europe: Conquest, Colonization, and Cultural Change, 950-1350.* Princeton, N. J.: Princeton University Press.
Bartley, Robert L. 1993. "The Case for Optimism." *Foreign Affairs* 72 (Sept.-Oct.): 2-9.
Bartusis, Mark C. 1992. *The Late Byzantine Army: Arms and Society, 1204-1453.* Philadelphia: University of Pennsylvania Press.
Bauer, Brian S. 1992. *The Development of the Inca State.* Austin: University of Texas Press.
Beattie, Hilary J. 1979. "The Alternative to Resistance: The Case of T'ung-ch'eng, Anhwei." In *From Ming to Ch'ing: Conquest, Region, and Continuity in Seventeenth-Century China,* ed. Jonathan D. Spence and John E. Wills, Jr. New Haven, Conn.: Yale University Press.
Bercé, Yves-Marie. 1990. *History of Peasant Revolts: The Social Origins of Rebellion in Early Modern France.* Trans. Amanda Whitmore. Ithaca, N.Y.: Cornell University Press.
Bernstein, Aaron. 1995. "The Wage Squeeze." *Business Week,* 17 July, 54-62.
Birdsell, Joseph B. 1973. "A Basic Demographic Unit." *Current Anthropology* 14: 337-50.
The Black Scholar. 1995. 25 (Winter).
Blanton, Richard E., Stephen A. Kowalewski, Gary Feinman, and Jill Appel. 1981. *Ancient Mesoamerica: A Comparison of Change in Three Regions.* New York: Cambridge University Press.
Bloch, Marc. 1961. *Feudal Society,* 2 vols. Trans. L. A. Manyon. London: Routledge & Kegan Paul.
Blum, Jerome. 1978. *The End of the Old Order in Rural Europe.* Princeton, N.J.: Princeton University Press.
Blumenthal, Uta-Renate. 1988. *The Investiture Controversy: Church and Monarchy from the Ninth to the Twelfth Century.* Trans. Uta-Renate Blumenthal. Philadelphia: University of Pennsylvania Press.
Bollen, Kenneth A. 1980. "Issues in the Comparative Measurement of Political Democracy." *American Sociological Review* 45: 370-90.
———. 1993. "Liberal Democracy: Validity and Method Factors in Cross-National Measures." *American Journal of Political Science* 37: 1207-30.
Bollen, Kenneth A., and Robert W. Jackman. 1985. "Political Democracy and the Size Distribution of Income." *American Sociological Review* 50: 438-57.
Bonney, Richard. 1991. *The European Dynastic States: 1494-1660.* Oxford, Eng.: Oxford University Press.

Boxley, R. F. 1971. "Farm Size and the Distribution of Farm Numbers." *Agricultural Economics Research* 23: 87–94.
Branigan, Keith. 1970. *The Foundations of Palatial Crete: A Survey of Crete in the Early Bronze Age.* London: Routledge.
Braudel, Fernand. 1982. *The Wheels of Commerce.* Vol. 2 of *Civilization and Capitalism, 15th–18th Century.* Trans. Siân Reynolds. New York: Harper and Row.
———. 1984. *The Perspective of the World.* Vol. 3 of *Civilization and Capitalism, 15th–18th Century.* Trans. Siân Reynolds. New York: Harper and Row.
"Breakthroughs." 1995. *Discover* 16 (September): 22.
Bremer, Stuart A. 1992. "Dangerous Dyads: Conditions Affecting the Likelihood of Interstate War, 1816–1965." *Journal of Conflict Resolution* 36: 309–41.
Briggs, Asa. 1983. *A Social History of England.* London: Weidenfeld & Nicolson.
Bronfenbrenner, Urie. 1960. "Freudian Theories of Identification and their Derivatives." *Child Development* 31: 15–40.
Browne, Malcolm W. 1994. "What Is Intelligence, and Who Has It?" Review of *The Bell Curve* by Richard J. Herrnstein and Charles Murray. In *New York Times Book Review*, 16 October, 3, 41, 45.
Brumfiel, Elizabeth. 1976. "Regional Growth in the Eastern Valley of Mexico: A Test of the 'Population Pressure' Hypothesis." In *The Early Mesoamerican Village*, ed. Kent V. Flannery. New York: Academic Press.
———. 1995. "Heterarchy and the Analysis of Complex Societies: Comments." In *Heterarchy and the Analysis of Complex Societies*, ed. Robert M. Ehrenreich, Carole L. Crumley, and Janet E. Levy. Arlington, Va.: American Anthropological Association.
Brundage, Burr C. 1963. *Empire of the Inca.* Norman: University of Oklahoma Press.
Brunner, Otto. 1992. *Land and Lordship: Structures of Governance in Medieval Austria*, 4th rev. ed. Trans. Howard Kaminsky and James Van Horn Melton. Philadelphia: University of Pennsylvania Press.
Budge, E. A. Wallis. 1977. *The Dwellers on the Nile: The Life, History, Religion, and Literature of the Ancient Egyptians.* New York: Dover.
Burkhart, Ross E., and Michael S. Lewis-Beck. 1994. "Comparative Democracy: The Economic Development Thesis." *American Political Science Review* 88: 903–10.
Butzer, Karl W. 1976. *Early Hydraulic Civilization in Egypt.* Chicago: University of Chicago Press.
———. 1984. "Long-Term Nile Flood Variation and Political Discontinuities in Pharaonic Egypt." In *From Hunters to Farmers*, ed. John D. Clark and Steven A. Brandt. Berkeley: University of California Press.
Cadogan, Gerald. 1976. *Palaces of Minoan Crete.* London: Barrie and Jenkins.
Cahen, Claude. 1970. "Economy, Society, Institutions." In *The Cambridge History of Islam.* Vol. 2, *The Further Islamic Lands, Islamic Society, and Civilization*, ed. P. M. Holt, Ann K. S. Lambton, and Bernard Lewis. Cambridge, Eng.: Cambridge University Press.

Cameron, Averil. 1993. *The Later Roman Empire: A.D. 284-430*. Cambridge, Mass.: Harvard University Press.
Canetti, Elias. 1973. *Crowds and Power*. Trans. Carol Stewart. Middlesex, Eng.: Penguin Books.
Carneiro, Robert L. 1970. "A Theory of the Origin of the State." *Science* 169: 733-38.
———. 1987. "Cross Currents in the Theory of State Formation." *American Ethnologist* 14: 756-70.
Castells, Manuel. 1997. *The Information Age: Economy, Society and Culture*. Vol. 2, *The Power of Identity*. Oxford, Eng.: Blackwell.
Castleden, Rodney. 1990. *Minoans: Life in Bronze Age Crete*. London: Routledge.
Chaitin, Gregory J. 1987. *Algorithmic Information Theory*. Cambridge, Eng.: Cambridge University Press.
Champernowne, D. G. 1953. "A Model of Income Distribution." *The Economic Journal* 63: 318-51.
Chan, Steve. 1984. "Mirror, Mirror on the Wall. . . . Are the Freer Countries More Pacific?" *Journal of Conflict Resolution* 28: 617-48.
———. 1997. "In Search of Democratic Peace: Problems and Promise." *Mershon International Studies Review* 41: 59-91.
Chang, Kwang-chih. 1980. *Shang Civilization*. New Haven, Conn.: Yale University Press.
———. 1986. *The Archaeology of Ancient China*, 4th ed. New Haven, Conn.: Yale University Press.
Charanis, Peter. 1967a. "Economic Factors in the Decline of the Byzantine Empire." In *The Decline of Empires*, ed. S. N. Eisenstadt. Englewood Cliffs, N.J.: Prentice-Hall.
———. 1967b. "Social Structure and Economic Policies in the Byzantine Empire." In *The Decline of Empires*, ed. S. N. Eisenstadt. Englewood Cliffs, N.J.: Prentice-Hall.
Chase-Dunn, Christopher, and Thomas D. Hall. 1997. *Rise and Demise: Comparing World-Systems*. Boulder, Colo.: Westview Press.
Chayanov, A. V. 1966. *The Theory of Peasant Economy*. Ed. Daniel Thorner, Basile Kerblay, and R. E. F. Smith. Madison: University of Wisconsin Press.
Chen Han-Seng. 1936. *Landlord and Peasant in China: A Study of the Agrarian Crisis in South China*. New York: International.
Chenery, Hollis B., and Moises Syrquin. 1975. *Patterns of Development, 1950-1970*. New York: Oxford University Press.
Cherry, John F. 1986. "Polities and Palaces: Some Problems in Minoan State Formation." In *Peer Polity Interaction and Socio-Political Change*, ed. Colin Renfrew and John F. Cherry. Cambridge, Eng.: Cambridge University Press.
Cherry, John F., and Colin Renfrew. 1986. "Epilogue and Prospect." In *Peer Polity Interaction and Socio-Political Change*, ed. Colin Renfrew and John F. Cherry. Cambridge, Eng.: Cambridge University Press.
Chipman, John S. 1976. "The Paretian Heritage." *Cahiers Vilfredo Pareto: Revue Européenne des Sciences Sociales* 14: 65-173.

Cioffi-Revilla, Claudio, and David Lai. 1995. "War and Politics in Ancient China, 2700–722 B.C." *Journal of Conflict Resolution* 39: 467–94.

Cioffi-Revilla, Claudio, and Todd Landman. 1996. "Rise and Fall of Maya Polities in the Ancient Mesoamerican System." Boulder: Long-Range Analysis of War Project, Department of Political Science, University of Colorado.

Clark, Colin. 1972. "The Extent of Hunger in India." *Economic and Political Weekly* 7: 2019–27.

Clements, Ronald E., ed. 1989. *The World of Ancient Israel: Sociological, Anthropological, and Political Perspectives*. New York: Cambridge University Press.

Cobo, Father Bernabe. 1979. *History of the Inca Empire: An Account of the Indians' Customs and their Origin Together with a Treatise on Inca Legends, History, and Social Institutions*. Ed. and trans. Roland Hamilton. Austin: University of Texas Press.

Coggins, R. J. 1989. "The Origins of the Jewish Diaspora." In *The World of Ancient Israel*, ed. R. E. Clements. Cambridge, Eng.: Cambridge University Press.

Cohen, Ronald. 1978. "State Foundations: A Controlled Comparison." In *Origins of the State*, ed. Ronald Cohen and Elman R. Service. Philadelphia: Institute for the Study of Human Issues.

Collingwood, R. G. 1994. *The Idea of History*, rev. ed. Oxford, Eng.: Oxford University Press.

Collins, James B. 1994. *Classes, Estates, and Order in Early Modern Brittany*. Cambridge, Eng.: Cambridge University Press.

Conrad, Geoffrey W., and Arthur A. Demarest. 1984. *Religion and Empire: The Dynamics of Aztec and Inca Expansion*. Cambridge, Eng.: Cambridge University Press.

Converse, Philip E. 1969. "Of Time and Partisan Stability." *Comparative Political Studies* 2: 139–71.

Cook, Sherburne F. 1946. "Human Sacrifice and Warfare as Factors in the Demography of Pre-Colonial Mexico." *Human Biology* 18: 81–102.

Cordy, Ross. 1986. "Relationships Between the Extent of Social Stratification and Population in Micronesian Polities at European Contact." *American Anthropologist* 88: 136–42.

Cornwall, Julian. 1977. *Revolt of the Peasantry, 1549*. London: Routledge & Kegan Paul.

Cose, Ellis. 1993. *The Rage of a Privileged Class*. New York: HarperCollins.

Cowgill, George L. 1979. "Teotihuacan, Internal Militaristic Competition, and the Fall of the Classic Maya." In *Maya Archaeology and Ethnohistory*, ed. Norman Hammond and Gordon R. Willey. Austin: University of Texas Press.

———. 1983. "Rulership and the Ciudadela: Political Inferences from Teotihuacan Architecture." In *Civilization in the Ancient Americas*, ed. Richard M. Leventhal and Alan L. Kolata. Albuquerque and Cambridge, Mass.: University of New Mexico Press and Peabody Museum of Archaeology and Ethnology, Harvard University.

Crawford, Harriet. 1991. *Sumer and the Sumerians*. Cambridge, Eng.: Cambridge University Press.

Crenshaw, Edward. 1992. "Cross-National Determinants of Income Inequality: A Replication and Extension Using Ecological-Evolutionary Theory." *Social Forces* 71: 339–63.

———. 1995. "Democracy and Demographic Inheritance: The Influence of Modernity and Proto-Modernity on Political and Civil Rights, 1965 to 1980." *American Sociological Review* 60: 702–18.

———. 1997. "Democracy and Proto-Modernity: Technology Influences on the Growth of Political and Civil Rights." In *Inequality, Democracy, and Economic Development*, ed. Manus I. Midlarsky. Cambridge, Eng.: Cambridge University Press.

Crumley, Carole L. 1987a. "A Dialectical Critique of Hierarchy." In *Power Relations and State Formation*, ed. Thomas C. Patterson and Christine W. Gailey. Washington, D.C.: American Anthropological Association.

———. 1987b. "Historical Ecology." In *Regional Dynamics: Burgundian Landscapes in Historical Perspective*, ed. Carole L. Crumley and William H. Marquardt. San Diego, Calif: Academic Press.

———. 1993. "Analyzing Historic Ecotonal Shifts." *Ecological Applications* 3: 377–84.

———. 1995. "Heterarchy and the Analysis of Complex Societies." In *Heterarchy and the Analysis of Complex Societies*, ed. Robert M. Ehrenreich, Carole L. Crumley, and Janet E. Levy. Arlington, Va.: American Anthropological Association.

Culbert, T. Patrick, ed. 1973a. *The Classic Maya Collapse*. Albuquerque: University of New Mexico Press.

———. 1973b. "The Maya Downfall at Tikal." In *The Classic Maya Collapse*, ed. T. Patrick Culbert. Albuquerque: University of New Mexico Press.

———. 1988. "The Collapse of Classic Maya Civilization." In *The Collapse of Ancient States and Civilizations*, ed. Norman Yoffee and George L. Cowgill. Tucson: University of Arizona Press.

Dahl, Robert A. 1971. *Polyarchy: Participation and Opposition*. New Haven, Conn.: Yale University Press.

———. 1989. *Democracy and Its Critics*. New Haven, Conn.: Yale University Press.

Dahl, Robert A., and Edward R. Tufte. 1973. *Size and Democracy*. Stanford, Calif.: Stanford University Press.

Davies, James C. 1962. "Toward a Theory of Revolution." *American Sociological Review* 27: 5–19.

Davies, Nigel. 1980. *The Aztecs: A History*. Norman: University of Oklahoma Press.

———. 1982. *The Ancient Kingdoms of Mexico*. New York: Penguin Books.

Davis, James C. 1962. *The Decline of the Venetian Nobility as a Ruling Class*. Baltimore: Johns Hopkins University Press.

De Montmollin, Olivier. 1989. *The Archaeology of Political Structure: Settlement Analysis in a Classic Maya Polity*. Cambridge, Eng.: Cambridge University Press.

de Pradt, D. de Fourt. 1800. *La Prusse et sa Neutralité*. London: G. Cowie.

Derman, Cyrus, Leon J. Gleser, and Ingram Olkin. 1973. *A Guide to Probability Theory and Application*. New York: Holt, Rinehart and Winston.

De Ste. Croix, G. E. M. 1981. *The Class Struggle in the Ancient Greek World from the Archaic Age to the Arab Conquests.* London: Duckworth.

Deutsch, K. W., S. A. Burrell, Robert A. Kann, Maurice Lee, Martin Lichterman, Raymond E. Lindgren, Francis L. Loewenheim, and Richard W. Van Wagenen. 1957. *Political Community and the North Atlantic Area.* Princeton, N.J.: Princeton University Press.

Deutsch, Morton. 1985. *Distributive Justice.* New Haven, Conn.: Yale University Press.

Diakonoff, I. M. 1991. "The City-States of Sumer." In *Early Antiquity,* ed. I. M. Diakonoff. Chicago: University of Chicago Press.

Diamond, Larry. 1992. "Economic Development and Democracy Reconsidered." In *Reexamining Democracy: Essays in Honor of Seymour Martin Lipset,* ed. Gary Marks and Larry Diamond. Newbury Park, Calif.: Sage.

Dickinson, H. T. 1985. "Government and Politics: England and Wales, 1701-1783." In *The Cambridge Historical Encyclopedia of Great Britain and Ireland,* ed. Christopher Haigh. Cambridge, Eng.: Cambridge University Press.

Diehl, C. 1967. "Forms of Political Conflict in the Byzantine Empire." In *The Decline of Empires,* ed. S. N. Eisenstadt. Englewood Cliffs, N.J.: Prentice-Hall.

Dix, Robert H. 1967. *Colombia: The Political Dimensions of Change.* New Haven, Conn.: Yale University Press.

Dixon, William J. 1993. "Democracy and the Management of International Conflict." *Journal of Conflict Resolution* 37: 42-68.

Dockès, Pierre. 1982. *Medieval Slavery and Liberation.* Trans. Arthur Goldhammer. London: Methuen.

Dominguez, Jorge I. 1978. *Cuba: Order and Revolution.* Cambridge, Mass.: Belknap.

Dovring, Folke. 1973. "Distribution of Farm Size and Income: Analysis by Exponential Functions." *Land Economics* 49: 133-47.

Downing, Brian M. 1992. *The Military Revolution and Political Change: Origins of Democracy and Autocracy in Early Modern Europe.* Princeton, N.J.: Princeton University Press.

Doyle, Michael W. 1983. "Kant, Liberal Legacies, and Foreign Affairs, Part 1." *Philosophy and Public Affairs* 12: 205-35.

———. 1986. *Empires.* Ithaca, N.Y.: Cornell University Press.

Drennan, Robert D., and J. A. Nowack. 1984. "Exchange and Sociopolitical Development in the Tehuacan Valley." In *Trade and Exchange in Early Mesoamerica,* ed. Kenneth G. Hirth. Albuquerque: University of New Mexico Press.

Duby, Georges. 1968. *Rural Economy and Country Life in the Medieval West.* Trans. Cynthia Postan. Columbia: University of South Carolina Press.

Dutta, M. 1966. "On Maximum (Information-Theoretic) Entropy Estimation." *Sankhya,* Series A. 28 (Dec.): 319-28.

Dwyer, Edward B. 1971. "The Early Inca Occupation of the Valley of Cuzco, Peru." Ph.D. diss., Department of Anthropology, University of California, Berkeley.

Earle, Timothy. 1997. *How Chiefs Come to Power: The Political Economy in Prehistory.* Stanford, Calif.: Stanford University Press.

Easton, David. 1965. *A Framework for Political Analysis.* Chicago: University of Chicago Press.

Egnal, Marc. 1988. *A Mighty Empire: The Origins of the American Revolution.* Ithaca, N.Y.: Cornell University Press.

Ehrenreich, Robert M., Carole L. Crumley, and Janet E. Levy, eds. 1995. *Heterarchy and the Analysis of Complex Societies.* Arlington, Va.: American Anthropological Association.

Ehrlich, Paul R., Anne H. Ehrlich, and John P. Holdren. 1977. *Ecoscience: Population, Resources, Environment,* 2nd ed. San Francisco: Freeman.

Eisenstadt, S. N. 1963. *The Political Systems of Empires.* New York: The Free Press.

———, ed. 1986. *The Origins and Diversity of Axial Age Civilizations.* Albany: State University of New York Press.

Eldredge, Niles. 1985. *Time Frames: The Evolution of Punctuated Equilibria.* Princeton, N.J.: Princeton University Press.

Elias, Norbert. 1982. *Power and Civility.* Vol. 2, *The Civilizing Process.* Trans. Edmund Jephcott. Oxford, Eng.: Basil Blackwell.

Ember, Carol R., Melvin Ember, and Bruce Russett. 1992. "Peace Between Participatory Polities: A Cross-Cultural Test of the 'Democracies Rarely Fight Each Other' Hypothesis." *World Politics* 44: 573-99.

Engels, Friedrich. 1940. *On Historical Materialism.* New York: International Publishers.

Erman, Adolf. 1971. *Life in Ancient Egypt.* Trans. H. M. Tirard. New York: Dover.

Esposito, John L., and John O. Voll. 1996. *Islam and Democracy.* New York: Oxford University Press.

Everitt, Alan. 1969. *Change in the Provinces: The Seventeenth Century.* Leicester, Eng.: Leicester University Press.

Farrar, Cynthia. 1988. *The Origins of Democratic Thinking: The Invention of Politics in Classical Athens.* Cambridge, Eng.: Cambridge University Press.

Feder, Jens. 1988. *Fractals.* New York: Plenum.

Fein, Helen. 1979. *Accounting for Genocide.* New York: Free Press.

Feller, William. 1968. *An Introduction to Probability Theory and Its Applications,* Vol. 1, 3rd ed. New York: Wiley.

Fiedel, Stuart J. 1992. *Prehistory of the Americas,* 2d ed. New York: Cambridge University Press.

Fine, John V. A. 1983. *The Ancient Greeks: A Critical History.* Cambridge, Mass.: Harvard University Press.

Finlay, Robert. 1980. *Politics in Renaissance Venice.* New Brunswick, N.J.: Rutgers University Press.

Finley, M. I. 1973. *The Ancient Economy.* Berkeley: University of California Press.

———. 1981. *Early Greece: The Bronze and Archaic Ages,* rev. ed. London: Chatto and Windus.

———. 1982. *Economy and Society in Ancient Greece*. Ed. Brent D. Shaw and Richard P. Saller. New York: Viking.

———. 1983. *Politics in the Ancient World*. New York: Cambridge University Press.

Fischer, Claude, Michael Hout, Samuel R. Lucas, Martin S. Jankowski, Ann Swidler, and Kim Voss. 1996. *Inequality by Design: Cracking the Bell Curve Myth*. Princeton, N.J.: Princeton University Press.

Flannery, Kent V., Joyce Marcus, and Stephen. A. Kowalewski. 1981. "The Preceramic and Formative of the Valley of Oaxaca." In *Handbook of Middle American Indians; Supplement 1: Archaeology*, ed. Jeremy Sabloff. Austin: University of Texas Press.

Fleischmann, M., D. J. Tildesley, and R. C. Ball, ed. 1989. *Fractals in the Natural Sciences*. Princeton, N.J.: Princeton University Press.

Flender, Harold. 1963. *Rescue in Denmark*. London: W. H. Allen.

Fogelman, Eva. 1994. *Conscience and Courage: Rescuers of Jews During the Holocaust*. New York: Doubleday.

Food and Agriculture Organization. 1955. *Report on the 1950 World Census of Agriculture*. Vol. 1, *Census Results by Countries*. Rome: FAO.

———. 1966. *Report on the 1960 World Census of Agriculture*. Vol. 1, Part A, *Census Results by Countries*. Rome: FAO.

———. 1981. *1970 World Census of Agriculture: Analysis and International Comparison of the Results*. Rome: FAO.

Foster, George M. 1967. *Tzintzuntzan: Mexican Peasants in a Changing World*. Boston: Little, Brown.

Fox, John. 1991. *Regression Diagnostics*. Newbury Park, Calif.: Sage Publications.

Frankfort, Henri. 1971. "The Last Predynastic Period in Babylonia." In *The Cambridge Ancient History*. Vol. 1, Part 2A, *Early History of the Middle East*, ed. I. E. S. Edwards, C. J. Gadd, and N. G. L. Hammond. Cambridge, Eng.: Cambridge University Press.

Freud, Sigmund. 1953. "Three Essays on the Theory of Sexuality." In *The Standard Edition of the Complete Psychological Works of Sigmund Freud*, ed. J. Strachey. London: The Hogarth Press.

Frick, F. S. 1989. "Ecology, Agriculture and Patterns of Settlement." In *The World of Ancient Israel*, ed. R. E. Clements. Cambridge, Eng.: Cambridge University Press.

Fried, Morton H. 1967. *The Evolution of Political Society: An Essay in Political Anthropology*. New York: Random House.

———. 1978. "The State, the Chicken, and the Egg; or, What Came First?" In *Origins of the State: The Anthropology of Political Evolution*, ed. Ronald Cohen and Elman R. Service. Philadelphia: Institute for the Study of Human Issues.

———. 1983. "Tribe to State or State to Tribe in Ancient China?" In *The Origins of Chinese Civilization*, ed. David N. Keightley. Berkeley: University of California Press.

Friedman, Jonathan. 1981. "Notes on Structure and History in Oceania." *Folk* 23: 275–95.

———. 1982. "Catastrophe and Continuity in Social Evolution." In *Theory and Explanation in Archaeology: The Southampton Conference, ed. Colin Renfrew, Michael J. Rowlands, and Barbara Abbott Segraves. New York: Academic Press.

Friedman, Philip. 1957. *Their Brothers Keepers*. New York: Crown.

Fuhrmann, Horst. 1986. *Germany in the High Middle Ages, ca. 1050-1200*. Trans. Timothy Reuter. Cambridge, Eng: Cambridge University Press.

Futia, Carl A. 1982. "Invariant Distributions and the Limiting Behavior of Markovian Economic Models." *Econometrica* 50: 377-408.

Gadd, C. J. 1971a. "The Cities of Babylonia." In *The Cambridge Ancient History*. Vol. 1, Part 2A. *Early History of the Middle East*, ed. I. E. S. Edwards, C. J. Gadd, and N. G. L. Hammond. Cambridge, Eng.: Cambridge University Press.

———. 1971b. "The Dynasty of Agade and the Gutian Invasion." In *The Cambridge Ancient History*. Vol. 1, Part 2A, *Early History of the Middle East*, ed. I. E. S. Edwards, C. J. Gadd, and N. G. L. Hammond. Cambridge, Eng.: Cambridge University Press.

Gardiner, Alan. 1961. *Egypt of the Pharaohs*. New York: Oxford University Press.

Gardner, Howard. 1995. "Self-Raising Power." *The Times Higher Education Supplement*, 28 July, 15.

Gastil, Raymond D. 1988. *Freedom in the World: Political Rights and Civil Liberties, 1987-1988*. New York: Freedom House.

Gates, Henry L., Jr. 1994. "Why Now?: The Peculiar Timing of This Apologia." *The New Republic* 211 (Oct. 31): 10.

Gentz, Friedrich von. 1806. *Fragments on the Balance of Power*. London: Herries.

Gernet, Jacques. 1982. *A History of Chinese Civilization*. Trans. J. R. Foster. New York: Cambridge University Press.

Gibbons, Jean D. 1971. *Nonparametric Statistical Inference*. New York: McGraw-Hill.

Gilman, Antonio. 1981. "The Development of Social Stratification in Bronze Age Europe." *Current Anthropology* 22: 1-23.

Gilpin, Robert. 1981. *War and Change in World Politics*. New York: Cambridge University Press.

Glazer, Nathan. 1994. "The Lying Game: Some Truths Are Maybe Not Worth Knowing." *The New Republic* 211 (Oct. 31): 15-16.

Gleick, James. 1987. *Chaos: Making a New Science*. New York: Viking.

Goffart, Walter. 1980. *Barbarians and Romans A.D. 418-584: The Techniques of Accommodation*. Princeton, N.J.: Princeton University Press.

Goldstone, Jack A. 1983. "Capitalist Origins of the English Revolution: Chasing a Chimera." *Theory and Society* 12: 143-80.

Good, I. J. 1963. "Maximum Entropy for Hypothesis Formulation, Especially for Multi-Dimensional Contingency Scales." *Annals of Mathematical Statistics* 34 (Sept.): 911-34.

Goodman, Martin. 1987. *The Ruling Class of Judaea: The Origins of the Jewish Revolt Against Rome, A.D. 66-70*. New York: Cambridge University Press.

Gordon, Sarah. 1984. *Hitler, Germans, and the 'Jewish Question.'* Princeton, N.J.: Princeton University Press.

Gould, Stephen Jay. 1985. *The Flamingo's Smile: Reflections in Natural History.* New York: W. W. Norton.
Graham, J. Walter. 1987. *The Palaces of Crete,* rev. ed. Princeton, N.J.: Princeton University Press.
Grant, Michael. 1971. *Atlas of Ancient History 1700 B.C. to 565 A.D.* New York: Dorset Press.
———. 1978. *The History of the Greeks.* New York: Scribner.
———. 1987. *The Rise of the Greeks.* New York: Collier Books.
Greene, Kevin. 1986. *The Archaeology of the Roman Economy.* Berkeley: University of California Press.
Grimal, Nicolas. 1992. *A History of Ancient Egypt.* Trans. Ian Shaw. Oxford, Eng.: Blackwell.
Gulick, Edward V. 1955. *Europe's Classical Balance of Power.* New York: W. W. Norton.
Gumbel, E. J. 1958. *Statistics of Extremes.* New York: Columbia University Press.
Gunn, Joel D. 1994. "Global Climate and Regional Biocultural Diversity." In *Historical Ecology,* ed. Carole L. Crumley. Sante Fe, N.M.: School of American Research Press.
Gunn, Joel D., and Richard E. W. Adams. 1981. "Climatic Change, Culture, and Civilization in North America." *World Archaeology* 13: 85-100.
Gunn, Joel D., William J. Folan, and Hubert R. Robichaux. 1995. "A Landscape Analysis of the Candelaria Watershed in Mexico: Insights into Paleoclimates Affecting Upland Horticulture in the Southern Yucatan Peninsula Semi-Karst." *Geoarchaeology: An International Journal* 10: 3-42.
Gurr, Ted R. 1970. *Why Men Rebel.* Princeton, N.J.: Princeton University Press.
Haas, Jonathan. 1982. *The Evolution of the Prehistoric State.* New York: Columbia University Press.
Hacker, Andrew. 1994. "White on White: The Double Standards of Racial Counting." *The New Republic* 211 (Oct. 31): 13-14.
Hadenius, Axel. 1992. *Democracy and Development.* Cambridge, Eng.: Cambridge University Press.
Haghayeghi, Mehrdad. 1996. *Islam and Politics in Central Asia.* New York: Saint Martin's Press.
Hallie, Philip. 1979. *Lest Innocent Blood Be Shed.* New York: Harper and Row.
Hamblin, Robert L., and B. L. Pitcher. 1980. "The Classic Maya Collapse: Testing Class Conflict Hypotheses." *American Antiquity* 45: 246-67.
Hamby, Russell R. 1986. "Coffee and Conflict in Colombia: Spatial, Temporal, and Class Patterns of *La Violencia.*" In *Inequality and Contemporary Revolutions.* Monograph Series in World Affairs, vol. 22, bk. 2, ed. Manus I. Midlarsky. Denver: Graduate School of International Studies, University of Denver.
Hammond, Norman. 1974. "The Distribution of Late Classic Maya Major Ceremonial Centers in the Central Area." In *Mesoamerican Archaeology: New Approaches,* ed. Norman Hammond. Austin: University of Texas Press.

———. 1988. *Ancient Maya Civilization*. New Brunswick, N.J.: Rutgers University Press.

Hardy, Melissa A. 1979. "Economic Growth, Distributional Inequality, and Political Conflict in Industrial Societies." *Journal of Political and Military Sociology* 7: 209-27.

Harris, Marvin. 1977. *Cannibals and Kings: The Origins of Cultures*. New York: Random House.

———. 1981. *America Now: The Anthropology of a Changing Culture*. New York: Simon and Schuster.

Harrison, E. J. 1928. *Lithuania, 1928*. London: Hazel, Watson and Viney.

Harvey, B. F. 1985. "English Society." In *The Cambridge Historical Encyclopedia of Great Britain and Ireland*, ed. Christopher Haigh. Cambridge, Eng.: Cambridge University Press.

Hassan, Fekri A. 1986. "Desert Environment and Origins of Agriculture in Egypt." *Norwegian Archaeological Review* 19: 63-76.

———. 1988. "The Predynastic of Egypt." *Journal of World Prehistory* 2: 135-85.

Hassig, Ross. 1992. *War and Society in Ancient Mesoamerica*. Berkeley: University of California Press.

Hastorf, Christine A. 1990. "The Ecosystem Model and Long-Term Prehistoric Change: An Example from the Andes." In *The Ecosystem Approach in Anthropology: From Concept to Practice*, ed. Emilio F. Moran. Ann Arbor: University of Michigan Press.

Haviland, William A. 1967. "Stature at Tikal, Guatemala: Implications for Ancient Maya Demography and Social Organization." *American Antiquity* 32: 316-25.

Heath, Dwight B., Charles J. Erasmus, and Hans C. Buechler. 1969. *Land Reform and Social Revolution in Bolivia*. New York: Praeger.

Herr, Larry G. 1993. "What Ever Happened to the Ammonites?" *Biblical Archaeology Review* 19 (Nov.-Dec.): 26-35.

Herr, Richard. 1989. *Rural Change and Royal Finances in Spain at the End of the Old Regime*. Berkeley: University of California Press.

Herrnstein, Richard J., and Charles Murray. 1994. *The Bell Curve: Intelligence and Class Structure in American Life*. New York: The Free Press.

Hexter, J. H. 1960. "The Wealthy Parliamentary Gentry—and the Reality of Ideology." In *The Origins of the English Civil War: Conspiracy, Crusade, or Class Conflict?*, ed. Philip A. M. Taylor. Lexington, Mass.: D. C. Heath.

Hickey, Daniel. 1986. *The Coming of French Absolutism: The Struggle for Tax Reform in the Province of Dauphiné, 1540-1640*. Toronto: University of Toronto Press.

Hilton, Rodney. 1990. *Class Conflict and the Crisis of Feudalism: Essays in Medieval Social History*, rev. ed. London: Verso.

Hintze, Otto. 1975. "Military Organization and the Organization of the State." In *The Historical Essays of Otto Hintze*, ed. Felix Gilbert. New York: Oxford University Press.

Hirschman, Albert O. 1981. *Essays in Trespassing: Economics to Politics and Beyond*. Cambridge, Eng.: Cambridge University Press.

———. 1996. "Two Hundred Years of Reactionary Rhetoric: The Futility Thesis." In *Living as Equals*, ed. Paul Barker. Oxford, Eng.: Oxford University Press.

Hirth, Kenneth G. 1984. "Early Exchange in Mesoamerica: An Introduction." In *Trade and Exchange in Early Mesoamerica*, ed. Kenneth G. Hirth. Albuquerque: University of New Mexico Press.

Historical Statistics of the United States, Colonial Times to 1970. 1975. Washington, D.C.: U. S. Department of Commerce, Bureau of the Census, U.S. Government Printing Office.

Hodgson, Marshall G. S. 1974a. *The Classical Age of Islam*. Vol. 1 of *The Venture of Islam: Conscience and History in a World Civilization*. Chicago: University of Chicago Press.

———. 1974b. *The Expansion of Islam in the Middle Periods*. Vol. 2 of *The Venture of Islam: Conscience and History in a World Civilization*. Chicago: University of Chicago Press.

Hoffman, Michael A. 1991. *Egypt Before the Pharaohs: The Prehistoric Foundations of Egyptian Civilization*, rev. ed. Austin: University of Texas Press.

Holborn, Hajo. 1959. *A History of Modern Germany*. Vol. 1, *The Reformation*. Princeton, N.J.: Princeton University Press.

Hollingsworth, Thomas H. 1965. *The Demography of the British Peerage*. London: London School of Economics.

Holmes, Steven A. 1996. "Income Disparity Between Poorest and Richest Rises." *New York Times*, 20 June, A1, A18.

Homer-Dixon, Thomas F., Jeffrey H. Boutwell, and George W. Rathjens. 1993. "Environmental Change and Violent Conflict." *Scientific American* 268, 2: 38–45.

Hopkins, Keith. 1978. *Conquerors and Slaves*. Cambridge, Eng.: Cambridge University Press.

Hosler, D., Jeremy A. Sabloff, and D. Runge. 1977. "Simulation Model Development: A Case Study of the Classic Maya Collapse." In *Social Process in Maya Prehistory*, ed. Norman Hammond. London: Academic Press.

Hourani, Albert. 1991. *A History of the Arab Peoples*. Cambridge, Mass.: Harvard University Press.

Hsu, Cho-yun. 1965. *Ancient China in Transition: An Analysis of Social Mobility, 722–222 B.C.* Stanford, Calif.: Stanford University Press.

———. 1980. *Han Agriculture: The Formation of Early Chinese Agrarian Economy (206 B.C.–A.D. 220)*. Ed. Jack L. Dull. Seattle: University of Washington Press.

Huang, Ray. 1990. *China: A Macro History*. Armonk, N.Y.: M. E. Sharpe.

Hucker, Charles O. 1975. *China's Imperial Past: An Introduction to Chinese History and Culture*. Stanford, Calif.: Stanford University Press.

Hughes, Malcolm K., and Henry F. Diaz. 1994. "Was There a 'Medieval Warm Period', and If So, Where and When?" In *The Medieval Warm Period*, ed. Malcolm K. Hughes and Henry F. Diaz. Dordrecht, The Netherlands: Kluwer Academic Publishers.

Humphreys, R. Stephen. 1991. *Islamic History: A Framework for Inquiry*, rev. ed. Princeton, N.J.: Princeton University Press.

Huntington, Samuel P. 1968. *Political Order in Changing Societies*. New Haven, Conn.: Yale University Press.
———. 1984. "Will More Countries Become Democratic?" *Political Science Quarterly* 99: 193-218.
———. 1991. *The Third Wave: Democratization in the Late Twentieth Century*. Norman: University of Oklahoma Press.
———. 1993a. "The Clash of Civilizations?" *Foreign Affairs* 72 (Summer): 22-49.
———. 1993b. "If Not Civilizations, What?: Paradigms of the Post-Cold War World." *Foreign Affairs* 72 (Nov.-Dec.): 186-94.
———. 1996. *The Clash of Civilizations and the Remaking of World Order*. New York: Simon and Schuster.
Hyams, Edward, and George Ordish. 1963. *The Last of the Incas: The Rise and Fall of an American Empire*. New York: Dorset Press.
Issar, Arie S. 1995. "Climatic Change and the History of the Middle East." *American Scientist* 83: 350-55.
Jacobsen, Thorkild. 1943. "Primitive Democracy in Ancient Mesopotamia." *Journal of Near Eastern Studies* 2: 159-72.
Jaggers, Keith, and Ted Robert Gurr. 1995. "Tracking Democracy's Third Wave with the Polity III Data." *Journal of Peace Research* 32: 469-82.
Jaynes, E. T. 1957. "Information Theory and Statistical Mechanics." *Physical Review* 106 (May): 620-30.
Jaynes, Gerald D., and Robin M. Williams, Jr., eds. 1989. *A Common Destiny: Blacks and American Society*. Washington, D.C.: National Academy Press.
Jeffrey, L. H. 1976. *Archaic Greece: The City-States ca. 700-500 B.C.* London: Methuen.
Johnson, Allen W., and Timothy Earle. 1987. *The Evolution of Human Societies: From Foraging Group to Agrarian State*. Stanford, Calif.: Stanford University Press.
Johnson, Gregory A. 1975. "Locational Analysis and the Investigation of Uruk Local Exchange Systems." In *Ancient Civilization and Trade*, ed. Jeremy A. Sabloff and C. C. Lamberg Karlovsky. Albuquerque: University of New Mexico Press.
Johnson, Norman L., and Samuel Kotz. 1970. *Continuous Univariate Distributions*, vol. 1. Boston: Houghton Mifflin.
———. 1977. *Urn Models and Their Application: An Approach to Modern Discrete Probability Theory*. New York: Wiley.
Jones, A. H. M. 1964. *The Later Roman Empire, 284-602: A Social, Economic, and Administrative Survey*, vol. 2. Baltimore: Johns Hopkins University Press.
———. 1966. *The Decline of the Ancient World*. New York: Longman.
———. 1986. *Athenian Democracy*. Baltimore: Johns Hopkins University Press.
Jürgens, Hartmut, Heinz-Otto Peitgen, and Dietmar Saupe. 1990. "The Language of Fractals." *Scientific American* 263 (2): 60-67.
Kaegi, Walter E. 1992. *Byzantium and the Early Islamic Conquests*. New York: Cambridge University Press.

Kaplan, Morton A. 1957. *System and Process in International Politics*. New York: Wiley.
Kasarda, John D. 1988. "Jobs, Migration, and Emerging Urban Mismatches." In *Urban Change and Poverty*, ed. Michael G. H. McGeary and Laurence E. Lynn, Jr. Washington, D.C.: National Academy Press.
Keep, John. 1995. "Watching the Russia-watchers." Review of *The Dream That Failed: Reflections on the Soviet Union*, by Walter Laqueur. In *The Times Literary Supplement* 4818 (Aug. 4): 8.
Kees, Hermann. 1977. *Ancient Egypt: A Cultural Topography*. Ed. T. G. H. James. Trans. Ian F. D. Morrow. Chicago: University of Chicago Press.
Keightley, David N., ed. 1983. *The Origins of Chinese Civilization*. Berkeley: University of California Press.
Kemp, Barry J. 1989. *Ancient Egypt: Anatomy of a Civilization*. London: Routledge.
Kernan, Beatrice. 1995. "Piet Mondrian." Museum of Modern Art Exhibition, Oct. 1, 1995–Jan. 23, 1996.
Kerr, Richard A. 1998. "The Hottest Year, by a Hair." *Science* 279 (5349): 315
Kleinbaum, David G., Lawrence L. Kupper, and Keith E. Muller. 1988. *Applied Regression Analysis and Other Multivariable Methods*, 2nd ed. Boston: PWS-Kent.
Kleinrock, Leonard. 1975. *Queuing Systems*. Vol. 1, *Theory*. New York: John Wiley.
Kramer, Samuel N. 1963. *The Sumerians: Their History, Culture, and Character*. Chicago: University of Chicago Press.
———. 1981. *History Begins at Sumer*, 3rd ed. Philadelphia: University of Pennsylvania Press.
LaFeber, Walter. 1983. *Inevitable Revolutions: The United States in Central America*. New York: W. W. Norton.
LaFree, Gary, and Kriss A. Drass. 1996. "The Effect of Changes in Intraracial Income Inequality and Educational Attainment on Changes in Arrest Rates for African Americans and Whites, 1957 to 1990." *American Sociological Review* 61: 614–34.
Landes, David S. 1998. *The Wealth and Poverty of Nations: Why Some Are So Rich and Some So Poor*. New York: Norton.
Lane, Frederic C. 1973. *Venice: A Maritime Republic*. Baltimore: Johns Hopkins University Press.
Langford, Paul. 1988. "The Eighteenth Century (1688–1789)." In *The Oxford History of Britain*, ed. Kenneth O. Morgan. New York: Oxford University Press.
Lanning, Edward P. 1967. *Peru Before the Incas*. Englewood Cliffs, N.J.: Prentice-Hall.
Lapham, Lewis H. 1988. *Money and Class in America: Notes and Observations on Our Civil Religion*. New York: Weidenfeld & Nicolson.
Lasch, Christopher. 1995. *The Revolt of the Elites and the Betrayal of Democracy*. New York: W. W. Norton.
Lasswell, Harold D. 1936. *Politics: Who Gets What, When, How*. New York: McGraw-Hill.
Laszlo, Ervin. 1987. *Evolution: The Grand Synthesis*. Boston: New Science Library.

Layne, Christopher. 1994. "Kant or Cant: The Myth of the Democratic Peace." *International Security* 19 (Fall): 5-49.

Lemann, Nicholas. 1991. *The Promised Land: The Great Black Migration and How It Changed America*. New York: Knopf.

Lenski, Gerhard. 1966. *Power and Privilege*. New York: McGraw-Hill.

Leventhal, Gerald S., Jurgis Karuza, Jr., and William R. Fry. 1980. "Beyond Fairness: A Theory of Allocation Preferences." In *Justice and Social Interaction*, ed. G. Mikula. New York: Springer-Verlag.

Lewis, Bernard. 1987. "Introduction." In *Islam, From the Prophet Muhammad to the Capture of Constantinople*. Vol. 1, *Politics and War*, ed. and trans. Bernard Lewis. New York: Oxford University Press.

———. 1993a. *The Arabs in History*, 6th ed. Oxford, Eng.: Oxford University Press.

———. 1993b. *Islam and the West*. New York: Oxford University Press.

Lichbach, Mark I. 1989. "An Evaluation of 'Does Economic Inequality Breed Political Conflict?' Studies." *World Politics* 41: 431-70.

———. 1990. "Will Rational People Rebel Against Inequality?: Samson's Choice." *American Journal of Political Science* 34: 1049-76.

———. 1995. *The Rebel's Dilemma*. Ann Arbor: University of Michigan Press.

Lijphart, Arend. 1984. *Democracies: Patterns of Majoritarian and Consensus Government in Twenty-One Countries*. New Haven, Conn.: Yale University Press.

Lim, Richard. 1995. *Public Disputation, Power, and Social Order in Late Antiquity*. Berkeley: University of California Press.

Lindblom, Charles E. 1977. *Politics and Markets: The World's Political-Economic Systems*. New York: Basic Books.

Lintott, Andrew. 1982. *Violence, Civil Strife, and Revolution in the Classical City*. London: Croom Helm.

Lipset, Seymour M. 1959. "Some Social Requisites of Democracy: Economic Development and Political Legitimacy." *American Political Science Review* 53: 69-105.

Livermore, Harold. 1966. *A History of Spain*, 2nd ed. London: George Allen & Unwin.

Löfstedt, Ragnar. 1995. "Hot Tips for a Tardy Planet." *The Times Higher Education Supplement* 21 July, 21.

London, Perry. 1970. "The Rescuers: Motivational Hypotheses About Christians Who Saved Jews from the Nazis." In *Altruism and Helping Behavior*, ed. Jacqueline Macaulay and Leonard Berkowitz. New York: Academic Press.

Lot, Ferdinand. 1961. *The End of the Ancient World and the Beginnings of the Middle Ages*. New York: Harper Torchbooks.

Lotka, Alfred J. 1939. *Théorie analytique des associations biologiques*, vol. 2. Paris: Actualités scientifiques et industrielles, No. 780.

Lowe, John W. G. 1985. *The Dynamics of Apocalypse: A Systems Simulation of the Classic Maya Collapse*. Albuquerque: University of New Mexico Press.

Lye, Keith, and Shirley Carpenter. 1987. *Encyclopedia of World Geography*. New York: Dorset.

Mackinder, Halford J. 1919. *Democratic Ideals and Reality*. London: Constable.
MacMullen, Ramsay. 1988. *Corruption and the Decline of Rome*. New Haven, Conn.: Yale University Press.
Mahan, Alfred T. 1890. *The Influence of Sea Power Upon History, 1660-1783*. Boston: Little, Brown.
Major, J. Russell. 1980. *Representative Government in Early Modern France*. New Haven, Conn.: Yale University Press.
Malefakis, Edward E. 1970. *Agrarian Reform and Peasant Revolution in Spain: Origins of the Civil War*. New Haven, Conn.: Yale University Press.
Mallory, J. P. 1989. *In Search of the Indo-Europeans: Language, Archaeology, and Myth*. London: Thames and Hudson.
Mandelbrot, Benoit B. 1960. "The Pareto-Lévy Law and the Distribution of Income." *International Economic Review* 1: 79-106.
———. 1961. "Stable Paretian Random Functions and the Multiplicative Variation of Income." *Econometrica* 29: 517-43.
———. 1982. *The Fractal Geometry of Nature*. San Francisco: Freeman.
Mann, Michael. 1986. *The Sources of Social Power: A History of Power from the Beginning to A.D. 1760*, vol. 1. New York: Cambridge University Press.
Mansfield, Edward, and Jack Snyder. 1995. "Democratization and War." *Foreign Affairs* 74 (Summer): 79-97.
Maoz, Zeev, and Nasrin Abdolali. 1989. "Regime Types and International Conflict, 1816-1976." *Journal of Conflict Resolution* 33: 3-35.
Maoz, Zeev, and Bruce Russett. 1993. "Normative and Structural Causes of Democratic Peace, 1946-1986." *American Political Science Review* 87: 624-38.
Marcus, Joyce. 1973. "Territorial Organization of the Lowland Classic Maya." *Science* 180: 911-16.
———. 1976. "The Iconography of Militarism at Monte Albán and Neighboring Sites in the Valley of Oaxaca." In *The Origins of Religious Art and Iconography in Pre-Classic Mesoamerica*, ed. Henry B. Nicholson. Los Angeles: Latin American Center, University of California, Los Angeles.
———. 1992. *Mesoamerican Writing Systems: Propaganda, Myth, and History in Four Ancient Civilizations*. Princeton, N.J.: Princeton University Press.
Martens, Georg F. von. 1795. *A Summary of the Law of Nations*. Trans. William Cobbett. Philadelphia: Thomas Bradford.
Martines, Lauro. 1988. *Power and Imagination: City-States in Renaissance Italy*. Baltimore: Johns Hopkins University Press.
Matthew, H. C. G. 1988. "The Liberal Age (1851-1914)." In *The Oxford History of Britain*, ed. Kenneth O. Morgan. Oxford, Eng.: Oxford University Press.
Matz, F. 1973. "The Maturity of Minoan Civilization." In *The Cambridge Ancient History*. Vol. 2, part 1, *History of the Middle East and the Aegean Region ca. 1800-1380 B.C.*, ed. I. E. S. Edwards, C. J. Gadd, N. G. L. Hammond, and E. Sollberger. Cambridge, Eng.: Cambridge University Press.

McAlister, Lyle N. 1984. *Spain and Portugal in the New World, 1492-1700*. Minneapolis: University of Minnesota Press.

McKay, Derek, and H. M. Scott. 1983. *The Rise of the Great Powers: 1648-1815*. London: Longmans.

McNeill, William H. 1963. *The Rise of the West: A History of the Human Community*. Chicago: University of Chicago Press.

———. 1976. *Plagues and Peoples*. Garden City, N.Y.: Anchor Press.

———. 1982. *The Pursuit of Power*. Chicago: University of Chicago Press.

Menezes, S. L. 1993. *Fidelity and Honour: The Indian Army from the Seventeenth to the Twenty-First Century*. New Delhi: Viking.

Métraux, Alfred. 1970. *The History of the Incas*. Trans. George Ordish. New York: Schocken Books.

Midlarsky, Elizabeth, and William Suda. 1978. "Some Antecedents of Altruism in Children: Theoretical and Empirical Perspectives." *Psychological Reports* 43: 187-208.

Midlarsky, Manus I. 1978. "Analyzing Diffusion and Contagion Effects: The Urban Disorders of the 1960s." *American Political Science Review* 72: 996-1008.

———. 1979. "Random and Systematic Inequality: A Cross-National Analysis." Paper delivered at the Annual Meeting of the American Political Science Association, Washington, D.C.

———. 1982. "Scarcity and Inequality: Prologue to the Onset of Mass Revolution." *Journal of Conflict Resolution* 26: 3-38.

———. 1983. "The Balance of Power as a 'Just' Historical System." *Polity* 16: 181-200.

———. 1984. "Political Stability of Two-Party and Multiparty Systems: Probabilistic Bases for the Comparison of Party Systems." *American Political Science Review* 78: 929-51.

———. 1985. "Helping During the Holocaust: The Role of Political, Theological, and Socioeconomic Identifications." *Humboldt Journal of Social Relations* 13 (Fall-Winter and Spring-Summer): 285-305.

———. 1988a. *The Onset of World War*. Boston: Unwin Hyman.

———. 1988b. "Rulers and the Ruled: Patterned Inequality and the Onset of Mass Political Violence." *American Political Science Review* 82: 491-509.

———. 1989. "A Distribution of Extreme Inequality with Applications to Conflict Behavior: A Geometric Derivation of the Pareto Distribution." *Mathematical and Computer Modelling* 12 (No. 4-5): 577-87.

———. 1992a. "The Origins of Democracy in Agrarian Society: Land Inequality and Political Rights." *Journal of Conflict Resolution* 36: 454-77.

———. 1992b. "Reversing the Causal Arrow: Domestic and International Sources of Early Democracy." Paper delivered at the 1992 Annual Meeting of the American Political Science Association, Chicago.

———. 1993. "Hierarchical Equilibria and the Long-Run Instability of Multipolar Systems." In *Handbook of War Studies*, ed. Manus I. Midlarsky. Ann Arbor: University of Michigan Press.

———. 1995. "Environmental Influences on Democracy: Aridity, Warfare, and a Reversal of the Causal Arrow." *Journal of Conflict Resolution* 39: 224–62.

———. 1997. "Systemic War in the Former Yugoslavia." In *Wars in the Midst of Peace*, eds. David Carment and Patrick James. Pittsburgh. Pa.: University of Pittsburgh Press.

———. 1998. "Democracy and Islam: Implications for Civilizational Conflict and the Democratic Peace." *International Studies Quarterly* 42: 485–511.

Midlarsky, Manus I., and Ted Hopf. 1993. "Polarity and International Stability." *American Political Science Review* 87: 173–80.

Midlarsky, Manus I., and Kenneth Roberts. 1985. "Class, State, and Revolution in Central America: Nicaragua and El Salvador Compared." *Journal of Conflict Resolution* 29: 163–93.

Miller, Abraham H., Louis H. Bolce, and Mark Halligan. 1977. "The J-Curve Theory and the Black Urban Riots: An Empirical Test of Progressive Relative Deprivation Theory." *American Political Science Review* 71: 964–82.

Miller, Arthur G. 1986. "From the Maya Margins: Images of Postclassic Politics." In *Late Lowland Maya Civilization: Classic to Postclassic*, ed. Jeremy A. Sabloff and E. Wyllys Andrews V. Albuquerque: University of New Mexico Press.

Miller, J. Maxwell, and John H. Hayes. 1986. *A History of Ancient Israel and Judah*. Philadelphia: Westminster Press.

Millon, René. 1988. "The Last Years of Teotihuacán Dominance." In *The Collapse of Ancient States and Civilizations*, ed. Norman Yoffee and George L. Cowgill. Tucson: University of Arizona Press.

Mintz, Alex, and Nehemia Geva. 1993. "Why Don't Democracies Fight Each Other?: An Experimental Study." *Journal of Conflict Resolution* 37: 484–503.

Modelski, George. 1983. "Long Cycles of World Leadership." In *Contending Approaches to World System Analysis*, ed. William R. Thompson. Beverly Hills, Calif.: Sage.

Moore, Barrington, Jr. 1966. *Social Origins of Dictatorship and Democracy*. Boston: Beacon Press.

Morgan, T. Clifton, and Sally H. Campbell. 1991. "Domestic Structure, Decisional Constraints, and War." *Journal of Conflict Resolution* 35: 187–211.

Morley, Sylvanus G. 1946. *The Ancient Maya*. Stanford, Calif.: Stanford University Press.

Morley, Sylvanus G., and George W. Brainerd. 1983. *The Ancient Maya*, 4th ed. Rev. Robert J. Sharer. Stanford, Calif.: Stanford University Press.

Morrill, John. 1985. "Government and Politics: England and Wales, 1625–1701." In *The Cambridge Historical Encyclopedia of Great Britain and Ireland*, ed. Christopher Haigh. Cambridge, Eng.: Cambridge University Press.

———. 1988. "The Stuarts (1603–1688)." In *The Oxford History of Britain*, ed. Kenneth O. Morgan. New York: Oxford University Press.

Morris, Ian. 1987. *Burial and Ancient Society: The Rise of the Greek City-State*. Cambridge, Eng.: Cambridge University Press.

Morrison, Donald G., Robert C. Mitchell, and John N. Paden. 1989. *Black Africa: A Comparative Handbook*, 2nd ed. New York: Paragon House.

Mosca, Gaetano. 1939. *The Ruling Class*, ed. Arthur Livingston. New York: McGraw Hill.
Moseley, Michael E. 1975. *The Maritime Foundations of Andean Civilization*. Menlo Park, Calif.: Benjamin Cummings.
———. 1992. *The Incas and their Ancestors: The Archaeology of Peru*. London: Thames and Hudson.
Muller, Edward N. 1985. "Income Inequality, Regime Repressiveness, and Political Violence." *American Sociological Review* 50: 47-61.
———. 1988. "Democracy, Economic Development, and Income Inequality." *American Sociological Review* 53: 50-68.
Muller, Edward N., and Mitchell A. Seligson. 1987. "Inequality and Insurgency." *American Political Science Review* 81: 425-51.
Muller, Edward N., Mitchell A. Seligson, Hung-der Fu, and Manus I. Midlarsky. 1989. "Land Inequality and Political Violence." *American Political Science Review* 83: 577-95.
Muller, Herbert J. 1961. *Freedom in the Ancient World*. London: Secker & Warburg.
Murray, Charles, and Richard J. Herrnstein. 1994. "Race, Genes, and I.Q.: An Apologia." *The New Republic* 211 (Oct. 31): 27-37.
Nagel, Jack H. 1974. "Inequality and Discontent: A Nonlinear Hypothesis." *World Politics* 26: 453-72.
———. 1976. "Erratum." *World Politics* 28: 315.
Negev, Avraham. 1986. *The Archaeological Encyclopedia of the Holy Land*. Nashville, Tenn.: Thomas Nelson.
Nejad, Hassan M. 1986. "Inequality in an Urban Revolution: The Case of Iran." In *Inequality and Contemporary Revolutions*. Monograph Series in World Affairs, vol. 22, bk. 2, ed. Manus I. Midlarsky. Denver: Graduate School of International Studies, University of Denver.
Neshamit, Sarah. 1977. "Rescue in Lithuania During the Nazi Occupation." In *Rescue Attempts During the Holocaust*, ed. Yisrael Gutman and Efraim Zuroff. Jerusalem: Yad Vashem.
Nicholas, David. 1992. *The Evolution of the Medieval World: Society, Government, and Thought in Europe, 312-1500*. London: Longman.
Nicholson, E. W. 1970. *Preaching to the Exiles*. Oxford: B. H. Blackwell.
Nicolle, David. 1994. *Yarmuk, 636 A.D.: The Muslim Conquest of Syria*. London: Reed International.
Niles, Susan A. 1987. *Callachaca: Style and Status in an Inca Community*. Iowa City: University of Iowa Press.
Nissen, Hans J. 1988. *The Early History of the Ancient Near East: 9000-2000 B.C.* Trans. Elizabeth Lutzeier and Kenneth Northcott. Chicago: University of Chicago Press.
Norton, Augustus R. 1995. "The Challenge of Inclusion in the Middle East." *Current History* 94 (Jan.): 1-6.
Oates, Joan. 1977. "Mesopotamian Social Organization: Archaeological and Philologi-

cal Evidence." In *The Evolution of Social Systems*, ed. J. Friedman and M. J. Rowlands. London: Duckworth.

Ober, Josiah. 1989. *Mass and Elite in Democratic Athens: Rhetoric, Ideology, and the Power of the People*. Princeton, N.J.: Princeton University Press.

Oliner, Samuel P., and Pearl M. Oliner. 1988. *The Altruistic Personality: Rescuers of Jews in Nazi Europe*. New York: The Free Press.

Olson, Mancur, Jr. 1965. *The Logic of Collective Action: Public Goods and the Theory of Groups*. Cambridge, Mass.: Harvard University Press.

———. 1987. "Why Some Welfare-State Redistribution to the Poor Is a Great Idea." In *Democracy and Public Choice: Essays in Honor of Gordon Tullock*, ed. Charles K. Rowley. Oxford, Eng.: Basil Blackwell.

Olzak, Susan, Suzanne Shanahan, and Elizabeth H. McEneaney. 1996. "Poverty, Segregation, and Race Riots: 1960 to 1993." *American Sociological Review* 61: 590–613.

Oppenheim, A. Leo. 1977. *Ancient Mesopotamia*, rev. ed. Chicago: University of Chicago Press.

Oquist, Paul H. 1980. *Violence, Conflict, and Politics in Colombia*. New York: Academic Press.

Ostrogorsky, George. 1969. *History of the Byzantine State*. Trans. Joan Hussey. New Brunswick, N.J.: Rutgers University Press.

Owen, John M. 1994. "How Liberalism Produces Democratic Peace." *International Security* 19 (Fall): 87–125.

Pagels, Heinz R. 1982. *The Cosmic Code*. New York: Bantam Books.

Pal, Agaton P. 1963. *The Resources, Levels of Living, and Aspirations of Rural Households in Negros Oriental*. Diliman, Quezon City: Community Development Research Council, University of the Philippines.

Paldiel, Mordecai. 1993. *The Path of the Righteous: Gentile Rescuers of Jews During the Holocaust*. Hoboken, N.J.: KTAV Publishing House.

Pareto, Vilfredo. 1935. *The Mind and Society: A Treatise on General Sociology*, vol. 1. Ed. Arthur Livingston. Trans. Andrew Bongiorno and Arthur Livingston. New York: Dover Publications.

———. 1964. *Cours d'économie politique*, ed. G. H. Bousquet and Giovanni Busino. Geneva: Droz.

Park, Kun H. 1986. "Income Inequality and Political Violence." In *Inequality and Contemporary Revolutions*, Monograph Series in World Affairs, vol. 22, bk. 2, ed. Manus I. Midlarsky. Denver: Graduate School of International Studies, University of Denver.

Parvin, Manoucher. 1973. "Economic Determinants of Political Unrest: An Econometric Approach." *Journal of Conflict Resolution* 17: 271–96.

Pasternak, Burton. 1978. "The Sociology of Irrigation: Two Taiwanese Villages." In *Studies in Chinese Society*, ed. Arthur P. Wolf. Stanford, Calif.: Stanford University Press.

Patterson, Thomas C., and Christine W. Gailey, eds. 1987. *Power Relations and State Formation*. Washington, D.C.: American Anthropological Association.

Paulsen, A. C. 1981. "The Archaeology of the Absurd: Comments on 'Cultural Materialism, Split Inheritance, and the Expansion of Ancient Peruvian Empires.'" *American Antiquity* 46: 31–7.

Payne, James L. 1989. *Why Nations Arm.* Oxford, Eng.: Basil Blackwell.

Perotti, Roberto. 1996. "Growth, Income Distribution, and Democracy: What the Data Say." *Journal of Economic Growth.* 1: 149–87.

Peterson, Wallace C. 1994. *Silent Depression: The Fate of the American Dream.* New York: W. W. Norton Press.

Pineda, Rosa F. 1988. "The Late Preceramic and Initial Period." In *Peruvian Prehistory: An Overview of Pre-Inca and Inca Society*, ed. Richard W. Keatinge. Cambridge, Eng.: Cambridge University Press.

Porter, Bruce D. 1994. *War and the Rise of the State: The Military Foundations of Modern Politics.* New York: The Free Press.

Proskouriakoff, Tatiana. 1960. "Historical Implications of a Pattern of Dates at Piedras Negras, Guatemala." *American Antiquity* 25: 454–75.

———. 1963. "Historical Data in the Inscriptions of Yaxchilan, Part I." *Estudios de Cultura Maya* 3: 149–67. Mexico: Universidad Nacional Autónoma de México.

———. 1964. "Historical Data in the Inscriptions of Yaxchilan, Part II." *Estudios de Cultura Maya* 4: 177–201. Mexico: Universidad Nacional Autónoma de México.

———. 1993. *Maya History.* Ed. Rosemary A. Joyce. Austin: University of Texas Press.

Pulleyblank, Edwin G. 1984. *Middle Chinese: A Study in Historical Phonology.* Vancouver: University of British Columbia Press.

Putnam, Robert D. 1993. *Making Democracy Work: Civic Traditions in Modern Italy.* Princeton, N.J.: Princeton University Press.

Quilter, Jeffrey, and Terry Stocker. 1983. "Subsistence Economies and the Origins of Andean Complex Societies." *American Anthropologist* 85: 545–62.

Raven, Susan. 1993. *Rome in Africa*, 3rd ed. London: Routledge.

Rawls, John. 1971. *A Theory of Justice.* Cambridge, Mass.: Harvard University Press.

Ray, James L. 1995. *Democracy and International Conflict: An Evaluation of the Democratic Peace Proposition.* Columbia.: University of South Carolina Press.

Raymond, J. Scott. 1981. "The Maritime Foundations of Andean Civilization: A Reconsideration of the Evidence." *American Antiquity* 46: 806–21.

Renfrew, Colin. 1972. *The Emergence of Civilization: The Cyclades and the Aegean in the Third Millennium B.C.* London: Methuen.

———. 1982. "Polity and Power: Interaction, Intensification, and Exploitation. In *An Island Polity: The Archaeology of Exploitation in Melos*, ed. Colin Renfrew and Malcolm W. Wagstaff. Cambridge, Eng.: Cambridge University Press.

———. 1986. "Introduction: Peer Polity Interaction and Socio-Political Change." In *Peer Polity Interaction and Socio-Political Change*, ed. Colin Renfrew and John F. Cherry. Cambridge, Eng.: Cambridge University Press.

Renfrew, Colin, and John F. Cherry, eds. 1986. *Peer Polity Interaction and Socio-Political Change.* Cambridge, Eng.: Cambridge University Press.

Rice, Prudence M. 1986. "The Peten Postclassic: Perspectives from the Central Peten Lakes." In *Late Lowland Maya Civilization: Classic to Postclassic*, ed. Jeremy A. Sabloff and E. Wyllys Andrews V. Albuquerque: University of New Mexico Press.

Richardson, Lewis F. 1960. *Statistics of Deadly Quarrels*. Pittsburgh: Boxwood.

Riots, Civil and Criminal Disorders. 1967. Hearings Before the Permanent Subcommittee on Investigations of the Committee on Government Operations, United States Senate, 90th Congress, First Session, part I. Washington, D.C.: U.S. Government Printing Office.

Roberts, C. Paul, and Takako Kohda, eds. 1967. *Statistical Abstract of Latin America, 1966*. Los Angeles: University of California.

Roberts, Kenneth, and Manus I. Midlarsky. 1986. "Inequality, the State, and Revolution in Central America." In *Inequality and Contemporary Revolutions*, ed. Manus I. Midlarsky. Denver: Graduate School of International Studies, University of Denver.

Rosenthal, A. M. 1995. "American Class Struggle." *New York Times*, 21 March, 21(A).

Rostovtzeff, M. 1928. *A History of the Ancient World*, vol. 2. Trans. J. D. Duff. Oxford, Eng.: Clarendon Press.

———. 1960. *Rome*. Ed. Elias J. Bickerman. Trans. J. D. Duff. New York: Oxford University Press.

Rowe, John H. 1985. "La Constitución Inca del Cuzco." *Histórica* 9: 35–73.

Rubinson, Richard, and Dan Quinlan. 1977. "Democracy and Social Inequality: A Reanalysis." *American Sociological Review* 42: 611–23.

Rucker, Rudy. 1982. *Infinity and the Mind: The Science and Philosophy of the Infinite*. New York: Bantam.

Rueschemeyer, Dietrich, Evelyne H. Stephens, and John D. Stephens. 1992. *Capitalist Development and Democracy*. Chicago: University of Chicago Press.

Rummel, Rudolph J. 1983. "Libertarianism and International Violence." *Journal of Conflict Resolution* 27: 27–71.

Runnels, Curtis N. 1995. "Environmental Degradation in Ancient Greece." *Scientific American* 272 (3): 96–99.

Russett, Bruce M. 1964. "Inequality and Instability: The Relation of Land Tenure to Politics." *World Politics* 16: 442–54.

———. 1993. *Grasping the Democratic Peace: Principles for a Post-Cold War World*. Princeton, N.J.: Princeton University Press.

Russett, Bruce M., and Harvey Starr. Forthcoming. "From Democratic Peace to Kantian Peace: Democracy and Conflict in the International System." In *Handbook of War Studies II*, ed. Manus I. Midlarsky. Ann Arbor: University of Michigan Press.

Sabloff, Jeremy A. 1990. *The New Archaeology and the Ancient Maya*. New York: Scientific American Library.

Sabloff, Jeremy A., and Gordon R. Willey. 1967. "The Collapse of Maya Civilization in the Southern Lowlands: A Consideration of History and Process." *Southwestern Journal of Anthropology* 23: 311–36.

Saggs, H. W. F. 1989. *Civilization Before Greece and Rome*. New Haven, Conn.: Yale University Press.

Sahota, Gian S. 1978. "Theories of Personal Income Distribution: A Survey." *Journal of Economic Literature* 16: 1-55.

Samuelsson, Kurt. 1968. *From Great Power to Welfare State: 300 Years of Swedish Social Development*. London: Allen & Unwin.

Sanders, William T. 1973. "The Cultural Ecology of the Lowland Maya: A Reevaluation." In *The Classic Maya Collapse*, ed. T. Patrick Culbert. Albuquerque: University of New Mexico Press.

———. 1977. "Environmental Heterogeneity and the Evolution of Lowland Maya Civilization." In *The Origins of Maya Civilization*, ed. R. E. W. Adams. Albuquerque: University of New Mexico Press.

Sanders, William T., and Barbara J. Price. 1968. *Mesoamerica: The Evolution of a Civilization*. New York: Random House.

Saul, Frank P. 1973. "Disease in the Maya Area: The Pre-Columbian Evidence." In *The Classic Maya Collapse*, ed. T. Patrick Culbert. Albuquerque: University of New Mexico Press.

Schele, Linda, and David Freidel. 1990. *A Forest of Kings: The Untold Story of the Ancient Maya*. New York: William Morrow.

Schoville, Keith N. 1978. *Biblical Archaeology in Focus*. Grand Rapids, Mich.: Baker Book House.

Schwartz, Barry. 1983. "George Washington and the Whig Conception of Heroic Leadership." *American Sociological Review* 48: 18-33.

Schweller, Randall L. 1992. "Domestic Structure and Preventive War: Are Democracies More Pacific?" *World Politics* 44: 235-69.

Scott, Franklin D. 1988. *Sweden: The Nation's History*, enlarged ed. Carbondale: Southern Illinois University Press.

Scullard, Howard H. 1991. *A History of the Roman World: 753-146 B.C.*, 4th ed. London: Routledge.

Sen, Amartya. 1997. *On Economic Inequality*, enlarged ed. Oxford, Eng.: Clarendon Press.

Service, Elman R. 1975. *Origins of the State and Civilization: The Process of Cultural Evolution*. New York: W. W. Norton.

Sharer, Robert J. 1977. "The Maya Collapse Revisited: Internal and External Perspectives." In *Social Process in Maya Prehistory: Studies in Honour of Sir Eric Thompson*, ed. Norman Hammond. London: Academic Press.

———. 1994. *The Ancient Maya*, 5th ed. Stanford, Calif.: Stanford University Press.

Shirley, Edward G. 1995. "Is Iran's Present Algeria's Future?" *Foreign Affairs* 74 (May-June): 28-44.

Sigelman, Lee, and Miles Simpson. 1977. "A Cross-National Test of the Linkage Between Economic Inequality and Political Violence." *Journal of Conflict Resolution* 21: 105-28.

Sijes, B. A. 1977. "Several Observations Concerning the Position of the Jews in Occupied Holland During World War II." In *Rescue Attempts During the Holocaust*, ed. Yisrael Gutman and Efraim Zuroff. Jerusalem: Yad Vashem.

Simon, Julian L. 1990. *Population Matters: People, Resources, Environment, and Immigration*. New Brunswick, N.J.: Transaction.

Sisk, Timothy D. 1992. *Islam and Democracy: Religion, Politics, and Power in the Middle East*. Washington, D.C.: United States Institute of Peace Press.

Skinner, G. William. 1978. "Cities and the Hierarchy of Local Systems." In *Studies in Chinese Society*, ed. Arthur P. Wolf. Stanford, Calif.: Stanford University Press.

Skocpol, Theda. 1979. *States and Social Revolutions: A Comparative Analysis of France, Russia, and China*. Cambridge, Eng.: Cambridge University Press.

Slack, Paul. 1985. "A Divided Society." In *The Cambridge Historical Encyclopedia of Great Britain and Ireland*, ed. Christopher Haigh. New York: Cambridge University Press.

Smith, Michael E., and Mary G. Hodge. 1994. "An Introduction to Late Postclassic Economies and Polities." In *Economies and Polities in the Aztec Realm*. Studies on Culture and Society, vol. 6, ed. Mary G. Hodge and Michael E. Smith. Albany, N.Y.: Institute for Mesoamerican Studies.

Snodgrass, Anthony M. 1977. *Archaeology and the Rise of the Greek State*. Cambridge, Eng.: Cambridge University Press.

———. 1986. "Interaction by Design: the Greek City State." In *Peer Polity Interaction and Socio-Political Change*, ed. Colin Renfrew and John F. Cherry. Cambridge, Eng.: Cambridge University Press.

Soisson, Pierre, and Janine Soisson. 1987. *Life of the Aztecs in Ancient Mexico*. Trans. David Macrae. Barcelona: Productions Liber.

Sourdel, Dominique. 1970. "The Abbasid Caliphate." In *The Cambridge History of Islam*. Vol. 1, *The Central Islamic Lands*, ed. P. M. Holt, Ann K. S. Lambton, and Bernard Lewis. Cambridge, Eng.: Cambridge University Press.

Sparrow, Colin. 1982. *The Lorenz Equations: Bifurcations, Chaos, and Strange Attractors*. New York: Springer.

Speck, William A. 1985. "Disorder to Stability: Britain and Ireland, 1625-1783." In *The Cambridge Historical Encyclopedia of Great Britain and Ireland*, ed. Christopher Haigh. New York: Cambridge University Press.

Spence, Michael W. 1984. "Craft Production and Polity in Early Teotihuacan." In *Trade and Exchange in Early Mesoamerica*, ed. Kenneth G. Hirth. Albuquerque: University of New Mexico Press.

Spring, David. 1977. "Landed Elites Compared." In *European Landed Elites in the Nineteenth Century*, ed. David Spring. Baltimore: Johns Hopkins University Press.

Sprout, Harold, and Margaret Sprout. 1962. *Foundations of International Politics*. Princeton, N.J.: Van Nostrand.

Spufford, Margaret. 1974. *Contrasting Communities: English Villages in the Sixteenth and Seventeenth Centuries*. Cambridge, Eng.: Cambridge University Press.

———. 1976. "Peasant Inheritance Customs and Land Distribution in Cambridgeshire from the Sixteenth to the Eighteenth Centuries." In *Family and Inheritance: Rural Society in Western Europe 1200–1800*, ed. Jack Goody, Joan Thirsk, and E. P. Thompson. Cambridge, Eng: Cambridge University Press.

Stager, Lawrence E. 1996. "The Fury of Babylon: Ashkelon and the Archaeology of Destruction." *Biblical Archaeology Review* 22: 56–69, 76–77.

Starr, Chester G. 1982. *The Roman Empire, 27 B.C.–A.D. 476: A Study in Survival*. New York: Oxford University Press.

———. 1986. *Individual and Community: The Rise of the Polis, 800–500 B.C.* New York: Oxford University Press.

———. 1991. *The Origins of Greek Civilization: 1100–650 B.C.* New York: Norton.

Starr, Harvey. 1991. "Democratic Dominoes: Diffusion Approaches to the Spread of Democracy in the International System." *Journal of Conflict Resolution* 35: 356–81.

Starr, Harvey, and Benjamin A. Most. 1978. "A Return Journey: Richardson, 'Frontiers,' and Wars in the 1946–1965 Era." *Journal of Conflict Resolution* 22: 441–67.

Statesman's Year-book: Statistical and Historical Annual of the States of the World for the Year 1914. 1914. London, Macmillan.

Statesman's Year-book: Statistical and Historical Annual of the States of the World for the Year 1983–84. 1983. New York: St. Martin's Press.

Statesman's Year-book: Statistical and Historical Annual of the States of the World for the Year 1990–91. 1990. New York: St. Martin's Press.

Statesman's Year-book: Statistical and Historical Annual of the States of the World for the Year 1991–92. 1991. New York: St. Martin's Press.

Statistik des Deutschen Reichs. 1936–37, 1944. Berlin: Verlag für Sozialpolitik, Wirtschaft und Statistik.

Steindl, Josef. 1965. *Random Processes and the Growth of Firms: A Study of the Pareto Law*. New York: Hafner.

Steiner, Jean-François. 1967. *Treblinka*. Trans. Helen Weaver. New York: Simon and Schuster.

Stern, Fritz. 1977. "Prussia." In *European Landed Elites in the Nineteenth Century*, ed. David Spring. Baltimore: Johns Hopkins University Press.

Stevens, William K. 1998. "New Evidence Finds This Is Warmest Century in 600 Years." *New York Times*, 28 April, F3.

Stockton, David. 1990. *The Classical Athenian Democracy*. New York: Oxford University Press.

Stone, Elizabeth C., and Paul Zimansky. 1995. "The Tapestry of Power in a Mesopotamian City." *Scientific American* 272 (4): 118–23.

Stone, Lawrence. 1965. *The Crisis of the Aristocracy, 1558–1641*. Oxford, Eng.: Oxford University Press.

Strayer, Joseph R. 1970. *On the Medieval Origins of the Modern State*. Princeton, N.J.: Princeton University Press.

Summers, Robert, and Alan Heston. 1984. "Improved International Comparisons of

Real Product and Its Composition: 1950-1980." *Review of Income and Wealth* 30: 207-62.

Tabacco, Giovanni. 1989. *The Struggle for Power in Medieval Italy: Structures of Political Rule*. Trans. Rosalind B. Jensen. Cambridge, Eng.: Cambridge University Press.

Tainter, Joseph A. 1988. *The Collapse of Complex Societies*. Cambridge, Eng.: Cambridge University Press.

Tanter, Raymond, and Manus I. Midlarsky. 1967. "A Theory of Revolution." *Journal of Conflict Resolution* 11: 264-80.

Tawney, Richard H. 1960. "The Gentry Take the Power to Which Their Economic Success Entitles Them." In *The Origins of the English Civil War: Conspiracy, Crusade, or Class Conflict?*, ed. Philip A. M. Taylor. Lexington, Mass.: D. C. Heath.

Taylor, Charles L., and Michael C. Hudson. 1972. *World Handbook of Political and Social Indicators*, 2nd ed. New Haven, Conn.: Yale University Press.

Taylor, Charles L., and David A. Jodice. 1983. *World Handbook of Political and Social Indicators*, 3rd ed, 2 vols. New Haven, Conn.: Yale University Press.

Taylor, William B. 1972. *Landlord and Peasant in Colonial Oaxaca*. Stanford, Calif.: Stanford University Press.

Thompson, J. Eric S. 1954. *The Rise and Fall of Maya Civilization*. Norman: University of Oklahoma Press.

———. 1970. *Maya History and Religion*. Norman: University of Oklahoma Press.

Thurow, Lester C. 1995. "Companies Merge; Families Break Up." *New York Times* 3 September, E11.

Tierney, John. 1990. "Betting the Planet." *New York Times Magazine*, 2 Dec., 52-82.

Tilly, Charles. 1990. *Coercion, Capital, and European States, A.D. 990-1990*. Oxford, Eng.: Basil Blackwell.

———. 1998. *Durable Inequality*. Berkeley: University of California Press.

Townsend, Richard F. 1992. *The Aztecs*. London: Thames and Hudson.

Toynbee, Arnold J. 1946. *A Study of History* (abridgment of vols. 1-6). New York: Oxford University Press.

Tozer, Henry F. 1974. *Lectures on the Geography of Greece*. Chicago: Ares.

Treadgold, Warren. 1988. *The Byzantine Revival, 780-842*. Stanford, Calif.: Stanford University Press.

Trevor-Roper, Hugh R. 1960. "Poor and Discontented Gentry Rebel Against Established Institutions." In *The Origins of the English Civil War: Conspiracy, Crusade, or Class Conflict?*, ed. Philip A. M. Taylor. Lexington, Mass.: D. C. Heath.

Trigger, Bruce G. 1965. *History and Settlement in Lower Nubia*. New Haven, Conn.: Yale University Publications in Anthropology, No. 69.

Turan, Ilter. 1991. "Religion and Political Culture in Turkey." In *Islam in Modern Turkey: Religion, Politics and Literature in a Secular State*, ed. R. Tapper. London: I. B. Tauris.

Uchitelle, Louis. 1998. "The Middle Class: Winning in Politics, Losing in Life." *New York Times*, 19 July, Section 4, pp. 1, 16.

United Nations. 1982. *Demographic Yearbook 1980*. New York: United Nations Department of International Economic and Social Affairs, Statistical Office.

Vanhanen, Tatu. 1990. *The Process of Democratization: A Comparative Study of 147 States, 1980–88*. New York: Taylor and Francis.

Vattel, Emmerich de. 1870. *The Law of Nations*, vol. 3. Philadelphia: T. and J. W. Johnson.

Vinogradov, I. V. 1991. "The Predynastic Period and the Early and the Old Kingdoms in Egypt." In *Early Antiquity*, ed. I. M. Diakonoff. Chicago: University of Chicago Press.

Viorst, Milton. 1995. "Sudan's Islamic Experiment." *Foreign Affairs* 74 (May–June): 45–58.

Virginia Gazette. 1775. 1249 (15 July):3.

Vogt, Evon Z. 1971. "The Genetic Model and Maya Cultural Development." In *Desarrollo Cultural de los Mayas*, ed. Evon Z. Vogt and Aberto Ruz L., 2nd ed. Mexico City: Universidad Nacional Autonoma de Mexico, Centro de Estudios Mayas.

Wakeman, Frederic, Jr. 1975. *The Fall of Imperial China*. New York: Free Press.

———. 1979. "The Shun Interregnum of 1644." In *From Ming to Ch'ing: Conquest, Region, and Continuity in Seventeenth-Century China*, ed. Jonathan D. Spence and John E. Wills, Jr. New Haven, Conn.: Yale University Press.

Wallas, Chief James, and Pamela Whitaker. 1989. *Kwakiutl Legends*. Surrey, B.C.: Hancock House.

Waltz, Kenneth N. 1979. *Theory of International Politics*. Reading, Mass.: Addison-Wesley.

Ward, Lorne H. 1988. "Origins of the Class Structure in Pre-Etruscan Rome, ca. 750 B.C.–ca. 550 B.C." *Science and Society* 52: 413–40.

Warren, Peter. 1989. *The Aegean Civilizations*, 2nd ed. Oxford, Eng.: Equinox.

Weede, Erich. 1981. "Income Inequality, Average Income, and Domestic Violence." *Journal of Conflict Resolution* 25: 639–54.

———. 1986. "Comment: Income Inequality and Political Violence Reconsidered." *American Sociological Review* 51: 438–41.

———. 1987. "Some New Evidence on Correlates of Political Violence: Income Inequality, Regime Repressiveness, and Economic Development." *European Sociological Review* 3: 97–108.

Weiss, H., M. A. Courty, W. Wetterstrom, F. Guichard, L. Senior, R. Meadow, and A. Curnow. 1993. "The Genesis and Collapse of Third Millennium North Mesopotamian Civilization." *Science* 261: 995–1004.

Wellhausen, Julius. 1927. *The Arab Kingdom and Its Fall*. Trans. Margaret Weir. Calcutta: University of Calcutta.

Wesson, Robert G. 1967. *The Imperial Order*. Berkeley: University of California Press.

Whittaker, C. R. 1994. *Frontiers of the Roman Empire: A Social and Economic Study*. Baltimore: Johns Hopkins University Press.

Wilford, John N. 1991. "What Doomed the Maya? Maybe Warfare Run Amok." *New York Times*, 19 Nov., C1, C10.

———. 1993a. "Collapse of Earliest Known Empire Is Linked to Long, Harsh Drought." *New York Times*, 24 Aug., C1, C10.

———. 1993b. "'House of David' Inscription: Clues to a Dark Age." *New York Times*, 16 Nov., C9.

———. 1995. "Lost Capital of a Fabled Kingdom Found in Syria." *New York Times*, 21 Nov., C1, C5.

———. 1997. "Ancient Graves of Armed Women Hint at Amazons." *New York Times*, 25 Feb., C1, C6.

Wilkie, James W., and Adam Perkal, eds. 1986. *Statistical Abstract of Latin America*, vol. 24 (for 1985). Los Angeles: University of California.

Wilkinson, Richard G. 1973. *Poverty and Progress*. New York: Praeger.

———. 1996. *Unhealthy Societies: The Afflictions of Inequality*. London: Routledge.

Willetts, R. F. 1965. *Ancient Crete: A Social History from Early Times Until the Roman Occupation*. London: Routledge.

Willey, Gordon R. 1987. *Essays in Maya Archaeology*. Albuquerque: University of New Mexico Press.

Willson, Stephen J. 1986. "A Use of Cellular Automata to Obtain Families of Fractals." In *Chaotic Dynamics and Fractals*, ed. Michael F. Barnsley and Stephen G. Demko. Orlando, Fla.: Academic Press.

Wilson, David J. 1981. "Of Maize and Men: A Critique of the Maritime Hypothesis of State Origins on the Coast of Peru." *American Anthropologist* 83: 93–120.

Wilson, John A. 1951. *The Culture of Ancient Egypt*. Chicago: University of Chicago Press.

Winter, Marcus C. 1984. "Exchange in Formative Highland Oaxaca." In *Trade and Exchange in Early Mesoamerica*, ed. Kenneth G. Hirth. Albuquerque: University of New Mexico Press.

Wittfogel, Karl A. 1957. *Oriental Despotism: A Comparative Study of Total Power*. New Haven, Conn.: Yale University Press.

The World in Figures, 5th ed. 1988. Editorial information compiled by *The Economist*. Boston: G. K. Hall.

Wright, Henry T. 1986. "The Evolution of Civilizations." In *American Archaeology Past and Future: A Celebration of the Society for American Archaeology, 1935-1985*, ed. David J. Meltzer, Don D. Fowler, and Jeremy A. Sabloff. Washington, D.C.: Smithsonian Institution Press.

Wright, Henry T., and Gregory A. Johnson. 1975. "Population, Exchange, and Early State Formation in Southwestern Iran." *American Anthropologist* 77: 267–89.

Wrightson, Keith. 1982. *English Society: 1580-1680*. New Brunswick, N.J.: Rutgers University Press.

Yahil, Leni. 1977. "The Uniqueness of the Rescue of Danish Jewry." In *Rescue Attempts During the Holocaust*, ed. Yisrael Gutman and Efraim Zuroff. Jerusalem: Yad Vashem.

Yerushalmi, Yosef Hayim. 1989. *Zakhor: Jewish History and Jewish Memory*. New York: Schocken Books.

Zaborowski, Wojciech. 1986. "Dichotomous Class Images and Worker Radicalism." In *Social Stratification in Poland: Eight Empirical Studies*, ed. Kazimierz M. Slomczynski and Tadeusz K. Krauze. Armonk, N.Y.: M. E. Sharpe.

Zuidema, R. Tom. 1990. *Inca Civilization in Cuzco*. Trans. Jean-Jacques Decoster. Austin: University of Texas Press.

INDEX

In this index an "f" after a number indicates a separate reference on the next page, and an "ff" indicates separate references on the next two pages. A continuous discussion over two or more pages is indicated by a span of page numbers, e.g., "57-59." *Passim* is used for a cluster of references in close but not consecutive sequence.

Abbasid empire, 11, 164f, 179-84, 277
Abundance: infinite, 19f, 286f; relative, 20f, 287
Act of Settlement, 157
Adab, 61
Adams, Richard E. W., 78, 81, 126, 200
Administrative hierarchy, 28ff
Aegean civilizations, 72, 186, 198, 211
Afghanistan, 223, 273
Africa, 63, 197, 222f, 226, 236, 278, 288. *See also* North Africa
African-Americans, 6, 147, 242-47, 267, 275
Age of the polity as predictor of democracy, 209, 214-20 *passim*
Aggad, 51, 56, 62, 67, 87, 277
Agnew, Spiro T., 268
Agricultural density, 157, 187ff, 201, 209, 214-21 *passim*, 305
Ahab, 132f
Ahuitzotl, 143
Ai, 59
Ajami, Fouad, 305
Albert the Bear, 173
Albrecht of Livonia, 174
Albrecht von Hohenzollern, 175
Algeria, 206, 236
Allende, Salvador, 242
Amen-hotep, 138
Ames, Aldrich, 269
Ammon, 89, 127-37 *passim*
Amon, Temple of, 137ff, 166
Amos, 130f, 133
Amsterdam, 31, 307
Anarchy, interstate, 302
Anderson, Benedict, 303
Anderson, Perry, 100, 161
Andes, 8, 54f, 83-87
Angell, Norman, 48
Angola, 236

Antisemitism, 250-59 *passim*
Arabs, 102, 109, 141, 180, 182f
Arameans, 133
Argentina, 305
Aristocracy, 81, 108f, 200, 304. *See also* Land inequality; Nobility
Aristotle, 72, 186, 188, 191
Armenians, 107
Army, role of: Roman, 101f; Byzantine, 108f; Spanish, 163; Muslim, 183. *See also* Military force size, as predictor of democracy
Aron, Raymond, 302
Ascanians, 173
Ashton, Robert, 155
Assyria, 128-33 *passim*
Atauhualpa, 144ff
Athens, 58, 80, 306; democracy in, 72, 186-93, 202, 211, 223ff, 269, 303; comparison with Rome, 151-55; land inequality in, 157, 186-93
Atkinson, A. B., 52
Attica, 188f, 211
Augsburg, Peace of, 178
Australia, 236, 304
Austria, 178, 211
Austria-Hungary, 41, 221
Autocracy, 193-96, 210
Aztecs, 10, 51, 89f, 118, 274, 279, 303; fall of, 141-44

Babylon, 61f, 128f, 134
Baghdad, 181, 183
Balazs, Etienne, 111
Balkans, 226, 301
Baltic region, 174f
Bank of England, 158
Banks, Arthur S., 209, 216
Barkay, Gabriel, 131f
Bar Kochbah rebellion, 136

340 / Index

Barraclough, Geoffrey, 166, 169
Bartlett, Robert, 173
Bartley Robert L., 304
Basil II, 107f
Bauer, Brian S, 86
Bavaria, 175
Becan, 121
Bell Curve, The (Herrnstein and Murray), 276; responses to, 308
Berawan (Borneo), 68
Bill of Rights: English, 157; U.S., 227
Bipolarity, 39, 42f
Black Death, 7
Blacks, *see* African-Americans
Blanton, Richard E., 79
Bloch, Marc, 168
Bohr, Niels, 257
Bolivia, 242
Bollen, Kenneth A., 207ff, 216
Bonney, Richard, 159, 171, 176
Books of Chilam Balam, 118
Borders: sea, 210ff, 216f, 222–234; land, 224
Bosnia, 223
Boutwell, Jeffrey H., 193
Boxley, R. F., 21
Branigan, Keith, 70, 72, 202
Braudel, Fernand, 4f, 31f
Brezhnev, Leonid, 280
Britain, 27, 141, 146, 226f, 288. *See also* England
British colonial heritage, as predictor of democracy, 11, 213–20 *passim*, 304
Bronfenbrenner, Urie, 251
Brumfiel, Elizabeth, 56
Bulgaria, 252
Burgundy, 169
Butzer, Karl W., 65
Buyeds (Iranian), 183
Byron, George Gordon, Lord, 129
Byzantium, 9f, 89f, 104–10, 117, 141f, 144, 264, 274f, 279

Calakmul, 122–26
Caliphate, 183
Cameroon, 236
Canada, 192, 236
Cañaris, 145
Canetti, Elias, 301
Caracalla, 102f

Caracol, 122–25
Carneiro, Robert L., 53f, 194
Carolingian kingdom, 166, 171, 264
Carpenter, Shirley, 209, 212
Castells, Manuel, 268
Castleden, Rodney, 73
Catholic Church, 101, 161–67 *passim*, 174f, 255, 257, 264
Catholics and English succession, 157
Celts, 303
Chad, 236
Champernowne, D. G., 293f
Chanca, 86
Chang, Kwang-chih, 75, 198, 203
Charisma, 268
Charlemagne, 168, 171. *See also* Carolingian kingdom
Charles I (England), 156
Chase-Dunn, Christopher, 54, 303
Chenery, Hollis B., 42, 302
Cherry, John F., 70, 73
Chichen-Itza, 125f, 279
Chiefdom, 8, 51, 197, 301
Chile, 242
Chimu, 85
Ch'in, 51, 76f, 87, 111, 203
China, 5, 8, 10, 111, 231, 274, 285; core Chinese cities, 36ff; state origins of, 47, 51–56 *passim*, 73–79, 89, 110–17; clans, 74–77; landlords and peasants, 97; decline of, 110–17, 127, 136; comparison with Judah, 136; democracy in, 176, 197f, 203, 210; comparison with Rome, 115ff, 136, 279
Ch'ing dynasty, 115
Ching-t'ien (well-fields), 112
Chi-square goodness of fit statistic, 31–37 *passim*, 238, 243f
Chou Pen-hsiung, 74
Chou dynasty, 111
Christianity, 99, 128, 159, 174, 254. *See also* Catholic Church, Lutheran Church
Chün-t'ien-fa, 113
Circumscription, 53f, 84, 196
Civilization, definition of, 55f
Civilizational conflict, 204–7, 227
Civil wars: Byzantine, 109; English, 155–60 *passim*, 190; Spanish, 163f
Class struggle, 14, 143
Cleisthenes, 189

Climate, 126f, 277
Clinton, Bill (William Jefferson), 268
Cobo, Father Bernabe, 145
Cohen, Ronald, 199
Collective action theories, 301
Collinearity, 214, 220f, 304
Collingwood, R. G., 47
Collins, James B., 160
Colombia, 242
Communism, 267f, 277f
Concordat of Worms, 168
Congo, 236
Conrad IV, 171
Conrad, Geoffrey W., 85, 146
Cook, Sherbune F., 142
Cooperation, 12, 247-60 *passim*; paradox of, 267
Copan, 124f
Copenhagen, 252-57 *passim*
Correlations (bivariate, partial, multiple), 213-20
Corruption, 101ff, 274; paradox of, 267ff
Cortés, Hernán, 141-44
Costa Rica, 211, 242
Counter-Reformation, 178
Cowgill, George L., 82, 201
Cozumel, 201
Crawford, Harriet, 200
Crenshaw, Edward, 221, 305
Crete, Minoan, 8, 55, 198, 202, 210; state origins of, 68-73
Croatia, 15, 301
Cromwell, Oliver, 155
Crowds and equality, 301
Crumley, Carol L., 56, 301
Crusades, 174, 227
Cuba, 234
Cyclades, 211, 225

Dahl, Robert A., 193, 213
Damascus, 133, 181
Davidic kingdom, 89, 128, 133
Davies, James C., 302
Davies, Nigel, 143
Demarest, Arthur A., 85, 146
Democracy, 10ff, 17, 61-73, 76f, 84, 185; failures of, 11, 176ff; rudimentary, 61, 72, 76-77, 82, 197-204; and land inequality, 176-78, 185-93; environmental influences on, 185, 193-96; and Islam, 185, 204-7, 224-28 *passim*; and war, 196-98; indexes of, 207-9; predictive variables for, 209-13, 221-27; culture and diffusion of, 213, 222, 226. *See also* Athens: democracy in; Liberal democracy
Denmark, 51, 251-57, 260, 307
Depopulation, 7, 99, 104f
De Pradt, Abbé, 38
De Rivera, Primo, 163, 195
De Ste. Croix, G. E. M., 14, 98
Desamortizacion, 163
De Vattel, Emmerich, 38
Difference principle (Rawls), 231
Diocletian, 93, 96-99, 116f, 143, 264, 279
Distributions: exponential, 5, 9, 17,19-24 *passim*, 31-34 *passim*, 49-88 *passim*, 234-44, 285-88, 306; fractal (EI), 5, 7ff, 11, 16, 24-38 *passim*, 49-88 *passim*, 234-44, 288-94, 306, 308; income, 12, 147, 233, 306; geometric, 23f; multinomial, 285; Gaussian, 294. *See also* Fractal formations; Land inequality
Dockès, Pierre, 96
Dominican Republic, 211
Donatists, 100
Don Carlos, 163
Dos Pilas, 123
Dovring, Folke, 21
Downing, Brian M., 304
Doyle, Michael W., 146, 197
Drennan, Robert D., 82
Duby, Georges, 176f
Düsseldorf, 258f
Dutch shipping, 31ff, 83

Earle, Timothy, 5, 51, 303
Easton, David, 3
Economic development, 188, 210, 214-21, 224, 227f, 233, 302, 304, 308
Ecuador, 35f
Edict of Nantes, 250
Egalitarianism, 250, 305
Egypt, ancient, 8ff, 54f, 71, 73, 105, 131, 146; state origins of, 62-68, 87, 153, 196, 280; decline of, 90, 133, 137-41, 166, 274, 277; comparison with ancient Israel, 137-42
Egypt, modern, 206f, 223, 266
Ehrenreich, Robert M., 56

Ehrlich, Paul R., 275f
Eisenstadt, S. N., 141
Elias, Norbert, 172
El Salvador, 234f, 237, 242, 306
Engels, Friedrich, 13f, 53, 275
England, 14, 31, 170, 172, 176, 196, 211, 225, 266; democratization in, 155–60, 190ff; contrast with Germany and Prussia, 167, 172–73. *See also* Britain
Environmental influences on state development, 126f, 181, 184, 193–96, 277–78; and threat of war, 11, 210ff; paradox of, 269f. *See also* Borders; Precipitation
Equal-fields concept, 114, 136
Equality, *see* Inequality
Equal opportunity, 18, 285ff
Equiprobability, 285f, 288
Erman, Adolf, 138
Esposito, John L., 207
Ethnocentrism, 250
Etruscans, 93, 152, 188
Euphrates River, 57f, 69, 181
Europe, 38ff, 48, 117, 186, 194, 221f, 227, 273, 236, 305
European Community, 213, 222. *See also* European Union
European Economic Community, *see* European Community
European location, as predictor of democracy, 213–20 *pasim*
European Union, 52, 213, 222f
Everitt, Alan, 156
Exkuseia, 109f
Exodus, 136
Exponential distribution, *see* Distributions, exponential

Farrar, Cynthia, 269
Fascism, 153
Fein, Helen, 307
Ferdinand VII, 163
Fideicommissum (Venice), 92
Filangieri, Gaetano, 92
Fine, John V. A., 187
Finley, M. I., 72, 93, 152f, 186–89, 202, 305
Flannery, Kent V., 78
Fogelman, Eva, 248
Fortifications, 59f, 69, 77, 86, 130, 202
Foster, George M., 235

Fractal expansion, *see* Fractal (EI) formations
Fractal (EI) formations, 8ff, 67, 72, 86, 93, 110, 140f, 170, 173ff, 179–84, 263ff. *See also* Distributions: fractal (EI)
France, 7, 170, 226, 236, 250, 288, 301; comparison with England, 159–62; comparison with Germany, 165f
Franco, Francisco, 163f
Frankish kingdom, 90
Frederick I, 169f
Frederick II, 170f
Frederick William, 171
Freidel, David, 121, 125
Freud, Sigmund, 251
Fried, Morton H., 51f, 77, 301
Friedman, Jonathan, 49, 57
Fu, Hung-der, 191
Fuglsang-Damgaard, Bishop, 254f
Futia, Carl A., 294

Gabon, 236
Gailey, Christine W., 56
Gamma (statistical measure), 240
Gardner, Howard, 232
Gastil, Raymond D., 207ff, 216
Gauls, 152, 303
Germanic tribes, 96, 100, 116, 272
Germano-Roman empire, 11, 165–78, 277
Germany, 5, 7, 11, 177, 221, 226, 274, 288, 303, 308; Nazi, 12, 135, 249–60 *passim*, 307. *See also* Germano-Roman empire; Prussia
Gilgamesh epic, 60, 198, 200
Gilman, Antonio, 72
Gilpin, Robert, 302
Gini index of inequality, 40, 209, 233, 240–41, 288. *See also* Land inequality
Girsu, 61
Global warming, 76, 278
Glorious Revolution, 155, 157, 190
Golden Bull (1356), 171
Gordon, Sarah, 258
Gould, Stephen Jay, 13
Gozo, 21f, 306
Gracchi, Gaius and Tiberius, 95f, 154f
Great Society, 243
Great Wall of China, 77
Greece: ancient, 14, 72, 99; modern 211
Greek city-states, 10, 87, 89, 117, 127, 187f,

269, 303-4. *See also* Athens; Sparta; Thebes
Gregory VII, 167ff
Gregory IX, 170
Grimal, Nicolas, 139
Gross Domestic Product (GDP), *see* Economic development
Gross National Product (GNP), *see* Economic development
Guatemala, 119
Gulick, Edward V., 38
Gunn, Joel D., 126
Gurr, Ted R., 192, 302
Guttman scale, 125

Habsburgs, 90, 172, 175
Hall, Thomas D., 54, 303
Hamblin, Robert L., 120
Hammond, Norman, 125
Han dynasty, 117; Eastern, 111-15 *passim*; Western, 111ff, 115
Harris, Marvin: *America Now*, 263
Hasmoneans, 136
Hassan, Fekri A., 64, 67
Hastorf Christine A., 86
Haviland, William A., 119
Hawai'i, 51
Health, and inequality, 147
Henry II, 167
Henry III, 167
Henry IV, 167, 169
Henry VI, 169f
Heraclius, 106
Herihor, 139
Herodotus, 130
Herr, Richard, 195
Herrnstein, Richard J., 276
Heston, Alan, 210
Heterarchy, 56, 302-3
Hexter, J. H., 155
Hierankopolis, 64, 67
Hierarchy, 57f, 302f. *See also* Stratification
Hilton, Rodney, 176
Hindus, 147
Hintze, Otto, 48
Hirschman, Albert O., 235
Hirth, Kenneth G., 82
Hobbes, Thomas, 5
Hodgson, Marshall G. S., 180-83
Hoffman, Michael A., 65-68 *passim*

Hohenstaufen, 169f, 172
Hohenzollern, 172, 175
Holborn, Hajo, 165
Holland, *see* Netherlands
Holocaust, 12, 248-60 *passim*, 275
Homer-Dixon, Thomas F., 193
Honduras, 35
Hsaio-Wen, 113
Hsu, Cho-yun, 112, 115f
Huang, Ray, 115
Huáscar, 144ff
Hucker, Charles O., 74
Hudson, Michael C., 209
Huguenots, 250
Hungary, 211
Huntington, Samuel P., 204-7, 224, 304f
Hyams, Edward, 145
Hydraulic civilization, 194ff, 304
Hyksos, 138

Iceland, 211, 225
Identification, among societal groups, 5, 12, 105, 232f, 248-60 *passim*, 275, 303, 307
Ideology, 204-7. *See also* Christianity; Islam; Judaism
Immigration, 272, 302
Inca, 10, 51, 85f, 89f, 141, 303; fall of, 144ff
Income distribution, *see* Distribution: income
India, 205, 288, 305
Indo-Europeans, 281
Indonesia, 272
Indus Valley, 54, 69, 272
Inequality, 8, 107f, 134f, 153, 287f; and scarcity, 5, 18-43 *passim*, 74f, 84ff, 126f, 243-60 *passim*, 278-81; and state survival, 7, 278-81; patterned, 12, 25ff, 231-47 *passim*, 259, 275; and corruption, 101ff, 267ff; and democracy, 176ff, 189-92, 218f, 221ff, 265f, 273-78; and gender, 199; paradox of, 265f. *See also* Distributions; Land inequality
Innocent III, 170
Innocent IV, 170
Investiture Contest, 167f, 177
Ionia, 225
Iran, 206f, 232, 266
Iraq, 207

Ireland, 211, 213
Irene (Byzantine Empress), 107
Irrigation, 58, 61, 75, 86. *See also* Hydraulic civilization
Islam, 11, 128, 147, 179-83 *passim*, 208; democracy and, 185, 204-7, 214-20 *passim*, 224-28 *passim*, 272. *See also* Muslims
Israel, ancient, 9f, 142, 166, 205, 274; decline of, 89f, 127-37; inequality in, 132f. *See also* Jews; Judaea
Israel, modern, 128, 135f, 225, 277
Italian-Americans, 147
Italy, 10, 41, 117, 167-71 *passim. See also* Venice

Jamaica, 211, 213
James II, 157f
Japan, 41, 111, 236, 249, 273, 305
Jaynes, Gerald D., 244
Jeffrey, L. H., 304
Jericho, 59
Jeroboam II, 133
Jerusalem, 59, 129f, 134f, 258
Jews, 12, 128, 135ff, 205, 247-60, 277, 307f. *See also* Israel, ancient
Jodice, David A., 208ff
Johnson, Allen W., 5
Johnson, Lyndon B., 243
Jones, A. H. M., 95, 100f
Jordan, 225
Josephus, 130, 135
Judaea, 105, 135
Judah, 10, 127-37. *See also* Israel, ancient
Judaism, Rabbinic, 128, 135
Justinian I, 106

Kaegi, Walter E., 105f
Kan (China), 76f, 197, 203
Kant, Immanuel, 17, 197, 227, 304
Kaplan, Morton, 39
Karl XI, 191
Kazakhstan, 281
Keep, John, 308
Kemp, Barry J., 139
Kenya, 236
Khariji, 180
Kinship structures, 74, 77f, 301. *See also Kan* (China)
Kirghiz, 5

Kish, 62
Kissinger, Henry, 308
Knights Templar, 174
Knossos, 69ff, 202
Koch curve, 289f, 294
Kowalewski, Stephen A., 78
Kramer, Samuel N., 198
Kristallnacht, 255

Lachish, 130
LaFeber, Walter, 306
Lagash, 61f, 81
Lai, David, 76
Landes, David S., 304
Landholdings, 22ff, 156, 163f, 176-83, 268. *See also* Land inequality
Land inequality, 12, 23f, 81, 100, 110, 116, 157, 160, 164, 289, 307; Russian, 33f; Venetian, 91ff; Roman, 93-95; Chinese, 97; Byzantine, 108f; Israelite, 132f; and democracy, 176ff, 185-93, 218-24 *passim*; and political violence, 233-42. *See also* Athens: land inequality
Landlordism, 112
Landowners, 97, 109, 147, 191
Landtage, 5, 11, 177f, 274
Langford, Paul, 157f
Languedoc, 159, 176-77
Lanning, Edward P., 83
Lapham, Lewis H., 306
Lasch, Christopher, 273, 276
Lasswell, Harold D., 3
Latifundia, 96f, 115f, 185
Latin America, 12, 197, 222, 226, 235, 236-42, 289, 305
Latvia, 174
League of Verona, 169
Lemann, Nicholas, 243
Lenin, V. I., 14, 268
Lenski, Gerhard, 193
Leo VI, 107
Le Patourel, John, 174
Levy, Janet E., 56
Lewis, Bernard, 179f, 206
Liberal democracy, 207, 264; index, 207ff, 213-28 *passim*
Liberalism, 226-27, 304
Libya, 207
Lichbach, Mark I., 192, 301
Limited good, 235

Lintott, Andrew, 192
Lipset, Seymour M., 193
Lithuania, 251-58, 260
Log-exponential distribution, *see* Distributions: fractal (EI)
Lombard League, 169f
Lords, *see* Nobility
Lorenz curve, 288
Lot, Ferdinand, 96
Lothar, 173
Louis the Pious, 171
Louis XIV, 158, 161
Lowe, John W.G., 120f
Lublin Union, 256
Lugalzaggesi, 62
Lung-shan culture, 75f
Luther, Martin, 178
Lutheran Church, 175, 254
Lye, Keith, 209, 212

Macedon, 51, 87, 141
Mackinder, Halford J., 193
MacMullen, Ramsay, 98, 101f
McNeill, William H., 4f, 51-67
MAD (mutually assured destruction), 248f
Magdeburg, Archbishop of, 175
Magna Carta, 197
Mahan, Alfred T, 193
Major, J. Russell, 162
Malaysia, 206, 211, 272
Malefakis, Edward, 195
Malta, 21f, 306
Manchus, 116
Mandelbrot, Benoit B., 289, 294
Mann, Michael, 58, 304
Mansfield, Edward, 305
Manzikert, battle of, 109, 144
Marcus, Joyce, 78
Markov chain, 293
Markovian process, 28
Martines, Lauro, 91
Marwanids, 180
Marx, Karl, 5, 13f, 53, 191, 275
Mashkan-shapir, 199
Matz, F., 71
Mawali, 180
Maximum likelihood method, 306
Maya, 55, 87, 279; decline of, 10f, 89f, 117-27, 277; Formative and Late Formative periods, 80f; Classic period, 80-82; democracy in, 81, 200f; Southern Lowlands, 117, 126; Putun (Chontal), 120, 124; Petén, 124; Puuc, 125; Northern Lowlands, 125f
Mazdak, 182
Mecca, 180
Medina, 180
Melanesia, 49
Merimda, 65
Mesoamerica, 8, 47, 54f, 198, 210; state formation in, 77-83; democracy in, 81, 200f; state dissolution in, 117-27, 141-44. *See also* Aztecs; Maya; Mexico, Valley of
Mesopotamia, 8, 47, 54f, 68, 76, 141, 180ff, 193, 196, 210; state formation in, 57-63 *passim*, 73f; democracy in, 198f. *See also* Abbasid empire; Aggad; Sumer; Umma; Uruk
Messenia, 69
Mexico, Valley of, 78, 81f, 87, 119, 122, 142
Michael I, 107
Micronesia, 59
Middle East, 104ff, 117, 222f, 277. *See also* Near East
Midlarsky, Elizabeth, 251
Midlarsky, Manus I., 191, 212, 302
Military force size, as predictor of democracy, 211f, 218f, 304
Ming dynasty, 111, 114
Minoan civilization, *see* Crete, Minoan
Minos, King, 71f, 202
Moche, 84
Moctezuma II, 143
Modelski, George, 302
Moghuls, 147
Mondrian, Piet, 16
Mongols, 111, 114, 116
Monte Albán, 79-82, 87
Moore, Barrington, Jr., 191
Morocco, 212
Mosca, Gaetano, 53
Moseley, Michael E., 83f
Mozambique, 236
Muhammad, 180, 182
Muller, Edward N., 191, 209
Multicollinearity, *see* Collinearity
Multipolarity, 10, 38-43 *passim*, 87, 124f, 127, 147

Muslims, 104-10 *passim*, 205, 227, 264, 277, 279. *See also* Islam
Myanmar, 302
Mycenae, 73, 202

Naples, 267
Naranjo, 122-25
Narmer, 64, 67
National debt, 158
Near East, 73, 130f, 198. *See also* Middle East
Nebuchadnezzar, 129
Nehemiah, 134f
Netherlands, 4, 31ff, 83, 158, 307
New England, 192
New Zealand, 236, 305
Nicaragua, 232, 234, 306
Nicholas, David, 176
Nicholson, E. W., 134
Nicophorus I, 107
Nigeria, 236, 305
Nile River region, 62-68 *passim*, 87. *See also* Egypt, ancient
Nissen, Hans J., 60
Nixon, Richard M., 268, 308
Nobility, 6, 160ff, 174, 176ff, 191. *See also* Aristocracy; Land inequality
Nomes (Egypt), 66, 87
Nordmark, 173
Normans, 170-74 *passim*
North Africa, 99f
Nowack, J. A., 82
Nüremberg, 4
Nushirvan, 182

Oaxaca, Valley of, 78-82, 142f
O'Donnel, Leopoldo, 163
Oligarchy, 224, 302
Oliner, Samuel P., 248
Oliner, Pearl M., 248
Olmec, 200
Olson, Mancur, Jr., 301
Omari, 65f
Omri, 130ff
Oppenheim, A. Leo, 200
Ordinary least-squares method, 19, 216-19, 306
Ordish, George, 145
Orozco, Francisco de, 143
Orthodox Church (Russian), 277
Ostrogorsky, George, 108

Ostrogoths, 105
Otto of Brunswick, 170
Otto I, 166f
Otto II, 166
Otto III, 166
Ottoman Empire, 90, 141

Pakistan, 207
Paldiel, Mordecai, 248
Palenque, 124-27
Palestine, 105f
Panama, 35
Papua New Guinea, 211
Paretian exponent, 292
Pareto, Vilfredo, 52f, 244, 308
Pareto distribution, *see* Distributions: fractal (EI)
Pareto-Lévy distribution, *see* Distributions: fractal (EI)
Parliament (English), 14, 155-59 *passim*, 178, 190, 192
Party systems, 305
Passover Seder, 136
Patrocinium, 100
Patterned inequality, 110, 231-47 *passim*. *See also* Inequality
Patterson, Thomas C., 56
Payne, James L., 304
Peasants, 9, 107, 111, 114, 116, 166, 185, 188, 191, 233-42 *passim*, 274, 305; middle, 97, 159, 176ff; rich and poor, 97, 176; and the social problem, 153, 159
Peer polity interaction, 55, 301
Perotti, Roberto, 191, 233
Persia, 104f, 136, 141. *See also* Sasanid Empire
Peru, 35f, 51, 242
Philip of Hesse, 172
Philistines, 129, 134, 140
Phoenicians, 132
Pilsudski, Józef Klemens, 221
Pisistratus, 154
Pitcher, B. L., 120
Pizarro, 141f, 144
Plato, 186f
Pliny, 95, 102
Plutarch, 94f
Poland, 175, 221, 256, 267, 305
Political rights index, 12, 207ff, 213-28 *passim*
Political violence, *see* Violence, political

Politics: definitions of, 3
Polity III index, 208f, 213-28 *passim*
Population, 69f, 92f, 104, 213; density, 59f, 66f, 69, 83f, 119-32, 192, 198; growth, 74, 78, 80, 84, 156, 159, 187ff, 192, 301, 307; displacement, 129; size (log), as predictor of democracy, 214-20 *passim*. *See also* Violence, political
Porter, Bruce D., 304
Portugal, 27
Potlatch state, 143, 305
Precipitation, 194ff, 210, 216ff, 223f, 304
Predictability of long-term political trends, 15f, 279-81, 301f
Price, Barbara J., 194
Primogeniture, 92, 111, 156, 160, 166, 172
Pristine states, 8, 54-55, 198
Priuli (diarist), 91
Pronoiars, 108
Proskouriakoff, Tatiana, 118
Prussia, 11, 32, 165f, 172-76
Prussians (native), 174f
Ptah (Egyptian god), 138
Ptolemies, 105
Purim, 136
Putnam, Robert D., 267
Pyrrhus, 152

Rabbinic Judaism, *see* Judaism, Rabbinic
Rainfall, 194ff. *See also* Precipitation
Rameses XI, 139
Random access, 18
Random variables, 291f
Rathjens, George W., 193
Rawls, John, 39, 231, 301
Raymond, J. Scott, 84
Redistribution, 50, 53, 70f
Reformation, 177f
Regression coefficient (*b*), 214-20 *passim*
Relative abundance, 21
Religion, *see* Christianity; Islam; Judaism
Renfrew, Colin, 55, 71, 73, 198, 211, 302
Resettlement, 28f
Revolution, etiology of, 302
Revolutions, 164, 191f, 234, 256
Richard I, 170
Riksdag, 190f
Roberts, Kenneth, 302
Rohatyn, Felix, 274ff
Roman Climate Optimum, 126
Romanus Lecapenus, 108

Rome, 6, 8f, 80, 91, 126, 162, 165-66, 264; curial class in, 5, 97f, 103; decline of, 56, 93-105, 268f, 272ff; comparison with Byzantium, 89f, 107; large estates in, 94-110 *passim*; Senate of, 95, 98; depopulation in, 99, 147; comparison with China, 115ff, 136, 279; comparison with Judah, 129, 136; comparison with Egypt, 139ff; comparison with Aztecs, 143f; comparison with Athens, 151-55; comparison with Soviet Union, 278ff
Rosario polity, 80
Rueschemeyer, Dietrich, 222
Russett, Bruce M., 191
Russia, 33, 135, 164, 221, 256, 277, 281. *See also* Soviet Union

Sabloff, Jeremy A., 120
Salamis, battle of, 154
Salinization, 181
Samaria, 129, 131ff
Samnites, 152
Sanders, William T., 80, 194
Sargon, 62
Sargon II, 129
Sasanid Empire, 181f
Saul, Frank P., 119
Sawad, 181f
Saxons, 166f
Scarcity, 10, 286ff; and inequality, 5, 18-43 *passim*, 74f, 84ff, 126f, 243-47, 265, 278-81
Schele, Linda, 121, 125
Schwartz, Barry, 302
Scott, Franklin D., 191
Sea borders, *see* Borders: sea
Seleucid Greeks, 136
Seligson, Mitchell A., 191, 209
Semites, 62, 67
Sen, Amartya, 302
Sennecharib, 129
Serbia, 15, 301
Serbs, 205
Service, Elman R., 53
Shang dynasty, 74-77, 203
Shantung, 75
Sharer, Robert J., 118, 120
Shih Tan, 112
Shiites, 180
Sicily, 170
Sierpinski gasket, 25ff

Sigismund II, 175
Sijes, B. A., 307
Simon, Julian L., 275f
Singapore, 220
Sisk, Timothy D., 305
Skinner, G. William, 37f
Slack, Paul, 156
Slavs, 147, 173f
Snodgrass, Anthony M., 186
Snyder, Jack, 305
Social Democratic Party (Denmark), 252f
Solomonic kingdom, 89, 128, 133
Solon, 153, 190, 192; reforms of, 157, 187ff
Somalia, 195, 223
Somoza family, 232, 234
South Carolina, and land inequality, 14
Soviet Union, 48, 197, 207, 223, 253, 256, 269, 273, 308; comparison with Rome, 278ff
Spain, 11, 27, 105, 141, 162ff, 195
Sparta, 69, 87, 127, 154, 187
Split inheritance, 144
Sprout, Harold, 193
Sprout, Margaret, 193
Sri Lanka, 211, 213
Stalin, Joseph, 14, 268
Starr, Chester G., 5, 154
State: expansion of, 7, 48; formation of, 8, 17; dissolution of, 8ff, 15; origins of, 47–88 *passim*; survival of, 278–81. See also under individual countries and regions by name
States-General, 177f
Stefan, Metropolitan of Sophia, 255
Stephens, Evelyne H., 222
Stephens, John D., 222
Stockton, David, 153–54
Stone, Elizabeth C., 199
Stone, Lawrence, 156
Stratification, 16, 51–88 *passim*, 200, 202, 279, 301
Strayer, Joseph R., 7, 301
Suda, William, 251
Sudan, 207
Sui dynasty, 113
Sulla, 94
Sumer, 8, 56, 67, 72f, 79, 87, 117, 120, 277; Late Uruk period, 35ff; state origins of, 57–62; rudimentary democracy in, 198ff

Summers, Robert, 210
Sung dynasty, 114
Susa, 58
Sweden, 49, 190–91, 252–53
Swidden agriculture, 119
Switzerland, 49, 225
Swordbrothers, 174f
Syria, 105f, 133, 223
Syrquin, Moises, 42, 302

t-test of significance, 214–220 *passim*
Tainter, Joseph A., 120
T'ang dynasty, 113f
Tau-b (statistical measure), 240f
Ta-wen-k'ou culture, 75
Tawney, Richard H., 155
Taylor, Charles L., 208ff
Taylor, William B., 142f
Templehof, 174
Temples, Egyptian, 137–41, 166
Teotihuacan, 81f, 87, 122, 200
Teutonic Knights, 174f
Thebes, 64, 87, 127, 137, 139
Themes (Byzantine provincial system), 106, 264
Thompson, Eric J., 120
Tigris River, 57f, 69, 181
Tikal, 121–27, 201
Tilly, Charles, 52, 197
Tlaxcalans, 143f
Toynbee, Arnold J., 272
Trade, 67, 70f, 73, 120, 122, 188, 210; Trade/GNP ratio, 214–20 *passim*
Treadgold, Warren, 107
Trevor-Roper, Hugh R., 155
Tribes, 77f
Trigger, Bruce G., 63
Trotsky, Leon, 268
Tseng Ying-lin, 115
Tufte, Edward R., 213
Tunisia, 212
Tunnel effect, 235
Turkey, 272
Turks: Seljuk, 109, 144; Ottoman, 147, 227
Two-party system, 14

U-function, inverted, 265f
Ubaid culture, 57
Umayyads, 180f

Umma, 61f, 81, 206
United States, 41, 52, 111, 236, 294, 302, 307; democracy in, 159, 191, 225ff; urban disorders in, 242–47; inequality in, 269, 273f, 276ff, 280; Congress, 280
Ur, 62, 81
Urban disorders, *see* United States: urban disorders in
Urbanization, 192, 254, 304, 307f
Urkesh, 199
Uruguay, 242, 305
Uruk, 57–61, 200. *See also* Sumer

Variance Inflation Factor (VIF), 214
Venice, 4–6, 90–93, 143, 274
Verdun, Treaty of, 171
Victory, Duke of, 163
Violence, political, 8ff, 12, 185, 192, 210, 275, 306; as predictor of democracy, 214–20 *passim*, 233–47 *passim*.
Vogt, Evon Z., 81, 200
Voll, John O., 207
Von Gentz, Friedrich, 38
Von Martens, Georg, 38

Wallace, Alfred R., 18
Waltz, Kenneth N., 3
Wang Mang, 113
Wanka cultures (Peru), 51, 86
War, 10, 76f, 80, 122, 126f, 301; and the state, 6f, 47–88 *passim*; and democracy, 196–203; threat of, 210ff, 224f, 269f. *See also* Borders: sea; Wars
Ward, Lorne H., 94
Warring States period, 76
Wars: Carlist, 162; Croatian, 15; of Devolution, 161; Dutch, 161; Franco-Spanish, 161; Iran-Iraq, 48; of the League of Augsburg, 155, 158, 161f; of the League of Cambrai, 91; Macedonian, 301; Napoleonic, 11, 49; Peasants, 178; Peloponnesian, 87; Peninsular, 162; Persian Gulf, 48; Punic, 152, 154; Serbo-Croatian, 301; Spanish-American, 163; of the Spanish Succession, 11, 155, 158, 162; Thirty Years, 161, 178; World War I, 33, 48f, 164, 221, 249, 256, 301; World War II, 48f, 226, 243, 248–60 *passim*, 266, 301, 303; Yom Kippur, 223. *See also* Civil wars
Warsaw Ghetto revolt, 136, 303
Washington, George, 159, 302
Watergate scandal, 268
Weber, Max, 268
Weede, Erich, 192
Wei dynasty, 113
Weiss, Harvey, 277
Wesson, Robert G., 9
Westphalia, Peace of, 178
Whites, American, 147, 245–47
Whitewater scandal, 268
Whittaker, C. R., 97
Willetts, R. F., 73
Willey, Gordon R., 82, 120
William the Conqueror, 172
William of Orange, 157f
Williams, Robin M., Jr., 244
Wilson, David J., 84
Wilson, John A., 66, 138
Winter, Marcus C., 79
Wittfogel, Karl A., 58, 193–96, 224, 304
Wrightson, Keith, 196
Wu, Emperor, 112

Yad Vashem, 248
Yahil, Leni, 256
Yarmuk, battle of, 106
Yathrib, 180
Yaxchilan, 124
Yellow River, 69
Yerushalmi, Yosef Hayim, 135
Yuan dynasty, 114
Yucatan, 124, 201
Yugoslavia, 48, 223

Zabalam, 61
Zaire, 236
Zimansky, Paul, 199

Library of Congress Cataloging-in-Publication Data

Midlarsky, Manus I.
   The evolution of inequality : war, state survival, and democracy
in comparative perspective / Manus I. Midlarsky.
      p.   cm.
   Includes bibliographical references and index.
   ISBN 0-8047-3376-7 (cl. : alk. paper) : ISBN 0-8047-4170-0 (pbk. : alk paper)
   1. Equality.   2. Democracy.   3. Social classes.   4. Wealth.
I. Title.
JC575.M53   1999
323.42—dc21   98-35062

∞ This book is printed on acid-free paper.

Original printing 1999
Last figure below indicates year of this printing:

06 05 04 03 02 01